Essays on
John Maynard Keynes

Essays on
John Maynard Keynes

edited by
MILO KEYNES

CAMBRIDGE UNIVERSITY PRESS
1975

CAMBRIDGE UNIVERSITY PRESS
Cambridge, New York, Melbourne, Madrid, Cape Town, Singapore, São Paulo

Cambridge University Press
The Edinburgh Building, Cambridge CB2 2RU, UK

Published in the United States of America by Cambridge University Press, New York

www.cambridge.org
Information on this title: www.cambridge.org/9780521205344

First published 1975
Reprinted 1975, 1976
First paperback edition 1979
Reprinted 1980
Re-issued in this monochrome digitally printed version 2005

A catalogue record for this publication is available from the British Library

Library of Congress catalogue card number: 74-12975

ISBN-13 978-0-521-20534-4 hardback
ISBN-10 0-521-20534-4 hardback

ISBN-13 978-0-521-29696-0 paperback
ISBN-10 0-521-29696-X paperback

The frontispiece in this work, produced in colour for the original publication,
has been replaced with a black and white image for this digital reprinting.

Contents

CONTENTS

CONTENTS

Illustrations

Frontispiece: Maynard and Lydia Keynes in 1935. Oil painting by William Roberts

Acknowledgements

Many have helped in the preparation of this book, either by discussion or by correspondence, and thanks are especially due to Lord Annan, Quentin Bell, Sir Isaiah Berlin, Lord Blake, Lord Butler, Lord Crawford and Balcarres, Lord Franks, Sir Frederic Harmer, Michael Holroyd, Robert Jackson, Lord Kahn, Sir John Masterman, James Meade, Sir Edward Playfair, Sir Dennis Proctor, Lord Robbins and Sir Duncan Wilson. Particular and essential help has been provided by Sir Austin Robinson, George Rylands, Donald Moggridge and Tim Munby, and their care and enthusiasm have allowed the easy preparation of this book.

Permission to quote from *Old Friends* (1956) by Clive Bell was given by Professor Quentin Bell and the publishers, Chatto and Windus Ltd of London and the University of Chicago Press. Lord Crawford and Balcarres kindly allowed me to search in his father's unpublished diary and to extract three passages. The essay by C. R. Fay on 'The undergraduate' originally appeared in *John Maynard Keynes – a Memoir*, prepared by direction of the Council of King's College, Cambridge and privately printed in Cambridge (1949). The greater part of the essay by Joan Robinson 'What has become of the Keynesian Revolution?', is taken from her Presidential Address, Section F, British Association Meeting, 1972, which appeared in *After Keynes*, Basil Blackwell, Oxford (1973). The essay 'How Keynes came to America' by John Kenneth Galbraith originally appeared in the *New York Times Book Review*, 16 May 1965, and was republished in *Economics, Peace and Laughter* (1971), and is here again reprinted by permission of Houghton, Mifflin Company, Boston, and André Deutsch, London. The essay 'Bretton Woods' by Richard N. Gardner originally appeared under the title 'The Political Setting' and is reprinted from *Bretton Woods Revisited*, edited by A. L. K. Acheson, J. F. Chant and M. F. J. Prachowny (1972), by permission of the University of Toronto Press and Macmillan, London and Basingstoke. The essay entitled 'The international negotiator' by Sir Frank Lee appears by permission of the Controller of H.M. Stationery Office. Angelica Garnett permitted use of letters from her mother, Vanessa Bell, in the essay 'The picture collector'. Much of the essay by A. N. L. Munby on 'The book collector' also appeared in the King's College *Memoir*. It is here reprinted with the College's permission with corrections and extensive additions.

It is worth pointing out that each of the essays was written by the first person who was asked to do it; this truly exceptional response must be due to the subject of the book.

Preface

John Maynard Keynes died aged sixty-two on Easter Sunday, 1946. In the past twenty-eight years much has been written about his influence on economics, but beyond this he has become one of the most famous men of this century. The volume of writing on him has increased in recent years, but little of it has been about the man himself, and what there is was done by economists. Immediately after his death Austin Robinson wrote about him for the *Economic Journal* (Vol. 57, 1947), and A. C. Pigou for the *Proceedings of the British Academy* (Vol. 32, 1947). The official biography, *The Life of John Maynard Keynes* by R. F. Harrod, appeared in 1951 and has remained the main source of information. Two books published in 1967, *Keynes and After* by Michael Stewart and *The Age of Keynes* by Robert Lekachman, gave short accounts of him, and another was published in *The Times* in March 1972 by Roy Jenkins.

This volume is intended for the general reader as well as for economists. It tries to provide a picture of the life of Maynard Keynes and his wide-ranging interests. The book is, in fact, a biography by many authors; each contribution is written by an expert in the field it covers. The range of Maynard's activities may surprise many.

Maynard Keynes was very happily married to the Russian ballerina, Lydia Lopokova, and in the writings about him her role in his life has been unduly neglected. Two of the essays try to give some idea of her personality and her great qualities. If he were still alive, Maynard would have been ninety-one this year; one reason for producing this book now is that if it had been delayed it would have been harder to obtain some of the contributions, particularly from his own contemporaries. A favourite member of the Bloomsbury Group and intimate friend of Maynard for forty years was Duncan Grant, who at the age of eighty-nine is still painting and has been able to supply details for the essay on Maynard as a picture collector. He continues to live and work, as he has done since 1916, at Charleston, a farmhouse in Sussex a few hundred yards from Maynard's and Lydia's house at Tilton. He appears in one of the illustrations, and two of the portraits reproduced are by him. Another is by the wood engraver Gwen Raverat, both author and illustrator of *Period Piece* (1952). She was a member of the Darwin family in Cambridge and knew Maynard in his early years. Her sister married Maynard's younger brother Geoffrey, my father, who has contributed at the age of eighty-six.

The essays on economic subjects contain new material, especially from the war years. The 'essay' composed from three entries in the private diary of the late Earl of Crawford and Balcarres is an interesting comment on the 'establishment' attitude to Maynard and to the publication of *The Economic Consequences of the Peace* in 1919. Sir Frank Lee's letter describing Maynard Keynes at an international negotiation in the United States in 1944 can be augmented by an extract from the diary kept by Lord Robbins at the Bretton Woods negotiations of 1944, which sums up Keynes's brilliance and the power of his personality: 'Keynes was in his most persuasive mood; and the effect was irresistible. At such moments I often find myself thinking that Keynes must be one of the most remarkable men that has ever lived – the quick logic, the birdlike swoop of intuition, the vivid fancy, the wide vision, above all the incomparable sense of the fitness of words, all combine to make something several degrees beyond the limit of ordinary human achievement.'

Cambridge, 1974   Milo Keynes

The surname 'Keynes' is pronounced 'Kaynes' as it is in several place-names in England, such as Horsted Keynes and (I hope) Milton Keynes.

Chronology and Bibliography

Contributors

R. B. Braithwaite – Emeritus Knightbridge Professor of Moral Philosophy, University of Cambridge; Fellow of King's College, Cambridge

Richard Buckle – writer; ballet critic of *The Sunday Times*

Earl of Crawford and Balcarres (1871–1940) – Lord Privy Seal, 1919

Nicholas Davenport – Financial Correspondent of the *Spectator*; previously Financial Correspondent of the *New Statesman*

N. H. Dimsdale – Fellow and Praelector in Economics, The Queen's College, Oxford

Howard Elcock – Lecturer in Political Studies, University of Hull

C. R. Fay (1884–1961) – late Reader in Economic History, University of Cambridge; Fellow of Christ's College, Cambridge, 1908–22

John Kenneth Galbraith – Professor of Economics, Harvard University

Richard N. Gardner – Henry L. Moses Professor of Law and International Organisation, Columbia University

David Garnett – author

Mary Glasgow – First Secretary-General of the Arts Council

Duncan Grant – painter

Norman Higgins (1898–1974) – First General Manager (later Managing Director), Arts Theatre, Cambridge

Harry G. Johnson (1923–1977) – Professor of Economics, the London School of Economics and Political Science; Fellow of King's College, Cambridge, 1950–6

Sir Geoffrey Keynes – retired consulting surgeon; Honorary Fellow, Pembroke College, Cambridge, and Darwin College, Cambridge

Sir Frank Lee (1903–71) – Joint Permanent Secretary of the Treasury, 1960–2; late Master of Corpus Christi College, Cambridge

Paul Levy – writer; one of the Strachey Trustees

J. E. Meade – Emeritus Professor of Political Economy, University of Cambridge; Senior Research Fellow, Christ's College, Cambridge; Nobel Prize Winner

xvii

D. E. Moggridge – University Lecturer in Economics, Cambridge;
Fellow of Clare College, Cambridge; part editor of *The Collected
Writings of John Maynard Keynes*

A. N. L. Munby (1913–74) – Librarian and Fellow, King's College,
Cambridge

A. F. W. Plumptre – Visiting Professor, Carleton University School
of International Affairs; formerly Assistant Deputy Minister of
Finance, Ottawa, and an Executive Director of the International
Monetary Fund, Washington

Sir Austin Robinson – Emeritus Professor of Economics, University
of Cambridge; Fellow of Sidney Sussex College, Cambridge

Joan Robinson – Emeritus Professor of Economics, University of
Cambridge; Fellow of Newham College, Cambridge

George Rylands – retired Senior University Lecturer in English,
University of Cambridge; Fellow of King's College, Cambridge;
Chairman of the Cambridge Arts Theatre Trust since the death
of Lord Keynes

Richard Shone – writer

Robert Skidelsky – Associate Professor of History, School of Advanced Studies at Washington, D.C., the Johns Hopkins University

Charles Wilson – Professor of Modern History, University of Cambridge; Fellow of Jesus College, Cambridge

PART ONE

I

Maynard and Lydia Keynes

MILO KEYNES

I only began to know my uncle Maynard well when I was seventeen; but after that I saw much of him until he died five years later. My first knowledge of him was mainly at second hand, for as children we spent Easters at Tilton when he and my aunt Lydia were safely away. Tilton is a hamlet on the edge of the South Downs, adjoining the village of Firle near Lewes in Sussex. Here Maynard died in 1946. The countryside is beautiful and it has always been a marvellous place in which to stay.

We got to know the atmosphere of the farmhouse and to wonder about its absent owners – a house with many pictures (a Degas drawing hung in the lavatory); its glimpses of the ballet world; the strangely painted gramophone (by Vanessa Bell or Duncan Grant); the damp library which Maynard had added across a small courtyard a few years earlier containing the portrait of Maynard and Lydia by William Roberts which is the frontispiece to this book; the vestigial garden with a veranda looking out onto the slopes of the South Downs. On this veranda Lydia used to sunbathe stark naked though a footpath crossed in front of it only a few yards away. When someone once asked if this might not cause embarrassment, Maynard replied 'No – a passer-by simply couldn't believe his eyes.'

As children we saw Maynard and Lydia occasionally at family parties, which seemed to be held more frequently as my grandparents got older and older. I only remember two early stories about Maynard. On one occasion he told me that the reason that Lydia wore her hair in a bun was so that I could undo it. As a six-year-old I was delighted. Later, (presumably) in 1936, we were walking on the Downs and I kept in front but sufficiently close to hear what the grown-ups were talking about. Maynard was saying that the King was seeing a great deal of the American divorcée, Mrs Simpson, and it was going to lead to trouble. My memory is one of astonishment that he could possibly know what was going on in such high places. After his illness in 1937 Maynard and Lydia used to lunch with my grandparents every Sunday when they were in Cambridge during

Term, and I was very often allowed to join them in those last five years. My grandfather died at ninety-seven; he had been married sixty-seven years and had kept a record 227 terms in continuous residence in the University. My grandmother died aged ninety-six. Both his parents outlived Maynard and were able to attend the memorial service for him in 1946 at Westminster Abbey.

To me, Maynard was a wonderful and understanding uncle, and I can echo about him the words of Walter Map, servant of Henry II, who wrote of the King that he was 'one upon whom men gazed closely a thousand times yet took occasion to return'. My first independent visit to Tilton was marked by my realisation that I seemed for the first time in my life to have worked out my own answer instead of having replied with the remark I might have supposed was expected. Maynard had given the impression of really wanting to know what I thought. It was on that occasion, too, that he taught me how to eat a peach, though how there was a peach to eat on that December evening in wartime England escapes me. He showed an interest in me as a human being even though I was only aged seventeen, and in his presence I felt I excelled myself and perhaps even occasionally became interesting. Harold Nicolson mentioned in a review of Roy Harrod's biography that Maynard 'would gaze at us with his probing, gentle eyes, as if we had said, or were about to say, something supremely important'.

The illustrations in this book give, I think, a good idea of Maynard's appearance over the years, but obviously it is impossible to recapture in writing his gestures, especially of his hands, and the sound of his soft, persuasive voice. He occasionally stammered, and sometimes in the quickness of his replies words became lost. He was a fine broadcaster, speaking slowly and very distinctly, and the B.B.C. has a recording of one of his broadcasts of which there is a copy in the Library at King's College, Cambridge.

Nor is it easy to describe his conversation and enjoyment of wit. In *Old Friends*, a book of personal recollections, Clive Bell wrote: 'what I miss is his conversation. It was brilliant: that is an obvious thing to say but it is the right thing. In the highest degree he possessed that ingenuity which turns commonplace into paradoxes and paradoxes into truisms, which discovers – or invents – similarities and differences, and associates disparate ideas – that gift of amusing and surprising with which very clever people, and only very clever, can by conversation give a peculiar relish to life.' Bell continues his somewhat critical account that 'in argument he was bewilderingly quick, and unconventional. His comment on any subject under discussion, even on a subject about which he knew very little, was apt to be so lively and original that one hardly stopped to enquire whether it was just. But in graver mood, if asked to explain some technical business, which to the amateur seemed incomprehensible almost, he would with good-humoured ease make the matter appear so simple that one knew not whether to be more amazed at his intelligence or one's own stupidity. In moments such as these I felt sure that Maynard was the cleverest man I had ever met; also, at such moments, I sometimes felt, unreasonably no doubt, that he was an artist.' Bell ends his essay on Maynard Keynes with the view that 'his supreme virtue was his deeply affectionate nature. He liked a great many people of all sorts and to them he gave pleasure, excitement and good counsel; but his dearest friends he loved passionately and faithfully and, odd as it may sound, with a touch of humility.'

Characteristically, when writing and reading, Maynard would lie on a bed or chaise-longue, and one day, returning from a walk, I asked him what he was reading. It was a book from his library, *A Collection of Emblemes* (1635) by George Wither (1588–1667), a minor poet and pamphleteer. 'It is odd', he said, 'that today I know a great deal about Wither and his writings, but next week I shall know nothing.' His memory was prodigious, but it was, unlike that of less gifted people, selective. His interest in detail was great, as was his enjoyment of simple things – like paradoxes. He wrote to the Editor of the *New Statesman and Nation*, 'The inevitable never happens. It is the unexpected always.' And another letter stated that 'words ought to be a little wild, for they are the assaults of thought upon the unthinking'.

Clive Bell describes how Maynard detested the political dishonesty of Lloyd George (commonly known as 'The Goat'), and how he once cut out a newspaper photograph of him in full evening dress, smothered in ribbons, speaking at a banquet in Paris and wrote on it: 'Lying in state'. On another occasion, after a comment that Lloyd George appeared to show so many different personalities to others, someone wondered what he would be like when he was alone in a room. Maynard's quick reply, 'There would be nobody there', is famous. He was pleased to find the perfect reply to the letters he so frequently received asking his opinion on some article, paper, or book: 'Dear X, thank you for sending me your article (paper, or book). I shall lose no time in reading it, yours sincerely, J. M. K.' And once he asked Lydia, 'What are you thinking about?' 'Nothing', said Lydia; 'I wish I could', replied Maynard.

James Meade says that for Maynard it was a major sin to think of a good remark and then suppress it, and Harold Nicolson thought that his passion for dialectics inspired his provocative paradoxes. On the same theme, Roy Harrod in his biography quotes an account of Maynard by the diplomat Sir Eyre Crowe in 1919: 'His opinions are in a perpetual state of progress, and therefore of apparent flux. He never shrinks from paradox and sometimes seems to aim at it for its own sake.' Bertrand Russell wrote in his autobiography covering the years 1872 to 1914 that 'Keynes's intellect was the sharpest and clearest that I have ever known. When I argued with him, I felt that I took my life in my hands, and I seldom emerged without feeling something of a fool. I was sometimes inclined to feel that so much cleverness must be incompatible with depth, but I do not think this feeling was justified.' This seems to me fairer than the remark Harold Nicolson quoted in his diary in 1951 that Russell found Keynes 'obviously a nice man, but I did not enjoy his company. He made me feel a fool.'

Kingsley Martin, Editor of the *New Statesman and Nation* (in which Maynard had had an interest), wrote in his obituary notice, 'Keynes was the most formidable of antagonists, ruthless and sometimes unscrupulous in argument, and always unsparing of all that seemed to him silly and insincere. A mutual friend once remarked that in conversation when Keynes was present there was never any point in saying anything because he always thought of a better remark than yours before you had time to think of it. His wit was shattering and his capacity for rudeness unequalled.' Harold Nicolson mentioned that 'Keynes was impatient, iconoclastic, rude. Yet although with incisive cruelty he would snub the eminent, he never snubbed the humble or the young.' Clearly Maynard was not always an easy companion.

I have quoted these accounts by men who knew him because I think they partially explain why Maynard was so often accused of arrogance, shared, according to Nicolson, by others of the Cambridge élite – which of course included Bertrand Russell. Austin Robinson discusses the question of academic arrogance elsewhere in this book, but what he writes does not cover the view of a recent autobiographer (who is not an economist) that he had rarely met anyone more smug or more arrogant. Perhaps this author is not using the word 'arrogant' in the sense of unjustified self-confidence, and certainly I have nowhere else heard of Maynard being called smug. Many may have found him alarming, but usually this impression soon disappeared, and could easily have been due to a previous knowledge of his eminence and brilliance. Clive Bell thought that Maynard 'was not pretentious; he made no boast of his superior knowledge and expected no praise for it, he merely assumed it'. I think that, particularly when younger, Maynard could be contemptuous of those who did not share his interests. Crowe said of him, in 1919, 'He can bring a converging series of arguments to bear upon a single point, so that he succeeds in making everything else seem to have a minor interest to other persons.'

Maynard had a severe cardiac infarction in 1937, when he was looked after by the remarkable Dr J. Plesch and spent several months' convalescence at Ruthin Castle, a medical centre in Wales. After this he lived for nine years with angina-of-effort and had several 'heart attacks' before the final one in 1946. Lydia became a stern and faithful scourge of anyone who occupied Maynard's time unnecessarily or for too long. Luckily, as a member of the family I was considered outside the edict, and was included in the weekly visit to the Cambridge Arts Theatre and any entertainment afterwards. Maynard and Lydia had a flat in St Edward's Passage near the Arts Theatre. It was King's College property and, when it was being converted for them, wooden panels with carved Tudor roses were discovered lining the walls of the main room. Though the flat was rather bleak and underused, it was adequate for their visits to Cambridge in term-time. Maynard, of course, also had the rooms in King's College which were decorated by Duncan Grant and Vanessa Bell with panels depicting the 'triposes'.* The panels have recently been renovated, but are at present covered and are not on view.

Maynard's and Lydia's London house was at 46 Gordon Square, in Bloomsbury, an address that is mentioned several times in this book. I only knew it after Maynard's death, when it had been subdivided. As at my grandparent's home in Cambridge, the house next door had been bought and room stolen from it to enlarge the main house. It seems to me, however, that the most important place in which they lived – where, indeed, Lydia still lives – was Tilton.

Lydia was born in St Petersburg on 21 October 1891, daughter of Vasili Lopukhov, usher at the Imperial Alexandrinsky Theatre. Her adored mother, Constanza Douglas, member of a Scottish–German family, came from the Baltic States to St Petersburg as a housekeeper, and never spoke Russian well. Two brothers and one sister became dancers, and one of the brothers, Fyodor, who died in Leningrad in 1973, was a very distinguished Russian choreographer and ballet director. The Lopukhovs derived from Tambov and the name is that of a flower, a burdock ('one which puffs out', Lydia told me). A more correct rendering of her name is 'Lopukhova', but Diaghilev used to simplify the spelling of his dancers' names, and Lydia's became 'Lopokova'. Accepted into the Imperial School of Ballet at the age of nine after an exam, she has always spoken highly of the education there and the training she received. At one time it was said that the members of the School stole Pavlova's

* Photographs are available in King's College Library.

ballet shoes out of admiration and worship of her. Lydia says this was nonsense, for there was a whole basketful of her discarded shoes in the corner, and it was a waste not to use them.

Maynard first met Lydia at a party given by the Sitwells in October 1918. At that time she was enthralling the London audiences by her performances for the Diaghilev Russian Ballet Company in *The Good-humoured Ladies*. Maynard lived with her for some time before they married in 1925 (see illustration), and 'Bloomsbury' got to know her. However, after the wedding his Bloosmsbury friends did not entirely approve of her: Duncan Grant and Vanessa Bell, though they liked her, found her interruptions with trivia about the ballet very annoying while they were painting at Gordon Square. Lydia would not settle down to a serious conversation, or if she did, would ruin it by a humorous remark. Bloomsbury found her unsound from their standpoint on the eternal verities, morality, religion, the soul and, particularly, on politics and public affairs, and was worried for Maynard when she married him. Perhaps, too, they felt that he had become less available to them. I think, also, that they tried to assume control over Maynard's conscience and felt they had the right to dictate his actions. Maynard hated surrendering his conscience to them as keenly as earlier, in the First World War, he had objected to surrendering it to the State. Clearly Lydia thought that Vanessa despised her, and years later when I took her over from Tilton to neighbouring Charleston, where Clive and Vanessa Bell lived with Duncan Grant, I sensed that she was shy of Vanessa's possible judgements of her. Bloomsbury, however, early discovered her gaiety and infectious laughter.

On one occasion E. M. Forster, returned from lunching with Lydia in the Cambridge flat, chucklingly told how he had just written down her last remark to him. She had warned him not to slip down the steep stairs on leaving – he was then aged nearly eighty – and had added 'I once did that, and believe me I paid the price.' Morgan Forster was aware that Bloomsbury had taken long to understand Lydia, saying 'How we all used to underrate her!' With time Bloomsbury ceased to be worried, because she always remained amusing on her own subjects, and because she obviously made Maynard extremely happy.

In an article in *The Times* in 1972 Roy Jenkins described Maynard's marriage to Lydia as 'surprisingly successful', but I believe that anyone who has ever met Lydia would not find the success of their marriage strange. Cecil Beaton has correctly described her as 'that most stimulating and entertaining of all human beings'; it was wonderful for me to find Maynard still amused by her, laughing with her and at her after so many years. At the time of his death he was still unable to tell what she would say or do next. The stories about her are fascinating, and her cunning misuse of the English language legendary. Maynard had primed her before she first met my mother, granddaughter of Charles Darwin, by explaining about *The Origin of Species*. But Lydia was not to be outdone: she said 'So you are the granddaughter of the man who wrote *Genesis*.' Once when I threatened to call on her she said that I might, but that I was not to stay too long 'as chatting is so boring'.

The family tells how when Diaghilev asked her if she would dance in *The Sleeping Beauty* ballet – probably having already decided to change its name as it sounded too much like a pantomime – he said that if she accepted he would have to alter the name to *The Sleeping Princess* because of her little nose. The ballet persisted under that name for years, and Lydia has recently confirmed the story. On one occasion she had left the Company, and her manager asked Diaghilev to take her back. 'Yes', he answered, 'if it is the same Lopokova I knew.' She has never shown off or asserted her greatness as a dancer. She once told me that one day she overheard Diaghilev shouting at someone. She remarked to him that he never seemed to shout at her, and he replied, 'No, and I never shall.' Some time later, however, her shoe-lace became undone on the stage and spoilt the dance as Diaghilev was watching from the wing, and he, furious, started shouting at her dresser, though not at her. 'And everyone knows that a dancer does up her own shoes,' Lydia added. One day after Lydia had been dancing in *The Good-humoured Ladies*, Eleonora Duse, who had been in the audience, came backstage. Lydia curtseyed to her and, taking her white gloved hand, kissed it leaving a mark on it from her painted lips. 'I will treasure this glove', said Duse, and to Lydia this was the supreme compliment.

Some years after Maynard's death she tried to provide an electric fire for Tamara Karsavina, 'because it is not right that the Firebird should be cold in winter'. But, she was asked, had she not danced the Firebird too? 'Yes', she replied quickly, 'but I was only the fried-bird.' She recently remarked about Maynard, simply: 'He gave gaiety to life.' After he died she said it would take ten years for her to recover, and it did.

Lydia has said that in art only the first-rate matters, but when she goes to a poor performance she almost invariably tries to find something of merit in it to mention to the performer – because she never would tell a lie, and I have not heard her speak badly about any artist. I have never met any member of the Bloomsbury Group (but admittedly did not meet Lytton Strachey) as humorous and verbally witty as Lydia. Her humour is not malicious even though

7

she may be outrageous. I think that Bloomsbury may have been puzzled by the absence of malice and by the genuine happiness of her wit, which they sometimes took for stupidity. One day after reading some letters of Virginia Woolf, she said with amazement in her eyes, 'Oh! how intelligent she was! I see now how terribly stupid she must have thought me.'

I think that I was probably the last person ever to dance with Lydia! She must have been in her sixties; a friend was playing a Chopin waltz on the 'crummy' piano at Tilton bought for Benjamin Britten to use, when she entered in a dressing-gown with her constant cigarette. She started dancing *Les Sylphides*. '*Lift*', she said in a hopeful way, and I became her partner. When it was over she returned to the housework. Dignity is not one of her vices. Once in a heat-wave in New York she was found sitting naked inside the refrigerator in the hotel suite. When one arrives at Tilton it is common to find her coats hanging on the outside of the front door 'to protect them from the moth', as she explains. She always bluntly claims to dislike economists, and, when asked by Marie Rambert had she ever read *The Economic Consequences of the Peace*, she replied, 'There is no need to understand it; for me it is just like Bach.' She has never read Roy Harrod's biography of Maynard, and will presumably never read *this* book.

In 1951, Picasso came over to England to attend an international Communist meeting which was suddenly banned: the only person he saw before returning to France was Lydia Lopokova. They lunched together, and Lydia asked him whether it was true that his son was a pimp. 'Yes', replied Picasso, 'but he is *so* charming.' Later he sent her an inscribed photograph of his drawing of her and Massine (Plate 5a). He wished to give her a present.

After Maynard's death Lydia used to give memorable meals at Gordon Square, often following performances at Covent Garden. She would tear off hunks of cold chicken for each of the guests and then put the carcass on her own plate. We would all laugh and talk endlessly, eat with our fingers and napkins, and get happier and more profound as the wine flowed. Lydia might interrupt the meal by rising from the table to illustrate some steps in a ballet, especially if Frederick Ashton or Balanchine were there.

She once described the experience of ageing: 'Every day a little bit of me flies away, like a bird.' She is old now and in quiet retirement at Tilton, where few ever see her. I have written at length here about Lydia because it is such a pleasure to write about this unique person, my aunt, and because in the writings about Maynard her importance has been unduly neglected.

2

A personal view

AUSTIN ROBINSON

This is the book I have always wanted to see written. Apart from the small and very inaccessible *Memoir* produced for King's College, most of what has been written about Maynard Keynes has been written by economists like myself and filtered through the eyes and perspectives of an economist. But as this book brings out so well, he was very many things beside an economist. Indeed if by 'economist' one means a creator of pure economic theories I feel far from certain that we economists have an unique claim upon him. If, obeying the too familiar cliché, I look around for his monument, is it *The General Theory*? Or is it the International Bank and Fund? Is it the fact that almost every nation today shapes its annual budget in terms of criteria that no nation had ever used when he helped to frame Kingsley Wood's budget of 1941? Is it the fact that for more than a quarter of a century the world economy has grown faster than in any other epoch largely through following policies that he initiated to avoid deep depressions? Is it the fact that we in the United Kingdom have an Arts Council, a vigorous ballet and the regular chance of seeing Shakespeare as it should be done? Is it the fact that he left great collections of books and paintings? There are indeed monuments here enough for many men.

What sort of a person was he, this versatile polymath, this academic who was through his adult life a man of action, this intimate both of 'Bloomsbury' and of those that inhabit the corridors of power? I have always found it difficult to write about him and to convey my own, necessarily limited, picture of him to a generation that never knew him. I start full of determination to dissect him coldly and objectively. In a page or two it becomes painfully obvious that I regard him as a person quite unlike other people, that I am launched again into an essay in hagiology. My difficulty is that I want to see Keynes reassessed by another generation. For reassessed he must be. Most of Keynes's contemporaries and the teachers of my own generation are gradually disappearing into the mausoleum of the history of economic thought. Keynes is still alive. Twenty-eight years after his death a great deal of current academic economics is still about him and his ideas. A great deal of economic policy-making is a debate about the reconciliation of Keynesian policies with the control of inflation. He is, almost as when he was alive, one of the protagonists, quoted by politicians as holy writ. An economist of today finds himself arguing with someone who cannot argue back. But as soon as Harry Johnson or Paul Levy or Robert Skidelsky starts reappraising him I find an irresistible urge to chip in and say, 'Oh, but you have got him all wrong. He was not a bit like that.' It seems to me therefore that those of us who knew him have a duty to our successors and the reappraisers to make sure that they can at least know all that is possible to record about him.

I saw Keynes first when someone took me to one of the later lectures in the course that he gave on 'Economic aspects of the Peace Treaty' during the weeks before the publication of *The Economic Consequences of the Peace* in December 1919. I date from that my own conversion to the faith of the economists. What most impressed me was the very obvious depth of his dedication to the problems of the world and his hatred of failure to avert foreseeable disaster. It was this dedication that inspired and fired his pupils of my generation.

During the next two years I got to see him much more closely, since, thanks to Ryle Fay, I was made quite early a member of his Political Economy Club, meeting weekly in King's. It would be easy to say that Keynes dominated those meetings. But I think that would be wrong, or at least very much too simple. It was never impossible for us undergraduates to argue with him. He did not lay down the law and frighten us into agreeing with him. He loved argument, he could occasionally be carried away by his own argument into preposterous conclusions and laugh them off. He was delighted when we developed our own arguments. He let us talk and normally intervened only at the very end. If he dominated us, it was in quite a different way. We gradually came to see things very much as he would see them, to accept his valuations of what were the priorities, and to accept his conclusions for action because he had led us to make them our conclusions. But his mind was always the quickest. His thinking was more radical and less circumscribed by unconscious limitations of political or institutional assumptions. And not infrequently we were discussing something about which Keynes was still developing ideas that he would be publishing in a week or two, and we had the excitement of feeling ourselves on the fringes of policy-making.

As undergraduates those of us who attended his Club were, almost to a man, Keynesians in whatever were the issues of the moment, but Keynesians because we had made ourselves Keynesians. I, like a few others, stayed on in Cambridge and became his very much junior colleague. It was at this stage of achieving maturity that some of us, at least, found the necessity to stand back, to escape from our self-imposed surrender and to try to see him more objectively. I myself, as a young fellow of Corpus, found myself in danger of being dominated by a much more aggressively and consciously dominating personality, Will Spens – a Disraelian Tory where Keynes was then a Gladstonian liberal, a high-church ecclesiastical politician where Keynes was an atheist with a devotion to King's Chapel, a former scholar of King's of Keynes's own vintage, who knew him well. It was under pressure from Spens that I found myself trying to rethink the dogmas of the Cambridge school of liberal economists of which Keynes was then the popular preacher, if Pigou was the high-priest with Dennis Robertson as his acolyte. I am glad that I had this short period of doubt and rethinking, followed by a period remote from it all in India. When I came back to work in Cambridge two and a half years later I could feel that I had lost the fear that I was being dominated by Keynes and was free to form my own judgements. But I think my own case was not an isolated one. Others also found the necessity to stand back and to get out for a period from under his shadow. What was more important was that most of us, having recovered our own initiative, came back and learned a more independent, a less subservient, relation. I think that another generation equally needs at some stage to stand back, to appraise with detachment, and to recover its own independent judgement. But when I look at my friends and colleagues I cannot help cataloguing them into those still in the phase of uncritical adulation, those struggling for independence and those who have won through.

Harry Johnson finds Keynes arrogant. Was he? I find myself wanting to say 'No.' But I am not always sure that I know what he is meaning by arrogant. Did he use his authority and position to make argument with him difficult? To overawe those, particularly his juniors, who disagreed with him? I would say emphatically 'No.' He was easier to argue with than many who have entrenched themselves in doctrinal positions today. He was more patient and more prepared to meet argument and to face the difficulties of someone who differed from him. I think that Lionel Robbins, reviewing the volume of the *Collected Writings of John Maynard Keynes* which publishes the correspondence leading up to *The General Theory*, has put his finger on the vital point. 'To those who know Keynes', he writes, 'only by *The General Theory* and his more polemical ephemeral publications, I imagine that among the most revealing features of this correspondence will be its open-mindedness and friendly good temper. In public controversy, often, Keynes followed his conviction that words should be a little wild, an assault on the complacent intellect . . . But the correspondence reveals another aspect of his many-sided character, a patience in argument, a willingness to admit imperfections of exposition, even a humility before ultimate problems which was no less genuine than his flashes of public arrogance or rudeness when confronted with those whom he regarded as fools.'

I would myself put the same thing a little differently. Keynes was always in the ultimate a man of action. When he was clearing his thinking and working out his proposals for action with those whose intellectual honesty he respected he was, to take Lionel Robbins' words, patient in argument. But, when his thinking was cleared and he moved over into the phase of political persuasion and into the battleground with entrenched authority, he did not hesitate to assault with the weapons of which he was a master – wit, sarcasm, ridicule, the biting phrase, the contemptuous exaggeration which punctured the pompous and pierced the more sensitive skin of the civil servant who too loyally defended the indefensible.

I would not want to deny that he inflicted wounds, or even that on occasion he irritated and made enemies of those that it might have been possible and better to make his friends. He clearly offended his American counterparts in the First World War. But more generally, was ever a battle fought without a casualty? Could he have better achieved his objects by humility and diffidence? Or would he – as I would believe – have been gently elbowed aside and forgotten by the safely entrenched establishment?

For whom did Keynes reserve the whips and scorpions? In my experience they were reserved for those who preferred authority to argument, oratory to orderly thinking, or were intransigent in advocating policies which he firmly believed to be wrong-headed. I attended countless meetings with him of the Cambridge Faculty, the Royal Economic Society, in the Treasury, on government missions, where we were discussing policies among a group of rational people. I have only one memory of a verbal lambasting, when an over-zealous representative of a small department was obstinately resisting the small sacrifice necessary to make a much larger negotiation successful. Almost always among those whom he respected it was by argument, persuasion and charm that he carried his point.

One cannot discuss his relations with academic colleagues without mention of the tragedy of his relations with Dennis Robertson, and Harry Johnson refers to this. I share the misery of others over the break between two, both of whom had been my close friends – a break which in my view has been greatly exaggerated by recent writers. I would want to urge any who wish to understand to read for themselves the long correspondence over the years between them in *Collected Writings*, Vol. xiii, and especially their comments, half light-hearted half very serious, on each other's habits of thought and work made in 1936 (Vol. xiv, pp. 94–5). May I make one general point? Keynes ordinarily bore no animosity towards those who differed from him intellectually. He wanted to convince them and was sorry when he failed. He was arguing over these years with Hawtrey and with Pigou. With both he failed to convince; I would go further and say that he failed to achieve a meeting of minds. With both he remained, despite intellectual differences, on terms of close personal friendship.

With Dennis Robertson his relations were for two reasons very different. First, as he stresses in the letter I have mentioned, 'I certainly date all my emancipation from the discussions between us which preceded your *Banking Policy and the Price Level*.' He believed right up to publication of *The General Theory* that Dennis was really in agreement with him, if he could only bring himself to say so. Second, and more important, Dennis, an immaculate scholar, had been for years in a sense the keeper of his conscience. If he could convince Dennis, he felt that he was right. I find it harder to look at this through Dennis Robertson's eyes. In retrospect I think Robertson felt more acutely than any of us imagined at the time the constant strain of being used as Keynes's conscience. Inevitably Keynes was arguing vigorously in defence of his ideas. And Robertson, who was curiously diffident for one of his great ability, was unsure whether he was yielding to good argument or to pressure of friendship, and unsure whether Keynes's attempts to restate really met the legitimate points that he made. One recalls what he had written to Keynes ten years earlier, when they were both arguing about his *Banking Policy and the Price Level*: 'I am afraid of being swayed into publishing by the desire to avoid disappointment and loss: but I am also afraid of being swayed against publishing by my tendency to believe you are always right! Sometimes when I have stood out against this weakness I have been justified!...I am so unconfident that I should always like to put at the top of everything that I write "Nobody must believe a word of what follows." Is that a hopeless frame of mind?'

I believe, that is to say, that when Robertson decided to take a chair in London in 1939 he was anxious to be released from the still continuing responsibilities of being the keeper of the conscience, the touchstone. I have always thought that, in the very last stages of

The General Theory, Robertson was quarrelling with Keynes not about the intellectual content of Keynes's economic model but about Keynes's way of presenting it in the book and his emphasis – his over-emphasis if you will – on its departure from the orthodoxies of Marshall and Pigou, where Robertson, himself a scholar rather than an evangelist, would have emphasised the continuity and development. That apart, all of us who knew Robertson well knew one feature of his make-up – his preference for being right in a minority of one to being an activist as member of a majority. Keynes was, as I see it, confronted with the dilemma of so emasculating the presentation of the book as to reduce – as he felt – its impact on the world, or failing in the last stages to win Robertson's acquiescence – knowing the latter I would doubt whether it could have been enthusiastic support. For better or for worse Keynes chose to achieve his impact.

But the story does not end here. Over the years after the appearance of *The General Theory* Keynes and Robertson continued to correspond over things that both of them were writing. When war came they were closely collaborating in the Treasury. At Bretton Woods Robertson played a key role. Keynes's comment after it to some of us was 'It was an absolute blessing to have one person there with a completely first-class mind.' When, in 1944, Pigou retired and the electors offered the chair to Keynes he declined in a letter pressing the claims of Robertson. While Keynes was alive there was, I am convinced, no break between them that could not have been mended. The antipathy of Robertson was not to Keynes himself living, but after his death to some of his younger friends and colleagues and their more radical interpretations of Keynesian policies, which differed increasingly widely from his own more and more right-wing liberal views.

Was Keynes arrogant in quite another sense? Did he, to a much greater extent than he realised, embody and even propagate the assumptions of the generation in which he was born and brought up – born a Victorian, brought up an Edwardian, surviving into the first beginnings of a new world that he had not fully visualised? Here I believe he is less impregnable and I, just a Victorian, educated an Edwardian and a Georgian, am ill-equipped to judge him through neo-Elizabethan eyes. It was a world in which a voter was allowed to choose between Herbert Asquith, the Craven Scholar from Balliol College, Oxford, and Arthur Balfour, the Etonian intellectual from Trinity College, Cambridge, as to who should exercise responsibility for Sir Robert Chalmers or Sir John Bradbury, who ruled the Treasury, and their Oxford and Cambridge counterparts through every level of a civil service recruited on the best principles of meritocracy by competitive examination in subjects which only Oxford and Cambridge could teach.

Into this narrow world of a benevolent avuncular bureaucracy, administered by a conscientious but narrowly inbred élite and responding to their intellectual valuations, Keynes had entered by the time-honoured channel of success in competitive examination at the age of fourteen for an Eton scholarship. From then on he was one of them, friend of the Asquiths, protégé of Margot, welcome guest at political house parties, adopted into the world that produced the future prime ministers, permanent secretaries and rulers of the Empire. He could not live in that hot-house of College at Eton, in that limited society of scholarship winners, for five years without taking on some of the values and assumptions of even the very critical young of his time.

But this was, I think, a slow process and one must not visualise him as becoming overnight a precocious, cynical, irreverent, insufferable, adolescent genius. When I first read, a year or so back, the schoolboy diaries which he kept for a short time in his early Eton days, what surprised me was not his precocious brilliance and sophistication but his schoolboy interest in the things that ordinary boys enjoy – bicycle rides during the holidays with his brother, playing golf at Royston with his father, playing fives and rowing, watching and criticising the crowned heads of Europe at Queen Victoria's funeral, being bored by bad sermons.

But by the time he left Eton he was half-way, I think, to his ultimate personality. One can visualise him as he was when he first arrived in King's with the help of the eyes of Ryle Fay. Already a book collector, proud of the trophies he has bought from David, already something of a polymath. Sophisticated far beyond the level of the ordinary undergraduate. Already familiar with and far from over-awed by the Fellows of King's – many known to him as his father's friends or as his own seniors at Eton. Proposing soon after his arrival the secularisation of the King's College Mission in London.

I have deliberately said 'half-way'. For what clearly changed all his thinking most over the next few years was his friendship with Lytton Strachey, Bertrand Russell, G. E. Moore and the Society of Apostles, first in Cambridge and later, with new additions, in Bloomsbury. The immensity of their influence over him at this moment in his life is beyond question. I have found the chapter on this by Paul Levy printed in this book quite fascinating. I had no share in this side of his life and am in no position to embroider it. But I cannot help wondering whether Paul Levy has interpreted quite rightly Keynes's changing relations to his Bloomsbury friends.

That he and they were wholly of one way of thinking when he first became one of them in the Cambridge of 1903-8 seems absolutely clear. But as the years went on I feel less certain. Paul Levy writes as if this was a religious brotherhood with a joint responsibility for each other's souls and consciences and as if, when Lytton and others of them found the immorality of war and the duty of complete pacificism paramount, they had a right to demand of him that he should resign from the Treasury. I wonder whether one cannot find a hint of his own attitude of mind in the letter which he wrote to the Local Tribunal which considered his application for exemption from military service on grounds of conscientious objection. He did not make his claim, as did several of his friends, on the principle that war was always wrong. He made it on the ground that he had 'a conscientious objection to surrendering my liberty of judgement on so vital a question as undertaking military service. I do not say that there are not conceivable circumstances in which I should voluntarily offer myself for military service ... I am not prepared on such an issue as this to surrender my right of decision, as to what is or is not my duty, to any other person, and I should think it morally wrong to do so.' I myself believe that he was as far from surrendering his conscience even to his friends as from surrendering it to the dictates of the State.

Inevitably one asks oneself how far in later life Keynes moved away from Bloomsbury. And move he quite certainly did, partly one suspects because of their failure to accept and welcome Lydia, partly because he became more involved in other worlds and in their senses of values – values much nearer to those from which he and his fellow offspring of the élite establishment had tried to escape by creating this new and private élite of their own.

Paul Levy begins his chapter with the picture of them sitting happily around on the lawn at Tilton. What were they doing on that occasion? Were they, as a superficial reading of his chapter might seem to suggest, engaged in happy and carefree literary reminiscence of themselves when young? Or were they, as I myself would think, engaged in something altogether more serious? For me, as for anyone primarily concerned about Keynes himself, the whole interest is focused in the last nine or ten pages of 'My Early Beliefs' (pages 442-50 as printed in *Collected Writings*, Vol. x, *Essays in Biography*) where, after picturing and interpreting the young Apostles as they had been in those earlier years with nostalgic understanding, he turns to look at them again through eyes that are thirty years older. For as I see it what he was engaged in doing that afternoon was to use the text of Bunny Garnett's reflections on D. H. Lawrence and Lawrence's antipathy to themselves to ask not only how, thirty years later, they really saw themselves as they had been, but also how far they had moved on and away from those earlier beliefs and values.

And what does he find? One can never compress or summarise him, and here least of all; a reader must go back to those pages for himself. Perhaps a dozen sentences here must serve: 'It seems to me looking back, that this religion of ours was a very good one to grow up under. It remains nearer the truth than any other that I know, with less extraneous matter and nothing to be ashamed of ... It is still my religion under the surface ... I see no reason to shift from the fundamental intuitions of *Principia Ethica* ... But we set on one side the part [of *Principia Ethica*] which discussed the duty of the individual to obey certain rules ... We were not aware that civilisation was a thin and precarious crust erected by the personality and the will of a very few and only maintained by rules and conventions skilfully put across and guilefully preserved ... It did not occur to us to respect the extraordinary accomplishment of our predecessors in the ordering of life (as it now seems to me to have been) or the elaborate framework which they had devised to protect this order ... As cause and consequence of our general state of mind we completely misunderstood human nature, including our own ... this pseudo-rational view of human nature led to a thinness, a superficiality, not only of judgement, but also of feeling ... Our comments on life and affairs were bright and amusing, but brittle ... because there was no solid diagnosis of human nature underlying them ... If, therefore, I altogether ignore our merits – our charm, our intelligence, our unworldliness, our affection – I can see us as water-spiders, gracefully skimming, as light and reasonable as air, the surface of the stream without any contact at all with the eddies and currents underneath.'

Was Keynes engaged in saying gently and with a twinkle in his eye to his old friends 'This is how I now see us. Do you also see us in the same way? Or have I, as I now am, really ceased to be one of you?'

If he had changed already to this extent in 1938, over the next eight years, as he became increasingly the man responsible in the corridors of power for our economic policies, so he became more and more absorbed into the establishment. Not that he had ever, since 1919, ceased to be effectively a member of the establishment. Though he criticised and attacked them in public he was throughout the inter-war years constantly engaged in personal correspondence with his old colleagues in the Treasury, trying out his ideas on them, occasionally flying kites for them to see whether particular policies would command support, a member of innumerable advisory committees so that he came near to sharing in the Treasury policy-making and their policy-making often reflected his thinking. Over the years the whole character of the establishment had changed. What had happened? Had the establishment taken over Keynes? Or had Keynes taken over the establishment?

I have read with great interest Robert Skidelsky's chapter on the political reception of Keynesian ideas. He does well to remind economists, who are somewhat prone to forget it, that new ideas have not only to be evolved in the ivory towers of the academics but also sold to the establishment both of the civil service and of the politicians. Why, he asks, were Keynesian ideas for dealing with a crisis of unemployment unacceptable in 1929 and acceptable in 1946?

When I try to understand his answers I find myself, however, considerably puzzled. He sees Keynes as 'guilty of treating power questions as intellectual questions . . . failing to recognise the power obstacles in the way of acceptance of his ideas ... What made Keynes's *Essays in Persuasion* "so uniformly unpersuasive" to John Strachey was their lack of any analysis in terms of interests. . . . Keynes's attack on the "faulty thinking" of the bankers in 1925 ignored the fact that "when their own interest was concerned the bankers and city merchants showed no lack of understanding" . . .'

Was Keynes in fact so imperceptive? Was the only way of battling with interests to ally oneself with another opposed group of interests? If the bankers, who claimed to be acting in the national interest, were in fact acting in their private interest, surely the most effective attack on them was to show the outside, political and administrative world, that they were, in effect, abusing their powers. If civil servants, in a similar position of responsibility, were acting against the national interest, they too were most vulnerable to public demonstration of their errors. This, I believe, is what Keynes was doing. When he comes to the need to rethink the classical ortho-doxies of *laissez-faire*, Robert Skidelsky credits Keynes with per-ceiving that it was economic orthodoxy and not the clash of eco-nomic interests which was the barrier to acceptance of his ideas. I agree.

But how came it that what was impossible in 1929 was possible in 1946? Robert Skidelsky argues, if I understand him right, that in 1929 Keynes was a voice in the wilderness, with no sufficient link with the establishment, beginning to urge the break with exaggera-ted internationalism and with rigid *laissez-faire*. He writes of the 'attitude gap between Keynes and the establishment'. Here, I cannot help thinking, he is wrong.

First, I think he forgets that Keynes himself was evolving

throughout this period. He was not in 1929 himself a complete and final 'Keynesian'. His own ideas of the relation of the British economy to the world economy were changing. But I do not think they were ever as simple as Skidelsky's analysis would have us believe. He quotes the Macmillan Report as typical of establishment thinking and of the 'terrifying implications' when it 'condemned a policy of devaluation which it recognised might help Britain's "domestic situation" for fear of the damage it might do to world trade and finance – this with almost three million unemployed'. He seems to have forgotten that it was Keynes who largely drafted the Macmillan Report, and has forgotten also Keynes's still strong internationalism in the *Treatise on Money*. Equally I think he forgets that Keynes, through his life, hated the exporting of unemployment. What was Bretton Woods about if it was not the creation of a world in which countries did not close their eyes to the repercussions of their actions on others? His whole attitude to the mutual interrelations of national and international policies and objectives was, I think, much more complex than Skidelsky thinks.

Second, I think that Skidelsky underrates the closeness of Keynes's relations with the Treasury through the 1920s and 1930s. He was, as I have said, in close touch with them throughout and not infrequently in what he published he was pressurising the establishment of the party politicians towards and not against the thinking of many in the Treasury. Once again I think the situation was much more complex than Skidelsky supposes. If one wishes to shift the action of the Treasury one must shift two things: their own internal attempts at rational thinking, which is largely an intellectual process; the willingness of their political masters to accept a new line of thinking and policy – the latter to be achieved through public discussion and argument. Keynes was operating at both these levels.

When Skidelsky comes to the final acceptance of Keynesian ideas he finds it in the fact that in wartime (after the replacement of peacetime generals) 'the second requirement is to replace many peacetime politicians and civil servants by new men whose ideas, personalities and interests have previously disqualified them for normal politics'. These were the people among whom I worked for nine years. The civil servants who played the central parts had been there in the 1930s. The new ideas came partly, it is true, from the heavy infiltration of academics, much less from the industrialists, valuable as they were in making an administration run. But so far as we were using new ideas or accepting new attitudes, I would myself want to say that the main source of them was Keynes. Of the political establishment, Churchill was sublimely unaware in all but very occasional detail of what happened on the economic front.

Was it Anderson, the great administrator, who changed political ideas – he was not a political animal? Oliver Lyttelton apart, who was no political theorist, the other ministers were mostly the politicians of the 1930s. If they were now receptive to new ideas, I would myself argue that this was largely a consequence of all that Keynes had done and written in popular as well as academic form over the years.

Let me come back now to my original question. Was Keynes by the end of his life just a skilful and persuasive apologist for the outmoded establishment of his day? Must he be rejected by those who, living forty or fifty years later, feel that they have a different set of values? Has Keynes dated in the way that for me Alfred Marshall has dated, so that I read him with my critical hackles always half-raised?

I cannot answer this question with confidence. For if he has dated, so to an even greater extent have I. But this I think one can say. The economic issues of today are very much the economic issues that he forty years ago was trying to tackle. Is anything more topical than trying to see just how far we can go towards preventing excessive inflation without depending on the sanctions of unemployment? Or than trying to see how one can best combine the virtues of reasonably predictable exchange-rates with the avoidance of excessively over-valued or under-valued currencies? He overrated, perhaps, our advance towards the millennium and did not, perhaps, foresee how large a part in the economies of our grandchildren would be played by public expenditure on health and education, making progress towards adequate and better distributed personal incomes slower than it might be. Nor, I think, did he see the full implications of continuing high levels of employment on relative incomes and the increasing need to compensate adequately those doing unpleasant or boring jobs. He was indeed too little interested in the distribution of income. But I do not think he has become irrelevant because he was writing about trivialities – far from it.

Were the solutions that he visualised the solutions that belonged to a world of carefree capitalism and government by a meritocratic establishment? He was, I would concede, concerned firstly with the problems of his own time, with making a system work which has itself considerably changed over the past forty years, so that our problems are not exactly his problems, and the best solutions today are not necessarily those that he advocated. The problems of preventing inflation in an over-full economy are not those of preventing the cruelties of unemployment in the 1930s. He left us, perhaps, too little precise guidance as to how he would have handled our very different problems. But more generally we can still learn from him

20

how to tackle these problems. His problems, like ours today, were very largely the problems of how to make an economy run which is neither crudely capitalist nor purely socialist but a mixture between the two. But I do not think that because he, always a seeker after the politically just practicable solution, was anxious to find ways of making the politico-economic system of the day work better, he was on a longer time-scale anxious to perpetuate it. One can see his mind at work on these problems in 'Economic Possibilities for our Grandchildren' (*Collected Writings*, Vol. IX, pp. 321–32), written as early as 1928, where he outlines an almost Marxian state of bliss, to be reached perhaps in a century, in which all goods become free, leisure is more important than production, the economics of scarcity is subordinated to enjoyment, and avarice is a vice. If, on a more mundane level he is concerned to cobble the contemporary economic system, I would want to argue that he was more anxious to create an economic system that would work within the given political framework than to determine the political framework.

He belonged, let me admit it, to a generation that had not yet learned the need to apologise for being more than normally endowed with intelligence or more than normally appreciative of the arts. He was proud of his Eton connections, of his Fellowship of King's. He was conscious that he, like others of his closest friends, possessed minds of unusual power. But he did not vaunt this. It was natural that he should draw these friends from a circle with similar intellects and similar interests. He was not, I think, as frighteningly contemptuous of others less well endowed as Strachey and others of that group. I do not think he was an intellectual snob. It is sometimes said of him that he did not suffer fools gladly. I do not think it was the honest fools that he did not tolerate so much as the pretentious and the pseudo-intellectual. In his relations with those younger than himself he was frightening only in the sense that he set himself and us standards of rational argument and conduct that one was afraid that one might fail to attain.

Having said all this, have I contributed anything to a picture of him? He is, as I said earlier, very difficult for any one person to picture, because one saw him and remembers him primarily in one aspect of his life.* That apart, the difficulty is that for many of us who were his pupils he became a sort of ideal of what we would like to make of ourselves, an apotheosis of our own ambitions. As a conventional 'do-gooder', I cannot fail to see him as the perfect

---

* I owe a number of ideas, here and elsewhere, to his economist niece Polly Hill, who lived at 46 Gordon Square with him and Lydia during the war and saw much more of him in his leisure moments than any other of his friends or relations.

'do-gooder', identifying the things that the world most needs to have done and using all his brains and persuasion to get them done. But that, so far as it was there, was only a fraction of him, and partly at least submerged in all the other aspects.

I myself remember his quickness of mind – many of the best things he wrote, he wrote with extreme rapidity. He took things in with equal rapidity. He told me once, when I was saying I wanted more time to think about a particular book, that he believed that one could always get the essentials out of any book (we were talking about economics) in two hours, if one knew how to do it. He got through a vast amount because he wasted very little time. He had no interest that I remember in technology for its own sake, in cars or aeroplanes except as means of transport, in how industrial processes worked, or in the scientific development of new techniques. He was no reader of 'who dunnits' and the rubbish with which many of us waste time or rest our tired minds. With Pigou, I could and did gossip about the latest Agatha Christie, or cricket, or climbing, or a dozen other trivialities; but I never remember gossiping with Keynes in that sort of way. In later life he had, as I remember, no interest in sport. If one was travelling with him one gossiped, so far as one gossiped at all, about work, friends and about books. When younger he had been a brilliant bridge player, but he seldom, as far as I know, played in his later years. He enjoyed good food and good wine. If he wanted to rest, he rested with a book that most of us would regard as serious. He was eternally watching and playing the markets, on his own behalf as well as for King's, the Royal Economic Society and his friends. He was not, as I may perhaps be suggesting, a perpetually serious person – it was always fun, always exciting to be in his company – but his frivolities were half-serious frivolities.

Of all the contributions to this volume by those who have known him, the letter of Frank Lee about a chaotic Washington negotiation, in which as it happens I took some small part, rings to me truest. It brings out his power of discarding inessentials to fasten on the essentials. But above all, with the attention focused on the detail of a single such task, it will make clearer than any amount of generalisation, the burden and strain that such a negotiation threw onto him personally. My own recollections are principally of the worries of Lydia and myself lest he might collapse under it. I was living in the same hotel and eating with them. Whenever we could, Lydia and I tried to take him out for an hour or two into the country. I was myself engaged on the munitions side of the negotiation and saw nothing of the financial and trade negotiations in which he was primarily concerned. But I heard all about it from

Keynes himself and my various friends who were involved. And I travelled back with him and Lydia, helping to get the material together for the necessary report to the Cabinet. On the long journey back by sea on a transport crowded with American troops he stayed almost the whole time in his cabin, first resting and then writing the brilliant account of it all which will in due course appear in the *Collected Writings*.

I have often wondered how many others beside myself have stumbled on that curiously prophetic 'Sonnet to J. M. K.' that Tennyson, himself one of the earliest of the Cambridge Apostles, wrote for another Apostle some fifty years before John Maynard Keynes was born. The second J. M. K., as he told me when I asked him after I first found it, had known it since boyhood:

Sonnet to J. M. K.
(1829–30)

My hope and heart is with thee – thou wilt be
A later Luther, and a soldier priest
To scare church-harpies from the master's feast;
Our dusted velvets have much need of thee;
Thou art no sabbath-drawler of old saws,
Distill'd from some worm-cankered homily;
But spurr'd at heart with fieriest energy
To embattail and to wall about thy cause
With iron-worded proof, hating to hark
The humming of the drowsy pulpit-drone
Half God's good sabbath, while the worn-out clerk
Brow-beats his desk below. Thou from a throne
Mounted in heaven wilt shoot into the dark
Arrows of lightnings. I will stand and mark.

3

A private view by a Cabinet Minister, 1919

EARL OF CRAWFORD AND BALCARRES

Three passages from the unpublished private diaries of David, 27th Earl of Crawford and Balcarres (1871–1940), Lord Privy Seal in 1919.

9 April 1919, written on return to London from Paris. Of the British personnel Lloyd-George, of course, is the dominant personality, but he appears to have made little impact upon the retina of Paris. On the whole they are over inclined to depreciate him, and just now they show no particular friendliness because they say that he is doing scanty justice to the Italian and French claims.... Now that we have gained our points we are fatigued by the applications of other countries who were not skilful enough to get their claims discussed during the earlier stages. People can't help laughing at Lloyd-George's witty sallies, many of which go the round of the Paris salon.... Neither does the British mission as a whole show much enthusiasm towards the P. Minister. They slave away, produce admirable data, statistics, résumés, argumentations – but they well know that he won't read them and that good labour is lost.... One day I attended a meeting of the supreme Economic Council. There were 52 people present, a sort of miniature parliament! Half the items on the agenda were scimped and the other half postponed....
I often wonder how we have got so wrong about indemnities. Hewins* says Germany can pay our debts, and being a Professor in status and pompousness, was taken at his word with lamentable results. Keynes too, I fancy, the Cambridge economist should have restrained the extravagance of ministerial promises. Keynes is the Treasury man in Paris – clear headed, self confident, with an unerring memory and unsurpassable digestion. But while he is one of the most influential of men behind the scenes, I cannot help thinking that he looks at large political problems too much from the aspect of currency and exchange; and that in large affairs his advice is often based upon premises which may be correct in technique,

* W. A. S. Hewins (1865–1931), political economist; first Director of the London School of Economics.

24

but utterly misleading in practice. This is an impression which emanates from Keynes's schemes, though his word is all too often taken for gospel. He is a wonderful fellow, but has passed his life in cloister and has had no experience in handling men or in assessing their temperaments.

22 December 1919. Keynes's book on the Economic results of the Peace Treaty will attract attention. I don't like it – I mean I find it distasteful that a man (apparently of military age) should enjoy a safe and cushy job and then write a book criticising his official superiors – his government's policy. Though Keynes may say that his criticism is based on common knowledge there can be no doubt that his position at the Treasury and afterwards in Paris gives réclame to his words which the book would not receive under different authorship . . . How is it that clever men, and Keynes is among the cleverest I know, are often so tactless – say such unwise things?

5 January 1920. I went to Christie's hoping to buy a hearthrug. There I saw the most unholy gang of Rag and Bone merchants running up the prices and bidding eagerly for all sorts of rubbish. . . One Englishman I saw – excluding the auctioneer – namely Keynes. I told him he was wrong in stating in his book that Orlando* can't understand English. In point of fact I quite satisfied myself on the point a few months ago when I dined with him at the Travellers' Club. He understands English very well though he speaks it hopelessly – his French likewise is pretty poor. Keynes was surprised – and to surprise so dogmatic a prig is quite an achievement! But why should Orlando have pretended he didn't understand English? – why, I replied, does Cambon† pretend he doesn't understand English? The unsophisticated Keynes dimly perceived that these astute Latins were playing with him – and that he had been deceived by a very palpable device. 'I must put that right in the new Edition of my new book' – yes, I murmured, but it would have been still better not to have had to make corrections on this . . . and other points.

* V. E. Orlando (1860–1952), Prime Minister of Italy, 1917–19.
† J. M. Cambon (1845–1935), French diplomat; one of the signatories of the Treaty of Versailles.

4

The early years

GEOFFREY KEYNES

John Maynard Keynes was born in Cambridge on 5 June 1883 at 6 Harvey Road, rather less than four years before my own appearance on the scene. In family life even this relatively short interval can create an important division between brothers. All my young days were lived under the shadow of a much more intellectual and forceful character in the person of my elder brother – not that he was ever unkind or even domineering; the division was the natural result of a situation where the elder was leading not so much by virtue of a few years between them, but rather by inborn advantages of mind and body. We were not close friends and my view of him was rather that of an eminent acquaintance to whom I looked up as a superior and rather distant being.

Our parents had married in 1882, my father, University Lecturer in Moral Science, having resigned his Fellowship at Pembroke College in order to unite his fortunes with Florence Ada Brown, one of the early students at Newnham College. Both of them belonged to the congregationalist circles who attended the services at Emmanuel Chapel in Trumpington Street opposite Pembroke. My father took his bride to live in a newly built semi-detached house on the outskirts of the town. At the end of Harvey Road to the East was Fenner's cricket ground. Not far away to the South were open fields where our butcher, Mr Bulman, grazed his cattle. The house and small garden were without charm or character, but the place suited our unexacting standards, and my mother died there seventy-six years later at the age of ninety-six. Our home was unmistakably and inevitably 'Victorian' in character. The walls of the rather dark dining-room were clad in deep blue and crimson Morris paper of such quality that it never needed renewal during our tenancy. The furnishings were undistinguished, but comfortable, some having stood in my father's rooms in Pembroke. The pictures were conventional specimens of period taste, the most vividly remembered being a large reproduction of Raphael's 'Virgin and Child', such as might have been seen in a hundred other homes of the same class. In the narrow hall was a print of Reynolds's 'Garrick between Comedy and Tragedy'. The few oil paintings had been bought in Salisbury by my grandfather, John Keynes, who had prospered as a market gardener specialising in the culture of roses and dahlias. He had been advised by a friend regarded as a connoisseur of pictures, but, apart from a modest canvas by Morland, his purchases have proved of small interest. Our home surroundings afforded no aesthetic stimulus of modernity or novelty to our expanding consciousness, but Maynard was fully able to get the best out of his contacts with our academic society. Home was, then, all middle-class comfort and security without luxury, making an ideal, if rather neutral, atmosphere in which a highly individual and intelligent mind like Maynard's could develop unfettered by parental dominance or prejudice.

Our parents, as I now look back on them, had a lovable aura of perfect integrity and goodness without stuffiness or pomposity; they were affectionate without sentimentality, and were careful not to interfere with the personalities of their children, while always fostering any worthwhile interests as soon as they discerned them. My father, in any situation of uncertainty, assumed a settled attitude of being 'prepared for the worst' though he never had justification for pessimism at any point in Maynard's career. He always took a deep interest in our school work and set great store by our marks and position in class, and this stimulated a sense of competition in Maynard, who enjoyed his own capacity for learning and leaping ahead of the other boys. His relations with his father were very close and he was devoted to his mother throughout his life. There was never in our family any of the now so frequent antagonism between the generations.

I have no memories of Maynard's taking part in nursery life, for he had passed out of this stage before I was old enough to be conscious of his presence. He moved in another sphere and it is impossible to imagine him under the dominance of a nurse or governess. He had the reputation in the family of having always been able to get the better of them in an argument, though being much too intelligent and sensible to be conventionally 'naughty'. My mother has recorded that his mind set itself difficult problems from an early age. 'Who invented Time?' he asked at the age of six. 'How did things get their names?' 'Just now', he said, 'my brain is wondering how it thinks. It ought to know.'

Both our parents had been brought up in fairly strict noncon-formist principles, my mother's father, Dr John Brown, being the congregationalist pastor of Bunyan Meeting in Bedford and a cele-brated preacher. Maynard felt great admiration for his grandfather and was always pleased with the thought that his great-great-grandfather on Mrs Brown's side, Thomas Ford, had lost his life in 1768 as a smuggler of brandy in an encounter with the excise-men at Lancing on the Sussex coast. Our great-grandfather, David Ford, had made his peace with the Almighty for his father's sins by becoming minister at the charming congregationalist Chapel in Long Melford, where he lies buried under an enormous inscribed slab of stone. Our Christmas holidays, when we were children, were always spent at The Manse in Bedford, where Sunday observance was strictly enforced. Even the most innocent game of cards, such as snap, was forbidden on the Sabbath and the family went through the daily formality of morning prayers, while we knelt at horse-hair chairs with the female staff in the background. At Harvey Road this ritual was not observed and we enjoyed a more relaxed view of religious duties and observances. In Cambridge the whole family attended every Sunday morning the service at Emmanuel Chapel and listened to a highly intellectual sermon lasting for any-thing up to three-quarters of an hour. To me this seemed to be interminable, though Maynard was certainly more interested, and in his teens at Eton he regularly recorded the preacher and his opinion of the sermon in his diary, sometimes in forthright terms. On a Sunday in February 1901 he wrote: 'The Reverend X preached. He was wholly abominable and altogether loathsome. His words were imbecile, devoid of taste, thoroughly offensive, and without eloquence. His delivery was loud and raucous. His matter turgid, execrable, and senseless. The British Empire has often been maligned; imperialism has often been besmirched by its adherents, but never as the Reverend X defiled it today.'

He felt always an intellectual interest in religion, but, like each of us at the age of seventeen or eighteen, passed painlessly into a natural state of agnosticism. Rather surprisingly, when we had all ceased to go to Sunday services our parents followed suit, without any discussion or outward show of uneasiness. It is certain that neither Maynard nor his juniors were subjected to any sort of pressure in matters of religion, each taking his or her own course.

Maynard and I both went at the age of nine to St Faith's School in the Trumpington Road, where Ralph Goodchild was headmaster, but owing to the four years between us we did not overlap and I have no memories of him in those surroundings. Goodchild had a very high opinion of Maynard's abilities. He was, he said, 'head and shoulders above all the other boys both mentally and physically', for he was growing very fast, and he was not at all surprised when Maynard became a King's Scholar at Eton College in July 1897. While the family waited anxiously for news of the results of the examination, my father had of course made up his mind to face failure. When the telegram came through announcing his success we happened to be all standing together in the garden at Harvey Road. I vividly remember how, with a small boy's impulsive enthusiasm, I flung my arms around Maynard's neck only to be pushed impatiently away. He was too old, being already fourteen, for such demonstration of affection.

There can be no doubt that at St Faith's he was regarded almost with awe by his schoolfellows. The stories of his slave, who walked behind him carrying his books in return for help and protection, and of the other boy with whom he had 'a commercial treaty', sealed with blood and enacting that he should not approach at any time nearer than fifteen yards, are not apocryphal. I can still name the second one.

At home at Harvey Road Maynard was treated with admiring respect by us all, though sometimes it seemed to us younger ones that he was perhaps given too much consideration when he developed his habit of staying up late at night and refusing to come down to breakfast before the middle of the morning without any protest from those in nominal authority.

When distinguished guests came to luncheon my sister and I usually kept a respectful silence. Maynard, on the other hand, was ready from an early age to join in learned discussions. Particularly clear in my memory are the exchanges with the philosopher, W. E. Johnson, who was a frequent visitor. I can still hear the high-pitched drawl of his voice raised in, to me, incomprehensible argument, with Maynard joining in whenever he saw an opening. The schoolboy was already shaping for the role of junior temporary civil servant, who was afterwards to tell a Prime Minister at a high-powered meeting, 'With the utmost respect, I must, if you ask my opinion, tell you that I regard your account as rubbish.' I was often reminded of his early passages with Johnson when, in later years, I listened to him arguing with Wittgenstein.

In the 1890s the Harvey Road children were enjoying to the full the recent introduction of the 'safety bicycles' and were dashing in gangs around the roads in the neighourhood, but I do not remember Maynard's taking part in this pastime. In 1892 he had himself begun to ride a bicycle before the rest of us and at the age of nine had been involved in a collision with a hansom cab, actually in Harvey Road. He was not seriously injured, but was shocked and frightened and I (aged five) can well remember seeing him dashing past the dining-room window and up the front steps in a frantic effort to reach the safety of home. He had suffered laceration of a finger, which had to be cleaned and dressed under an anaesthetic by our family doctor, a traumatic experience for a small boy. This resulted in a permanent slight deformity of the injured finger, and this may have influenced his life-long interest in other people's hands, which he regarded as an important index of character.

Although he did not join in the more rowdy amusements of his juniors, he took an interest in our more sophisticated pleasures at home. My father was a dedicated stamp collector, operating on a large scale. This resulted in his having a great number of miscellaneous stamps not needed for his albums and of these he would make a pile to be distributed to his children on Sunday afternoons. This operation was known as a 'choice', each choosing one stamp in turn, so that fair division was achieved without noise or tears, a very wise parental device. Maynard took his part in this, though his collecting of stamps did not attract him beyond his early teens. Another curious form of collecting, in which we all took part, was the accumulation of steel pen-nibs, of which there was a great variety then available, recommended by the jingle:

> The Pickwick, the Owl and the Waverley pen,
> They come as a boon and a blessing to men.

My father always used quill pens, for which he had a special cutter, but we preferred the steel nibs, Maynard as a schoolboy writing in an individual, though neat and legible, hand. He took very little interest in the entomological collection which my father and I were forming over a long period. This was of such enormous attraction to me, spread as it was over several counties and later over most of the countries of Europe, that I could not understand his indifference. He was never attracted by any form of nature study, though as a schoolboy he was already collecting a large number of small books, such as Elzevirs and Aldines, and he was immensely proud of owning a fine copy of the enormous Baskerville Bible, given him by a friend of the family. His book collecting was greatly helped by the presence of Gustave David at his celebrated bookstall in the market-place. David traded on the unusual principle of selling cheaply what he had bought cheaply, whatever it might be, and many of his prices were quite extraordinarily low. Maynard was always grateful for his help given in this way, and saw to it in the old man's declining years that he was able to trade in a convenient shop on King's College property in St Edward's Passage, which his son Hubert still occupies.

Maynard was normally cheerful, witty and full of self-confidence. He occasionally had fits of adolescent depression, which he called 'natural sadness', but they did not last long or disturb the happiness of the family of which he was so important a part. Long and serious 'word-games' were a favourite method of getting through wet days during summer holidays, though Maynard naturally was apt to come out top. Family magazines were also much favoured, my sister Margaret providing most of the graphic features. Maynard was totally unable to draw, but could turn out humorous pieces in prose, verse or doggerel with the greatest ease. The wit was not of a very high order, but the exercise kept us occupied and amused; it was not intended to be an exhibition of intellectual precocity. On the other hand the correspondence which he maintained at regular intervals with his sister, who was at Wycombe Abbey School, was full of good fun, affectionate and sympathetic, with many shrewd comments on his own affairs.

Margaret, less than two years younger than Maynard, was more nearly on an equality with him than I could be. She possessed a strong personality with much originality and humour. As a pioneer in the organisation of homes for old people, she received the order of C.B.E. in later life and, as wife of Professor A. V. Hill, F.R.S., a Nobel prize winner for physiology, raised a large and clever family of children and grandchildren. She and Maynard felt a great mutual respect, and as adolescents they shared such social recognition as Cambridge offered, while I was left behind as too young – not that I felt any jealousy of my elders. It may seem odd, but I do not recall any family squabbling. Maynard's supremacy was accepted and there was no ground for quarrels to disturb our happiness, a reflection, perhaps, of the perfect harmony between our parents; a tribute, too, to our mother who directed all our lives with loving tact and understanding.

My father, first as Secretary of the Local Examinations Board and for many years of the Council of the Senate, and later as Registrary of the University, lived a carefully ordered life. He became an outstanding adminstrator, though not allowing any of this to spill over into family affairs. It is often forgotten that he was of considerable distinction in the intellectual disciplines of philosophy and economics, author of standard books on *Formal Logic* and *The Scope and Method of Political Economy*. Maynard felt the utmost respect for his father's qualities of mind, and it cannot be a matter for surprise that he so soon developed evidence of similar qualities in his own mind, whether due to personal example or hereditary tendencies. The people who visited the house were naturally those who had the same intellectual interests or academic responsibilities and they would also have had their influence.

All through his Eton schooldays Maynard spent his holidays with his family at Cambridge or, during the long summer vacation, in Yorkshire, Cornwall or Devon. He played a great deal of golf at Royston or the Gog Magog links, usually with his father, or sometimes with eminent family friends such as Professor Henry Sidgwick. As I have said he was not really interested in any form of natural history, yet he would often accompany me on long bicycle rides round Cambridge even when the object was to catch butterflies or to find fossils at Upware in the fens. On one occasion he thought it worthwhile to record in his diary that we amused ourselves by riding 23 miles in a circle round the town never going more than 4 miles from the perimeter – an example of his fondness for statistics.

In the winter months evening parties were fashionable, with dancing as the chief entertainment, always an old-fashioned programme of waltzes, polkas, lancers, with perhaps a barn dance or a 'Sir Roger de Coverley' as a cheerful finale. But Maynard was frankly bored by this kind of 'enjoyment', and wrote in his diary on 31 December 1900: 'I went to my dancing class again; it is a nuisance, but like most nuisances it is not eternal. If people will ask one to parties, I suppose one must learn to dance, but it is certainly one of the poorest ways of wasting time known. Everybody says I am sure to like it when I get older. Perhaps I shall. People have got used to castor oil; having cut my own tail I shall want to perpetuate the practice in order to get other people to cut theirs. This is the last day of the Nineteenth Century and I have been 17 and a half years in it.'

While at Eton Maynard kept a daily record of the number of hours he worked – three or four were regarded as a poor effort; eight or nine were satisfactory. Often he would take time off to do some research in the College library, learning the use of reference books and historical records in an attempt to unravel the details of the Keynes family history since 1066 when our ancestor, William de Cahagnes, arrived in England with King William. One of my own grandsons, also as a schoolboy, has carried on the investigation from where Maynard left it off, bringing it almost to completion.

Whatever the number of hours that Maynard worked, no time was wasted. His mind worked quickly and he possessed to a high degree the power of concentration. He also worked steadily at home and was allowed to share his father's study, a tribute to the son's habitual quiet attention to the subject in hand, for the father was extremely sensitive to any kind of disturbance. At school he was the ideal pupil if he respected the teacher. His tutor, Gurney Lubbock, soon discovered this and provided the foundation of the wide culture for which Maynard afterwards became famous. Whether working or playing he lived intensely in the present and entered with zest into everything that Eton offered him – unless it had any taint of militarism. On 2 February 1900 he wrote to his sister: 'Most extraordinary martial ardour has seized the school. The head gave us a solemn oration a few days ago telling us that in a national crisis like the present it was the duty of all to join the volunteers. The result has been over a hundred recruits, but I am one of the very few who have not joined. Pa and ma didn't seem keen, I wasn't keen, and I didn't see that I should be conferring a very great benefit on my country if I did join the Eton Dogshooters. All the same I wavered considerably and only escaped by a hair's breadth.'

Maynard's letters to his father from Eton were not like the duty letters written home by the average schoolboy. They exhibit the close and happy relations he always enjoyed with his parents, being filled with lively details of school events, his hopes and disappointments, sometimes including descriptions of historical events such as the celebration of the relief of Mafeking in May 1900. Sir Roy Harrod has quoted extensively from these letters and they need not be repeated here, but he did not quote the following passages from Maynard's diary concerning the death and funeral of Queen Victoria, an event sensed by many people as the beginning of a new era, coinciding so neatly as it did with the first year of a new century. Maynard was deeply impressed by the scene as his description shows.

Tuesday 22 January 1901, Cambridge. The Queen died at 6.30 this evening. The previous bulletins left little room for hope, but the tolling of the Roman Catholic Church [which stands at the end of Harvey Road] as we sat down to dinner did not seem any less sudden.

Saturday 2 February 1901, Eton. We marched to Windsor for the fourth time since I have been here and it goes without saying that this was by far the greatest occasion of all. There was no early school, and after chapel Dundas and I went to Windsor to see what there was to be seen. An immense crowd was in the act of congregating, but it was possible for anyone who did not want a pew to walk about a good deal. I have never seen so many policemen in my life. I was told afterwards there were a thousand. Troops were arriving almost continuously and we saw the blue-jackets and the Oxford Shooters and the Beefeaters. I saw Pole-Carew who was in command exceedingly well. At 12.30 we paraded in the School yard and marched through a very private part of the Castle grounds to the Long Walk which we lined, shooters and non-shooters alternately. Beyond the gates was a dense mass of uplifted faces, a battery behind them, and then another crowd stretching down the Long Walk at a distance of at least a mile from any point of the procession. At 2.15 the minute guns began booming out, that the funeral cortège had reached Windsor station. About ten minutes later the advance portion of the escort of Life Guards arrived and the last of the procession was not past before 3. Amongst the notabilities of the procession were the Kings of Belgium, Portugal, Greece, Germany, England, the heirs of Russia, Norway and Sweden, Italy, Germany, Austria, Siam etc., etc., but of the whole number the Kaiser was the only one who was not an ordinary man; he was the only one who could have been nothing but a King. Roberts I saw very distinctly; he looked very careworn, and was, to my mind, the most sorrowful figure of the whole procession. The royalties came so close together that it was impossible to take in more than half. The King of Portugal was very grotesque with an enormous pot belly. I liked the look of the German Crown Prince, and the Crown Prince of Sweden not as bad as his photographs. The King did not look either young or healthy. The Duke of Cambridge looked very old indeed and could not walk without assistance. The whole spectacle was indescribably grand, but amidst all the brilliant uniforms the coffin itself stood out most gorgeously. The crowds in the extreme distance must have been able to see that. Of the rest I was most pleased with the small band of picked Germans, the long string of aged generals and admirals, and the beefeaters. The only blot was the French mission; they chatted and strolled along as if they were smoking cigarettes on their native boulevards. No one can have seen the procession better than we did; we were on the very edge of a path about half the width of an ordinary road. The gun carriage was dragged by bluejackets as the artillery horses refused at the last moment.

I made my maiden speech in College Pop, holding that 'Woman is *not* more fitted to rule than man'. I was on the winning side by one vote.

Monday 4 February. The actual interment at Frogmore took place to-day, and the King asked us to go. The Head, however, refused on the ground of the shortness of the notice given. We are, as may be imagined, angry with him.

Though he seldom failed to win any prize or scholarship for which he was able to compete, Maynard was not always at his books. There was time for innumerable hard-fought games of fives or squash racquets and he enjoyed rowing. He was above all an adept at the 'wall game', peculiar to Eton and demanding great powers of physical endurance and indifference to pain. It was all in line with his determination and persistence in getting his own way in life and keeping faith in his own judgement. Yet he never entertained pre-

34

tensions that he was an athlete or admired the prowess of others. He was respected by his contemporaries for his varied qualities and he enjoyed in his last year at school being a member of the Etonian élites when he was elected to the Society known as 'Pop'. By this time the younger masters such as Geoffrey Winthrop Young, were discovering that they had in their midst a boy who possessed the intellect and poise of a brilliant adult, and it was no surprise when he was elected to an Eton scholarship at King's College, Cambridge, in 'Mathematics and Classics', characteristically combining two unrelated subjects, in both of which he excelled. He had told his father beforehand: 'I have entered myself for £40 at King's, as I want to go there anyhow. There is nowhere else worth going to at Cambridge which comes on later. And I do not want to go to Oxford at any price.' As usual he had proved irresistible. This was in November 1901.

School friendships had been of great importance to him throughout his time at Eton and I became familiar with the names of many of them – Dilly Knox, Robin Dundas, Granville Hamilton, Swithinbank, Mackworth Young, Tom Balston, and others. By the end of July 1902 he had passed his nineteenth birthday and was more than ready to leave Eton; yet he found the break was a severe wound to his feelings. Near the end of his time he wrote to his father a very long letter, ending: 'Last night I received a vote of thanks in College Pop, which I think I desired perhaps more than anything else that remains to be got here. Eton has been much kinder to me than I deserve.'

On 30 July he wrote in his diary, 'I have come out first again in the certificate, but Knox, the next man, of course gets the scholarship. As I am proscribed by last year's 'ship from anything this year, the Head sent for me and gave me *Fors Clavigera* in 7 vols. as a present from him. My tutor has given me as a leaving book Lecky's *England in 18th. cent.*, 7 vols., blue morocco. Dinner with Goodhart and many farewells; but no sentiment is allowed in this diary.'

35

5

The undergraduate

C. R. FAY

Since I never called him Maynard till long after the war of 1914–1918 and find it strange to refer to him now in my lectures as Lord Keynes, I will call him what we called him then (just as we called Dick-in-son Dickinson) – Keynes. A troublesome name, to be sure, for if I have interrupted Canadian and American friends once for pronouncing it Keens, I have done it twenty times ('Kaynes: and not Professor, just Mister').

When I arrived in the Lane for Little-go on 1 October 1902, there was only one other person on the staircase; and as I descended from my about-to-be furnished rooms, he asked me to come in and have some tea. 'My name's Keynes. What's yours?' He had a moustache and fancy waistcoat, a beautifully carved desk and a wicker basket, with a pair of gloves in it. He asked me if I liked the place, and I said 'Rather', and to keep the ball rolling I lugged in O.B. whereupon he said 'I was at Eton, too'.

It was surely strange that the first person I met at King's was the most brilliant man I have ever met or can hope to meet. I make for him the claim that he was greater than Alfred Marshall and the equal of Adam Smith, and had what Adam Smith also had, an uncanny power of 'going along with' you or it. He suffered fools and foolish thoughts, not gladly but patiently and kindly. A Puritan in soul and bodily habit, he yet was fond of sumptuous things, of old books, social breakfasts, *de luxe* travel and *petits chevaux* (when we were at Biarritz in 1907 he lost his spare cash on a system, so that for the last three days we were confined to piquet, his hotel coupons against my French francs): and fond above all of being in the swim. Not for years (not indeed till his tremendous article of September 1914 in the *Economic Journal* when he exposed the poltroonery of the bankers) did I recognise his stature.

As an undergraduate he did many things, and once out of bed worked really hard, trying to keep up with Page in Mathematics and always finding time for his other interests, literary, social and political. Through his father and Sidgwick (a boyhood friend who told him Limericks on the Royston links) he imbibed the atmosphere of the Moral Sciences, which then was a nursery of economists; and from the time I knew him he took an interest in the Stock Exchange, which is but an exercise in Probability. Neither Page nor I was his bosom friend. This was our Classic, R. A. Furness, whose familiarity with Rabelais and Sterne *et hoc genus omne* caused Page to blush, me to feel inferiority complex and Keynes to be enviously competitive. As I was in my first year something of a Rugger celebrity, he often talked games with me, and especially of his wall-scraping role in the Eton Wall Game. Later we used to play golf at Royston, at which he was the worst player I have known with the exception of Wedd, whose method was: first to miss the ball, then to talk to it, then to refill his pipe, and finally to wave through the pair behind.

All through his undergraduate days Keynes was as happy as the rest of us, for how can I express the freedom we enjoyed at King's: no gate fines, no pestering from that damnable thing now called supervision (I exclude the coaching, which sometimes he cut, and my weekly essay, through which the O.B. slept), attending what lectures we pleased, such as McTaggart's at Trinity, into which Keynes roped me, and paying for none. But I thought it a bit offensive when in his second year, having bought a standard edition of Burke, he proceeded to win the Members' Prize for English Essay on the Political Philosophy of Burke (1904). By this time, however, he was a Union light, and seemed to know most people at Trinity; and if I had been asked what his best speech was, I would have recalled his début in the College Hall at King's in his first year, when he followed Meredith and others in helping to down a College Mission with religious tests in London: of which I and others reaped the harvest, by obeying the invitation of Reddaway to play, instead, undenominational cricket with the College tenants.

It rankled with Keynes that the Dean would not allow him to read the lessons in Chapel, unless he promised regular attendance on Sunday mornings, which he would not. For he loved to read aloud and I remember well how, when he stayed with us at Liverpool (in those days I was slated for the Church), he explained on the way to church that Huxley had exploded Christianity and in the afternoon, while I smoked, he read to me *Will o' the Mill*.

When he came back to Cambridge in 1909 he was just the same, only more so. (I believe that at that moment he would have gone to Trinity, though nowhere else, if they had been shrewd enough to invite him.) Quite obviously he would in a few years be running the College; and if the Economics Tripos did not offer a fair field to Money, then the Economics Tripos must be, and duly was, reformed.

6

The Kingsman

GEORGE RYLANDS

'I've had a good look round the place and come to the conclusion that it's pretty inefficient.' Thus spake the Freshman J. M. Keynes in 1902, as C. R. Fay records. What would his verdict have been had he gone to Trinity, as one of his Eton ushers urged – mathematics at King's being then at a low ebb? Trinity would still be the Trinity that has been and ever will be; but King's as we have known it for half-a-century, could never have come into being. The Freshman was lodged in the confined and unlovely Lane buildings, reached from Chetwynd Court by a subterranean passage, and known inevitably as 'the Drain'. Sixty-five years later that huddle of sunless premises – the old tutor's house, the backside of the Bull Hotel, tenement habitations, the lane with the double twist, the Chetwynd lecture room, were all swept away in a grandiose scheme, in alliance with St Catharine's; the lane was shifted and straightened, the kitchens reconstructed and modernised, Chetwynd Court extended and humanised, eighty bed-sitters and four sets occupied, the prolific mulberry in Webb's Court uprooted. Keynes had asked in his Will that the governing Body should remember two things dear to his heart: the Arts Theatre which he created and the Drain where he had pronounced upon the inefficiency of his College. Thanks to the Keynes estate the ambitious and costly operation was carried out and a bust of Keynes presides over a concert room in the complex named after him. He and I had walked over the site several times not long before his death; the City had been consulted about moving the services under the Lane; there had been pourparlers with St Catharine's. Towards the end of the war considerable improvements (mainly sanitary) had taken place beyond the Drain to accommodate personnel of the United States Forces. Meanwhile all along the Backs a large motor transport unit of our own R.A.F. had parked their vehicles, sharing the College kitchens and various services. I have a letter from Keynes, dated 10 December 1942, which is highly characteristic. He had collapsed terrifyingly at the end of Founders' Dinner and been taken up to my rooms and put to bed. He writes, 'You and Weller were extraordinarily kind to me on the 5th. I must be more careful another time, since it is exactly what happened the year before. It seems to be a sort of fainting fit plus sickness which comes on me when too much food and drink are added to too much work. The heart suddenly decides that it will only perform part of its duties. Fortunately, although I am such a nuisance, it does not seem to do me much harm. I was quite well next morning, though I decided to spend the day resting a bit, and have been quite well since.' He then proceeds to business, the fainting fit not having impaired his remarkable memory: 'There was one point I wanted to add to your argument with Weller, which I was listening to just before I gave way, and had not the strength to utter. It seems to me to be quite true that our profits from housing the R.A.F. are taxable. You were alleging that they were certainly considerable. That was what I wanted to query.' He went on to consider the proper allocation of receipts, the share of College services, liabilities arising out of capital expenditure in the past, and so on; and advised me to lay all the facts before the Revenue.

I got to know Keynes in a bursarial context during the war years when for the second time a World War claimed him and I was appointed acting Bursar. At weekends whenever possible he would come down and interrogate me and his bursarial clerk (Mr Jack Peters, now Third Bursar and a Fellow, as Keynes had always said that he should and would be). He would scrutinise the Mundum Books and tell me that I had erred in allowing a cottager a shilling for mending a tap – 'That's the tenant's responsibility' – and he meant it. Some time would be spent in the College office but there were regular morning conferences when he 'received', propped up in bed, surrounded by letters and reports and files. He would lay these down and look one in the eye and give his entire attention – one knew that not a moment might be wasted – to one's problem. As I departed he picked up his papers refocusing on the precise point where he had left off. He possessed an abnormal power of switching from one subject to another. There would however be time on these visits, after he had satisfied himself, with Peters's cooperation, on whatever graver issues had transpired, for a gossip which he much enjoyed. We talked of course much about the Arts Theatre, plans, programmes and frustrations, and about College personalities. But he also greatly enjoyed hearing about my domestic troubles as Steward. The College housed a diversity of squatters: dons and students of Queen Mary College, the Home Guard H.Q., the Provost Marshall's Office, all ranks of the services, distinguished visitors. He loved to be amused, and there was plenty to laugh at (albeit wryly); for instance the attitude to ration books of senior fellows – one would consume a month's marmalade at a breakfast; another rebelled at dollops of whale.

Memorable to me in the war was a visit with him and Mr Davis of James Styles and Whitlock (to whom Keynes was a hero of heroes) to survey an extensive freehold estate on either side of Putney Hill, let on ground rents for unexpired periods. We perambulated streets of small houses, explored the grounds of Victorian mansions which had been converted into girls' schools and suchlike, and assessed the potentialities of a large and partly derelict nursery garden. It was to prove, as he anticipated, a most profitable investment. I seem to remember Keynes considering for a moment – he had of course to get back to Whitehall – whether a taxi was justified rather than public transport on such an occasion. My memory may be libelling him but it is undeniable that although he believed with Francis Bacon that 'Money like muck is not good unless it be spread', he also subscribed to the adage: 'Take care of the pence and the pounds will take care of themselves'. He favoured munificent gestures but often chided the College Council for dissipating small sums 'because they didn't like to say No'. In fact he could be parsimonious and as Steward and Bursar I had to exert my powers of persuasion to secure increases in salaries and wages. Mr Peters recollects that between the wars he was mainly blamed by the staff for the poor wage rates. 'In times of crisis they were led to believe that substantial increases would not be in the national interest. But when he was urging the housewife to go out and spend and thus help the economy, the staff did not benefit by more generous treatment.' In the same way, he was intransigent over the King's College School, when I was in charge of its finances. The School had always been run on a shoe-string; buildings and equipment were sorely needed if the School was to survive and be an honour to the College. Keynes accepted the fact that the choristers were part of the Royal Foundation but insisted that the School should stand on its own feet. Loans at a reasonable rate of interest were in order but not subsidies. I must add however to any strictures on his closeness that he was ever reluctant to indulge himself; and not long before his death when he was a wealthy man he asked me whether I thought it was extravagant of him to purchase a rare Elizabethan book – it may have been *The Faerie Queene*.

How formidable was he as a Fellow and Officer of the College? I feared his disapprobation as I was proud of a word of praise. Both were rare. He would always listen to one's arguments, sympathise with one's aspirations and often yield when he realised that one felt deeply on the matter. I do not think I was afraid of him. Harold Nicolson, reviewing Roy Harrod's biography, wrote: 'If he contradicted his subordinates he did so in a voice so soft and beautiful that his remarks were robbed of all asperity. Yet when he argued with statesmen or financial magnates his sentences were as thongs; scouring dissimulation, stupidity and untruth. His juniors would sit there aghast, actually trembling with delight. His, certainly, was the most compelling personality that I have ever encountered.'

Sir Dennis Proctor's account of Keynes at the Treasury reinforced this. 'The moment he came into contact with anyone who knew his job and could show that he was doing it, his attitude was one of respect, almost of humility. He would accept correction immediately from anyone, however lowly placed in the official hierarchy, if he felt he was an authority on the subject in hand. The only thing he could not stand was the supine attitude and the predilection for the line of least resistance. One usually felt a mugwump after a talk with Keynes, even though he may not himself have thought one was.'

If I was not afraid of him when elected an amateur Bursar, acting as his lieutenant and stand-in (although not infrequently conscious of mugwumpery), it was because I had been his confidant and ally over the foundation and early years of the Arts Theatre and he respected my experience, as actor and director in the fortunes of the Marlowe Dramatic Society. We shared a passion for the stage, Shakespeare and the English poets. This concord was sealed, as it were, in December 1930, when Maynard sponsored the presentation of Lopokova in eight performances of a 'Masque of Poetry and Music' at the London Arts Theatre Club. They had taken to reading poetry aloud together and she was nursing aspirations as an actress which were later to be realised when she played Olivia in *Twelfth Night* at the Old Vic and in the roles of Nora and Hilda Wangel in an Ibsen season of four plays. The Masque, entitled 'Beauty, Truth and Rarity', was a collaboration between Lydia, Constant Lambert, Frederick Ashton and myself. She and I had performed part of Milton's *Comus* at a party in my College rooms, repeated in Gordon Square, with Michael Redgrave and Robert Eddison (undergraduates) as the two brothers. This provided one item. Then Maynard and Lydia had discovered that exquisite period piece, *A Lover's Complaint*, which Shakespearean scholars unaccountably neglect. To these were added a dialogue of Youth and Age arranged from the Old Testament, and the 'Debate of the Infernal Peers' from *Paradise Lost*. Donald Beves of King's (the best amateur player in Cambridge for four decades) and three undergraduates took part with me: Peter Hannen, who died young, gifted son of Nicholas; Geoffrey Toone, a future actor; Wynyard Brown, a successful dramatist to be. For the music, Constant Lambert arranged two ballets: 'A Passionate Pavan' by Dowland with epigraph from Campion, 'Follow your saint, follow with accents sweet'; and 'Dances on a Scotch theme', founded on symphonies of William Boyce (1710–79). Frederick Ashton, who had recently created *Pomona* and was working on Walton's *Façade*, was the choreographer. With him in support of Lopokova danced Harold Turner who with Karsavina had danced the virtuoso role in *Le Spectre de la Rose*. The costumes were designed by William Chappell and photographs taken by Cecil Beaton.

Looking back on this aesthetic adventure which Keynes sponsored nearly forty-five years ago, I see it as a fertile seed which bore fruit not long after in his munificent gift to Cambridge of an Arts Theatre; and I have digressed from my appointed theme to recall it, not only for its own sake, but because it shows his appreciation and encouragement of undergraduate acting; because also it united Maynard and myself in tastes and interests outside and beyond College matters. And perhaps the Masque was a candle throwing its beams forward and afar to C.E.M.A. and the Arts Council.

Therefore, as I have said, when I was bidden to stand in as Bursar, I was not afraid of Keynes. I had served with him on several major College committees for nearly ten years. At meetings of the College Council he would sit at the end of the long table (the Provost presided in the middle) looking through a pile of papers, writing letters rapidly; yet he never missed a point in the discussions; biding his time until the clever, the muddlers, the trimmers, and the dissidents had said their say. Then he would sum up the situation (often with astringency) and propose a vote which the Provost and the majority gratefully accepted. His tongue was wondrously persuasive and his mind worked so speedily that his reasoning could seem too plausible to be true. But, when Keynes was absent, Provost Sheppard took an unconscionable time in reminiscence and digression. On the Fellowship Electors, whose tempo was very properly geared to slow motion, Keynes might be less effective and did not always win the day. Intellectually brilliant persons are on occasion most dogmatic on those subjects in which they are less expert and profound. One thing which he detested, to which Committees are prone, was what he called the principle of equal injustice for all; by this he signified a consciously high-minded refusal to do something generous and beneficial for x because you are not in a position to do it for y or z. His star performance, which all members of the Governing Body took pains not to miss, was given each November at the Annual Congregation when he delivered his 'Chancellor of the Exchequer' speech. Had things been different, had it not been that 'He narrow'd his mind/And to *College* gave up what was meant for mankind', his budget speeches might have made House of Commons history.

Jack Peters, who was his right-hand man before as well as during the war and who, I surmise, was never fully aware of Keynes's high opinion of him, complements my impressions of him in College business with his own experience in the College office over two decades:

When I joined the staff of King's as a lad in the mid-twenties, we juniors had little contact with the Bursar. He gave the impression of being an unapproachable sort of man, and during his short weekend visits within Full Term he was jealously guarded by the then Bursar's Clerk. We were led to believe that he was something of a terror: this was not entirely untrue; for he was a hard taskmaster with his fast dictation and the inevitable request for the work to be available within a specified time. His soft 'r' gave some difficulty with shorthand and any hesitation in transcribing a letter would be brushed aside: 'Your shorthand is your music and the typewriter your piano; it should be as easy as that.' Until one got used to him he seemed very hard to please. I remember twenty-two commas (most of them unnecessary) being inserted in one letter as a lesson in punctuation! But he was ready to praise when the circumstances called for recognition. Good handwriting fascinated him, but his own pencilled drafts were often brought to me to decipher. [In due course Jack Peters was the *only* man who could decipher Provost Sheppard and Professor Pigou.]

He had remarkable powers of persuasion – both the spoken and the written word – and it was hopeless to contradict him unless one had some cast-iron facts; even these had to be presented in the right order to carry any weight. Second thoughts did not impress, and he had a remarkable memory. [N.B. Inferior to J. P., who became, and is, the College's Memory.]

Ambiguous laws and some interpretations of them irritated him beyond measure, and a close examination of the College's files would reveal his views on a variety of legal opinions. He respected College procedures but he hated red tape. When a Government Department suggested the creation of a Sinking Fund to replace the purchase price of a small property held on a 999-year lease, he offered to send a penny stamp, which accumulated at 3% would, he calculated, amount to £250,000 on the expiration of the long residue of the lease. His proposal was not accepted but he had made his point and the original demand was greatly abated.

Like so many others I owe much to this remarkable man and his early training followed by his friendly encouragement over some twenty years which laid a firm foundation for a later period. In the war years when he had perforce delegated much of his College work, although his interest never wavered, he had mellowed. He seemed far more approachable and without betraying national secrets would talk to me about some of the personalities he had met in the course of his Government duties.

T. S. Eliot, five years Keynes's junior, who admired him as an artist in expository prose and because 'unlike some other brilliant

44

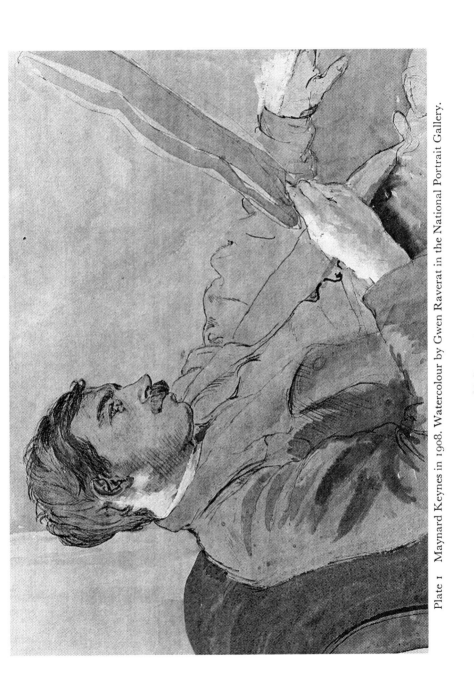

Plate 1   Maynard Keynes in 1908. Watercolour by Gwen Raverat in the National Portrait Gallery.

(a)

(b)

(c)

Plate 2 (a) and (b): Maynard Keynes's parents in 1905: John Neville
Keynes and Florence Ada Keynes; (c) the three Keynes children in 1889:
on the left, Margaret (later Mrs A. V. Hill) aged 4; in the middle, Geoffrey
aged 2½; on the right, Maynard aged 6.

scholars he had continued throughout his life to feed and exercise his mind by wide reading in English and other literature', ruefully confesses in *East Coker*:

> So here I am, in the middle way, having had twenty years
> Twenty years largely wasted, the years of *l'entre deux guerres* –
> Trying to learn new words, and every attempt
> Is a wholly new start and a different kind of failure.

Those years for Keynes (ever ready to make a new start, shrugging off failure, blandly capable of changing his mind and saying so), those years for King's were the great ones. Hugh Durnford, Domus and Estates Bursar at that time, wrote:

Perhaps they were the happiest years for him. In those years he did not often go abroad. He shuttled between Cambridge and London in Full Term. In vacations, when there were no pupils and no Statutory attendances required, he was only there in an emergency. . . . It seemed as if he needed the pulse and movement of the College working in all its arteries to keep him happy; that he shunned a depleted Hall, a skeleton High Table, and courts emptied of undergraduates. Not that he saw a great deal of them, or they of him. . . . But with the Fellows it was quite otherwise. . . . He sat amongst them in his hour of relaxation in the Combination Room after dinner, playing patience and accessible to all. Since there were many – and the expansionist in him always wished that there were more – the variety of his discussions would have tired a normal man who had been working on his 'big stuff' almost all day. He had a great, an almost incredible power of switch, from an abstruse economic point to the fine interpretation of a Statute or an estate matter, and he produced his opinion on the dot without taking his eye off the cards.

It was natural then that, as Bursar in charge of successive and far-reaching alterations in College financial policy and in the seeking of 'unusual powers' without which they would have been unworkable, he should have had his colleagues behind him; or that when he proposed amendments or motions in his own name as an individual Fellow, he was likely to carry the day. To the younger progressives, there was to hand an older authoritative progressive, on whose ideas they could hardly improve: with the older Fellows knowledge of the man and the logic of the argument prevailed over inherent apprehensions.

Looking back at what Keynes did to enrich the College materially and equip it for its further progress in other spheres, Durnford states that nothing worried him more as a Cambridge don than the keeping of Collegiate resources in a stocking. 'Nothing, as he would say, in those days appeared to worry some Colleges less!' I myself well remember in the war his inviting the Bursars of all the Colleges to an informal meeting in King's when he urged upon them greater enterprise in investment policy, more adventurous expenditure, far more generous assistance by the wealthier foundations to their less well-endowed sisters. The response was chilly. Keynes was a devotee of Wordsworth (he gave me a first edition of *The Excursion*), but he did not believe that 'getting and spending we lay waste our powers'.

Durnford also noted that 'he was a friend of preservation as few Bursars could dare to be and the College followed his lead on permanently restricting building on much of its Grantchester land. ... He also started the fashion of derailing Cambridge. On his individual motion the ugly railings along the whole College front were replaced by a low wall, on which he hoped 'men might sit and dogs not misbehave'.

Might not Keynes have said with the Divines (and T. S. Eliot): 'In my end is my beginning'? The progress of the Cambridge child, son of a future Mayor of the City and of the Registrary of the University, from the Eton K.S. to the negotiator at Bretton Woods, was constant and, as it were, ordained. In the College *Memoir* Hugh Durnford carries us back from 1939, when I became Keynes's bursarial subaltern, to 1919 and his own appointment as Second Bursar. Bursarial arrangements had been discussed by a special committee who recommended that he should be asked to undertake duties in connection with College finances and accounts. This was the aftermath of the *démarche* he had made with the support of certain younger Fellows in 1912, within eighteen months of his election; but he was already a member of the Estates Committee and of the Fellowship Electors (the most high-powered of the College committees). On that occasion the *enfant terrible*, as he may have seemed to some Victorian survivals, attacked the holding of large cash balances and won the day. His second proposal, that the domestic catering departments should be integrated, was also successful. But a third and more revolutionary motion, the raising of the Fellowship Dividend from £120 to £130 a year was defeated. However he was elected to the Council at that meeting and presently served on a committee to consider a letter of resignation from the Bursar, who interpreted what had occurred as a vote of no confidence. Then the war intervened. Keynes put aside his 'Theory of Probability' which had occupied him as a Fellowship dissertation from 1906 to 1908 and joined the Treasury. Thus his potentialities were to be discerned in his attitudes and activities and ambitions before he was thirty. As wise Nestor says in Shakespeare's 'War and Peace' (*Troilus and Cressida*):

> And in such indexes, although small pricks
> To their subsequent volumes, there is seen
> The baby figure of the giant mass
> Of things to come at large.

As Bursar, Keynes's two main reforms and innovations were firstly, the establishment of the Chest – a single fund into which various free moneys and balances could be concentrated to the tune of some £30,000. It is characteristic of his remarkable memory that he noticed that a gift of £100 had been recorded in error as allocated to the Chest, whereas it had in fact been paid to the Senior Wine Account fifteen years earlier. By the time of his death the capital appreciation amounted to about £380,000. Secondly, the College agreed to the selling off of more than a few ancient estates in the West Country and East Anglia. At that time also the extensive Ruislip property was in the process of dispersion. However Keynes invested not only in property in the City, very profitably as it proved, but also in the ambitious purchase of some 3,000 acres of farmland in Lincolnshire. And when, owing to the agricultural depression, the low-lying land was tenantless and would have become derelict, he persuaded the College to stock it and nurse it and farm it on their own account. The decision was to cause the College a good deal of anxiety for many years, although the Bursar of Caius, Mr E. P. Weller, devoted his expertise to the management of the estate. I vividly remember attending the January Audit with the latter in the war, and the tenants' luncheon and the old people's Christmas party. Those Lincolnshire farms have all now been sold. Would Keynes have persuaded the College to hang on till better times? He would have been right.

Hugh Durnford wrote:

The Bursar, who had hitherto judged farms and farmers by their showing in valuers' reports or in the College accounts, began to go several better than his predecessors in his nearer acquaintance with the land. On his visits there was nothing perfunctory or superficial or merely social. Inappropriately dressed – the familiar blue serge and brown shoes – he was to be seen in his new element, in labourers' cottages or studying the points of stock or attending pig sales on the College farms. . . . His contact with men of the soil seemed at that time to have a wider repercussion. It was as if something which had been latent now burgeoned and that he was glad of it – a something of additional softness in his relations with men of ordinary but genuine mould. From now on it was a pleasure to him rather than a duty to sit next to a tenant at the College Audit feast. They could talk each other's language.

Two names spell King's for me: Sheppard and Keynes. How different in their origins, their careers, their temperaments; united in affection and appreciation of one another; at one in their devotion to the College. Sheppard brought me up to King's two terms early in January 1921, to act in the Greek play, the *Oresteia*, and took me to my first Gilbert and Sullivan the night I arrived. Keynes asked me to luncheon in that term in his rooms in Webb's Gateway, presided over by the austere murals of the Triposes, as depicted by Duncan Grant and Vanessa Bell. Oysters and hock! I balked at the former, and sole Colbert was immediately summoned from the College kitchens. Nearly twenty-five years later, next to me at a College Feast, he voiced his one regret that he had not drunk more champagne in his life.

For a physical image Hugh Durnford remembers him at Congregations, looking down the long table, each hand buried in its opposite sleeve, reviewing, prophesying, calculating. 'How well I recall those rapid movements of the head from side to side, from face to face, as if none were to be left out of his confidence: the sudden upward tilt of the chin with which he overcame his occasional stammer: the beam with which he invited general laughter at some mischievous thrust.' My pictures are of him propped up in bed and very wide awake; hunching his shoulders before the Combination Room fire; dancing a wild burlesque as the Prince Consort with Lopokova as Victoria at Gordon Square parties; placing an accusing finger on the shilling in the Mundum Book which I had allowed a cottager; smiling delightedly at a titbit of gossip I had saved for him. I never think of him as laughing, but the smile was that of a benign badger, depicted by Beatrix Potter.

On my last visit to Provost Sheppard in a nursing home (he was eighty-six) I talked about the College. 'What College?' he asked bewildered. The mental powers of the inspired Coleridgean lecturer on Homer and Aeschylus were 'frozen at their marvellous source'.

Keynes slipped peacefully away at his home in the Sussex Downs aged sixty-two, his work and warfare for the College and the country accomplished. The Book of Eccelesiasticus speaks for both these famous men:

Giving counsel by their understanding ... and by their knowledge of learning meet for the people, wise and eloquent in their instructions: Such as found out musical tunes, and recited verses in writing; Rich men furnished with ability, living peaceably in their habitations: these were honoured in their generations ... that have left a name behind them, that their praises might be reported.

7

On loving Lydia

RICHARD BUCKLE

Bloomsbury often missed the point. They missed it over Epstein, the raucous individuality of whose style in the years before the First World War was anyhow predestined to put them off; and when he failed to toe the tea-party line they plumped for the milder, minor talent of Frank Dobson. They missed it – at least, according to Osbert Sitwell – over Diaghilev's great production of *The Sleeping Princess*, mistaking a reaffirmation of classical virtue as a backward step in art. They missed it over Lydia Lopokova – all of them, that is, except Maynard Keynes, whose marriage to the ballerina aroused their incredulous disapprobation.

I find it hard to see why. It cannot have been for the eminently Victorian reason that she was a dancer. If Lytton Strachey had had an *affaire* with aerial Idzikovski – to name the most uxorious and least available of the Russian dancers – they would surely have been delighted. Was it because she was a woman? I wonder if they would have accepted more readily the beautiful and intellectual Karsavina. Possibly: but Karsavina, so aristocratic by instinct, so fastidious in the conduct of personal relationships, would probably not have accepted *them*. Lydia was indeed no beauty – merely a ravishing and exuberant creature – and no intellectual, though possessed of a quick intelligence, a passion for art and learning and, as her English improved, a gift for self-expression which it is odd to think they overlooked.

Virginia Woolf wrote to her sister, Vanessa Bell: 'I can foresee only too well Lydia stout, charming, and exacting; Maynard in the Cabinet; 46 Gordon Square the resort of dukes and prime ministers. Maynard, being a simple man, not as analytic as we are, would sink beyond recall long before he realised his state. Then he would awake, to find three children and his life entirely and forever controlled.' It was Vanessa Bell who ruled the roost in W.C.1. She painted a large decoration, which is still at Tilton, and which was either the advertisement for or the commemoration of an entertainment given in Gordon Square: it depicts Lydia taking a call, curtseying, and Maynard looking round the curtain like a ridiculous stage-door Johnnie. I think Lydia always remained a little afraid of Mrs Bell; and when she said to me, obviously expressing a conviction born of long experience, 'I do *not* like *women in power!*', although she was referring to Dame Ninette de Valois, perhaps she also had in mind the autocrat of the Bloomsbury tea-table.

I never saw Lydia dance. I saw her act once, and was embarrassed by her Russian accent: she was playing Célimène in a translation of *Le Misanthrope*. But when I had met and made friends with her in 1950 four years after Lord Keynes's death, as a result of observing her, reading one or two accounts of her dancing, and studying old photographs – or, better still, drawings by Picasso – I thought I could visualise exactly how she danced and in what her charm as a dancer had consisted. That I should be able to 'see' Lydia in certain ballets of Massine, without ever having really seen her, strikes me as odder than it sounds; for I could never quite imagine – to take only one example – what Pavlova's special magic was. Anyway, there can be no doubt that in 1919 the twenty-eight-year-old Lydia had London at her feet. Let me assemble a few words that others have written about her.

Cyril Beaumont's first sight of Lopokova was in the role of Mariuccia, the maid in *The Good-humoured Ladies*, Massine's ballet inspired by Goldoni, by the Commedia dell'Arte, by Longhi, Watteau and, yes, the silent cinema. 'I shall always remember her becoming white wig and panniered, ochre-coloured frock barred with red, and the violet bow at her breast; together with the little mannerism she had of tilting her head on one side and slightly arching her expressive eyebrows, while her lips perpetually trembled between a pout and a smile' A snapshot in words!

Osbert Sitwell too gave a good account of her in the Italian ballet. 'Her face . . . was appealing, inquisitive, bird-like, that of a mask of comedy, while, being an artist in everything, she comprehended exactly the span and the limits of her capacities: the personification of gaiety, of spontaneity, and of that particular pathos which is its complement, she had developed the movements of her hands and arms in a way that hitherto no dancer had attempted, thereby achieving a new step forward in technique. Her wit entered into every gesture, into everything she did.'

A year later came the first night of *La Boutique fantasque*. Of the can-can Lopokova danced with Massine (see plate 5a) Beaumont wrote: 'Lopokova had an extraordinary resemblance to a doll, for which her rounded limbs, plump features, curved lips and ingenuous expression were admirably suited. You could easily imagine her squeaking "Mam-ma!" "Pa-pa!" She whirled her leg and flirted her skirt with the utmost abandon, yet there was nothing vicious, nothing inelegant in her presentation, it was all deliciously mischievous, exuberant, light-hearted . . . At one point, for a few minutes only, her expression did change. This occurred when, after the shop is closed, she is raised high in the air on the crossed sticks of the Cossacks. As she was temporarily parted from her sweetheart she gazed at him with a look of ineffable love, which seemed to light up her whole face.'

'This great ballerina', wrote Osbert Sitwell, 'fair, with the plump, greenish pallor of arctic flowers, formed the perfect foil to the dark, grotesque quality which Massine instilled into his masterpieces of satiric dancing and choreography.'

Massine wrote: 'Lopokova knew instinctively the effect I was aiming at, and without a word from me would speed up her kicks or tilt her head coquettishly in response to my sinuous movements. Perhaps it was the contrast between the fluttering, pink-petticoated, mischievous Lopokova, taunting and being taunted, and her greasy and sinister-looking partner, which caused the can-can to be so well received.'

There exists a sheet of blotting-paper, scribbled over by Picasso, inscribed to Massine and dated 'Londres 1919', which brings to life that famous *pas de deux*. Between three marvellous studies of Lopokova's rounded ballet hands, the artist has flicked in with a sharp hotel pen three vivid impressions of the delirious duet. In one the ballerina is poised on point with drifting arms; in another she is supported by Massine holding her right arm above her head; in a third, as he kneels with one arm raised, she lies across his knee, hand cocked pertly under her chin, and in this one particularly the artist has perpetuated in a few scratchy strokes the charm of her chubby profile and her doll-like perfection of awkward grace (see plate 5b).

Lydia was a bit of a bolter. In 1910, having danced Columbine in Fokine's *Carnaval* for the first time in Berlin and Paris (only a year after graduating from the Imperial School in St Petersburg), she had signed up with an American impresario and left Diaghilev after only one season. When the Russian Ballet went to New York during the war they joined forces once again, so that she was on the spot for the new wave of creativity under Massine. (*Les Sylphides*, the Polovtsian dances from *Prince Igor*, and *Petrushka* were the Fokine ballets that she danced.) By then she had acquired a husband, Randolfo Barocchi, whose multi-lingual wit and vivacity are described by Beaumont, but whose other charms, to judge from photographs, would seen to be hidden. I never asked her about Barocchi, knowing how ballerinas dislike reference to their first husbands. Already, at the time of *La Boutique fantasque* in June

1919 in London, Beaumont, who had made friends with them both, saw signs of Lydia's dissatisfaction with Barocchi. 'When, from time to time, I went to greet Lopokova in her dressing-room, she would sometimes lean back in her chair, a wave of weariness would pass over her features, and she would murmur half plaintively, "*Kak yah oustala!*" (How tired I am!).' On 10 July she ran off to St John's Wood with a Russian officer, leaving a note for Diaghilev; and the hoardings announced 'Ballerina vanishes'. A few weeks later Diaghilev took her back, but she departed for the third time before the end of the year.

When Diaghilev brought his Ballet to the Prince's Theatre in 1921, Massine had left the company, but Lydia was welcomed back to dance the can-can, this time with Woizikovski. She was one of four ballerinas to take the part of Aurora in *The Sleeping Princess* at the Alhambra Theatre that winter, and she also danced the Lilac Fairy. She must have made a charming fairy godmother, although the famous solo for that character at the christening is designed, with its swooping leg movements, for a taller dancer. The Bluebird *pas de deux*, which she did with Idzikovski, was more suited to her. Lydia married Maynard Keynes in 1925. After that she returned to dance for Diaghilev only once, on the occasion of a gala in the presence of the King of Spain, at the Prince's Theatre in July 1927. But she created the role of the Milkmaid in Ashton's *Façade* for the Camargo Society in 1933, danced *Coppelia* for the new Vic–Wells in the same year, and played a part – as did her husband – in the establishment of ballet in England.

Lydia's colleague the other Lydia, the English dancer Hilda Munnings who became, as Lydia Sokolova, the most Russian of Russians, described the part Massine played in the fulfilment of Lopokova's destiny:

All choreographers must agree that there are certain dancers who excel in the particular type of movement they invent. Just as Karsavina and Tchernicheva were essentially Fokine dancers, so I am sure that Lopokova, Idzikovski, Woizikovski and myself were most suitable and adaptable to Massine's individual kind of ballet.... I responded to his type of movement because the whole system of it seemed to be part of me.... This applied also to Lydia in *Les Femmes de Bonne Humeur* and in the can-can from *Boutique*: nobody was ever able to give quite the same accent and flavour to the steps which Massine had invented for her. Leon Woizikovski understood and danced some of Massine's own roles almost as well as their creator; and what Stas Idzikovski did in the Scarlatti and Rossini ballets could never be repeated by anyone else. That is why these perfect ballets, although they are still done, are in a way *lost*, and when Massine ceased inventing his extraordinary movements for Lydia, Stas, Leon and myself we were lost too, and never did anything so great again.

It must have been in January 1950 that I was introduced to Lydia. An invitation to the ballet soon followed. I was then ballet critic of *The Observer* and ran a monthly magazine, which lost money.

6 Feb. 1950   King's College, Cambridge
Dear Mr Buckle
  It would be nice if you could come with me on Feb. 20 to glance at 'a new' Don Quixote. Afterwards we can have supper at Gordon Square.
  My brother in law Geoffrey Keynes and wife also coming.
                              With every best wish
                              Yours sincerely
                              Lydia Keynes.

We plunged into intimacy.

28 Feb. 1950   King's College
Dear Dicky (may I)
  You are *molto simpatico* as a private personality. I was so glad you came and I will gladly come with you again, only at the moment war damage is going on in Gordon Square, the windows clothed with tarpaulin, and I cannot live without light. Can you? How exciting it was to read you in *The Observer* when you became a public personality. The space was used wisely. Burra [the designer of De Valois's *Don Quixote*] is much better in black and white than on the stage, and your critique is only *one* worth reading, yet not harsh . . .
                              With every best wish
                              Yours
                              Lydia Keynes

When she was not at her flat in Cambridge or at Tilton in Sussex, Lydia camped out in the two ground-floor rooms of 46 Gordon Square. The fact that these were her regular London home in a house which belonged to her did not detract from an air of Polovtsian impermanence. As in all her homes the furniture was perfunctory, as if borrowed from a friendly warehouse. She entertained in the small high back-room at a table normally covered in oilcloth, where, among the piles of books and tins of food, one was surprised to find a cubist Picasso and Delacroix's sketch for the mural of 'Jacob Wrestling with the Angel' in the church of Saint-Sulpice. The upper part of the house was let to some society for Christian aid, and when the front-door bell rang Lydia would dart to answer it and ask an astonished young man 'Are you Christian?' The large front room which, with its large mirror, had used to be the practice room, was Lydia's bedroom. Into this I may have glanced, though hardly penetrated; but I was sure that when she fortified herself within her stronghold, becoming on the stroke of midnight a Russian peasant once more, she slept in a cupboard on top of a stove, under ten eiderdowns, with Pushkin and Dostoievsky.

Lydia was tiny, eager, birdlike, with a Dodo nose. She was totally uninterested in clothes, and usually had a scarf wound tightly round her head, as if her whole day were taken up with housework, which it wasn't. Her enthusiasm for art, nature, people and life was invigorating.

5 March 1950   King's College
Dear Dicky,

Thanks for the information ... I have seen Rosario and Antonio on the films – real good Spanish earth! My dry rut soon will be cured and then I shall turn up in London. . . .

         Yours,
         Lydia Keynes

26 March 1950   46, Gordon Square, W.C.1.
My dear Dicky

After talking to you I went to Sadler's Wells Rosebery Avenue and was pleased. *Carnaval* has been a nightmare, but this young company [the Sadler's Wells Theatre Ballet] has a kind of verve. Patricia Miller was a *good* China [Chiarina?] and David Poole attractive in a most difficult of roles [Pierrot].

Spanish Ballet [*El Destino* by Angelo Andes] was nonsense. Trico [Pirmin Trecu] superb. *Valse Noble, Sentimental* [Ashton's ballet to Ravel] very pleasing. Blair, Fifield in *Casse Noisette* very good. I came away with a feeling that trees do grow in every country.

When can you sup with me and bring Kirstein [naming four possible dates].

       All best wishes
       Lydia Keynes

With Lincoln Kirsten, George Balanchine and Frederick Ashton I dined with Lydia at 9 o'clock on 29 March.

When Nijinsky died on 8 April 1950 I wrote a short piece about him in *The Observer*, and I think I must have asked Lydia to write something for *Ballet* magazine, for I have a telegram which reads: 'Forgive cannot do it not a born writer rather talk with you when in London later Sunday article supreme and an obituary love Lydia Keynes.'

8 May 1950   Gordon Square
My dear Dicky

It was handsome of you to escort me in such a grand manner. Thank you. I felt like a lady, quite. Did I behave?

The critic was good and just in *The Observer*.

       Yours
       L.K.

24 May 1950   King's College
Dear Dicky
    I *was* pleased with the Ballet in *The Observer*. Your sense of humour! I
laughed till my mouth split (hare lip).
    Sadler's Wells fun is here. *Beauty and Beast* touching. Peggy van Pragh
[Praagh] is a dear.
    Please, let me know the address of L. Kirstein, to thank him for nylon.
    Admonition! Do not give up your paper. Economise, work harder, you
mustn't lose 10,000 Everyman.
                            All best wishes
                            Adieu
                                Yours ever
                                L.K.

Although I think I write more sense about ballet now, twenty
years after Lydia wrote those letters to me, I have no such appreciative reader today. Indeed, months go by without comment on
my articles in *The Sunday Times* from friend or foe.
    The summer of 1950 rises like steam from Lydia's next few letters.

8 June 1950   King's College
Dear Dicky
    ... For the last days I have been sweating like a dancer. I was so hot I
wished for nothing but sea shells around my neck, but that would be the
case for the Blue lamp. [I think she means she would be arrested for
indecency. Blue Lamp = Police station?] ...
                            Best love ...
                            Lydia Keynes

2 July 1950   Tilton, Firle, near Lewes, Sussex
Dear Dicky
    Where are you roaming? I am surrounded by broad beans, green peas
and weeds, my skin almost rattles from the sun, so rewarding and sudorous.
    I have got the tickets for July the 10th. Are you coming with me? Do
let me know.
                            Best love
                            Lydia Keynes

July 1950   Tilton
My dear Dicky
    ... The hay smells good and English country is beautiful, I circulate,
exist like a plant with two arms.
                            Best love,
                            Lydia Keynes

25 July 1950   Tilton
My dear Dicky
    Where are you? ... At the moment I am shelling broad beans, like a

Tibetan monk with his beads, I find life a melody, away from Oxford Street.

Best love,
Lydia Keynes

27 July 1950   Tilton
My dear Dicky
Although I am keen to see the new ballets, I am so stuck, cannot move to city life: half-naked creeping like a lizzard (non poisonous) amongst cabbages and beans, I forget the world in 'contemplative idleness'. I was annoyed last Sunday when *The Observer* was not delivered, can you supply with the copy of last Sunday (July 23) please? I cannot ask you to stay yet, as previous engagements are filling my week-ends.

Best love
Lydia Keynes

I was to visit Lydia at Cambridge before I stayed with her at Tilton.

9 Oct. 1950   King's College
My dear Dicky,
I am away from London to reach warm walls with my cold in the chest. I am well again, as everyday I eat roast beef. We all want you to visit Cambridge . . .

Best love . . .
L.K.

'We all', I supposed, were the Provost and Fellows of King's, breathless for my visit.

18 Feb. 1951   King's College
Dear Dicky,
. . . Your duel with puma [controversy with Ninette de Valois] was fun, but she might be annoyed just the same . . .
Now Noel Annan the fellow and a great friend is offering you his College rooms at King's for March 10, 11. Also there is a performance of *Coriolanus* by the Marlowe Society. I shall be buzy with the Festival of my mother in law [her 90th birthday party], for lunch and early afternoon, but in the evening Kahn and I will entertain you, and we might get Rylands, however there is still Sunday to meet my chums, and we shall look after you . . .

Best love.
L.K.

I had a crowded, enjoyable visit to King's, where there was a Roger Fry on every wall, and was welcomed by Provost Sheppard, the Annans, Richard Kahn (Lydia's trustee) and other distinguished dons. Lydia made rather a fool of me by telling me to wear a dinner jacket for a dinner party in college, as I turned out to be the only person in evening dress. Playing up to the role of London gigolo, in which I seemed to have been cast, I announced in an affected voice 'I bet I'm the only person at the table wearing cuff-links given him by a Fellow of King's.' This remark provoked various surmises, but nobody guessed that the donor was that austere sinologist Arthur Waley, who, admittedly, without the collaboration of Beryl de Zoete, then a close friend and regular contributor to my magazine, would hardly have dreamt of giving me a Christmas present.

At Tilton I was allowed to breakfast and write throughout the morning in bed. This, I felt, would not have been encouraged without the precedent of Maynard, who was known to have made his fortune by lying late in bed to read the newspapers. Maynard's principles were strictly adhered to. Gin and whisky were therefore not provided, though a glass of sherry was permitted before meals and wine was plentiful. (Once, meeting Lydia at Covent Garden and attempting to salute her with the usual kiss, I had been repulsed and admonished 'Maynard say no kissing in public.') Tilton was a white box-like farmhouse under the South Downs. The hall was stacked with tins of food, tribute from America, and with innumer-able pairs of shoes – for shoes held a sexual fascination for Lydia – she could not resist buying them, and on excursions to Lewes would stand spellbound outside a shoe-shop window. The furniture was as characterless as in the London flat – except for one piece painted by Duncan Grant, who lived with Vanessa Bell at Charleston, a field away; but the pictures were not only by these two stars of the Bloomsbury Pléiade, but by Sickert, Picasso, Braque, Cézanne, Renoir, Degas and Seurat. Sickert had told Lydia her head was like a pigeon's and I admired his profile of her in murky tones of green and purple. Lydia and I would meet for a jolly lunch, tended by two rosy elves, her housekeeper's children; then I walked on the Downs while Lydia rested and learned the poems of Shakespeare and Eliot by heart. I would stand, breathless from climbing, on Firle Beacon and survey to the North the iridescent landscape; then it was only a few steps southward over the high ground to a point from which I could see the Channel packet coming in to Newhaven. After dinner with Lydia and Logan Thompson, who farmed her land, I would settle down by the log fire in the apple-green drawing-room to talk about ballet. Lydia, with a big box of cigarettes beside her, and wrapped in rugs and jackets against the 'curly winds', would describe how she used to steal Pavlova's shoes in the old days in St Petersburg, for Pavlova had a rich protector to buy her plenty of shoes; then, filled with nostalgia for her Imperial past, she would run eagerly across to the upright piano and play a tinkling tune she had danced to in Theatre Street over forty years ago.

July 1951   Tilton
Dear flatterer
    You are a very easy amiable guest. Come again.
    Having my tooth pulled out it was necessary to see 'The point of departure'. Anouil [h] is always worth seeing. . . .
    Do not drink too much gin or sherry, stick to beer.
                        Best love
                          L.K.

7 Oct. 1951   Tilton
My dear Dickie
    A beautiful letter. Thank you. I shall never go to the theatres any more if I get your critique . . . In spite of your opinion I must have a look at Tamburlaine, even if it is a 'female bishop' [Could this be my description of Donald Wolfit?] makes me roar with laughter.
    Most of the day I am in the hills, learning poetry, bitten by invisible insects in the lower parts of my body. Still I have the taps of water to rinse me through and degrade the bites.
                        Best love.
                    Lydia Keynes

    Next February Lydia was not well and wrote: 'One day I hope I shall jump over the river like a fox, and then we shall both jump together.' In April 1953 she was expecting me 'to eat raspberries'. In January 1954: 'I am taking things easy this time of year, but the sun was full of mirth and that is why I am writing to you, feeling gay.' That August she lent some pictures to my Diaghilev exhibition in Edinburgh. 'The lorry has arrived last Thursday and took away five contributions as agreed . . . You probably do not notice that we have a weary summer, the winds rattle and I am glad I am not a cow in the meadows.' The exhibition came to London, and she would not leave Tilton to attend the opening, but later on I found her queuing up one morning before the doors were open, with a lot of boy-scouts. On Boxing Day: 'I mounted the hill today. It was misty and mystical. I felt I had done "good works" being on top.' In spring 1956 Lydia wrote: 'My staff left me after ten years so I cannot invite you at the moment. "Normal service will be resumed as soon as possible."' After 'giving up writing about ballet for ever' for a year or two, I joined *The Sunday Times*. In March 1960 Lydia encouraged me again: 'Were you tipsy when you wrote last Sunday's article? If so, you must drink more, it was one of your best.'
    When I consider the inspiration and delight Lydia's friendship afforded me – and the preceding extracts are from letters covering only our first decade – I cannot find it surprising that Lord Keynes loved her for more than twenty-five years.
    For years I was a regular visitor at Tilton, where Lydia still lives

(and learns); and I wrote the first act of my first play there. I gathered that other friends who popped in to amuse her were Frederick Ashton, Robert Helpmann and Vivien Leigh. Lydia used to say 'I like to be alone, yes I *do*! But I must have a man for Sunday Lunch.' There were certain aspects of her past life which she never discussed, and it is known that she neither helped Roy Harrod with his life of Lord Keynes, nor read it when it was published. I think that a slight fear of being betrayed and 'put into a book' tinged her friendship for me with reserve. Thanking me for my *Adventures of a Ballet Critic*, from which I have plucked a few sprigs to embellish this essay, she wrote 'I should think most saleable with so much inside information', implying that my material had been procured by stealth. And here I am – treacherously but lovingly – writing about her. Well, writers are spies; and it is too late now to choose a more honourable profession.

8

The Bloomsbury Group

PAUL LEVY

On Friday, 9 September 1938, a particularly fine day, a group of friends gathered in the garden of Tilton, Maynard Keynes's house in Sussex, to hear their host read a chapter of autobiography later called 'My Early Beliefs'. The occasion was a meeting of the Memoir Club, but the subject for this afternoon was rather special for some of the company: Keynes had been stimulated to write this piece by some remarks made by David Garnett, dealing with his friendship with D. H. Lawrence, which Garnett had read at the last meeting of the Club. Hearing Garnett's paper had recalled to Keynes Lawrence's hostility to himself and to his friends when they were young men at Cambridge, and by a process of association Keynes was led to reflect on what it was that made them the sort of young men they had been, and what Lawrence had found so objectionable.

It was an ordinary enough gathering, with Keynes, now a man of fifty-five, reclining to avoid over-taxing his heart, reading to his audience seated around him in the large, sunny garden. Looking around him, Keynes probably felt rather pleased with the setting; though he had not been aware of the fact when he first took Tilton, it had once belonged to the Keynes family, and he now considered himself, with more than faint irony, the rightful squire of Tilton. The dozen or so people present were all close friends, and most of them had good reason for the careful attention they paid to the paper Keynes was reading, for its subject was the ethical doctrines of the philosopher G. E. Moore. Three of the present company had been early friends of Moore and counted themselves among his original disciples. These were Keynes himself, Leonard Woolf, and Desmond MacCarthy. But everyone was interested in what Keynes had to say, as each of them felt his own life, or his friends' or parents' lives, had been influenced by Moore's teachings in *Principia Ethica*, a book that had been published almost exactly thirty-five years earlier, when Keynes was a twenty-year-old undergraduate.

It was near the end of the summer holidays and the whole party was staying in Sussex, for several of them had houses quite near to

Tilton, and the rest were their house-guests. The audience included Keynes's wife Lydia, who had finally become a member of the Memoir Club after years of exclusion from it. Among the neighbours present were Clive and Vanessa Bell and Duncan Grant from Charleston, which is only a few hundred yards distant from Tilton, and Leonard and Virginia Woolf whose Monk's House was in the nearby village of Rodmell. Other Sussex residents present were Quentin and Angelica Bell. The visitors to Sussex were David Garnett, E. M. Forster, Janie Bussy, and Desmond and Molly MacCarthy. Mrs MacCarthy was suffering doubly as she sat on the lawn; not only was she very, very deaf, and so had to strain to hear Keynes read, but she had also injured her ankle earlier that day while lunching at Monk's House and was in pain.

The relationships among those gathered on the lawn that afternoon were unusually close, and this is of some importance in understanding the effect of what Keynes read upon his audience and the tone of his paper. His listeners included not only neighbours, but people related by blood- and marriage-ties. Their friendships were both old and deep, and each member of the group was conscious of this. As youths, Maynard Keynes and Duncan Grant had been lovers; their friendship had endured and mellowed with the passage of time, leaving room for Keynes's passionate attachment to his wife and Grant's to Vanessa Bell. After the births of their sons, Julian and Quentin, Clive and Vanessa Bell had lived mostly apart for fourteen years; during this time Vanessa had lived with Duncan Grant at Charleston, and in 1918 they had a daughter, Angelica. Angelica herself was to marry another member of the group, David Garnett (who had been present at her birth), in four years' time. Several of the older members of the Memoir Club had reason to feel for their host gratitude as well as deep affection, as Keynes had more than once put his business acumen and developed political instinct at the service of his friends; his loyalties sprang from deep sources, and he had never spared himself when a friend was in need. Though aware of these facts and the feelings they occasioned, the younger members of the party nonetheless had slightly different feelings about their host. Janie Bussy, the niece of Lytton Strachey, was highly politicised, and held Trotskyite convictions; Quentin Bell considered himself a 'fellow-traveller'. The year, after all, was 1938: the Spanish Civil War was raging, and Quentin's brother Julian had been killed there only the year before; Chamberlain was Prime Minister, the Munich Pact was only twenty days in the future, and the beginning of the actual war less than a year. Fine as the day was, the young found it difficult to put aside their preoccupation with these facts; much as they recognised Keynes's genius and generosity, they found it hard not to disapprove, and even to resent his ties with the Establishment. For them, the concern of their elders for the past, as reflected in Keynes's choice of topic, must have seemed trivial, perhaps even wicked. There was no point, though, in boycotting the meeting; the Memoir Club was, in spite of being a venerable institution, always amusing and sometimes edifying. So many good friends were gathered in Sussex, and it was a glorious day.

The Memoir Club came into being precisely on 6 March 1920, according to Leonard Woolf[1] (though its Secretary, Molly MacCarthy, had called its first meeting late in 1919 in order to organise the Club). It may well have grown out of the earlier Novel Club which the same group of friends had founded to encourage Desmond MacCarthy to write the novel that his friends were convinced would be his most important work. This group collapsed, so the story goes, when it was discovered that the brilliant chapters that MacCarthy read aloud regularly at the Novel Club's meetings were nothing but blank sheets of paper. Many of the group of old friends who comprised the Novel Club and the Memoir Club had lived in the neighbourhood of the British Museum in the twenties; then their number had included Roger Fry and Saxon Sydney-Turner as regular participants. Why, one may wonder, would a group of friends, even very old friends, gather to read bits of autobiography to each other? They were mostly eminent people, certainly; the meeting that summer afternoon in Sussex included the two most important novelists, the most important art critic, literary critic, and economist in England; the stories of their lives were clearly of interest to more people than those who actually heard them read. But the answer to this question must be that the people present had a strong sense of themselves as a group. Most intellectuals thought of these people as forming the core of the Bloomsbury Group, and none of those seated in the spacious garden of Tilton was oblivious of this.

The characteristics of the Bloomsbury Group and the circumstances of its origin are tales too familiar to bear retelling. It is sufficient to say that it sprang from the undergraduate friendships at Cambridge of its male members, all of whom save Clive Bell and Thoby Stephen had been part of a secret discussion society called the Apostles, or just 'the Society'. Of course, not all these men were up at Cambridge at the same time; Fry was much older, and MacCarthy and Forster slightly older, than the others. If they were not all contemporaries at Cambridge, and not even all Apostles, what then did they have in common that led them all to Bloomsbury? A too brief answer is that they shared certain feelings about human relations and about works of art, in fact, certain elements of a philosophy. The origins of these attitudes they credited to G. E. Moore, and for this reason those who were present that afternoon in September 1938, listened with even more interest than usual to the paper read by Keynes, 'My Early Beliefs', for it was those beliefs that the Bloomsbury Group supposed themselves to share. The younger generation objected to this talk of the past, for they were keenly aware of the threat posed to civilisation by Nazi Germany and Fascism, and felt it self-indulgent to linger on the past when the present was so threatening. But no one in the audience was more aware of the danger menacing civilisation than Keynes himself; in talking about Moore's influence he intended, and so he was understood by the elder number of his listeners, to deliver a summing-up of what this threatened civilisation meant to him and to them. For Moore had inculcated in them, when they were undergraduates, Keynes said,[2] certain habits of feeling, and 'it is those habits of feeling, influencing the majority of us, which make this Club a collectivity and separate us from the rest'. Trying to recapture, thirty-odd years later, the feeling of what it was like to be associated with Moore, Keynes remarked that 'it was exciting, exhilarating, the beginning of a renaissance, the opening of a new heaven on a new earth, we were the forerunners of a new dispensation, we were not afraid of anything'.[3]

Maynard Keynes went up to King's College in the autumn of 1902: sometime in his first term he was called on in his rooms by two lean and ascetic looking men: they were Lytton Strachey and Leonard Woolf, and they had come to propose taking Keynes to tea with G. E. Moore. Keynes was being vetted for election to the Apostles. The meeting was a success, and Keynes was duly elected in February 1903, which was unusual, for he was still in his first year at University. Moore, though no longer officially an active member of the Society, was in fact its most important member. It was essential to secure his approval before proceeding to an election, and the Society was having some difficulty in finding suitable candidates, for Keynes was the sole new man elected in 1903. The officially active Apostles that year were Austin Smyth, (Sir) Ralph Hawtrey, H. O. Meredith, E. M. Forster, (Sir) John Sheppard, Strachey, Saxon Sydney-Turner, Woolf, and Leonard Greenwood; it was they who, with Moore's blessing, elected Keynes. The characteristics of the Society and the demands it makes upon its members are well known; Keynes was 'Apostolic' by nature, and soon drew his friends chiefly from their number, with the exception of two Trinity men, Thoby Stephen and Clive Bell, who were strangely never elected to the Apostles. One of the sporadic traditions of the

Society was that of the 'higher sodomy', a sort of ideological homosexuality, which manifested itself more in words than in deeds. With the advent of Strachey, and later Keynes, this tradition was powerfully reborn, and its emphasis on verbal behaviour may have shifted just a little. Certainly the next year found Strachey and Keynes conniving at the election of (Sir) Arthur Hobhouse, whose most Apostolic feature seems to have been his yellow hair and strong resemblance to the Hermes of Praxiteles; but unknown to each other, the older men were rivals for Hobhouse's affections. With extreme difficulty they succeeded in securing the election in his first year of this comely son of a Somerset squire. For some time following this election, which depended not a little on Moore's extreme innocence of such matters, Strachey thought he had Hobhouse's heart to himself. When he learned that Keynes was his chief rival for this very object he sank into miserable gloom, but rallied himself to deliver a terrible attack on Keynes at a meeting of the Apostles that took place only a week after Hobhouse's election. (This was in February 1905; there had been no suitable candidate the year before, and Hobhouse was thus the first Apostle to be elected since Keynes himself.) 'For it is one of his queer characteristics', said Strachey of Keynes, 'that one often wants, one cannot tell why, to make a malicious attack on him, and that, when the time comes, one refrains, one cannot tell why. His sense of values, and indeed all his feelings, offer the spectacle of a complete paradox. He is a hedonist and a follower of Moore; he is lascivious without lust; he is an Apostle without tears.'

In fact, Keynes's affair with Hobhouse was probably, as his letters to the younger man seem to show, as chaste as Strachey's own. But Strachey hit the mark in saying that the future economist was 'lascivious without lust', if by that he meant that Keynes had the makings of a sensualist, where he himself inclined to sentimentality. It is doubtful that Keynes had yet had any sexual experience; but it would later be true to say that he was capable of enjoying copulation without fancying himself in love, however passionate the language he might employ in addressing his lover. In this he was not in perfect sympathy with Strachey, whatever avowals of harmony of feeling each made to the other, for Strachey, until he was past his first youth, always prized the feeling of being in love more highly than the copulation that might or might not accompany it. This trait was revealed in Keynes's appearance, especially in his mouth which was full with thick lips, over which he wore (as a youth) a thin moustache, and in his piercing, brilliant and dark eyes, surmounted by long lashes and thickly luxuriant eyebrows. Keynes had a certain sense of his physical presence, which was magnetic and seductive, though he never considered himself attractive. This was not the presence of someone like his later friend David Garnett, who was aware of his own physical beauty, but of someone who was used to his own appearance and comfortable with his body. This last was shown by the economy with which Keynes used his hands, which he was capable of keeping perfectly at rest throughout a conversation, save when his talk demanded him to strike a deliberate attitude. He was capable of a physical repose that is the complement of a confident attitude, and his voice was silky and well-modulated. Though not good-looking in any conventional sense save for his eyes, these formidable attributes made Keynes attractive both to men and to women.

But Keynes could fall in love properly, as he was to show to Strachey's discomfiture, when, following the Hobhouse affair, he fell in love with Strachey's own special friend and cousin, Duncan Grant. In the summer of 1908 Keynes wrote to Strachey that he was in love with the young painter and that his feelings were returned; once again Strachey had to bow out of the dance after Keynes had cut in. Hobhouse had gone from Strachey to Keynes to Grant in the past; now Grant glided from Strachey to Keynes. Surely it is not too fanciful to see in this the beginning of the Bloomsbury Gavotte, a gracefully romantic dance in which the participants couple, separate, and go on to another, without ever having to leave the floor in search of a new partner. Unlike Strachey, Keynes never found it necessary to sit out a dance; this one, with Grant, lasted a particularly long time, until, the tempo slowing, the less intricate but perhaps deeper rhythm of friendship was assumed, to endure for life. Keynes was, in fact, bisexual, and in the years before his marriage had romantic dealings with people of both sexes; after his move from Cambridge to the India Office these were most often with other young people associated with Bloomsbury. Many of them were friends of Keynes before they entered upon a liaison with him, and, to his credit, all of them remained friends when passion had run its course.

Sometimes, though, his romantic interests were directed to people with whom intimacy involved some risk, either of exposure of unconventional sexual tastes or of exposure to a way of life so unlike his own as to be bewildering. In these relations Keynes showed two traits that were characteristic of his life and even of his work, his love of risk-taking and his genuine concern and kindness for the welfare of others. In his intimate dealings with people who belonged to a social class lower than his own there was always the danger, whether inadvertently or maliciously, of a revelation that could have injured his career and hurt his parents and their friends.

Though Keynes, and indeed all Apostles and members of the Bloomsbury Group despised the conventions that restricted sexual behaviour, all knew that defying these conventions was risky. But Keynes was by nature a gambler – in his human relationships, in his financial speculations, and at the tables of Beaulieu-sur-Mer and Biarritz. On the other hand his view of human nature was as generous as his own character, and he derived real pleasure from the material help his great gifts allowed him to give to all who knew him well, whether they were friends, lovers, employees, or Fellows of the same College. His generosity was magnificent, unfailing and universal; his attitude to humanity was avuncular. Though not a Christian Keynes practised Christian charity on a scale not conceived of by most believers.

For a time Keynes had close friendships with a group of young people he called the 'neo-pagans'. These included Ka Cox, Justin Brooke, the Olivier sisters, Rupert Brooke, Geoffrey Keynes and Virginia Stephen, who in September 1911 organised a camp in Devon. To the number of his pre-war friends should be added the names of James Strachey, Gerald Shove, Ferenc Békássy, Harry Norton, Cecil Taylor, G. H. Luce, and Ludwig Wittgenstein, all of whom were Apostles younger than Keynes. With the last he had a serious intellectual relationship like that of each of them to Bertrand Russell; and with Shove, as later with Frank Ramsey, he had common interests in economics. During the war he was to acquire the friendship of several young ladies, some ex-Cambridge students and some of them students at the Slade, many of whom were to become welcome additions to Bloomsbury. They were Faith Bagenal (later Mrs Hubert Henderson), Dora Carrington, Dorothy Brett, Alix Sargant-Florence (later Mrs James Strachey), and especially Barbara Hiles (later Mrs Nicholas Bagenal). Much of the story of Keynes's social life is told by a list of his addresses, for in those days the Bloomsbury Group was a geographical entity, and several of these young ladies shared lodgings with Keynes, as did Duncan Grant, Middleton Murry and Katharine Mansfield, Adrian and Virginia Stephen, Gerald Shove, Leonard Woolf, Clive and Vanessa Bell, Harry Norton, James Strachey and J. T. Sheppard – at 21 Fitzroy Square, 38 Brunswick Square, 10 Great Ormond Street, 3 Gower Street, and 46 Gordon Square.

The war years were dreadful for Keynes. Most of his friends were conscientious objectors, a position whose sincerity he never doubted and with which he was in sympathy though he could not embrace it himself. On behalf of these friends he worked tirelessly and selflessly, and more than once to good effect. While still at Cambridge he began to feel the horror that would increase as the war was prolonged, starting with the death of Freddie Hardman in November 1914, and the deaths of two King's undergraduates as well as Rupert Brooke in April 1915, and then a casualty on the other side, the Hungarian Ferenc Békássy in July. He nevertheless, and in the face of strong opposition from his best friends, accepted a post at the Treasury, where, by January 1917, as he wrote to Duncan Grant, 'I pray for the most absolute financial crash (and yet strive to prevent it – so that all I do is a contradiction with all I feel).' And in December that year he wrote to Grant: 'I work for a Government I despise for ends I think criminal.'

Keynes had only reached this position by a great deal of anguished soul-searching, and no other aspect of his life shows so clearly the influence of his Bloomsbury friends on his own thinking. Békássy's death, for example, was a more severe blow for the fact that it was Keynes who made it possible for him to return to Hungary to fight and be killed. It was Keynes who had raised the money for Békássy's passage while the banks were shut and no other funds were available. Keynes had pleaded with Békássy not to leave England, but he was determined to fight against Russia. (War was not declared between Britain and Austria–Hungary until the morning after he left.) David Garnett remonstrated with Keynes that he was not only sending a friend to his death but was helping to strengthen the enemy forces. Keynes took the view that Békássy's wish to go was absolute, and that his first duty was to help his friend before any considerations of patriotism. Keynes was certain then that the war could not, for economic reasons, last more than eighteen months, and this influenced Garnett[4] not to make an immediate decision about enlisting.

Bloomsbury found it difficult to despise the Germans, for they thought more often of Goethe and Bach than of Kaiser Bill; this pro-Germanism though was purely cultural – for German militarism they cared no more than for English jingoism. When the introduction of conscription threatened, Bloomsbury opinion hardened: were conscription to be introduced, the war which was ostensibly being fought against militarism would have made Britain a militaristic state. Clive Bell especially took the line that a negotiated settlement was the only way to preserve European civilisation from complete ruin. Argument raged in Bloomsbury. David Garnett said:

Maynard was in an exceptional position inasmuch as he was occupying a position of continually increasing importance in the Treasury, and was thus in possession of the secret facts with regard to the day-to-day conduct of the war. Much of what his closest friends said exasperated him, since they were ignorant of the facts and he was unable to use his knowledge to prove them mistaken. On the other hand his detailed information led him frequently to adopt a short-term view and he sometimes failed to see the major issues as clearly as his friends. When in 1918, the policy of British intervention in Russia came up my mother, Constance, was right and realistic, and Maynard, with all the detailed knowledge of day-to-day secret information, was wrong.[5]

Keynes was under pressure from his friends. One day in February 1916 Lytton Strachey put the conscientious objector's equivalent of the white feather on Keynes's dinner plate. It took the form of an extract from a vehemently militaristic speech by Charles Edward Montague, the formerly liberal jounalist who had dyed his grey hair and enlisted as a private soldier. Strachey told his brother James that he 'wrote on a piece of notepaper the following – "Dear Maynard, why are you still in the Treasury? Yours, Lytton." I was going to post it to him, but he happened to be dining at Gordon Square where I also was. So I put the letter on his plate. He really *was* rather put out when he read the extract.' Keynes said he had talked to Montague only two days earlier. Strachey demanded to know

what was the use of his going on imagining he was doing any good with such people? I went on for a long time with considerable virulence, Nessa, Duncan and Bunny sitting round in approving silence. . . . The poor fellow seemed very decent about it, and admitted that *part* of his reason for staying was the pleasure he got from being able to do the work so well. He also seemed to think he was doing a great service to the country by saving some millions per week. . . . He at last admitted that there *was* a point at which he *would* think it necessary to leave, but what that point might be he couldn't say. [22 February 1916]

Among the Bloomsbury conscientious objectors were not only the two Strachey brothers and David Garnett, but also Clive Bell, Adrian Stephen, Gerald Shove, Harry Norton and Duncan Grant. The last took a true pacifist position – that the use of violence was always wrong – and it was possible for Keynes to support him in this position without worrying about his own views. But the others tended to take up positions that demanded a response from Keynes. Lytton Strachey, for example, opposed this war specifically, on political and ethical grounds, while refusing to rule out the possibility of some future just war; to agree with him was to rule out the possibility of any cooperation with the war effort, even as a non-combatant in the Treasury. Clive Bell's opposition centred on the immorality of war as a means of pursuing national policies; no one who agreed with him could possibly work for the Treasury in wartime. David Garnett felt it was impossible to be a soldier, because no moral person could delegate to another his right of private judgement; he found it impossible to agree to obey orders without question, when those orders could possibly entail the commission of an atrocity. Only this last argument did not affect Keynes's position – he could after all resign from the Treasury. But he agreed in large measure with all three arguments.

With his customary generosity, Keynes rescued Garnett and Grant when they had made a hash of their first hearing for military service exemption at the Local Tribunal at Blything, and appeared in person for their Appeal Tribunal at Ipswich. He himself put Duncan Grant's case, intimidating the Tribunal members by clutching his official Treasury bag with the royal cipher and insisting that the procedures be carried on expeditiously as his presence was required at Whitehall. Grant was allowed non-combatant service, but Keynes insisted that he be given leave to appeal to the Central Tribunal. Garnett, whose hearing followed immediately, employed the same strategy with success. Keynes also supported the claims for exemption of several more friends, notably the two Strachey brothers. Still his own position grew more difficult.

He had promised Bloomsbury to refuse to attest under the Derby Scheme, and he did; but when he received notice to attend for calling-up procedures, he simply replied on Treasury notepaper that he was too busy to attend. He had kept faith with his friends in that he did not apply for exemption at all; but when this omission was discovered by a Treasury bureaucrat, Keynes repaired it without demur. Keynes's whole attitude seems to have been that the war having been started must be finished. But Strachey and others did not forget that Keynes had once said that he would resign his Treasury post if universal conscription was introduced. Clearly Keynes did agree with at least some of the arguments put forward by Bloomsbury, and Bloomsbury never ceased to feel that there was an inconsistency between these beliefs and Keynes's remaining at the Treasury where, it seemed obvious to them, his job must have involved calculating the cheapest way to kill Germans. David Garnett[6] tells of an episode that shows how tense Keynes's relations with his friends had become. One evening at Gordon Square, after having worked particularly late at the Treasury, Keynes, whose nerves must have been very frayed (for he could not possibly have doubted the sincerity of the friends whose exemptions he had worked so hard to secure), declared that he did not think anyone could have a genuine conscientious objection. When Vanessa Bell and Harry Norton attempted to argue with him, he snapped at them, 'Go to bed. Go to bed.' J. T. Sheppard, infuriated by this behaviour, said, 'Maynard, you will find it is a mistake to despise your old friends.' Keynes's irritability is perhaps understandable when it is remembered that of the members of Bloomsbury, Duncan

Grant alone made any attempt to sympathise with Keynes's difficult personal position. By 1917, as we have seen, this position was nearly intolerable; and yet it was just the fact that he did not give up his job at the Treasury that made him so useful to his friends.

Keynes felt this tension throughout the war. The strain finally became too great to be endured during the Paris Peace Conference, when the Allies insisted on Treaty terms of a meanness that was anathema to his generous nature and of a stupidity that was despicable to one of his intelligence. He had what we would now call a nervous breakdown and took to his bed in June 1919. He returned to London, and during his recovery wrote *The Economic Consequences of the Peace;* he resumed his life in Bloomsbury, and began paying frequent and momentous visits to the Russian ballet. Setting himself up to make some money by his financial gifts and his experience of such affairs gained in his time at the Treasury, he never refused investment advice to his friends – or to their parents, uncles, aunts or cousins. But in 1920 the combination of his generosity and his gambler's instincts resulted in his ruining not only himself but much of Bloomsbury, and even their distant relations, by speculation in currencies. It was not long before he recovered his losses and theirs, and in years to come he established his friends' financial security, as well as finding them jobs, buyers of paintings, and publishers. His energy was as terrific as his devotion to his friends was deep.

In the early summer of 1919, while Keynes was lying prostrate in Paris, the Diaghilev ballet was beginning a new season in London. The dancers and painters associated with the company found a warm welcome in Gordon Square, and pre-war Bloomsbury seemed to revive from its wartime despair. Recovered from his illness, Keynes joined in this new life, moving from Gordon Square to Charleston to King's, and by August he had re-assumed his natural role, and presided over a supper party at Gordon Square for thirty-two guests. This was to mark the end of the London season of the ballet, but the beginning of Keynes's post-war social life. There were visits to The Wharf, as the Asquiths' house guest – one in the company of Lytton Strachey – and to Garsington, as the guest of Lady Ottoline Morrell, where Keynes met several Oxford undergraduates whose presence was later to enliven many a Bloomsbury party. It was about this time that T. S. Eliot became acquainted with Bloomsbury, and Keynes plotted, without success, to have him appointed literary editor of the *Nation and Athenaeum,* of which he was a director. There was now another country outpost of Bloomsbury in the Mill House, Tidmarsh, where a syndicate of friends had installed Lytton Strachey. There he lived with the painter Dora Carrington, and after a time Ralph Partridge married her and became a permanent member of their household. In a letter to Carrington (4 September 1920) Strachey gives an amusing glimpse of life at Charleston, where he and Keynes were staying with the Bells:

> Typically, Maynard has insisted on ... you'd never guess what: altering the time! So that the clocks are one hour in advance even of summer time, with curious consequences. For one thing Jessie disapproves, won't have it, and has let the kitchen clock run down, so that the servants have *no* time. Then Clive is fitful on the subject, and insists upon always referring to the normal time; and altogether the confusion is extraordinary. How mad they all are! Maynard, though he sees what a rumpus it causes, persists. Vanessa is too feeble to put him down, and Clive is too tetchy to grin and bear it. The result is extremely Tchekhofesque. But luckily the atmosphere is entirely comic, instead of being fundamentally tragic as in Tchekhof. Everyone laughs and screams and passes on.[7]

From time to time Keynes had Strachey to stay with him at King's and introduced him to the new Apostles, F. L. (Peter) Lucas, W. J. H. (Sebastian) Sprott, and George (Dadie) Rylands, Richard Braithwaite, and Frank Ramsey; these young men had joined Keynes's close circle of Cambridge friends who were not economists (though Ramsey was in fact to make some important contributions to the subject), and all of them were to have distinguished academic careers. Keynes took Sebastian Sprott on a holiday to Algeria and Tunisia in the Easter vacation of 1921, where they were stoned by street urchins because they had given one of them an insufficient tip for cleaning their shoes. Keynes was certain the tip he had proffered was correct, and when Sprott suggested raising it to escape the wrath of the native boys Keynes firmly declined, saying, 'I will not be a party to debasing the currency.'[8] For Christmas of 1922 Keynes took Lopokova to stay in Tidmarsh with Strachey, Carrington and Ralph Partridge.

Still later in the twenties Bloomsbury acquired yet another centre at 52 Tavistock Square; there Leonard and Virginia Woolf lived over their Hogarth Press, and gave after-dinner parties, where the chief entertainment was conversation. Keynes often attended these parties, where the other guests might have included Strachey, Duncan Grant, Roger Fry, and sometimes Desmond MacCarthy or E. M. Forster. Less sedate parties were given by Duncan Grant in his studio at 8 Fitzroy Street; these were more like the all-night affairs that sometimes took place at 46 Gordon Square. It was at such a party that David Garnett saw Picasso chatting to Douglas Fairbanks Snr while Lytton Strachey introduced himself to Mary

Pickford; not all the guests at these parties were drawn from Bloomsbury or Cambridge![9]

In 1922 Keynes persuaded Lydia Lopokova to give up her
lodgings in the Waldorf Hotel, and to move, literally, into Bloomsbury. He arranged for her to take the ground floor of 41 Gordon
Square, where she would be living below Alix and James Strachey,
who remembered the whole house trembling when Lopokova practised her entrechats.[10] Keynes was not pleased to learn that
Lopokova had also used the Waldorf Hotel as her bank, and, as was
his habit for all his close friends, showed her how to make better
use of her earnings.[11]

His marriage in 1925 to Lydia Lopokova was his greatest and
most successful gamble. His Bloomsbury friends adored her as a
party-guest but had doubts about whether a prima ballerina could
possibly also have a suitable mind, and Keynes's relations with
Bloomsbury, even with Duncan Grant and Vanessa Bell, were for a
while distant. As for the Fellows of King's, they were, before
meeting Lopokova, unable to distinguish between one sort of dancer
and another. In time all these difficulties were overcome, and before
the beginning of the Second World War, Lydia Keynes was finally
welcomed even into the sanctum of the Memoir Club.

The courage of the gambler and the generosity of the saint were
characteristic of Keynes's public career; no less were they the source,
in his personal affairs, of his greatness as a human being.[12]

NOTES

1. Leonard Woolf, *Downhill All the Way* (London, 1967), p. 114.
2. J. M. Keynes, *Two Memoirs* (London, 1949), p. 81.
3. *Ibid.*, p. 82.
4. David Garnett, *The Golden Echo* (London, 1953), pp. 270-2.
5. David Garnett, *The Flowers of the Forest* (London, 1955), pp. 104-5.
6. *Ibid.*, pp. 148-9.
7. Letter from Lytton Strachey quoted in Michael Holroyd, *Lytton Strachey* (London, 1968), Vol. 2, p. 309.
8. R. F. Harrod, *The Life of John Maynard Keynes* (London, 1951), p. 304.
9. Michael Holroyd, *op. cit.*, Vol. 2, p. 486n.
10. *Ibid.*, pp. 371-2n.
11. R. F. Harrod, *op. cit.*, p. 309.
12. The author wishes to thank Professor Quentin Bell for his help in the preparation of this essay.

PART TWO

9

The influence of Keynes on the
economics of his time

D. E. MOGGRIDGE

Soon after the Second World War the American Economic Association commissioned one, and later two volumes in which specialists
surveyed 'contemporary economics' so as to 'provide the economist
outside a particular field with an intelligible and reliable account of
its main ideas . . . which have evolved during the last ten to fifteen
years'.[1] If one looks at the indexes to the two volumes which eventually appeared and ranks economists in terms of the number of
entries, the results of the first eight come out as follows: Keynes 98,
J. R. Hicks 56, A. Marshall 40, J. Schumpeter 39, O. Lange 39,
P. A. Samuelson 38, A. B. Lerner 37, A. C. Pigou 34. If one goes
deeper and follows up the page references, Keynes's contributions
prove to be the subject of parts of no fewer than fifteen of the
twenty-three chapters, including such unlikely candidates to the
modern eye as 'Value and Distribution'.[2] In one of the chapters,
one of the reviewers found Keynes's influence so persuasive that he
remarked, 'Tacitly this is perhaps Lord Keynes's greatest tribute:
his contributions need not be itemized even for non-specialists.'[3]

Perhaps the authors of the relevant surveys were biased in that
they all were in the vanguard of the 'Keynesian revolution',
although the balance by vintage of academic training proves
remarkably even. However, doubts on this score as to the extent of
Keynes's influence on the economics of his time dissolve somewhat
when one comes across the following remarks by Professors Pigou
and Marget, neither of whom could be counted amongst Keynes's
greatest admirers.

Those of us who disagreed in part with his analysis have, nevertheless,
undoubtedly been affected by it in our own thinking; and it is very hard
to know exactly where we stood before. Not a little of what we now believe
ourselves to have known all along, it may well be we owe to him.

. . .

Indeed if one needs further proof of the 'strangeness' of the Keynesian
episode, one need ask only at what other time since Adam Smith, a position

73

avowedly presented as revolutionary and heterodox, has become for so
large a number of professional economic theorists a new ('modern') orthodoxy in so short a period.[4]

These statements from Pigou and Marget, plus the treatment of
Keynes in the early post-war surveys illustrate the difficulties that
exist in an attempt to assess Keynes's contribution to the economics
of his time. Granted 'he was, beyond doubt or challenge, the most
interesting, the most influential and the most important economist of
his time'.[5] Granted his influence remains very much with us as
witnessed by two large-scale recent attempts to reassess aspects of
contemporary economic thought in relation to his initial contributions.[6] But how does one assess a direct contribution whose ramifi-
cations spilled over into several areas of theoretical and applied
economics, as well as economic policy, and which indirectly spread
further as it stimulated the work of others in both support and
reaction?[7] And how does one assess the work of a man whose contribution had such apparent effects yet who seemed 'to have left no
mark on pure theory', according to one of his early American
supporters – one whose introductory textbook reflected, as did its
post-war brethren, a profound change in the orientation of economics at least as taught to undergraduates?[8]

Perhaps the best way to begin an assessment is to look at Keynes's
interests and writing habits, for they affected the product he offered
his contemporaries and their assessment of him. First of all Keynes's
interests in economic theory were almost completely practical: he
was never much interested in pure theory except as a guide to action.
This concern with action, with practical results, influenced not only
his own work but also his students.[9] As Austin Robinson emphasised
on one occasion, remembering Keynes as a teacher:

[We] learnt something quite different from Keynes [than from Robertson
and Pigou] – that we had got to think about the world, we had got to care
about the world; that if we were going to get the problems of the world
straight we had got to do it by some fundamental hard thinking; . . . that
if *we* were not going to think about the world nobody else was.[10]

Schumpeter certainly caught much of Keynes's work when he
emphasised his 'vision'[11] and when in reviewing *The General Theory*
he wrote that 'everywhere he really pleads for a definite policy and
on every page the ghost of that policy looks over the shoulder of the
analyst, frames his assumptions, guides his pen'.[12] Keynes was almost
always, as he told J. R. Hicks in connection with *The General
Theory*, refraining 'from pursuing anything very far, my object
being to press home as forcibly as possible certain fundamental

(a)

(b)

c)

(d)

Plate 3   Maynard Keynes: (a) aged 3, (b) aged 12, (c) aged 15, (d) aged 19, in 1902.

Plate 4 The barge *Aholibah* at the May races, Cambridge, in 1911. Maynard Keynes wearing a boater has his hands on the wooden bar in the centre of the photograph, and his mother is standing behind him on his left. On the right, at the end of the barge, Virginia Woolf stands in a flowered hat, and two away from her nearer the centre stands Rupert Brooke with his left arm across his body.

opinions – and no more'.[13] Such an approach to economic theory is hardly likely to win plaudits from pure theorists.

Added to Keynes's approach to theory in economics were his habits of working. His 'economic thinking was, in reality, intuitive, impressionistic, and in a sense feminine'.[14] Thus in writing *The General Theory* Keynes obviously depended on the careful, constructive advice of Richard Kahn to move from intuition to final text, intuitive as that may still be.[15] As well, Keynes's working habits were such that he did not *normally* pay attention in a formal sense to the work of his predecessors before making up his mind. Granted this work was often part of his stock of mental capital, but it was unlabelled as to source. Only after he had made up his mind would the predecessors get acknowledgement or blame.[16]

These characteristics of Keynes's working as an economist had important consequences for his influence on his contemporaries – and his successors:

1. His work was rarely formally complete or consistent. He only constructed the basic tools for the job at hand – no more. The rest he left to 'time, experience and the collaboration of a number of minds'[17] often with unintended consequences.

2. Even where his work might have been formally correct in the round, Keynes's methods of exposition and habits of thought required a high degree of sympathetic cooperation from his readers. This plainly left his work open to a wide number of interpretations.

3. Keynes's wide reading, plus his formal neglect of his predecessors while writing, meant, when coupled with the industry of the academic world, that it was, and is, possible to find a precursor for almost every idea in his work, as numerous issues of economic journals and scholarly monographs have proved beyond doubt.

4. Keynes's controversialist tendencies, at times heightened for scientific effects, which were evident in even as austere a work as his *Treatise on Probability*, invited rejoinders and drove others back to original sources to check his and their arguments.[18]

These habits of thought, expositions and working, plus the twin forces of a thermidor and academic product differentiation inevitably led to a reaction against Keynes, which still prevails outside introductory textbooks – a reaction that began well before his death.[19] Only with the passage of time have come attempts at reappraisal largely by a generation that did not live through the 'revolution' but rather the subsequent reaction. These reappraisals, interestingly enough, often take Keynes's influence as coming in areas either ignored or dismissed by most of his contemporaries. However, they do not help us all that much in assessing Keynes's contribution to or influence on the economics of his time.

Keynes's passionate concern for the world and its ills provides the first clue to his influence on his contemporaries. For Keynes's concern with economic policy took him into most of the economic debates of his generation – Indian currency, reparations, international currency arrangements, unemployment policy, war finance and post-war reconstruction. Inevitably the atmosphere of public debate, pluss Keynes's undoubted skills as a controversialist, often generated heat rather than light. However, the issues and Keynes's contributions to their discussion, amongst other factors, brought to economics a generation of economists committed to the subject for what might be called Keynesian reasons as much as they brought policy involvement to economists on a scale previously unknown.

This concern with policy, with the active management of the economy, meant that Keynes always emphasised the need for operational economic constructs, as well as the need to keep clear the distinction between theoretical ideas and policy guidelines.[20] He also framed his theory, whenever possible, so as to be amenable to actually or potentially available statistics. This had several important effects on his contemporaries. First, they attempted to develop the relevant statistical series. The classic case here, as far as Britain is concerned, was the work on national accounting, which, building on earlier work by Bowley and Stamp, under the influence of the *Treatise, General Theory* and wartime needs, took on its recognisable post-war form in the hands of Clark, Rothbarth, Stone and Meade.[21] Second, Keynes's contemporaries attempted to estimate the size of the various parameters or the shapes of various relationships in the systems put up by Keynes. The most fruitful exercise in this area was perhaps Richard Kahn's attempt to sort out the relationship between the primary and secondary employment resulting from loan-financed public works schemes.[22] However, Keynes was also fortunate in working at the time of the early development of econometrics, for the estimation and testing of Keynesian relationships increased his influence amongst economists generally. Here one must note that, despite his often legitimate questioning of some of the attitudes and methods of early econometricians, Keynes encouraged investment in such research for its practical applications.[23] Finally Keynes's policy orientation, plus subsequent policy-making experience in most cases, left lasting influences on modern economic thought in the form of the now vast literature on the appropriate linking of policy instruments to policy goals.

This emphasis on policy and its associated questioning of many of the precepts of *laissez-faire* also had significant effects on the political economy of Keynes's period, as many of Keynes's contemporaries realised with some alarm. Thus T. E. Gregory attacked Keynes's *Economic Consequences of Mr Churchill* for making monetary policy a class issue and, hence, making managed money more difficult in future.[24] Similarly, in the course of the 1930s various economists, in Britain largely associated with the London School of Economics, decried the 'Keynesian' emphasis on tinkering, on management, on involvement with current issues and problems, and argued for a much more detached view of the economic organism and its working.[25] Keynes was hardly indifferent to the liberalism or neo-liberalism underlying these views of the nature of economics, but his innate optimism concerning human nature and the powers of rational persuasion led him to discount the fears of this 'neo-classical' view of the role of economics.[26] The net result was a greater questioning, a greater politicisation of economic debate, both in his lifetime and after. And this change in concerns naturally transferred itself to economic policy issue, as British debates on wartime policy and the shape of the post-war world accurately show.[27]

However, if Keynes had merely been an able economist interested in questions of economic policy, his influence on his contemporaries would hardly have been sufficient to merit the attention he gained, even in the economically disturbed period of the inter-war and war years.[28] Nor would it be sufficient to explain the radical changes in the teaching of economics by economists to their prospective professional successors that occurred between, say, 1920 and the late 1940s. For during this period there was a marked change in the allocation of time and space, in elementary textbooks, between the various branches of economics. Thus in the 1920s Taussig's *Principles* in its third edition devoted 36 of its 1,147 pages to the trade cycle and 192 pages to money and banking, while Carver's text devoted only 9 of its 584 pages to the previous subject.[29] However, in the 1940s Tarshis's text devoted over 200 of his 700 pages to national income and employment issues (excluding the foreign trade sector), plus 57 to money, while Samuelson's text in its first incarnation devoted 126 of its 608 to the former and 75 to the latter.[30] Surely there must have been some force behind this change beyond the policy views and personality of Keynes, for the magnitude and speed of the change are both historically remarkable.

The change that did occur, as James Meade points out elsewhere in this volume, at one level saw a reordering of the sequence of analysis – from the savings dog wagging the investment tail to an alternative system where changes in autonomous expenditure (investment, government expenditure and exports) affected savings through changes in the level of expenditure.[31] At the roots of this change in emphasis lay an attempt, as Keynes himself recognised in prefaces to later foreign editions of his *General Theory*, within the dominant English Marshallian tradition to take monetary economics into the short period, into the real world where markets adjust to changes at widely different speeds under the influence of uncertainty and where the analysis of a neutral money economy is irrelevant.[32] It was an attempt to change the previous economics of tranquillity or of confident foresight to an economics of uncertainty. In doing this he left economists with a series of concepts, which, although they often had precursors in the earlier literature, changed the way economists looked at the world whether they agreed with Keynes or not.[33] Keynes also left his contemporaries with the prospect at least of losing the pattern of unique, inevitable order which had characterised much of the 'orthodox' economics of his time – a pattern which, as yet, the efforts of post-Keynesian general equilibrium theorists have failed to restore, despite a long period of post-war complacency.[34]

However, not all of the refinements or deeper implications of this changed frame of reference passed into the economics of Keynes's contemporaries. Rather, as some critics who saw early-Keynesianism as a threat to Western liberal societies gleefully pointed out, in many circles the change in the focus of analysis reflected in the early post-war textbook treatments of the theory of income determination found itself grafted onto earlier traditions.[35] The most popular graft proved to be with the Walrasian general equilibrium tradition, then popular in America and undergoing a Hicksian revival.[36] This grafting produced a plant sufficiently robust for contemporary policy discussions and for elementary teaching, yet allowed a reconciliation between much of Keynes and the classics – on the classics' own ground, the barter economy. The reasons for the success of this graft are doubtless various, but amongst them must surely be the strength of the earlier tradition in a world of greater mathematisation of the subject and the strong belief that the Keynesian Revolution was about economic policy not economic theory.[37] As a result, however, many of the more important long-term implications of Keynes's approach to the real world were submerged, only to affect that generation of economists coming to maturity well after Keynes's death.Whether their reassessment of Keynes will have lasting effects on their contemporaries as a whole and the origins of the reassessments themselves are, of course, another story.

NOTES

1. *A Survey of Contemporary Economics*, Vol. I, ed. H. S. Ellis, Vol. II, ed. B. F. Haley (Philadelphia: Blakiston, 1948 and Homewood: Irwin, 1952, p. v of both volumes.
2. The full list of chapters concerned included Value and Distribution, Employment Theory and Business Cycles, Price and Production Policies, the Development and Use of National Income Data, Monetary Theory, Theory of International Trade, Economics of Labour, the Prospects for Capitalism, Economics of Growth, Economics of Consumption, International Finance, National Economic Planning.
3. G. Stigler, 'A Survey of Contemporary Economics', *Journal of Political Economy*, LVII (April 1949), p. 95.
4. A. C. Pigou, 'John Maynard Keynes 1883–1946', *Cambridge Review*, 18 May 1946, p. 381; A. Marget, *The Theory of Prices*, II (New York: Prentice Hall, 1942), p. xxii.
5. Pigou, 'John Maynard Keynes', p. 382.
6. A. Leijonhufvud, *On Keynesian Economics and the Economics of Keynes* (New York: Oxford University Press, 1968); P. Davidson, *Money and the Real World* (London: Macmillan, 1972).
7. In fact most observers have agreed that 'classical' or 'neo-classical' monetary theory did not exist as a formal analytical construct until worked out by expositors or critics of Keynes.
8. P. A. Samuelson, '*The General Theory* (1946)', in R. Lekachman (ed.), *Keynes' General Theory: Reports of Three Decades* (New York: St. Martin's, 1964), p. 326.
9. D. Bensusan Butt, 'Keynes's *General Theory*: Then and Now', mimeo 1967.
10. E. A. G. Robinson's concluding comment in D. E. Moggridge (ed.), *Keynes: Aspects of the Man and his Work* (London: Macmillan, 1974), p. 100.
11. J. A. Schumpeter, *History of Economic Analysis* (New York: Oxford University Press, 1954), pp. 41–3, 1171.
12. J. A. Schumpeter, 'Review of the General Theory of Employment, Interest and Money', *Journal of the American Statistical Association*, XXXI, 196 (December 1936), p. 792.
13. J. M. Keynes to J. R. Hicks, 21 June 1935.
14. E. A. G. Robinson, 'Could there have been a "General Theory" without Keynes?' in Lekachman (ed.), *Keynes' General Theory*, p. 90.
15. See *Collected Writings of John Maynard Keynes*, Vol. XIII, *The General Theory and After: Preparation*, ed. D. E. Moggridge (London: Macmillan, 1973).
16. Robinson, 'Could there have been a "General Theory"?', pp. 88–9.
17. J. M. Keynes, 'The General Theory of Employment', in *Collected Writings*, Vol. XIV, p. 111.
18. *Collected Writings*, Vol. VIII, p. 467.
19. See, for example, the Samuelson article referred to in note 8 above

and G. Haberler, '*The General Theory* after Ten Years', in Lekach-man (ed.), *Keynes' General Theory.*
20. See the discussion in D. E. Moggridge, 'Keynes: The Economist', in Moggridge (ed.), *Keynes: Aspects of the Man and his Work.*
21. See J. R. N. Stone, 'The Use and Development of National Income and Expenditure Estimates' in D. N. Chester (ed.), *Lessons of the British War Economy* (Cambridge: Cambridge University Press, 1951), pp. 83–5.
22. R. F. Kahn, 'The Relationship between Home Investment and Unemployment', reprinted in *Selected Essays on Employment and Growth* (Cambridge: Cambridge University Press, 1972).
23. Keynes was actively involved in most of the major statistical enterprises in Britain during his lifetime: the London and Cambridge Economic Service, the National Institute of Economic and Social Research and the Cambridge Department of Applied Economics.
24. T. E. Gregory, *The First Year of the Gold Standard* (London: P. S. King, 1926), pp. 18, 44–5, 93–4.
25. See D. Winch, *Economics and Policy: A Historical Study* (London: Fontana, 1972), ch. 9.
26. *Ibid.*, p. 203; Moggridge, 'Keynes: The Economist', pp. 68–9.
27. In particular the press and 'popular' academic discussions of Keynes's *How to Pay for the War* and the Coalition Government's 1944 Employment Policy White Paper bring this out clearly.
28. The scrapbooks kept by his mother provide ample evidence for his contemporary influence.
29. F. W. Taussig, *Principles of Economics*, 3rd ed. (New York: Macmillan, 1924); T. N. Carver, *Principles of Political Economy* (New York: Ginn, 1919).
30. L. Tarshis, *The Elements of Economics* (Boston: Houghton Mifflin, 1947); P. A. Samuelson, *Economics: An Introductory Analysis* (New York: McGraw-Hill, 1948).
31. This volume, pp. 82–8.
32. See *Collected Writings*, Vol. xiii and H. G. Johnson, 'The General Theory after Twenty-five Years', reprinted in *Money, Trade and Economic Growth* (London: Allen and Unwin, 1962).
33. See above note 4 for two leading examples of Keynes's period. The modern quantity theorists are in most ways more dependent on Keynesian constructs than on their predecessors in the same tradition, despite their claims to the contrary. See D. Patinkin, 'The Chicago Tradition, the Quantity Theory and Friedman', *Journal of Money Credit and Banking*, I, 1 (February 1969) and 'Friedman on the Quantity Theory and Keynesian Economics', *Journal of Political Economy*, lxxx, 5 (September–October 1972).
34. See, for example, F. H. Hahn, 'On the Foundations of Monetary Theory' in M. Parkin (ed.), *Essays in Modern Economics* (London: Longman, 1973).
35. See, for example, H. Hazlitt, *The Critics of Keynesian Economics* (Princeton: Van Nostrand, 1960), pp. 1–10; W. H. Hutt, *Keynesian-ism: Retrospect and Prospect* (Chicago: Regnery, 1963), ch. xix.

36. The classic examples here are, of course, J. R. Hicks, *Value and Capital* (London: Oxford University Press, 1939); D. Patinkin, *Money, Interest and Prices* (New York: Harper and Row, 1956).

37. See, for example, R. Lekachman, *The Age of Keynes* (New York: Random House, 1966).

IO

The Keynesian Revolution

JAMES MEADE

Was there ever a Keynesian Revolution and, if so, what was it? Any short answer to these questions, particularly if it is designed to be of interest to those who are not professional economists, is bound to be a gross oversimplification. Not only are the problems themselves of some technical complexity; but one of the outstanding features of Keynes's mind was its intuitive subtlety and flexibility. As a result commentators have found it easy to make quips about Keynes's inconsistencies, but the fact that Keynes was trying continuously to relate his very extensive experiences in the real world of affairs in an intuitive manner to the revision of standard economic theory was of the essence of his genius. His thinking never stood still and his critique of the existing corpus of economic doctrine was constructed out of many and various – and in some cases rather subtle – components.

In spite of this, one can, I think, pick out one rather simple and precise relationship which is the quintessence of Keynes's intellectual innovation. I shall concentrate solely on this one single feature, which has not only changed the typical economist's approach to his problems but has also had a far-reaching effect on government economic policies. There are in fact two distinct, though closely related, Keynesian Revolutions: first, the theoretical revolution in economic analysis; and, second, the practical revolution in governmental policies. I will discuss each of these in turn.

Keynes's intellectual revolution was to shift economists from thinking normally in terms of a model of reality in which a dog called *savings* wagged his tail labelled *investment* to thinking in terms of a model in which a dog called *investment* wagged his tail labelled *savings*. Let me explain. Investment is defined as the flow of expenditure of money on additions to the real capital equipment of the community (additions to plant, machinery, stocks of goods, houses etc.) and savings is defined as that amount of their flow of incomes which people decide not to spend on consumption goods (food, clothing and so on). Before the Keynesian Revolution a normal way of starting to think about the relationship between savings and investment would have been in terms of models of the following kind: out of given real incomes people decide to spend a certain amount on consumption goods: they save the remainder; these savings flow on to the money and capital markets and constitute what is directly or indirectly available for borrowing by entrepreneurs and others to spend on new capital equipment; if savings go up, more funds are available on the capital market; the cost of borrowing falls; accordingly more is spent on investment in real capital goods; if people do not decide to increase their savings, it is not possible to finance an increase in investment.

It was thinking of this kind which lay behind the notorious 'Treasury view' of the 1920s and early 1930s. At that time the United Kingdom was experiencing a period of heavy unemployment of labour and underutilisation of industrial capital equipment. Lloyd George and others (including Keynes himself) were advocating a policy of public works (i.e. public investment schemes) to put the unemployed to work. The Treasury view, which opposed these proposals, was that if savings were borrowed for public works there would be just so much less savings available on the capital markets to finance private investment. The result would be merely to substitute less productive public investment for more productive private investment.

There was clearly something wrong with this line of argument in a period of mass unemployment. In a period of full employment, when it is impossible to produce more goods and services in general, the argument would hold. If people are buying a given amount of consumption goods, then there is left over a certain amount of resources to produce capital equipment. In conditions in which these productive resources are fully employed, if the public sector takes up more of these investment resources. it must drain them from the private sector. But in a period of mass unemployment this conclusion does not necessarily hold. More goods and services can be produced for all uses. An increase in public investment does not necessarily imply any reduction in private investment or in consumption. The Treasury view was applying to conditions of mass unemployment a mode of thought that was suitable for conditions of full employment.

Keynes started at the other end. His reasoning ran on the following lines. Drop the assumption that there is a given level of real income. Suppose instead that we start with a given level of the flow of investment expenditures. This is sensible because investment is in fact influenced primarily by outside or 'exogenous' influences such as the confidence and expectations of businessmen in the case of private investment and governmental decisions in the case of public investment. These investment expenditures will generate the payment of wages, rents, interest, profits etc. to those engaged in producing the capital equipment in question. Those engaged in the production of these capital goods will save some of the incomes so earned but will spend the rest on consumption goods. The producers of these consumption goods will thus earn incomes, part of which they will save but part of which they will in turn spend on other consumption goods, thus generating still other incomes which will be partly saved and partly spent on consumption, and so on. This process will generate a converging series of ever diminishing waves of expenditures which will result in a finite level of demand for goods and services to meet both the original investment demand and the subsequent induced demands for consumption goods. The level of economic activity so generated may or may not be sufficient to provide full employment for the available productive resources in the community. If it is insufficient, why not do something to increase the original injection of the flow of investment expenditures into the system?

Such was the famous Keynesian Multiplier, expressing total income as a multiple of investment. This relationship could be expressed in another way. Investment expenditure could be regarded as an injection from outside of a flow of purchasing power into an income-generating system; savings could be regarded as a leakage of purchasing power out of this income-generating system. Given an initial injection of investment demand into the system, incomes would be generated by a succession of waves of induced demand for consumption goods until the resulting leakage out (savings) was equal to the original injection in (investment). The greater the level of investment and the lower the proportion of their income which people decide to save, the higher would be the level of the resulting effective demand for goods and services and so the demand for output and for the employment of labour.

It was an easy extension of this mode of thought to realise that private investment was not the only element of demand for goods and services that might best be regarded as an exogenous injection from outside into the income-generating cycle, and that savings was not the only possible leakage of purchasing power out of this income-generating cycle. Government expenditure on goods and services of all kinds also constitutes an injection of purchasing power into the system which can be exogenously determined by government policy; and corresponding to this injection there is a leakage of purchasing power out of the income-generating system in the form of the direct and indirect taxes which people must pay out of their increased incomes and expenditures. The demand for a country's exports may also be regarded as primarily determined by what is going on in other countries outside the country in question and thus may be regarded as representing another injection from outside of purchasing power into the system, and corresponding to this there is a leakage of purchasing power out of a country's income-generating process in so far as its citizens spend their incomes on imports rather than on home-produced goods. We may regard the system then as one in which

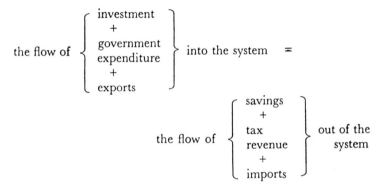

The left-hand side is the Keynesian dog and the right-hand side is the Keynesian tail. The inflow on the left-hand side, by a series of repercussions, raises the demand for consumption goods until incomes are earned on such a scale that there is an equal outflow on the right-hand side.

But how was one to judge between this Keynesian view and the then prevailing Treasury view? Suppose that a policy of substantial public works expenditures were adopted and that the increased borrowing for the finance of this programme did cause such an increase in the rate of interest and the general difficulty of acquiring finance that competing private projects were stifled, so that there was no net increase in investment. If this happened, then there would be no net additional investment to be financed but also no net additional finance in the form of savings generated through a Keynesian Multiplier. The Treasury view would be justified. Suppose, however, on the other hand that the public works expenditures did not supplant existing investment expenditures, then there would be a net additional injection of investment demand into the system which would generate additional incomes and so additional savings on a scale sufficient to finance the new public works. The Keynesian view would be justified. Both results might seem at first sight to be equally plausible. Is it a pure toss-up which happens?

Keynes argued for the validity of his view through his analysis of the basic nature of the money and capital markets. People hold money for two broadly distinguished purposes. First, they must hold a stock of active money to finance the turnover of their business, commercial, and domestic purchases and sales of goods and services. Second, they may well choose to hold additional sums of idle money as a liquid asset in preference to other forms of capital asset. It is true that if they hold idle money on which the yield is low or non-existent, they will lose the yield in interest or dividends or rents which they might have obtained if they had put their funds into other less liquid assets. But there are certain advantages in holding some part of their funds in the form of liquid money, which is a safe asset which can be used quickly and readily to meet unforeseen contingencies; and there will be an additional reason for holding money rather than other assets, if it is thought that the current market prices of such assets (such as security prices on the stock exchange) are on the high side so that they are more likely to fall than to rise in the near future. Such was Keynes's Liquidity Preference theory, expressing the fact that the higher the price of non-liquid assets such as Stock Exchange securities and the lower their yield, the greater would be the relative attraction of holding idle balances of liquid money instead of other income-earning assets.

Armed with this Liquidity Preference theory Keynes could justify the Keynesian view in the following way. Suppose that increased borrowing by the government through the sale of additional government bonds to finance a public works programme did initially tend to cause some fall in the price of such securities and thus some rise in the rate of yield on them. The Keynesian view would be substantially correct if a fall in security prices and a rise in interest rates (1) had little effect in discouraging other competing investment projects but (2) had much effect in inducing people who were holding idle liquid balances of money to purchase other assets such as securities which were now somewhat cheaper and provided a somewhat higher yield. For in this case the fall in security prices and the rise in interest rates would be quickly checked by those who were using their idle liquid balances for the purchase of these securities; and any small increase in interest rates which did nevertheless occur would have a negligible effect in cutting back existing investment projects. On the other hand, the Treasury view would be substantially correct if a fall in security prices and a rise in interest rates (1) had much effect in discouraging other competing investment projects but (2) had little effect in inducing people who were holding idle liquid balances of money to purchase securities which were now cheaper. For in this case there would be nothing to prevent a heavy decline in security prices and rise in interest rates; and this would have a very marked effect in cutting back on existing investment projects.

The Keynesian effect could, of course, always be made to operate by means of monetary policy. If, when the government issued new bonds to finance public works, there was not a sufficient shift out of existing liquid balances of idle money to prevent a substantial rise in the cost of borrowing, a suitable purchase of government bonds by the banking system with newly created money could play the necessary role in preventing any increase in the cost of borrowing or difficulty in finding finances for existing investment projects. In the absence of a suitable monetary policy the effect could in theory be partly of the Keynesian and partly of the Treasury variety; but it was Keynes's contention that in fact – particularly at a time of great economic depression with an excess of idle funds waiting for profitable outlets – the nature of the demands for money and for other capital assets was such to justify his view, even in the absence of an expansionary monetary policy.

Thus the Keynesian theoretical revolution can be expressed in terms of the combination of his Multiplier theory with his Liquidity Preference theory. It would, however, do a grave injustice to many earlier and contemporary economists to suggest that they were oblivious either of the fact that exogenously determined changes in such variables as investment could affect the level of activity in the economy or of the importance of the nature of the demand for money in influencing such effects. On the contrary, much analysis of the trade cycle and of other phenomena had been based on relationships of just this kind. But nearly all intellectual revolutions have their roots in the work of forerunners. It was Keynes's great contribution to start with investment wagging savings and to build modifications on to that model, rather than to start with savings wagging investment and to build modifications on to that model.

Since Keynes made us all think in these – at that time apparently topsy-turvy – terms, there has been much sophisticated work attempting to incorporate these and other relationships into dynamic models of the whole system; but nearly all such models start now from the basic Keynesian original.

Such in my opinion was the essence of Keynes's intellectual revolution. The revolution in practical governmental policy is of much greater importance and significance for the welfare of mankind. But it can be expressed and discussed in many fewer words. It is now universally recognised by governments, at least throughout the industrialised free-enterprise world, that it is one of their primary duties to control the level of total effective demand for goods and services. If demand is insufficient to provide full employment, it is the government's duty to raise it by stimulating the injections (investment, government expenditure, and/or exports) and/or by discouraging the leakages (by reducing the proportions of income saved, paid in taxes, or spent on imports). If demand is excessive, then it is the government's duty to restrain the injections and to encourage the leakages. This general task of controlling the level of total effective demand throughout the economy was not recognised to be a duty of government before the Second World War; it has been generally so recognised since the war.

How far is this revolution in government policy due to Keynes or how far simply to the bitter experience of the wastes of mass unemployment between the two world wars? One cannot give any precise answer to this question. But one can at least assert with confidence that Keynes's great intellectual contribution hastened the change and that the execution of this new governmental obligation is nowadays conceived in Keynesian categories.

The overall stabilisation of a modern economy must be thought of in two parts: first, a stabilisation of effective demand in the sense that the real demand for real goods and services of all kinds for all purposes must be kept at a level which will provide full employment, but not more than full employment, for the available real resources of labour, land, capital equipment etc. in the economy. But that, alas, as we are learning by bitter experience is not the whole of the story. In conditions of modern industrial and trade union organisation such a level of real demand has come to be habitually accompanied by an inflationary upsurge of money costs and prices. Keynes, if anyone, can be regarded as the architect of the system designed to maintain effective real demand at the full-employment level. Would that he were alive to exercise his ingenious and fertile mind on the problem to which the very success of his construction has in large measure contributed, – namely the problem of making a high and sustained level of *real* economic activity compatible with a restraint of those inflationary rises in *money* prices and wage rates which are so naturally demanded and so readily conceded in conditions of a sustained high level of demand for the goods and services in question.

I I

The reception of the Keynesian Revolution

ROBERT SKIDELSKY

In his biography of Keynes, Sir Roy Harrod reports a widely acclaimed speech delivered by his subject to the House of Lords in 1946, the year of his death. 'But Keynes had been talking in this style ... for some twenty-seven years. Why had his words not been listened to....?'[1] To suggest some answer to this crucial, though neglected, question is the purpose of this essay. Hopefully it will put us in a better position to understand why Keynes's message was more acceptable in 1946 than it had been in 1936 – or 1926.

The most usual explanation, implicit rather than explicit, is that until 1936 Keynes failed to establish a sound theoretical backing for his interventionist policy proposals. Thus the nearest Sir Roy Harrod himself comes to answering his own question is when he describes attending a lecture given by Keynes to the Liberal Summer School in 1924. 'Watching Keynes's enthusiasm on the one side and the comparative apathy of his audience on the other, I felt that there was some missing clue, something unexplained, that his statement needed amplification, that there was some message which he had failed to deliver. There was indeed a missing clue. The task of discovering that clue was to occupy the next twelve years of his life. What was lacking was an explanation in terms of fundamental economic theory of the causes of unemployment.'[2] The implication here is that had this 'missing clue' been discovered in 1924, the Keynesian Revolution would have taken place there and then.

Is this assumption plausible? Surely not. Politicians and their advisers may possess a theoretical understanding of how unemployment arises and how it may be ended without necessarily wishing, or even being able, to end it. Other values may rank higher than the achievement of full employment, especially if they are seen to conflict with it. Or, it may be that the ability of politicians to achieve full employment is frustrated by powerful groups outside or inside the nation whose interests are not served by it. Conversely, it may be that politicians will provide jobs for the unemployed without a theoretical understanding of how unemployment arises and without any secure intellectual guarantee that their actions will not, in fact, worsen the situation they are designed to remedy.*

How then has the idea that inadequate theory was the decisive barrier to Keynesian policies gained such wide currency? The basic reason, I believe, stems from the failure to distinguish between the theoretical and the political aspects of the Keynesian Revolution. To explain the triumph of Keynesianism as an intellectual enterprise there is little need to go outside the economics profession. Thomas Kuhn has provided the classic account of this type of revolution with his notion of a 'crisis' within a scientific community. The crisis arises from the discovery of a serious 'anomaly' which the existing 'paradigm' (or structure of concepts and empirical procedures) cannot explain.[3] This can readily be applied to the Keynesian Revolution considered as a scientific phenomenon. The anomaly which cannot be explained by means of the existing paradigm is pervasive mass unemployment. Ultimately a new paradigm is suggested. It is resisted by other members of the community. It slowly wins adherents and acceptance, completing the revolution and starting the new cycle. The only modification which suggests itself is that in the case of a social science the pressure to change the paradigm is more likely to come from outside the discipline than from within it.[4]

Explanation of the Keynesian Revolution as a political phenomenon requires a different conceptual apparatus. What we will need to explore are the political and social conditions favouring or inhibiting acceptance of Keynesian policies. It is the neglect of this dimension of historical explanation, and the unthinking and perhaps unconscious assumption that to explain the intellectual revolution is to explain the political revolution, that is the most marked feature of the historiography of the Keynesian Revolution.

Superficially, the reasons for this are not hard to find. The Keynesian Revolution has been written about mainly by economists, who are naturally most interested in its theoretical dimensions. Politicians themselves have often been happy to use the imperfections of economic theory as an excuse for their own mistakes.†

* The American, German and Swedish experiments in the 1930s are examples of 'Keynesian' policies unsupported by Keynesian theory. The Swedish Finance Minister who superintended the most successful of these experiments argued in a speech in London that no one knew why unemployment occurred but that was no argument for not trying to eliminate it. (*The Times*, 13 January 1937)

† When I interviewed surviving politicians of the Labour Government of 1929–31 I was struck by the unanimity with which they transferred the blame for their own failure to cope with unemployment to the inadequacy of existing economic science.

Historians, reluctant to probe deeper into political failures which came close to destroying Western democracy, have accepted too uncritically the politicians' defence of honest ignorance of the new economic wisdom. One suspects, too, that the emergence of social science as a major modern growth industry has reinforced the tendency of social scientists to emphasise the theoretical requirements for social action in order to justify the heavy investment of public funds in their activities.

A more fundamental reason remains largely unacknowledged. This is the unwillingness of historians and economists alike to recognise the connection between the Keynesian Revolution and the social phenomenon known as 'modernisation'. The travails of the less developed countries in their attempts to move from a pre-industrial to an industrial basis, with all the profound social, moral and political dislocation which this entails, are thought to have no counterpart in the relatively easy transition of advanced nations like Britain from a *laissez-faire* to a managed economic system. Nevertheless, it can be argued that the challenge to modern nations posed by the progressive breakdown of individualistic capitalism was as real, if not as severe, as those facing developing nations today. Keynes himself seemed to recognise this when he wrote in 1930: 'We are suffering, not from the rheumatics of old age, but from the growing-pains of over-rapid changes, from the painfulness of readjustment between one economic period and another.'[5] This 'painfulness' provoked precisely the resistance one would expect from the traditional forces in British life, taking their stand on a nineteenth-century normality which was assumed to be permanent. The ensuing drama may be accurately translated into economic theory (this I believe was the contribution of Keynes's *General Theory*) but it cannot be explained by it.

Unlike the historians of Keynesianism, Keynes himself did not believe that Keynesian theory was a prerequisite for Keynesian action. Keynesianism had its birth not in the search for a theoretical explanation of unemployment, but in Keynes's conviction that the 'doctrines of *laissez-faire* . . . have ceased to be applicable to modern conditions'.[6] Keynes undoubtedly believed that this practical argument, so vividly illustrated by continuing mass unemployment and world economic breakdown, should suffice to provide the necessary spur for action. His argument in essence was that the complex of conditions necessary to ensure the working of the nineteenth-century *laissez-faire* system was passing away. We may discern two lines of thought:

The first concerned the erosion of the social and psychological conditions which had sustained that system. It had rested upon the power of the middle class to determine society's income distribution in a manner highly favourable to itself. The resulting inequality of wealth received its moral sanction in the supposed 'saving' function of the possessing classes, itself rooted in the puritan psychology that dominated early capitalism. As Keynes wrote, 'the capitalist classes were allowed to call the best part of the cake theirs... on the tacit underlying condition that they consumed very little of it in practice'.[7] In this way, inequality of wealth, via capitalist 'abstinence', promoted the production of fresh wealth which would percolate through the whole society. In the twentieth century the unchallenged power of the capitalist class to determine the distribution of wealth had given way to the class struggle; and the old puritan psychology was giving way to a new hedonist one. Keynes seemed to regard the First World War as the crucial catalyst in both processes – it had, he wrote, 'disclosed the possibility of consumption to all and the vanity of abstinence to many' – though the impact on his own class and generation of G. E. Moore as well as the rise of industrial militancy in Edwardian England show that both developments were well under way before 1914.

The second line of thought had to do with the drying up of private investment opportunities. How far Keynes himself ever accepted the 'secular stagnation' thesis associated with his American follower Alvin Hansen is open to question. What he apparently did believe was that the nineteenth century had afforded exceptional opportunities for private investment which alone had overcome the inherent tendency, with an unequal income distribution, for the demand for goods to fall short of productive capacity. Such opportunities were not available in mature economies and in the generally unsettled conditions of the twentieth century: hence the need, as he put it in 1925, for 'some co-ordinated act of intelligent judgment' as to the proportions of the national income that should go into savings and consumption and as to the manner in which savings should be distributed.[8] A buoyant nineteenth-century demand, he wrote in *The General Theory*, had been maintained by population growth, new inventions, the opening up of new continents, the state of confidence, and the 'frequency of wars'.[9] Earlier he had stressed the importance of the 'uniformity of social and political conditions' as an essential ingredient in confidence.

The consciousness of changed conditions was thus the departure point of Keynesian economics. For example, changed psychological conditions meant that the traditional disciplines of capitalism would not work. Long before Keynes became convinced on theoretical grounds that wage reductions would not produce full employment he had realised that they could not, in fact, be applied. 'I know that in my country', he told an American audience in 1931, 'a really large cut of many wages . . . is simply an impossibility. To attempt it would be to shake the social order to its foundations.'[10] Similarly, free trade 'does not exist outside the field of pure hypothesis'.[11] Keynes, as one commentator has well put it, 'held the view that the economic structure is not a perfect fluid, but resembles, if not a solid, at least a sticky mass. His opponents generally believed it to be more liquid'.[12] These were clearly judgements about the real world. Taking a longer view, Keynes found attractive the hypothesis of an American scholar that one could distinguish between three stages of economic evolution: a pre-industrial era of scarcity marked by state control, an era of abundance culminating 'gloriously in the victories of *laissez-faire* and historical Liberalism' and a period of stabilisation marked by 'the transition from economic anarchy to a regime which deliberately aims at controlling and directing economic forces'.*

What then was the relationship between these views and the theoretical revolution with which Keynes is associated? *The General Theory* was in essence a translation into terms of economic theory of Keynes's perception of historical discontinuity. This translation proceeded in two stages. The first was his realisation in the 1820s that Say's Law did not hold good in the short run. As such this involved no formal breach with classical economics, which claimed to be a long-run theory. But to argue that the assumptions of *laissez-faire* might not hold good in a time span 'long enough to encompass the decline and downfall of nations' was clearly to question the whole utility of a theory which depended for its working on those assumptions, especially in an age when mass electorates looked to politicians to remedy intolerable conditions. The view that Say's Law might not hold good in the short run gradually evolved into the proposition that it was a 'special case' of a 'general theory': full employment equilibrium was only one of a number of possible states of equilibrium. Translated into historical terms this amounts to saying that the nineteenth century was a 'special case' in the history of economic evolution. The absence in Keynesian theory of any explicit historical dimension should not blind us to the practical and historical roots of Keynes's equations. It was because he felt that the kind of proposals he was advocating could be

* Keynes, *Essays in Persuasion*, pp. 334–5. The link between the Keynesian revolution and mercantilism is made explicit in ch. 23 of *The General Theory*. So also is Keynes's view that right theory is not a necessary condition for right action. 'The early pioneers of economic thinking may have hit upon their maxims of practical wisdom without having had much cognisance of the underlying theoretical grounds.' (p. 340)

overwhelmingly justified by practical considerations – that a Keynesian Revolution could and should occur without a formal Keynesian theory – that Keynes presented his case mainly through the medium of popular writings, and took part in drawing up the Liberal election manifesto of 1929.

How then did Keynes explain the public indifference to his message which reduced his voice to the 'croakings of a Cassandra who could never influence the course of events in time'? He attributed it primarily to an intellectual failure on the part of the British governing classes, a failure to 'grasp the significance of what is happening'. Its chief symptom was that slovenly habit of mind which relied uncritically on axioms or 'rules of thumb' for the conduct of public policy which, however appropriate they had been in the past, demanded the most critical scrutiny in the present. Keynes's well-known dictum about practical men being unconscious slaves to defunct economists should be seen not as an attack on bad economic theory but on the way in which inferior minds remained prisoners of a conventional wisdom which reality had rendered obsolete. 'Half the copybook wisdom of our statement is based on assumptions which were at one time true, or partly true, but are now less and less true by the day. We have to invent new wisdom for a new age.'[18]

Keynes's constant emphasis on thought – not theory – as a prerequisite for action has suggested an alternative explanation of his failure to exert political influence, which at least has the merit of shifting the discussion away from his theoretical imperfections. This is that he was guilty of treating power questions as intellectual questions. According to Robert Heilbroner '... it is clear enough where to look for the main sources of resistance to change. They are to be found in the structure of privilege inherent in all societies, against which the pressures of change pose their threats.'[14] Marxists were the first to attack Keynes for failing to recognise the power obstacles in the way of acceptance of his ideas. What made Keynes's *Essays in Persuasion* 'so uniformly unpersuasive' to John Strachey was their lack of any analysis of ideas in terms of interests. If his proposals to rescue capitalism were so sound, why had they never been applied?[15] This charge has recently been taken up by Sidney Pollard. Thus, according to Pollard, Keynes's attack on the 'faulty thinking' of the bankers in 1925 ignored the fact that 'when their own interest was concerned, the bankers and City merchants showed no lack of understanding. ...'[16] A. L. Rowse advised Keynes in 1932 that the 'right policy for him is to seek to put himself in relation with the political environment which alone can make his views effective'.[17]

Writers of this school see the main resistance to Keynesian

policies coming from powerful economic groups whose interests would have been harmed by them; Keynes's failure as a practical persuader lay in not directing his fire at these groups and concentrating his efforts on persuading other groups, such as the Labour Party, more inherently sympathetic to his ideas. But in order to be persuasive as an explanation of why Keynes had so little political influence in the inter-war years, this theory has to postulate the existence of frustrated radical forces only too eager to accept the new economic wisdom had it in fact been aimed in their direction. As an interpretation of British politics in the inter-war period this is hardly plausible. The problem was not to hurl the modernising forces against the reactionary ones but to *locate* the modernising forces themselves.

Keynes's scepticism about the Labour Party as an engine either of Keynesianism or of any radical change hardly seems exaggerated. Intellectually, the Labour Party at the time saw the issue largely in terms of capitalism versus socialism which, as Keynes pointed out, 'misses the significance of what is actually happening'.[18] This intellectual tendency increased, rather than diminished, in the aftermath of the slump. In practice, most Labour leaders 'agree at heart with their opponents' on economic matters. 'They have been totally out of sympathy with those who have had new notions of what is economically sound ... such as Mr Lloyd George or Sir Oswald Mosley or Mr Bevin or myself ... This puts the Labour Party in a hopeless position.'[19] Keynes perceptively saw that the socialist theory to which Labour politicians subscribed, as much as the bankers' capitalism which they followed in practice, were equally derived from 'nineteenth-century individualism'.[18] Not that Keynes found the other parties any better: they too were, with a few prominent exceptions, firmly rooted in the past; and the party battles were fought over the issues of the day before yesterday. Keynes put the matter perfectly accurately when he wrote, 'The historic party questions of the nineteenth century are as dead as last week's mutton; and whilst the questions of the future are looking up, they have not yet become party questions, and they cut across party lines.'[20] Whether Keynes ever believed that the 'questions of the future' would be party questions in quite the same way as the questions of the past is doubtful. He thought of 'Keynesianism' as a historical neccessity which once recognised would be generally accepted. The problem was to get people to hear the 'hoofbeat of history'.

Although Keynes was perfectly aware of the clash of economic interests* his perception that interests were not the decisive barrier

---

* Much of his *Tract on Monetary Reform* (1923) is taken up with showing how different economic groups stood to gain or lose from different economic

to acceptance of his ideas is well founded. It was not the clash of competing interests, but the absence of any real dissent from economic orthodoxy that was the most notable feature of the inter-war years. English society was adaptive in a number of ways, but when it came to the uncharted seas of Keynesian experiments, the drawbridges went up and the defenders stood firm on their ancient ways. When the new paths of thought encounter a resistance so resolute, so monolithic, it becomes not a problem of economic theory or economic interest, but a problem of political culture.

What do we mean by this? It can be conceived of in much the same way as Kuhn does his 'paradigm' in scientific thought, that is, as a body of concepts and rules of procedure established by achievements 'sufficiently unprecedented to attract an enduring group of adherents away from competing modes of . . . activity'. The British political culture consisted of a set of values and conventions of behaviour fortified by their unrivalled success in raising Britain to the pinnacle of nations. The century of *laissez-faire* against which Keynes rebelled was Britain's century. Under the impact of that colossal triumph, the protean, experimental forms of earlier British political life solidified into a stuffy set of axioms and conventions. Policies successful at the time acquired the status of 'fierce, quasi-religious dogma'.[21] The politics of accommodation gradually reached such a pitch of perfection that it became almost impossible to inject new issues into the political process: the last great period of ferment came in the years before the First World War. This was the background against which the Keynesian Revolution struggled for life.

The two critical values against which it had to make headway were the doctrine of economic internationalism and the doctrine of minimal government. These two doctrines were supported by all the major parties of the state. By internationalism is meant an economic theory postulating the international mobility of the factors of production, a set of moral beliefs, and a self-serving ideology of powerful groups whose fortunes are bound up with it. All three were ratified by a long and unbroken period of success. As a result of its early monopoly of industrial goods, Britain had locked itself into a system of world economy. Britain's first major industry, textiles, was created and sustained by foreign demand. Britain exported the

policies. His own suggestions would no doubt hurt the City in the short run which is why 'many conservative bankers regard it as more consonant with their cloth, and also as economising thought, to shift public discussion of financial topics off the logical on to an alleged "moral" plane, which means a realm of thought where vested interest can be triumphant over the common good without further debate'. (p. 68)

Industrial Revolution to Europe and America, while British capital, railways and steamships opened up the great primary producing areas of the world and integrated them with the manufacturing areas. The City of London became the world's financial centre, and the Bank of England in effect managed the international gold standard. By 1900 the direct employment of one British worker in every four had come to depend on the foreign demand for British goods and well over 50% of British savings had come to be invested abroad. At the same time internationalism had become for the thinking Englishman 'almost part of the moral law' as Keynes put it. International exchange of goods, knowledge, hospitality, would forge a worldwide community of interests which would make war unthinkable and unnecessary. The transnational and imperial links promoted by the proliferation of Britain's business created powerful vested interests in internationalism among politicians, bureaucrats, professional groups, financiers and businessmen.

These were enormous investments of financial, industrial, moral and intellectual capital. Their effect was to make it almost impossible for Britain's rulers to conceive of British economic life in *national* terms, that is to say as anything but a subordinate and integrated part of a system of world economy. This view came out in all its terrifying implications when the authoritative Macmillan Report of 1931 condemned a policy of devaluation which it recognised might help Britain's 'domestic situation' for fear of the damage it might do to world trade and finance – this with almost three million unemployed.[22] This is not to say that a 'Keynesian' policy in the inter-war years *necessarily* involved a choice between domestic and international objectives. Rather it involved a change of priorities. Keynes's message in effect was: look after the domestic economy and the international economy will look after itself. The view of bankers, industrialists, pundits and politicians of all three parties was: look after the international economy and the domestic economy will look after itself. This view implied domestic *laissez-faire* and assumed that the British economy could and should bear the burden of readjustment to unfavourable changes in the international environment. It thus ruled out of consideration any policies aimed specifically at tackling the unemployment problem within the national context.

Whether a Keynesian policy in the circumstances of the time would *in fact* have involved a choice between domestic and international objectives is debatable. It certainly would have meant scrapping the actual international policy pursued, particularly the return to the gold standard with an overvalued currency. A more interesting question is whether, even with a sensible exchange rate policy, British unemployment could have been mopped up consistently with the maintenance of free trade and free capital movements, in short, with the degree of dependence on foreign trade which Britain had acquired in the nineteenth century. Keynes himself seems to have thought not. Even before the return to the gold standard he was advocating a restriction on capital exports.[23] In the later 1920s he urged a policy of import substitution.* In 1931 he abandoned free trade.[24] In 1933, even after the devaluation of the pound, he wanted Britain to go 'homespun'.[25] Perhaps such views represent too pessimistic a reaction to the secular trend towards world industrialisation which was knocking out Britain's main export industries.† The point is that an important explanation for the attitude gap between Keynes and the Establishment is to be found not so much in economic theory or vested interest as in a way of thinking about Britain's relationship with the rest of the world which excluded the possibility of national self-determination as an appropriate goal of economic policy.

The breakdown of the world economy in 1931 weakened the inhibition against interfering with foreign trade, but not the equally potent objection to state interference in the domestic economy. Like economic internationalism, the doctrine of minimal government was in part an economic theory based on the efficiency of market forces, in part a political value, that of individual liberty, and in part the self-serving ideology of groups who felt their interests challenged by state intervention. Its roots lay in the parliamentary revolt against royal despotism and the later middle-class revolt against landed monopoly and corruption, of which classical economics was the theoretical expression. It was ratified by the belief that *laissez-faire* had been responsible for Britain's economic triumphs.‡ By the 1920s an increasing number of 'exceptions' testified to the fact that the 'normal' theory of government was breaking down; but the core of that theory – that government should not intervene to determine the level of economic activity – remained intact, and was even more

* See the Liberal Party's *Britain's Industrial Future* (1927), pp. 319–20, which Keynes helped to draft. In 1930, Keynes was strongly urging on the Economic Advisory Council a policy of agricultural development to lessen Britain's dependence on foreign foodstuffs.

† N. Kaldor's argument in the *Economic Journal* of March 1971 that heavy unemployment in Britain's traditional exports could have been eliminated by adopting a floating exchange rate appears to depend on a number of arguable assumptions.

‡ At the very least, this view was a serious over-simplification. Not only had the Lancashire cotton industry developed under tariff protection against Indian aid Irish cotton imports, but, as Eric Hibsbawn has pointed out (*Industry and Empire*, London, 1968), British industry in the late eighteenth century expanded into a colonial vacuum created by the British Navy.

stoutly defended by virtue of its erosion at the peripheries, and the threats which this posed.*

In the inter-war years, its classical economic formulation was the so-called 'Treasury view' that government expenditure was 'unproductive', serving only to deplete the capital stock available for investment. On close analysis of the actual arguments deployed, this turns out to be a rationalisation for a set of deep-seated administrative and political objections to the extension of state activity, centring on the practical difficulties of organising a public works programme, and the threat to local authorities, private property rights, and 'confidence'. Because Keynes himself attacked the Treasury view on theoretical grounds, historians have assumed all too readily that the issues involved were issues of theory rather than of political culture.

The popular presentation of the inter-war economic problem in terms of socialism versus capitalism, far from polarising attitudes towards the role of the state as might have been expected, in fact hardened them in opposition to state intervention to improve the economic performance of society. The business view of Keynesianism as the first step toward Bolshevism is perhaps understandable in the light of the Russian Revolution.† What is more surprising is that its theoretic commitment to state socialism never weakened the Labour Party's practical commitment to *laissez-faire*. Elie Halevy has explained this contradiction as a consequence of Labour's roots in nineteenth-century liberalism. 'Their idea was merely that of a limited monarchy, to control and limit the captains of industry and to get good conditions for those whose representatives they were. They are born parliamentarians. Now, if you go to the root of the idea of Parliament, the system is not one which wants to make the state strong, but one which wants to keep it weak for the sake of

---

* The 1920s were full of such exceptions. The big one was unemployment insurance, which was supposed to be self-financing, but which in fact became largely a dole, paid by the Exchequer. The Unemployment Grants Committee too was intended as purely temporary. In the 1930s the government financed industrial reorganisation, or 'rationalisation' on an *ad hoc* basis. It also developed price support policies for agriculture, and industrial Protection was designed to ensure the same result. Mr Donald Winch, *op. cit.*, has rightly drawn attention to the need to distinguish Keynesianism from other aspects of the general twentieth-century movement towards greater state interference in economic life. My argument is that the erosion of the accepted view at its peripheries strengthened, rather than weakened, the defence of the core of the doctrine.

† As Keynes remarked, 'The difficulty is that the Capitalist leaders in the City and in Parliament are incapable of distinguishing novel measures for safeguarding Capitalism from what they call Bolshevism.' (*Essays in Persuasion*, p. 327.)

liberty. That is the tragedy. The Labour leaders are men whose doctrine requires them to make the state stronger, and whose good British instinct is to make the state as weak as possible.'[26] The very gains won by the working class tended to diminish their disposition to look to the government to solve the economic problem. Powerful and well organised trade unions relied upon direct bargaining with employers to improve their lot in a system which has been aptly described as one of 'collective *laissez-faire*'; while the fact that the state provided extensive welfare weakened the call upon it to provide jobs as well.

Thus Keynes's demand that the state should step in to do the business which private enterprise claimed it was doing, but which in fact it was not doing, while posing an implicit challenge to classical economic theory and an explicit challenge to some vested interests, posed a much more fundamental challenge to the conventionally accepted ideas of the relationship of government to the economic process, and more generally to the nineteenth-century dichotomy between state and society. Once the idea of the economic self-sufficiency of society was impugned, then a whole set of consequential ideas – about the role of government, the scope and nature of individual liberty – came under fire. There was no knowing where it would lead. The main charge against the Lloyd George public works programme of 1929 was that it would involve 'dictatorship'.[27] With the rise of Communism and Fascism, the relationship of Keynesianism to political values became all-important.

The conventional ideas survived unscathed until well into the twentieth century, not just because they had been uniquely successful for so long, but because the British political system was uniquely successful in stifling public debate. Lord Snow has been only one of many who have pointed to the 'small size, the tightness, the extreme homogeneity of the English official world'.[28] This is partly a product of shared background; partly the result of the British genius for coopting dissent into the system of privilege. The result has been that English public life is run very much on a club basis (with parliament the best club in the country) and one of the rules of a well-ordered club is that no one makes a row. The most unpopular figure in English public life is someone who does just that: Keynes's reputation was severely damaged when he took his controversy with government officials over the Versailles Treaty to the public with his *Economic Consequences of the Peace*. Snow has a revealing comment on Tizard's defeat by Lindemann on the question of strategic bombing in the Second World War: 'He had adapted himself to play the game according to the rules of the English governing and administrative classes ... The result was, he surrendered a little too easily. A less disciplined character might have made more of a row, kicked over the applecart, risked a public scandal . . .'[29]

The consequence of the club system has been what Ian Gilmour describes as 'smooth government', government on the 'inside circle'. 'The essence of the British political system is that it is more important to travel peacefully than to arrive.'[30] A 'consensus of stagnation' replaces vigorous controversy. Robust critics are dismissed as dangerous extremists; and since the scope of controversy is defined by the political machines, a critic is under a strong compulsion either to express his views in such a way that no one need take any notice of them, or to vanish into the political wilderness. Gilmour has drawn a picture of the kind of official attitude that confronted Keynesian proposals in the inter-war years much more plausible than that which postulates a rejection on grounds of imperfect economic theory: 'The present policy may have obvious disadvantages, but who can guess the consequences of altering it? The devil we know is better than the devil we don't. If we go on as we are, it will probably end in disaster. But a change now will produce immediate trouble. The day of judgement may be on us soon, but not until we have changed our jobs and after the next election.' He adds, 'only when a policy is visibly in ruins is it altered; often not even then'.[31]

The tragedy in the inter-war period was that the politics of minimising conflict were perfected at precisely the moment when conflict had become particularly necessary. In part, of course, this was done precisely to avert it. The feeling of living on top of a volcano had never been far from the consciousness of Britain's governing élites. It was revived by the pre-war violence, the Russian Revolution, and the immediate post-war industrial unrest, and more generally by the rise of democracy and the politics of class. The fact that the economic problem of the time was posed in class terms instead of in terms of modernisation contributed to this atmosphere of insecurity. The Baldwin–MacDonald politics of decency and consensus were designed to dissipate this threat, and they succeeded remarkably well. Unfortunately, the consensus created was based on mass unemployment and the dole, rather than on full employment and growth. As A. J. P. Taylor writes, 'The very forces which made Great Britain peaceful and stable prevented her from becoming the country of the New Deal.'[32]

Even though the British political culture was highly resistant to change, we may ask why it was proof against the overwhelming *fact* of mass unemployment. The answer is that the existence of a new and unpleasant fact is not the same as the perception of the fact as a problem, and even if it is perceived as a problem, it may not be perceived as a crisis which has to be overcome if the system is to survive. In fact, the British political system survived the era of mass unemployment with comparative ease, even though the economy was thereby enfeebled, and entirely avoidable suffering inflicted on millions of people.

Mass unemployment was very slow to change the belief of all classes in the basic validity of the economic and political order under which they lived. Unemployment had existed since the beginning of the factory system. It only started to be perceived as a pervasive anomaly of the system in the 1880s, partly because of improved methods of measuring it, partly because it continued for longer and at a higher level than was considered 'normal'. This period produced not only the revival of socialism but, more significantly, in terms of economic policy, the first major assault on economic internationalism in Joseph Chamberlain's Tariff Reform Campaign of 1903. The boom years immediately before the First World War revived optimism and ratified the previous normality. In fact, the concept of normality only became fully articulated in the 1920s when it was clearly breaking down, as a defence against unwelcome change, and in reaction to the 'abnormal' interlude of war. This blinded people to the perception of the even deeper anomaly of continued unemployment in the inter-war years. In the 1920s everyone was busily trying to get back to the normality of 1913, having largely forgotten the conditions that gave rise to Chamberlain's campaign.

By the time it became clear that unemployment was not going to go away on its own, most people had learnt to live with it, particularly the unemployed, and the working class from which they sprang. This was not only because of the 'dole', and the function of unemployment in keeping up wages for those employed, but because of the extraordinarily low expectations of the mass of the British working class – a striking commentary on over a hundred years of industrialisation. There was thus little real pressure from below to force politicians to revise their accepted axioms of public policy.* This is one key difference between Britain and America in the 1930s. It was the 'discontinuity' of expectations created by the Depression that produced the political pressure in America for Roosevelt's New Deal. It was the depressing continuity of life for the mass of the British which helps explain the absence of such pressure in England.† Unemployment as a problem in economic theory may have

* This is the argument of W. G. Runciman, *Relative Deprivation and Social Justice: A Study of Attitudes to Social Inequality in Twentieth-Century England* (1966), esp. pp. 60–78.

† W. Kornhauser, *The Politics of Mass Society* (London, 1959), pp. 159–

been sufficient to produce a revolution in the discipline; unemployment was not a sufficient problem to society to produce a revolution in political ideas.

If it was not the prolonged experience of mass unemployment that finally broke the hold of nineteenth-century ideas, what was it? A strong case can be made out for war. 'Normal' life could coexist with unemployment; it could not with modern war. Therefore war meant the scrapping of normal life. As such, it could not fail to have a profound effect on men's perception of reality. Twentieth-century war has been the greatest of the modern engines of change.

Keynes's own experience at the Treasury in the First World War prepared him uniquely for his later accomplishments; as his old tutor Alfred Marshall wrote to him in 1917, 'You have a better chance than any economist has ever had in this country of rendering high services to the State on critical occasions . . .'[33] His proposal for a 'managed' currency to replace the 'automatic' gold standard sprang directly from his experience in managing the sterling–dollar exchange in the war. Equally, his part in the handling of government wheat purchases could well have implanted his first doubts about the 'sufficiency of commercial motives' in ensuring the national well-being.[34] To the war experience, too, must be attributed the development of Keynes's sense of realism, his outstanding quality as an economist: the realisation, as he puts it, that 'we live in the realm of the finite' where 'everything we do is *alternative* and not additional to something else'.[35] Experience of total war sharply challenged his previous views on government and society. 'We can only say that we have already extended the sphere of government control far beyond what would have been believed possible a short time back', he wrote in 1917,[36] and to his mother later that year: 'My Christmas thoughts are that a further prolongation of the war, with the turn things have now taken probably means the disappearance of the social order we have known hitherto. With some regrets I think I am not on the whole sorry. The abolition of the rich will be rather a comfort and serve them right anyhow.

160 notes: 'A *steady* level of poverty favors the stabilization of social and cultural relations. But if economic conditions are changing, then people are more likely to feel frustrated and insecure as they compare their lot with the one that has been held out to them as their legitimate condition. . . . Hence, countries undergoing economic growth, rather than economically stagnant ones, manifest the greater discontent when discontinuities in economic conditions occur.' Of course this is not a sufficient explanation of why America experienced a New Deal and Britain did not. We have to take into account the greater 'openness' of the American political system, the greater degree of crisis, and the absence of an explicit socialist challenge to the existing economic order.

What frightens me more is the prospect of *general* impoverishment.'[37]

War challenged far more fundamentally than mass unemployment the doctrines of economic internationalism and the minimum state. As far as the first is concerned, war demands greater self-sufficiency, in short, a reversion to mercantilism. It is thus the engine of national self-determination in the economic sphere. From the notion that national security cannot be entrusted to the free market, arises naturally the idea that national welfare may also be too valuable to be entrusted to it. This is particularly the case if war changes fundamental perceptions of the world we inhabit. Adam Smith and his supporters tended to assume perpetual peace and an automatic harmony of interests. The twentieth-century age of war has shattered this illusion. Britain and most other nations today accept the view that if national and international economic objectives conflict, national ones must take priority. This shift in priority is a necessary condition for the application of national Keynesian policies and it can clearly be traced back to the experience of war.

Even more dramatically has war broken the hold of the doctrine of the minimal state. Clearly the requirements of modern 'total' war involve the substitution of planning for market forces in allocating resources.* This itself may help to legitimise the role of planning by rooting it in practical success – though of course the necessary element of coercion it involves makes it unlikely to survive in peacetime except in an 'indicative' form. More specifically, the problems of war finance provided the first opportunity to test out the new Keynesian techniques of measuring and regulating the levels of aggregate income and output. Keynes himself had doubted whether it would be politically possible 'for a capitalistic democracy to organise expenditure on the scale necessary to make the grand experiment to prove my case – except in war conditions'.[38] The Second World War provided the necessary laboratory.

This willingness to experiment is connected with another effect of war: namely, the large-scale replacement of official personnel. If the first requirement for waging a successful war is to get rid of the peacetime generals, the second is to replace many peacetime politicians and civil servants by 'new men' whose ideas, personalities and interests have previously disqualified them for 'normal' politics.

* According to Horst Menderhausen, *The Economics of War* (1943), p. 36, 'The failure of collective wants and costs to find expression in prices under a system of private enterprise renders the price system imperfect. This imperfection may be tolerated by society as long as the neglected social considerations are of minor importance; but society cannot be tolerant of it in times of war – or of preparation for war. . . .'

The challenge of war demands the response not only of new ideas, but of new men capable of developing and implementing them. It thus shakes up the political culture in much the same way as a crisis shakes up a scientific 'paradigm'.*

Finally, war is crucial in establishing, or reinvigorating, the sense of a public purpose which transcends private purposes, and without which the notion of state responsibility for economic life cannot be legitimised. The need to keep labour contented dictates a policy of fair shares and even fairer promises which in turn arouse social expectations which cannot prudently be disappointed. Treasury accounting gives way to Keynes's conviction that 'what I can create, I can afford' – and suggests that that which is created once for war, may be re-created for peace. The abnormal expectations aroused by war help to define a new concept of peacetime normality.

It may be asked straightaway why the First World War failed to have these alleged effects. The reason is that it was still possible, and indeed usual, to regard the first war as an 'abnormality' with no relevance to peacetime life. It was not possible to take this view of the Second World War. Many people in 1918 wanted to get back to 1913; no one in 1945 wanted to return to 1939. The First World War was the 'war to end wars'. After two World Wars and the almost immediate outbreak of the Cold War it was impossible to go on thinking about the twentieth century as an era of peace, comparable to the nineteenth.† The promise to build a Land fit for Heroes could not be betrayed twice with impunity.

Lastly, the economic innovations of the First World War, substantial though they were, were not supported by the theoretical innovations which suggested how they might be tolerably applied in peace. In fact, the very crudeness of wartime finance between 1914 and 1918, especially in its failure to control inflation, provoked a reaction in favour of orthodox budgeting. It has been very far from my intention to suggest that Keynesian theory and the fiscal techniques to which it gave rise have not played a vital part in winning peacetime acceptance for Keynesian policies. Nor do I deny that the prolonged experience of mass unemployment and the shorter, though sharper, experience of depression played their part in discrediting the old ideas. My argument rather is that it required the

* Thomas Kuhn (*The Structure of Scientific Revolutions*, p. 89), writes; 'Almost always the men who achieve these fundamental inventions ... have been either very young or very new to the field whose paradigm they change ... for obviously, these are the men who, being little committed by prior practice to the traditional rules of normal science, are particularly likely to see that those rules no longer define a playable game ...'

† Consciousness of living in an age of war has been a prime factor in the American acceptance of Keynesianism.

Second World War to convince men in all sections of society that a 'new age' requiring a 'new wisdom' had indeed arrived to stay.

Perhaps I may be allowed to end on a note of scholarly doubt. Surveying the struggle of the Keynesian Revolution to establish itself in post-war Britain one is struck not by the completeness of its triumph, but by the tenacity of the old attitudes, and particularly by the continued resilience of the internationalist forces in British public life. One can only be grateful that the buoyancy of the world economy has protected the Keynesian credentials of our rulers from too searching a test; and the country from the consequences of the fragility of their new convictions. As it is, Britain has been able to stagger along under a burden of international pretensions which a true Keynesian would have ruthlessly cut away. Today we may be more inclined to date the triumph of the Keynesian Revolution from 1972 when Britain floated the pound, rather than from 1945; and to see this too not as a culmination, but as a new beginning.

NOTES

1. R. F. Harrod, *The Life of John Maynard Keynes* (London, 1951), p. 618.
2. *Ibid.*, p. 350.
3. Thomas Kuhn, *The Structure of Scientific Revolutions* (Chicago, 1962).
4. Donald Winch, *Economics and Policy* (London, 1969), p. 175. For a contrary view, see G. J. Stigler, 'The Influence of Events and Policies on Economic Theory' in *Essays in the History of Economics* (Chicago, 1965), pp. 16–30.
5. *Essays in Persuasion* (1963 ed.), p. 358.
6. *Ibid.*, pp. 329–30.
7. *Collected Writings of John Maynard Keynes*, Vol. II (London, 1971), p. 12.
8. *Essays in Persuasion* (London, 1931), p. 318.
9. *The General Theory of Employment, Interest and Money* (London, 1936), p. 307.
10. 'An Economic Analysis of Unemployment' in *Unemployment as a World Problem*, ed. Q. Wright (Chicago, 1932), p. 31.
11. *New Statesman*, 21 March 1931.
12. Walter A. Morton, *British Finance 1930–1940* (Madison, 1943), p. 61.
13. *Essays in Persuasion*, p. 337.
14. Robert L. Heilbroner, *The Limits of American Capitalism* (New York, 1965), p. 70.
15. John Strachey, *The Coming Struggle for Power* (London, 1932), p. 201.
16. Sidney Pollard's Introduction to *The Gold Standard and Employment Policies between the Wars* (London, 1970), p. 12.

(a)

b)

Plate 5   Drawings by Picasso of Lydia Lopokova and Léonide Massine in 1919:
(a) Lydia Lopokova and Léonide Massine in the *pas de deux* 'the can-can' from
La Boutique fantasque. Photograph of drawing inscribed by Picasso.
(b) Sketches on blotting paper (described in the text on page 51).
The present whereabouts of both these drawings is not known.

(b)

(a)

Plate 6   Lydia Lopokova (a) as the ballerina in the ballet *Petrushka*; (b) dancing in the open air at Garsington in 1925.

17. Quoted by Donald Winch, *op. cit.*, p. 341.
18. *Essays in Persuasion*, p. 316.
19. Draft of article which appeared in the *Political Quarterly*, April–June 1932.
20. *Ibid.*, p. 325.
21. Max Nicholson, *The System: The Misgovernment of Modern Britain* (London, 1967), p. 269.
22. *Macmillan Report*, para. 253.
23. *Nation and Atheneum*, 24 May, 7 June 1924.
24. *New Statesman and Nation*, 7 March 1931.
25. *Ibid.*, 8 July 1933.
26. Elie Halevy, *The Era of Tyrannies* (London, 1966), p. 258.
27. *Memoranda on Certain Proposals Relating to Unemployment* (1929), p. 23.
28. C. P. Snow, *Science and Government* (London, 1960), p. 51.
29. *Ibid.*, p. 89.
30. Ian Gilmour, *The Body Politic* (London, 1969), p. 14.
31. *Ibid.*, p. 198.
32. A. J. P. Taylor, *English History, 1914–1945* (Oxford, 1970), p. 286.
33. *Collected Writings*, Vol. XVI, p. 223.
34. *Ibid.*, p. 87.
35. *Ibid.*, pp. 156, 187.
36. *Ibid.*, p. 262.
37. *Ibid.*, p. 265.
38. Quoted by Donald Winch, *op. cit.*, p. 266.

12

Keynes and British economics

HARRY G. JOHNSON

Introduction

Some of the other contributors to this volume write with first-hand knowledge of the personality, life, professional work and amateur interests of John Maynard Keynes, and of the personal, social, and political milieu of his career. Lacking these advantages, and even the English upbringing that would have conditioned me into an understanding and acceptance of British standards for the assessment of his professional achievement, I attempt in this essay to present a rather impressionistic view of that accomplishment, looked at from outside both the United Kingdom and the historical epoch to which Keynes belonged. Much of what I shall have to say is not about Keynes himself so much as about the younger generation of Keynesians, who constitute the older generation of economists to the younger generation to which I belong. And since much of what I shall say on both counts is unflattering, I should emphasise, first, that these are personal views, though derived from considerable thought about the evolution of economics since the First World War; and second, that to trace the subsequent impact of a man's ideas on his subject and his society is not to hold him responsible for the consequences of his thoughts – by the opposite assumption, all the great thinkers who have influenced human history (including most notably Jesus Christ) would be guilty of crimes against mankind.

Keynes's contribution to economics – a reassessment

According to an admittedly drastically over-simplified but widely-propagated view of Keynes's professional contribution, the orthodox economic theory in which Keynes was trained held that the 'invisible hand' tended to produce automatically a state of full employment in the economy, unless prevented by worker insistence on too high a level of money wages. This was contrary to the facts of years of British experience of mass unemployment. Keynes produced an alternative theory that explained the facts, to the effect that the level of production and employment depends on the level of aggregate demand; aggregate demand is the sum of aggregate consumption (determined largely by aggregate demand itself in its alternative identity of aggregate income according to the 'fundamental psychological law' that when income rises consumption also rises but not by as much) and aggregate investment (influenced by business expectations and the rate of interest) with investment determining aggregate demand through its 'multiplier effect' on consumption; that the level of aggregate demand is normally not such as to produce full employment; and that money wage reductions can influence employment only indirectly, through their very uncertain effects on investment through the quantity of money in real terms and the equilibrium rate of interest, and through business expectations. Thus unbridled capitalism meant chronic unemployment, and the maintenance of satisfactory employment required policy management of the level of aggregate demand; and while Keynes himself was always confident of the powers of monetary policy to control the level of aggregate demand, both certain aspects of his theory and the apparent failure of 'easy money' to achieve economic recovery in the 1930s made it easy for his followers to read into the theory the need for control of aggregate demand by budgetary policy (setting the levels of taxes and government expenditure – 'fiscal policy', in American terminology).

In the light of historical hindsight and retrospect, the place of Keynes and of *The General Theory* in the evolution of economics appears very differently; and the above interpretation of it appears strongly circumscribed and biased by the peculiar economic and political situation of the early 1930s against the background of which *The General Theory* was written. To appreciate this point, it is necessary to refer to British economic and monetary history, the state of British academic economics at this time, and the character of Keynes himself. The first reference is relevant to explaining why no 'Keynesian Revolution' was really necessary (what was necessary, however, was for economists to apply the economics they had). The second two references are relevant to explaining why a Keynesian Revolution nevertheless occurred (and may indeed have been necessary after all, given the inability or refusal of economists to apply the tools of their trade to their society's most pressing social and economic problem).

To recapitulate the history briefly, the mass unemployment in Britain in the 1920s – which, far more than the additional mass unemployment in Britain and the novelty of mass unemployment in other countries created by the great depression after 1929, was the focus of Keynes's prolonged professional concern – was the result of two interacting forces, one inevitable but the other the result of a perverse act of policy decision by the British government. The inevitable force was Britain's gradual loss of her early nineteenth-century industrial supremacy, which some economic historians trace back to the 1890s and others to the 1870s. (Certainly Keynes's great teacher Alfred Marshall was contemporarily aware of Britain's relative decline and anxious about its implications.) The perverse decision was the return to the gold standard at the pre-war parity for sterling. This made British goods uncompetitive in money terms and necessitated a restrictive monetary policy to retain foreign capital and maintain foreign confidence in the pound, both of which necessitated mass unemployment which in turn aggravated the problems of industrial obsolescence. Somewhat paradoxically, however, the overvaluation of the pound meant a higher standard of living for both the upper class of civil servants and professional people (including academics) on the one hand, and rentiers and owners of established businesses and large estates on the other, while the majority of workers, who managed to obtain full-time employment, also reached a higher standard than they would probably have enjoyed with an appropriate lower exchange rate. The result was to preserve an increasingly tenuous myth of Britain as a wealthy and powerful country – with obvious implications both for foreign policy and for potential domestic social welfare policy – while widening the gap between the status of the unemployed and the employed and the social and political tensions associated with it. (There is, incidentally, an interesting parallel in economic policy views between that period of overvaluation with mass unemployment and precarious balance-of-payments equilibrium and Britain's chronic post-Second World War situation of overvaluation with full employment and a balance of payments deficit, in both cases a way out of the dilemma was sought in 'the rationalisation of industry' and in lower wages, though in the 1920s the argument was for reduction of money wages and in the 1950s–1970s for achievement of essentially the same result through increasing productivity to reconcile rising money wages with lower money prices and more recently through 'incomes policy'.)

Had the exchange value of the pound been fixed realistically in the 1920s – a prescription fully in accord with orthodox economic theory – there would have been no need for mass unemployment, hence no need for a revolutionary new theory to explain it, and no triggering force for much subsequent British political and economic history. The country would have been worse off than it remembered being before the First World War, due to the inevitable pressures of industrial obsolescence, and the large majority of the assuredly employed or otherwise provided with money income would have been worse off than they actually were, but this would have been more than offset by the gains of those who would have been employed instead of unemployed. With reasonably full employment in the 1920s, moreover, the economic adjustment to industrial obsolescence would probably have been both easier and more effective (involving less concentration on promoting the survival of traditional industries and the preservation of traditional markets for their products – including the Empire) and the political adjustment to Britain's declining importance in the world less crisis-torn and traumatic (for example, Britain might have joined the Common Market at the beginning, or else remained determinedly aloof from it).

The universal mass unemployment that struck the capitalist world after 1929, and enabled a theory developed for the special circumstances of Britain in the 1920s to become accepted as a universally applicable theory of the failure of unmanaged capitalism, can also be attributed to the perversity of monetary management, national and international. What began in 1929 as the depression phase of a normal short trade cycle was converted by the Federal Reserve's failure to prevent a collapse of the American money supply into an unprecedentedly deep and prolonged depression; and the American monetary collapse precipitated the collapse of the international gold exchange standard, including the adoption of a floating pound in 1931 under political crisis conditions that have inhibited rational discussion of exchange rate policy for sterling ever since. Keynes's *The General Theory* distracted attention from all this background – which fits without trouble into the orthodox tradition of economic theory, unless one rejects a great deal of work on the trade cycle as not belonging to that theory – by focusing on a closed economy and on mass unemployment as an equilibrium situation instead of a long-lagged adjustment to a severe monetary disturbance. Keynes's followers did extend his theory to an open economy, but regarded exchange rate adjustments – in the light of their 1930s experience of them – as of very doubtful efficacy in affecting employment and the trade balance. In this, they failed to distinguish between a devaluation by one country required to align its domestic price level with world market prices – the British problem of the 1920s – and a devaluation of all currencies against gold as one means (not necessarily the most efficient and least painful) of increasing world liquidity. (The same problem has recurred in recent years in the international monetary system, with respect to inflation, and equally eluded the understanding of many international monetary experts.)

In justice to Keynes, it must be recalled that when later confronted directly with the problem of international monetary reform, in the course of preparations for the Bretton Woods negotiations of 1944 that established the International Monetary Fund, he pioneered the intellectual foundations of a system vastly superior to the previous gold exchange standard. (One cannot really blame him for the fact that the I.M.F. system eventually developed internal strains very similar to those that destroyed the gold standard, with the result that it has recently been temporarily dropped in favour of a floating rate system and if reconstituted, as is probable, will incorporate arrangements for much greater exchange rate flexibility).

Had the policy-makers of the 1930s really understood what was occurring in the international monetary system and their own part in it, or the economists of the time understood it (as they could have done by developing available monetary theory) and explained it effectively, the Great Depression of the 1930s would have been nipped in the bud and *The General Theory* either not been written, or been received as one eccentric English economist's rationalisation of his local problems. Had Keynes been a different type of personality, he might have produced and published in the 1930s the international monetary reform plan he pioneered in the 1940s, together with an explicit rationale for the plan more firmly based in monetary theory than the I.M.F. Articles of Agreement (and still more, subsequent plans for international monetary reform) have ever been. As it occurred, however, the Great Depression and international monetary collapse set the stage for a view of capitalism and of appropriate government policy to manage it oriented towards the problems of Britain in the 1920s to become the majority view of economists in the Anglo-Saxon countries ever since.

I have argued that the sources of the problem of mass unemployment with which *The General Theory* was concerned lay in severe monetary disturbance created by perverse monetary policies, thoroughly reconcilable with the orthodox neo-classical tradition of monetary theory, and not in any inherent deficiency of capitalism requiring a new causal theory and a new set of policy prescriptions and governmental responsibilities. Clearly what is so obvious to economists now, two generations later, was not at all obvious to economists (or the accepted leaders among them) then. For this there are several reasons, applying either to economics in general or to British economics in particular.

We may begin with the quantity theory of money. In its simplest and broadest form, this theory asserts that in a closed economy the level of money prices will tend to proportion itself to the quantity of money in relation to the volume of transactions to be effected in a given period and the speed with which money turns over in trans-actions (this last factor can be formulated alternatively and more fruitfully in terms of the ratio the public wishes to hold between its money stock and the money value of its transactions per period). What makes the theory a theory and not a mere tautology is the assumption that the latter two factors are determined by other forces than the quantity of money itself; but this assumption makes the theory true only in a long enough time perspective for the assumption to be approximately valid. The classical and neo-classical economists, living in a world of normally slow economic change, could safely rely on the assumption and the theory, since in the long run the volume of transactions would be governed by the stock of productive resources accumulated from the past because competi-tion would tend to ensure full employment of those stocks and money-holding habits would be stable. Moreover, for various reasons those economists were primarily concerned with the allocative functions of relative prices and wages, and their main interest in monetary theory was to establish that in the long run money was 'neutral', merely casting a 'veil' over the results of the interaction of real wants and productive possibilities without affecting the 'real' equilibrium of prices and quantities towards which the operation of these forces tended; and in the circumstances of their pre-First World War times, this concentration was natural and reasonable.

For the few specialists in monetary theory, however, the quantity theory as expressed in the quantity equation described above was only a starting point. Their interest shifted increasingly towards 'the conditions of monetary equilibrium', i.e. the conditions under which money would have to behave or should be made to behave in order to perform merely as a veil and so as not to impede or distort the operation of the underlying 'real forces'. Work on this problem reached its full flower in the 1920s and early 1930s, with the work (in English) of Robertson, Keynes in *A Treatise on Money*, and Hayek, (in Dutch) of J. J. Koopmans, and beginning earlier (in Swedish) of Wicksell, and later Myrdal and others. This was a much shorter-perspective problem than that with which the earlier quan-tity theory was concerned, yet the theory continued to be built on the assumption of full employment as the condition to which the economy would approximate, though the shorter perspective made this assumption questionable, particularly in the case of severe monetary disturbances. In an important sense, *The General Theory* can be considered as a successful (and theoretically useful) chal-lenging of the relevance of the full employment approximation to the problem under analysis. In terms of the framework of present-day monetary–theoretic controversy, Keynes can be interpreted as insisting that both output and prices are variable in the short run relevant to monetary changes, and dramatising the need for analysis of the division of response to aggregate demand changes between prices and output by assuming, in opposition to classical and neo-classical theory, that quantities and not prices (except indirectly) respond to short-run changes in aggregate demand. In short, contemporary monetary theory was guilty of sticking to traditional assumptions in the face of the evidence that these were empirically invalid for the problem under examination; and it compounded this stupidity, when questioned, by seeking for reasons why mass unemployment constituted a real equilibrium (witness Robertson's attempt to convince the Macmillan Committee that mass unemployment was attributable to the satiation of human wants). In so doing, it paved the way for a revolution in monetary theory when what was called for was a drastic effort at application.

In similar but less obvious fashion, when international trade and investment are extensive the world as a whole becomes the closed economy of monetary theory, and the relevant variables are the world stock of money and the world price level. Recognition of this is implicit in Hume's price-specie-flow mechanism, and explicit in important neo-classical studies of such phenomena as the effects of the inflow of precious metals to Europe after the Spanish conquests in Latin America. But monetary theorists faced with the collapse of the 1930s were unable to make this intellectual leap, and instead tended to stop short at the limitations imposed on national stabilisation policy by adherence to the gold standard. As mentioned, Keynes's assumption of a closed national economy ruled international monetary phenomena out of the theoretical purview of *The General Theory*, and his followers naturally saw no reason to disturb their logically self-contained view of macroeconomics by introducing consideration of them in more than a peripheral way.

The failure of economists generally to understand the nature and sources of the Great Depression of the 1930s as a matter of international monetary collapse is probably considerably more excusable than the general failure of British economists to relate the mass unemployment of the 1920s to the maintenance of an overvalued exchange rate. For this latter failure there are many explanatory factors, such as the fact that Marshall never managed to write the intended monetary companion volume to his *Principles of Economics*, while his successor to the Cambridge chair, Pigou, was neither interested nor competent in the field; also responsible was the British tradition in monetary economics, which until very recent years was concerned with history and institutions rather than with theory, and with theory only as a part of historical and current policy debates. Something is attributable to the prestige of the Bank of England and its commanding social dominance at the time over politicians, civil servants and academics, a dominance that it has begun to lose only recently, long since its nominal nationalisation. Probably a considerable amount is attributable to the effects of the First World War. It slaughtered a significant proportion of the country's best young brains or made them, as erstwhile conscientious objectors, outcasts from their decision-taking class – alternative fates that Keynes's invaluability enabled him to escape gracefully, despite his early Apostolic beliefs. The war also created something of a national 'backs-to-the-wall' attitude which made loyalty to national policy decisions, right or wrong, a virtue, and made outspoken and sustained fundamental criticism of policies unpopular and a ticket of assignment to the political wilderness. Such criticism in any case consorted ill with the symbiotic, to some extent parasitic, relationship between the ancient universities and Whitehall and Westminster. (Both elements, national loyalty and symbiosism, have if anything strengthened since the Second World War, and have helped to squelch any fundamental debate over crucial policy decisions such as the failures to float the pound in 1951 and to devalue the pound in 1964, and the decision to enter the Common Market in 1971.) To be blunt, whatever the balance of the reasons, British economics lacked the confident grasp of applied monetary theory and the intellectual courage to insist that the exchange rate was crucial to Britain's problems and that continued overvaluation would make a solution impossible; instead, it joined the government in the hunt for ways around the impasse.

This brings us to the character of Keynes. Keynes was – without any intention of slurring him – an opportunist and an operator, the glowing exception being his expression of moral outrage in *The Economic Consequences of the Peace* – and even that redounded to his personal and professional benefit. He was also – and this helped – a brilliant applied theorist; but the theory was applied when it was useful in supporting a proposal that might win current political acceptance, and dropped along with the proposal when the immediate purpose had been served or had failed. Thus Keynes realised fully, and exposed brilliantly in *The Economic Consequences of Mr Churchill*, the adverse consequences for Britain of the return to the gold standard. But once that decision had become a part of the order of things, he absorbed it and turned to advocating public works as a way of increasing employment; and in 1931 he came out in favour of protection. These gyrations frequently made him seem inconsistent to his contemporaries; actually the examples cited can be easily reconciled by reference to the modern theory of second-best, but Keynes never spelled out such a theory. *The General Theory* represents the apotheosis of opportunism in this sense, in two ways. Mass unemployment had lasted so long that it appeared to the average man to be the natural state of affairs, which economics was powerless to explain and political processes powerless to alter; a new theory of its causes that promised an easy cure was thus virtually certain to sell, provided its author had impeccable professional credentials. But to be a new theory it had to set up and then knock down an orthodox theory, not merely explain what traditional theory really was and develop its application to the problem in hand – a procedure Keynes had applied frequently in his younger days but which in this case would have required a major effort of theory construction and probably made the product unsaleable to the relevant public anyway. It was far easier to set up the dry aridity of Pigovian reasoning and the labyrinthine alien Austrian logic of Hayekian capital theory as the targets, and to sacrifice the subtle and sensitive, intellectually more menacing but emotionally more vulnerable, personality of his former student Robertson to his coterie of young lions in the bitter in-fighting that followed the revolution.

To make these points is not to dispute that *The General Theory* is nevertheless one of the few classics in the history of economics. But its importance from the long-range point of view of the development of economics, as distinct from the contemporary and subsequent politics of economic policy in Britain and the United States lies not in its refutation of a classical 'orthodoxy' but in its application of capital theory to the theory of demand for money and the stimulus it provided to study of the dynamics of price and quantity adjustments to changes in aggregate demand.

Keynesianism and British Economics

There can be no doubt that, at least in the historical short run, the publication and reception of *The General Theory* gave British economics a prestige in the outside world that it had possessed up to and including the heyday of Marshall but which had been waning ever since, the publication of Joan Robinson's *Economics of Imperfect Competition* constituting the major exception to this generalisation. As time has passed, however, it has become increasingly apparent that Keynes's work in a sense marked the end of an era in British predominance in economics, an era which may be termed the Marshallian era and includes both Pigou's contributions to welfare economics and Cambridge work in the 1920s on the problem of reconciling the theory of the individual firm with the assumption of perfect competition. It has also become apparent that other important British work in the inter-war period, notably that of Hicks and Allen on general equilibrium systems and of Hicks on demand theory and welfare economics, work of at least comparable importance to Keynes's in monetary economics to the development of modern economics, was overshadowed by Keynes and unjustly denigrated by Keynes's Oxbridge followers – a misjudgement recently underlined by the award of the Nobel Prize in economics to Hicks. Finally, it is a fair generalisation not only that leadership in economics has decisively passed from Britain to the United States in the post-war period, but that Britain has contributed very little in the way of new ideas and directions to the process of scientific development of economics. The only exceptions that spring to mind, by this extremely stringent standard, are Harrod's extension of Keynesian economics to the context of economic growth, and, of relatively greater fundamental significance, Meade's monumental works on the theory of international economic policy.

For this there is a variety of general reasons, including the vastly superior numbers and resources of the American economists and the economies of specialisation and division of labour that size and wealth make possible, the exhaustion of the intellectual curiosity and energy of many of the active contributors of the 1930s in the service of the government during the war, the closing of ranks in loyalty to the national society in a country that felt itself far more beleaguered by uncontrollable internal and external economic forces in the post-Second World War peace than it had after the First World War, and the excessive preoccupation with current politics and policy problems generated thereby. But the nature of the Keynesian revolution and of Keynesian economics in its British version have played an important part. Two specific aspects have been especially influential: a view of the nature of scientific work and the character of progress in economics derived from the intellectual success of *The General Theory*, and the identification of Keynesian economics with left-wing politics. Both aspects, it should be emphasised, are the creation of the Keynesians, and quite contrary to the life-work of Keynes the economic scientist and the political stance of Keynes the political economist.

The view of economic science in question consists of positing an orthodoxy which is committed to defence of every aspect of the existing system and denies that any improvement on its performance is possible, and identifying as a contribution the use of clever reasoning to dispute the posited orthodoxy at some point. Thus economics becomes a crooked game, the winning of which by the 'good guys' requires intelligence but not sustained hard work. For most of his long professional career before *The General Theory* (he was in his fifties by the time it was published), Keynes put in the hard intellectual labour of learning monetary theory by study and application; and the book was presented as a challenge to orthodoxy, not merely for the strategic reasons discussed above, but because he honestly believed that he had found a crucial flaw in what his contemporaries regarded as orthodox economics. He was fortunate to be right, as least superficially – and superficiality represented as deeply as a very busy man could go into the foundations of monetary theory as then commonly understood. This made him an easy act to imitate but a very hard act indeed to follow. Unfortunately his followers have tried only too often to imitate the act without putting in the long hours of preliminary practice. Even where they have put in the practice, as is true of the most eminent of his Cambridge followers, the usefulness of their work to scientific progress has been largely vitiated by Procrustean forcing of it into the framework of a straw man of capitalist orthodoxy to be knocked down by the force of superior intellect. Thus Joan Robinson writes the most arid of technical capital theory in the belief that, contrary to all the empirical evidence, capitalism cannot possibly work, because she can to her own satisfaction make a nonsense of the concept of the production function and of distribution by marginal productivity; and Nicholas Kaldor goes one better than her by admitting that capitalism does work, but maintaining that it cannot possibly work according to orthodox theories of how it works, proper understanding of it requiring acceptance of revolutionary new but unverified theories of his own devising. Each derives support and satisfaction from the knowledge that there are eminent professional economists in the United States who are prepared to take their arguments seriously, little realising that if they did not exist it would be necessary for American economics to invent them to meet its own need for an orthodoxy against which to demonstrate its own scientific superiority.

The damage done to professional work by a methodology requiring an orthodoxy to assault unfortunately does not end with its stultifying effect on the work of those who espouse that methodology. The myth of a mindless but majority orthodoxy has to be given some degree of verisimilitude by the existence of a few professionally reputable specimens at whom the finger of scorn may be plausibly pointed. Since no young scholar can afford the professional risk and no senior mature scholar fancies the role, volunteers are not forthcoming and hapless innocents have to be pressed into service, willy-nilly. The results are personal and professional destruction or at least serious damage for the thinner-skinned scholars such as

Robertson, and the suppression of the free spirit of scientific enquiry by the use or threat of the witch-hunt. An economics profession in which people have to think 'before I dare to say what I think, I have to be sure that what I say will not damn me as hopelessly othodox' is not one likely to discover new and important scientific truths.

This baneful influence of concern about orthodoxy or heterodoxy as the hallmark of 'bad' or 'good' economics is vastly reinforced by the identification of Keynesian economics in Britain with left-wing or at least Labour Party politics, and the politicisation of economics that it has entailed. (Keynes is well known to have had strong Liberal sympathies, but he carefully kept out of party politics to protect his professional reputation, and while he consistently sought for solutions to current problems that might be acceptable politically there is no reason, so far as I know, to suspect him of ever having produced or endorsed a solution because it conformed to the credo of a party he favoured.) The evidence of politicisation ranges all the way from the scandal attending certain recent appointments to chairs at Cambridge, through the consensus version of accepted economic principles expressed by economic and financial commentators and journalists, and the significant failure of leading economists known to be Labour Party sympathisers to speak out in public against the decisions not to devalue in 1964 and 1966 and to seek entry to the Common Market in 1966, to the report by Samuel Brittan in his recent *Is There An Economic Consensus?* that an unexpectedly large number of academic economists gave the scientifically wrong answer to a question involving comparison of provision of below-cost public housing and direct social security payments to poor people and his suggested explanation that 'when they came to as politically charged a subject as homes for the poor, they dug in their heels and were determined to provide no comfort to the opponents of subsidised council building'. The adverse affects of political self-censorship on both the progress and propagation of scientific understanding and the professional reliability of economic advice on policy questions are too obvious to require further comment.

Keynesian economics and British economic policy

The success of the Keynesian Revolution and its defeat of orthodoxy, and the subsequent adoption of Keynesian policies of demand management, is widely credited with responsibility for the fact that the post-Second World War period has been characterised by the disappearance for some thirty years of the mass unemployment that characterised the British economy in the inter-war period. The critics of Keynesian economics implicitly concur by blaming the chronic inflation that has characterised the same period on the same adoption of Keynesian policies. The validity of the attribution in both cases is extremely doubtful. Other countries have had at least as good luck without following Keynesian policies or even knowing what they are – the 'new economics' won acceptance in the United States only as recently as the tax cut of 1964, and Japan's economic policy seems to have been orthodox in the extreme – and one can with fair plausibility attribute Britain's success to prosperity in the rest of the world coupled with the good fortune of a forced devaluation of the pound in 1949. Economic growth is a different story, but even there Britain has done far better than she did for many decades before, stretching back into the nineteenth century; and some would argue that she would have done still better by far had it not been for the crippling load of the mixture of perfectionist policies for industry and the regions and of Keynesian policies for employment inherited from her inter-war time of torment. (In any case, the promotion of economic growth was no part of Keynes's thinking, nor indeed of Keynesian economics until sometime in the later 1950s.) About the most one can say is that Keynes's demonstration that mass unemployment is an avoidable evil has been popularly accepted to the extent that the government could no longer get away with the egregiously deflationary errors of policy it committed in the inter-war period, and even this is not necessarily a plus point, since under post-war conditions the temptations have generally been to aim in the inflationary direction, and in a generally inflationary world environment the social costs of inadvertent errors in the deflationary direction have generally been low as compared with those of errors in the inflationary direction.

Leaving those issues aside, it is worthwhile calling attention to the naïveté of the concept of full employment as a policy goal, which has been one of the main legacies of Keynes and Keynesianism to economic policy-making in Britain and elsewhere. That goal, as Elizabeth Johnson points out in a forthcoming paper in the *Journal of Political Economy*, is very intimately related to Keynes's essentially aristocratic Victorian view of the economic requirements of a happy society. In that view, social happiness consisted of a job for everyone in his appointed place in life – Keynes was little concerned about providing more equal opportunities for advancement within the ordered hierarchy of employments, since in the typical fashion of successful men he believed that his society was so organised that anyone of merit, if only he exerted himself, could rise to the eminence he had himself attained. Social misery of a severe and completely avoidable kind resulted from the failure of society to keep demand high enough to provide the expected and deserved jobs. (This simple view, incidentally, is consistent with and indeed necessary to another of Keynes's beliefs, one which demarcates him sharply from post-war Keynesianism with its emphasis on the necessity of economic growth to the good society, namely his confidence that it would take no more than a generation or so of capital accumulation at the normal rate to satiate society's demands for goods and services and free man for the cultivation of the finer things of civilised life. There is in fact an obvious disagreement between first-generation and second-generation Keynesians on the issue of the importance of economic growth, reflecting a basic difference between aristocratic and democratic attitudes to the desire of the lower orders for improvement in their material standard of life.)

The identification of social welfare with full employment not only represents an extremely narrow aristocratic and paternalistic attitude to the workers, but leads to serious biases in attitudes on policy issues evident particularly in the pronouncements and writings of some of the leading British Keynesians. For one thing, by neglecting the role of voluntary unemployment in providing flexibility, capacity for adjustment to economic change, and the opportunity for self-betterment by obtaining a better job, as well as in permitting individuals to escape from the boredom of working the same number of hours doing the same thing week after week into the freedom of disposal of their own idle time, it leads to a serious exaggeration of the social loss from unemployment and the social benefit of full employment. If unemployment actually means both total waste of the lost labour time of the unemployed and the psychological and social demoralisation of the individuals concerned, then virtually no amount of inflation is too high a price to pay for full employment (and if inflation is bad for the balance of payments, no amount of interference with international transactions to control the balance of payments is too costly either). But, as a logical corollary, if full employment is such a great boon to the workers, they ought to show their gratitude for the full employment conferred on them by Keynesian policies by not making inflationary wage demands in the first place; and if nevertheless they irresponsibly persist in doing so, as some of them do, it is not only socially fair but in their own long-run interests, as they ought to see, to force an incomes policy on them.

For another thing, identification of social welfare with the single simple index of the unemployment percentage, and specifically disregard or denial of the manifold elements of voluntary choice that enter into the determination of the unemployment rate, leads to disregard of the fact that the unemployment percentage that corresponds in principle to what Keynes can be deemed to have in mind in the concept of full employment is not a social constant determinable by technical calculations based on aggregate labour market statistics but a variable changing in response to other kinds of change. Specifically, there are two major kinds of relevant changes which will tend to raise this unemployment rate. One is the provision of more generous social security benefits. The other is the general progress of affluence and increase in educational levels, which make it easier for individuals to finance voluntary unemployment out of past savings or the possible gains to be obtained by devoting time to the search for a better job. Improved social security is especially important as an alternative, and in many ways more sensible, method of presenting the socially evil consequences of unemployment than the Keynesian panacea of maintaining a high pressure of aggregate demand. One of the areas in which the naïveté of the Keynesian concentration on employment is most evident, incidentally, is that of regional variations in unemployment rates. It is extremely difficult to believe, after even the most cursory thought on the matter, that an abnormally high unemployment rate that has persisted in a region for several generations represents a failure of the competitive system to provide job opportunities, rather than some sort of social choice in favour of a lower probability of employment at high wages and a higher probability of leisure time in a broad sense, as against a greater certainty of employment and less individual free time.

Concluding observations

All in all, it is difficult to avoid the conclusion that Britain has paid a heavy long-run price for the transient glory of the Keynesian Revolution, in terms both of the corruption of standards of scientific work in economics and encouragement to the indulgence of the belief of the political process that economic policy can transcend the laws of economics with the aid of sufficient economic cleverness, in the sense of being able to satisfy all demands for security of economic tenure without inflation or balance-of-payments problems, or less obvious sacrifice of efficiency and economic growth potentialities. A good case could even be made to the effect that Keynes was too expensive a luxury for a country inexorably declining in world economic and political importance and obliged to scramble for dignified survival, to be able to afford.

13

What has become of the Keynesian Revolution?

JOAN ROBINSON

I

What was the dominant orthodoxy against which the Keynesian Revolution was raised? *The General Theory of Employment, Interest and Money* was not published till 1936 but the revolution began to stir in 1929, lurched forward in 1931 and grew urgent with the grim events of 1933.

In those years British orthodoxy was still dominated by nostalgia for the world before 1914. *Then* there was normality and equilibrium. To get back to that happy state, its institutions and its policies should be restored – keep to the gold standard at the old sterling parity, balance the budget, maintain free trade and observe the strictest *laissez-faire* in the relations of government with industry. When Lloyd George proposed a campaign to reduce unemployment (which was then at the figure of one million or more) by expenditure on public works, he was answered by the famous 'Treasury view' that there is a certain amount of saving at any moment, available to finance investment, and if the government borrows a part, there will be so much the less for industry.

In 1931, when the world crisis had produced a sharp increase in the deficit on the U.K. balance of payments, the appropriate remedy (approved as much by the unlucky Labour Government as by the Bank of England) was to cut expenditure so as to balance the budget. These were the orthodox views that prevailed in the realm of public policy.

In the realm of economic theory, orthodox doctrine comprised two distinct branches – *Principles* and *Money*. In the department of Principles, the main topic was the behaviour of markets under the influence of supply and demand and the determination of the relative prices of commodities and the relative earnings of 'factors of production'. In so far as there was anything that would nowadays be called a macro theory, that is, an analysis of the operation of the economy as a whole, it was dominated by the conception of a natural tendency to equilibrium under the free play of market forces. *General* unemployment was a contradiction in terms.

Marshall had a foxy way of saving his conscience by mentioning exceptions, but doing so in such a way that his pupils would continue to believe in the rule. He pointed out that Say's Law – supply creates its own demand – breaks down when there is a failure of confidence, which causes investment to fall off and contraction to spread from one market to another. This was mentioned by the way. It was not meant to disturb the general faith in equilibrium under *laissez-faire*.

The department of monetary theory was quite different. This dealt with the general price level and had to include awkward subjects like inflation and the trade cycle. According to this theory, movements in prices were determined by changes in the quantity of money. It is a strange fact that, when it came to pronouncing on public affairs, the economists everywhere derived their advice from the department of Principles and forgot all about Money. In those days (unlike now) the leading symptom of a recession was a fall in prices. If all that was needed to raise prices, and so get production going again, was to print some bank notes, why did not the economists advise their governments to do so at once? No. The money cranks were saying: It can all be done with a fountain pen, but the orthodox economists thought them very wrong. The orthodox line was that nothing can be done; that nothing should be done; that in good time, equilibrium will be restored.

Keynes started life as a monetary economist. When he was working on his *Treatise on Money*, he thought that he had to be concerned strictly with the general price level. He rejected the suggestion that his subject was connected with the problem of unemployment. But in 1929 he had descended from this high theoretical plane to practical policy, supporting Lloyd George's campaign for public works. The pamphlet which he wrote with Hubert Henderson, 'Can Lloyd George Do It?', sketches out the theory that investment generates saving, so that a budget deficit can reduce unemployment without causing inflation.

The analysis is very sketchy. R. F. Kahn took it up, worked out the theory of the multiplier in a more coherent manner, and persuaded Keynes that he and Henderson had been perfectly right. The ink was not dry on the first copies of the *Treatise* before Keynes began to acknowledge that employment was after all the central point. The quantity of money fell into place in the theory of interest rates. Changes in activity were seen to be governed by changes in expenditure on investment and the purchase of consumption goods.

The price level had nothing to do with banking policy, it depended on money-wage rates. So the old dichotomy was broken down and 'monetary theory' was absorbed into the analysis of output as a whole.

Meanwhile, the Nazis had been proving Lloyd George's point with a vengeance. It was a joke in Germany that Hitler was planning to give employment in straightening the Crooked Lake, painting the Black Forest white and putting down linoleum in the Polish Corridor. The Treasury view was that his unsound policies would soon bring him down. But the little group of Keynesians was despondent and frustrated. We were getting the theory clear at last, but it was going to be too late.

2

Recently, an account has appeared in Volume XIII of the *Collected Writings of John Maynard Keynes* of the upheavals and reformulations that lead from the *Treatise* to *The General Theory*. It will be seen that there were moments when we had some trouble in getting Maynard to see what the point of his revolution really was, but when he came to sum it up after the book was published he got it into focus.*

On the plane of theory, the revolution lay in the change from the conception of equilibrium to the conception of history; from the principles of rational choice to the problems of decisions based on guess work or on convention.

In traditional teaching, it was assumed 'that the amounts of the factors of production in use were given and that the problem was to determine the way in which they would be used and their relative rewards'. Keynes's contemporaries like their predecessors were still dealing with a system in which the amount of the factors employed was given and the other relevant factors were known more or less for certain. This does not mean that they were dealing with a system in which change was ruled out, or even one in which the disappointment of expectation was ruled out. But at any given time facts and expectations were assumed to be given in a definite and calculable form; and risks, of which, though admitted, not much notice was taken, were supposed to be capable of an exact actuarial computation. The calculus of probability, though mention of it was kept in the background, was supposed to be capable of reducing uncertainty to the same calculable status as that of certainty itself.

Keynes drew a sharp distinction between calculable risks and the uncertainty which arises from lack of reliable information. Since

* 'The General Theory of Employment', *Quarterly Journal of Economics*, February 1937. Reprinted in *Collected Writings*, Vol. xiv.

the future is essentially uncertain, strictly rational behaviour is impossible; a great part of economic life is conducted on the basis of accepted conventions.

Knowing that our own individual judgment is worthless, we endeavour to fall back on the judgment of the rest of the world which is perhaps better informed. That is, we endeavour to conform with the behaviour of the majority or the average. The psychology of a society of individuals each of whom is endeavouring to copy the others leads to what we may strictly term a *conventional* judgment . . . Being based on so flimsy a foundation, it is subject to sudden and violent changes. The practice of calmness and immobility, of certainty and security, suddenly breaks down. New fears and hopes will, without warning, take charge of human conduct. The forces of disillusion may suddenly impose a new conventional basis of valuation. All these pretty, polite techniques, made for a well-panelled board room and a nicely regulated market, are liable to collapse. At all times the vague panic fears and equally vague and unreasoned hopes are not really lulled, and lie but a little way below the surface . . .

Though this is how we behave in the market place, the theory we devise in the study of how we behave in the market place should not itself submit to market-place idols. I accuse the classical economic theory of being itself one of these pretty, polite techniques which tries to deal with the present by abstracting from the fact that we know very little about the future.

The existence of money is bound up with uncertainty, for interest-earning assets would always be preferred to cash if there was no doubt about their future value. In this light, the nature of interest becomes clear. Keynes was able to resolve a deep-seated confusion in traditional teaching by emphasising the distinction between the rate of interest, as the price of finance, and the rate of profit expected on an investment, for which he unfortunately devised a new term – *the marginal efficiency of capital*.

It is uncertainty that accounts for

the liability of the scale of investment to fluctuate for reasons quite distinct (a) from those which determine the propensity of the individual to *save* out of a given income and (b) from those physical conditions of technical capacity to aid production which have usually been supposed hitherto to be the chief influence governing the marginal efficiency of capital.

Once we admit that an economy exists in time, that history goes one way, from the irrevocable past into the unknown future, the conception of equilibrium based on the mechanical analogy of a pendulum swinging to and fro in space becomes untenable. The whole of traditional economics needs to be thought out afresh.

After the war, Keynes's theory was accepted as a new orthodoxy without the old one being rethought. In modern textbooks, the pendulum still swings, *tending* towards its equilibrium point. Market forces allocate given factors of production between alternative uses, investment is a sacrifice of present consumption, and the rate of interest measures society's discount of the future. All the old slogans are repeated unchanged.

How has this trick been worked? First of all, simplifications in Keynes's own exposition, which were necessary at the first stage of the argument, have been used to smooth the meaning out of it. Keynes sometimes talked of total output at full employment as though it was a simple quantity. Obviously, the maximum output that can be produced in a given situation depends on the productive capacity in existence of plant and equipment for labour to be employed with, and productive capacity exists in concrete forms available for producing particular kinds of output. The notion of 'the level of investment that will ensure full employment' presupposes the existence of productive capacity for investment and consumption goods in the right proportions.

Moreover, it presupposes a particular ratio of consumption to investment. But the level of consumption from a given total income depends upon its distribution between consumers, and this depends on the distribution of wealth among households, the ratio of profits to wages, relative prices of commodities and the system of taxation.

All this is ignored in the vulgarised version of Keynes's theory. At any moment, the textbook argument runs, there is a certain amount of saving per annum that would occur at full employment. Let the government see to it that there is enough investment to absorb that amount and then all will be well.

So we return to the classical world where accumulation is determined by saving and the old theory slips back into place. But here there is a difficulty. Investment every year is to be just enough to absorb the year's savings. What about the new equipment that it creates? Will that be just enough to employ the labour then available, when investment is absorbing saving next year? The long-period aspect of investment, that it creates capital goods, must be considered as well as the short-period aspect, that it keeps up effective demand.

Never mind! Never mind! cry the bastard Keynesians. We can pretend that capital goods are all made of putty. They can be squeezed up or spread out, without trouble or cost, to give whatever amount of employment is required. Moreover, there is no need to worry about mistaken investments or about technical change. Not only the putty added this year, but the whole lot, can be squeezed into any form that is needed so as to re-establish equilibrium instantaneously after any change.

There has been a lot of tiresome controversy over this putty. The bastard Keynesians try to make out that it is all about the problem of 'measuring capital'. But it has nothing to do either with measurement or with capital; it has to do with abolishing time. For a world that is always in equilibrium there is no difference between the future and the past, there is no history and there is no need for Keynes.

3

What about the influence of *The General Theory* on practical affairs?

There is a kind of simple-minded Marxist who has a great resentment against Keynes because he is held responsible for saving capitalism from destroying itself in another great slump. This is often made an excuse for not understanding the theory of effective demand, although Michał Kalecki derived pretty well the same analytical system as Keynes from Marx's premises. Moreover it implies that capitalists are so stupid that they would fail to learn from their experiences during the war that government outlay maintains profits, unless they had Keynes to point it out to them.

But what was the political tendency of *The General Theory*? Keynes himself described it as 'moderately conservative' but this was intended as a paradox, for the whole book is a polemic against established ideas. His own mood often swung from left to right. Capitalism was in some ways repugnant to him but Stalinism was much worse. In his last years, certainly, the right predominated. When I teased him about accepting a peerage he replied that after sixty one had to become respectable. But his basic view of life was aesthetic rather than political. He hated unemployment because it was stupid and poverty because it was ugly. He was disgusted by the commercialism of modern life. (It is true he enjoyed making money for his College and for himself but only as long as it did not take up much time.) He indulged in an agreeable vision of a world where economics has ceased to be important and our grandchildren can begin to lead a civilised life. But in that vision there is room for a rich man to enjoy his wealth in a civilised manner.

The argument of *The General Theory*, viewed in the perspective of the present time, appears to be partly progressive and partly the reverse. There is one element in Keynes's analysis which, in its own day, must clearly be regarded as having been on the progressive side, this is the theory that the level of prices in an industrial economy primarily depends on the level of money-wage rates.

The dominant official orthodoxy at the time of the great slump was maintained by those whom Keynes called the 'bumists', because they held that equilibrium would be restored when costs were reduced as much as prices. Their one and only remedy for the situation was to break the power of the trade unions and cut wage rates.

In 1925, after the establishment of an overvalued exchange rate of sterling, Keynes had argued that it would be impossible to cut wages without enormous industrial strife. (There was a general strike in 1926.) Now he argued that even if it were possible, it would do no good, because a cut in wages would only bring prices down. This would fail to improve the relation of costs to prices; real-wage rates would not be much altered one way or the other, but the basic situation would be made much worse by the loss of liquidity for the banks. (In 1933 the banking system in the U.S.A. collapsed dramatically.)

Keynes maintained that cutting wages was an unsound policy. (If the object was to get a competitive advantage in international trade it could always be better done by depreciating the exchange rate.) The trade unions were wiser economists than the orthodox school.

Nowadays, of course, the boot is on the other leg and trade unions are being reproached for raising wages. This is a misapplication of half-digested theory. It was an obvious rider to *The General Theory* that if we are to enjoy continuous near-full employment without changing the institutions and habits of industrial bargaining, we shall suffer from inflation. It is neither the fault of the trade unions, fulfilling their proper function of demanding a fair share in rising profits, nor of businessmen trying to preserve profits by raising prices when costs go up. It is the fault of an economic system inappropriate to the state of development of the economy. This seems to be dawning at last on official opinion. It would have been better if Keynes's theory of prices had been understood sooner.

There is another element in *The General Theory* which is more dubious; this is the conception of the marginal efficiency of capital. It seems to contain an undigested lump of what Keynes called classical theory. In one sense it means merely the expected rate of profit on investments that businesses are planning to make, but in another sense it means the real return to the economy as a whole that an increment of capital will bring.

In discussions of the immediate problem of unemployment, the confusion between the rate of profit on capital to the capitalist and the benefit of investment to society does not matter. Investment is being treated only as a way of raising employment today, without considering the future benefits to be drawn from an addition to wealth for the future. But when it comes to discussing long-run growth, the confusion in theory vitiates practical conclusions.

Keynes conceived of accumulation in the long run raising capital per head of the population and reducing the usefulness of further accumulation until no more investment would be needed for any important purpose. He took for granted that the rate of profit on capital would fall *pari passu* with the rate of return to society from investment. There is no suggestion that they are not necessarily the same thing or that what a business finds most profitable is not necessarily the best use of resources for the rest of the population.

In the last chapter of *The General Theory*, Keynes argued that fiscal and monetary remedies for unemployment will probably prove too weak and that a comprehensive socialisation of investment will be necessary, but he supposed that this does not involve any change in social objectives because the orthodox analysis of the allocation of resources according to 'marginal productivity' is perfectly acceptable. This element in *The General Theory* now seems retrograde, both intellectually and politically. It might be excused because in the 'long struggle to escape' from orthodox ideas Keynes simply had not time to escape from all of them.

In any case, his vision of long-run growth appears today to have been unrealistic rather than pernicious. At the time when *The General Theory* was being written, Keynes, projecting the situation of the slump into the future, threw out the suggestion that the need for accumulation could be overcome in thirty years of investment at the full-employment level, provided that wars were avoided and population ceased to grow. (He was taking an insular view. The Third World had not yet come to mind.) Alvin Hansen took this up and turned it into a horror story. With the closing of the frontier in North America, there would not be sufficient outlets for the saving that capitalism generates and chronic stagnation would set in. This was not Keynes's attitude. He welcomed the euthanasia of the rentier. He was only afraid that the prospect might be spoiled by failure to get the rate of interest to fall fast enough. Keynes was arguing that, if a private enterprise system cannot deal with potential abundance, we must turn it into a system that can. Certainly, the last chapter of *The General Theory* tries to make out that such a change could be easy and painless but it does not suggest, like Hansen, that if capitalism is incompatible with plenty, plenty ought to be sacrificed to keep capitalism going.

Of course, it has all turned out to be a daydream. The twenty-five years after the war that passed without a major recession has been called the Age of Keynes, but it was not much like his vision. It turned out closer to Kalecki's sardonic description of the régime of the political trade cycle.

Unemployment is a reproach to a democratic government. When

it gets too big, steps are taken to reduce it. Besides, unemployment is associated with low profits. But when unemployment falls too low, inflation sets in. So policy is always alternating between go and stop. This is not using resources for rational ends; it is making employment, or rather avoiding *much* unemployment, an end in itself.

When we were up against sound finance and the Treasury view, we had to argue that any expenditure is better than none. Dig holes in the ground and fill them again, paint the Black Forest white; if men cannot be paid wages for doing something sensible, pay them to do something silly. '"To dig holes in the ground", paid for out of savings, will increase, not only employment but the real national dividend of useful goods and services. It is not reasonable, however,' Keynes adds, 'that a sensible community should be content to remain dependent on such fortuitous and often wasteful mitigations when once we understand the influences upon which effective demand depends.'*

As it has turned out, employment has been kept up by expedients that are not just silly. The self-styled Keynesians in the United States boast of having overcome the rule of sound finance. The consequence has been to facilitate deficit expenditure on armaments; it has helped to keep up the Cold War and promoted hot wars here and there around the world.

Now, it seems that the bastard Keynesians' era is coming to an end in general disillusionment; the economists have no more idea what to say than they had when the old equilibrium doctrine collapsed in the great slump. The Keynesian Revolution still remains to be made, both in teaching economic theory and in forming economic policy.

* *The General Theory*, p. 220.

14

How Keynes came to America

JOHN KENNETH GALBRAITH

'I believe myself to be writing a book on economic theory which will largely revolutionize – not, I suppose, at once but in the course of the next ten years – the way the world thinks about economic problems.' Letter from J. M. Keynes to George Bernard Shaw, New Year's Day 1935.

The most influential book on economic and social policy so far in this century, *The General Theory of Employment, Interest and Money*, by John Maynard Keynes, was published in 1936 in Britain and a few weeks later in the United States. A paperback edition is available in the United States, and quite a few people who take advantage of this bargain will be puzzled at the reason for the book's influence. Though comfortably aware of their own intelligence, they will be unable to read it. They will wonder, accordingly, how it persuaded so many other people – not all of whom, certainly, were more penetrating or diligent. This was only one of the remarkable things about this book and the revolution it precipitated.

By common, if not yet quite universal agreement, the Keynesian Revolution was one of the great modern accomplishments in social design. It brought Marxism in the advanced countries to a total halt. It led to a level of economic performance that now inspires bitterend conservatives to panegyrics of unexampled banality. Yet those responsible have had no honours and some opprobrium. For a long while, to be known as an active Keynesian was to invite the wrath of those who equate social advance with subversion. Those concerned developed a habit of reticence. As a further consequence, the history of the revolution is, perhaps, the worst told story of our era.

It is time that we knew better this part of our history and those who made it, and this is a little of the story. Much of it turns on the almost unique unreadability of *The General Theory* and hence the need for people to translate and propagate its ideas to government officials, students and the public at large. As Messiahs go, Keynes was deeply dependent on his prophets.

The General Theory appeared in the sixth year of the Great Depression and the fifty-third of Keynes's life. At the time Keynes, like his great contemporary Churchill, was regarded as too clear-headed and candid to be trusted. Public officials do not always admire men who say what the right policy should be. Their frequent need, especially in matters of foreign policy, is for men who will find persuasive reasons for the wrong policy. Keynes had foreseen grave difficulty from the reparations clauses of the Versailles Treaty and had voiced them in *The Economic Consequences of the Peace*, a brilliantly polemical volume, which may well have overstated his case and which certainly was unjust to Woodrow Wilson.

Later in the twenties, in another book, he was equally untactful toward those who invited massive unemployment in Britain in order to return sterling to the gold standard at its pre-war parity with the dollar. The man immediately responsible for this effort, a highly orthodox voice in economic matters at the time, was the then Chancellor of the Exchequer, Winston Churchill, and that book was called *The Economic Consequences of Mr Churchill*.

From 1920 to 1940 Keynes was sought out by students and intellectuals in Cambridge and London; was well known in London theatre and artistic circles; directed an insurance company; made, and on one occasion lost, quite a bit of money; and was an influential journalist. But he wasn't really trusted on public questions. The great public trade union which identifies trustworthiness with conformity kept him outside. Then came the Depression. There was much unemployment, much suffering. Even respectable men went broke. It was necessary, however unpleasant, to listen to the candid men who had something to say. This is the terrible punishment the gods reserve for fair weather statesmen.

It is a measure of how far the Keynesian Revolution has proceeded that the central thesis of *The General Theory* now sounds rather commonplace. Until it appeared, economists, in the classical (or non-socialist) tradition, had assumed that the economy, if left to itself, would find its equilibrium at full employment. Increases or decreases in wages and in interest rates would occur as necessary to bring about this pleasant result. If men were unemployed, their wages would fall in relation to prices. With lower wages and wider margins, it would be profitable to employ those from whose toil an adequate return could not previously have been made. It followed that steps to keep wages at artificially high levels, such as might result from the ill-considered efforts by unions, would cause unemployment. Such efforts were deemed to be the principal cause of unemployment.

Movements in interest rates played a complementary role by insuring that all income would ultimately be spent. Thus, were people to decide for some reason to increase their savings, the interest rates on the now more abundant supply of loanable funds would fall. This, in turn, would lead to increased investment. The added outlays for investment goods would offset the diminished outlays by the more frugal consumers. In this fashion, changes in consumer spending or in investment decisions were kept from causing any change in total spending that would lead to unemployment.

Keynes argued that neither wage movements nor changes in the rate of interest had, necessarily, any such agreeable effect. He focused attention on the total of purchasing power in the economy – what freshmen are now taught to call aggregate demand. Wage reductions might not increase employment; in conjunction with other changes, they might merely reduce this aggregate demand. And he held that interest was not the price that was paid to people to save but the price they got for exchanging holdings of cash, or its equivalent, their normal preference in assets, for less liquid forms of investment. And it was difficult to reduce interest beyond a certain level. Accordingly, if people sought to save more, this wouldn't necessarily mean lower interest rates and a resulting increase in investment. Instead, the total demand for goods might fall, along with employment and also investment, until savings were brought back into line with investment by the pressure of hardship which had reduced saving in favour of consumption. The economy would find its equilibrium not at full employment but with an unspecified amount of unemployment.

Out of this diagnosis came the remedy. It was to bring aggregate demand back up to the level where all willing workers were employed, and this could be accomplished by supplementing private expenditure with public expenditure. This should be the policy wherever intentions to save exceeded intentions to invest. Since public spending would not perform this offsetting role if there were compensating taxation (which is a form of saving), the public spending should be financed by borrowing – by incurring a deficit. So far as Keynes can be condensed into a few paragraphs, this is it. *The General Theory* is more difficult. There are nearly 400 pages, some of them of fascinating obscurity.

Before the publication of *The General Theory*, Keynes had urged his ideas directly on President Roosevelt, most notably in a famous letter to the *New York Times* on 31 December 1933: 'I lay overwhelming emphasis on the increase of national purchasing power resulting from government expenditure which is financed by loans.' And he visited F.D.R. in the summer of 1934 to press his case, although the session was no great success; each, during the meeting, seems to have developed some doubts about the general good sense of the other.

In the meantime, two key Washington officials, Marriner Eccles, the exceptionally able Utah banker who was to become head of the Federal Reserve Board, and Lauchlin Currie, a former Harvard instructor who was director of research and later an economic aide to Roosevelt (and later still a prominent victim of McCarthyite persecution), had on their own account reached conclusions similar to those of Keynes as to the proper course of fiscal policy. When *The General Theory* arrived, they took it as confirmation of the course they had previously been urging. Currie, a highly qualified economist and teacher, was also a skilled and influential interpreter of the ideas in the Washington community. Not often have important new ideas on economics entered a government by way of its central bank. Nor should conservatives worry. There is not the slightest indication that it will ever happen again.

Paralleling the work of Keynes in the thirties and rivalling it in importance, though not in fame, was that of Simon Kuznets and a group of young economists and statisticians at the University of Pennsylvania, the National Bureau of Economic Research and the United States Department of Commerce. They developed the now familiar concepts of National Income and Gross National Product and their components of National Income and Gross National Product was the saving, investment, aggregate of disposable income and the other magnitudes of which Keynes was talking. As a result, those who were translating his ideas into action knew not only what needed to be done but how much. And many who would never have been persuaded by the Keynesian abstractions were compelled to belief by the concrete figures from Kuznets and his inventive colleagues.

However, the trumpet – if the metaphor is permissible for this particular book – that was sounded in Cambridge, England, was heard most clearly in Cambridge, Massachusetts. Harvard was the principal avenue by which Keynes's ideas passed to the United States. Conservatives worry about universities being centres of disquieting innovation. Their worries are surely exaggerated – but it has occurred.

In the late thirties, Harvard had a large community of young economists, most of them held there by the shortage of jobs that Keynes sought to cure. They had the normal confidence of their years in their ability to remake the world and, unlike less fortunate generations, the opportunity. They also had occupational indication of the need. Massive unemployment persisted year after year. It was degrading to have to continue telling the young that this was merely a temporary departure from the full employment norm, and that one need only obtain the needed wage reductions.

Paul Samuelson of M.I.T., who almost from the outset was the acknowledged leader of the younger Keynesian community, has compared the excitement of the young economists on the arrival of Keynes's book to that of Keats on first looking into Chapman's Homer. Some will wonder if economists are capable of such refined emotion, but the effect was certainly great. Here was a remedy for the despair that could be seen just beyond the Yard. It did not overthrow the system but saved it. To the non-revolutionary, it seemed too good to be true. To the occasional revolutionary, it was. The old economics was still taught by day. But in the evening, and almost every evening from 1936 on, almost everyone discussed Keynes.

This might, conceivably, have remained a rather academic discussion. As with the Bible and Marx, obscurity stimulated abstract debate. But in 1938, the practical instincts that economists sometimes suppress with success were catalysed by the arrival at Harvard from Minnesota of Alvin H. Hansen. He was then about fifty, an effective teacher and a popular colleague. But most of all he was a man for whom economic ideas had no standing apart from their use.

The economists of established reputation had not taken to Keynes. Faced with the choice between changing one's mind and proving that there is no need to do so, almost everyone opts for the latter. So it was then. Hansen had an established reputation, and he did change his mind. Though he had been an effective critic of some central propositions in Keynes's *Treatise on Money*, an immediately preceding work, and was initially rather cool to *The General Theory*, he soon became strongly persuaded of its importance.

He proceeded to expound the ideas in books, articles and lectures and to apply them to the American scene. He persuaded his students and younger colleagues that they should not only understand the ideas but win understanding in others and then go on to get action. Without ever seeking to do so or being quite aware of the fact, he became the leader of a crusade. In the late thirties Hansen's seminar in the new Graduate School of Public Administration was regularly visited by the Washington policy-makers. Often the students overflowed into the hall. One felt that it was the most important thing currently happening in the country, and this could have been the case.

The officials took Hansen's ideas, and perhaps even more his sense of conviction, back to Washington. In time there was also a strong migration of his younger colleagues and students to the capital, and Keynes himself once wrote admiringly of this group of young disciples. The discussions that had begun in Cambridge continued through the war years in Washington. One of the leaders, a close friend of Hansen's but not otherwise connected with the Harvard group, was Gerhard Colm of the Bureau of the Budget. Colm, a German refugee who made the transition from a position of influence in Germany to one of influence in the United States in a matter of some five years, played a major role in reducing the Keynesian proposals to workable estimates of costs and quantities. Keynesian policies became central to what was called post-war planning and designs for preventing the re-emergence of massive unemployment.

Meanwhile, others were concerning themselves with a wider audience. Seymour Harris, another of Hansen's colleagues and an early convert to Keynes, became the most prolific exponent of the ideas in the course of becoming one of the most prolific scholars of modern times. He published half a dozen books on Keynes and outlined the ideas in hundreds of letters, speeches, memoranda, Congressional appearances and articles. Professor Samuelson, mentioned above, put the Keynesian ideas into what became (and remains) the most influential textbook on economics since the last great exposition of the classical system by Alfred Marshall. Lloyd Metzler, now of the University of Chicago, applied the Keynesian system to international trade. Lloyd G. Reynolds, at a later stage, gathered a talented group of younger economists at Yale and made that university a major centre of discussion of the new trends.

Nor was the Harvard influence confined to the United States. At almost the same time that *The General Theory* arrived in Cambridge, Massachusetts, a young Canadian graduate student named Robert Bryce arrived from Cambridge, England. He had been in Keynes's seminar and had, as a result, a special licence to explain what Keynes meant in his more obscure passages. With two or three other Canadian graduate students, Bryce went on to Ottawa and to a succession of senior posts culminating in Deputy Minister of Finance. Canada was perhaps the first country to commit itself to a firmly Keynesian economic policy.

Meanwhile, with the help of the academic Keynesians, a few businessmen were becoming interested. Two New England industrialists, Henry S. Dennison of the Dennison Manufacturing Company in Framingham and Ralph Flanders of the Jones and Lamson Company of Springfield, Vermont (and later United States Senator from Vermont) hired members of the Harvard group to tutor them in the ideas. Before the war they had endorsed them in a book, in which Lincoln Filene of Boston and Morris E. Leeds of Philadelphia had joined, called *Toward Full Employment*. It was only slightly more readable than Keynes. In the later war years, the Committee for Economic Development, led in these matters by Flanders and the late Beardsley Ruml, and again with the help of the academic Keynesians, began explaining the ideas to businessmen.

In Washington during the war years the National Planning Association had been a centre for academic discussion of the Keynesian ideas. At the end of the war Hans Christian Sonne, the imaginative and liberal New York banker, began underwriting both N.P.A., and Keynesian ideas. With the C.E.D., in which Sonne was also influential, N.P.A. became another important instrument for explaining the policy to the larger public. (In the autumn of 1949, in an exercise of unparalleled diplomacy, Sonne gathered a dozen economists of strongly varying views at Princeton and persuaded them to sign a specific endorsement of Keynesian fiscal policies.)

In 1946, ten years after the publication of *The General Theory*, the Employment Act of that year gave the Keynesian system the qualified but still quite explicit support of law. It recognised, as Keynes had urged, that unemployment and insufficient output would respond to positive policies. Not much was said about the specific policies but the responsibility of the federal government to act in some fashion was clearly affirmed. The Council of Economic Advisers became, in turn, a platform for expounding the Keynesian view of the economy and it was brought promptly into use. Leon Keyserling, as an original member and later chairman, was a tireless exponent of the ideas. And he saw at an early stage the importance of enlarging them to embrace not only the prevention of depression but the maintenance of an adequate rate of economic expansion. Thus in a decade had the revolution spread.

Those who nurture thoughts of conspiracy and clandestine plots will be saddened to know that this was a revolution without organisation. All who participated felt a deep sense of personal responsibility for the ideas; there was a varying but deep urge to persuade. But no one ever responded to plans, orders, instructions, or any force apart from his own convictions. That perhaps was the most interesting single feature of the Keynesian Revolution.

Something more was, however, suspected. And there was some effort at counter-revolution. Nobody could say that he preferred massive unemployment to Keynes. And even men of conservative mood, when they understood what was involved, opted for the policy – some asking only that it be called by some other name. The Committee for Economic Development, coached by Ruml on semantics, never advocated deficits. Rather it spoke well of a budget that was balanced only under conditions of high employment. Those who objected to Keynes were also invariably handicapped by the fact that they hadn't (and couldn't) read the book. It was like attacking

Plate 7   After the Registry Office wedding in 1925
(*London News Agency Photo*).

(a)

Plate 8   Maynard Keynes in 1908 by Duncan Grant: (a) pencil drawing on an envelope; (b) oil painting at King's College, Cambridge.

the original Kama Sutra for obscenity without being able to read Sanskrit. Still, where social change is involved, there are men who can surmount any handicap.

Appropriately Harvard, not Washington, was the principal object of attention. In the fifties, a group of graduates of mature years banded together in an organisation called the Veritas Foundation and produced a volume called *Keynes at Harvard*. It found that 'Harvard was the launching pad for the Keynesian rocket in America'. But then it damaged this not implausible proposition by identifying Keynesianism with socialism, Fabian socialism, Marxism, Communism, Fascism and also literary incest, meaning that one Keynesian always reviewed the works of another Keynesian. More encouragingly, the authors also reported that 'Galbraith is being groomed as the new crown prince of Keynesism (sic)'. Like so many others in similar situations, the authors sacrificed their chance for credibility by writing not for the public but for those who were paying the bill. The university was unperturbed, the larger public sadly indifferent. The book evidently continues to have some circulation on the more thoughtful fringes of the John Birch Society.

As a somewhat less trivial matter, another and more influential group of graduates pressed for an investigation of the Department of Economics, employing as their instrument the visiting committee that annually reviews the work of the department on behalf of the governing boards. The Keynesian Revolution belongs to our history; so accordingly does this investigation.

It was conducted by Clarence Randall, then the exceptionally articulate head of the Inland Steel Company, with the support of Sinclair Weeks, a manufacturer, former Senator and tetrarch of the right wing of the Republican Party in Massachusetts. In due course, the committee found that Keynes was, indeed, exerting a baneful influence on the Harvard economic mind and that the department was unbalanced in his favour. As always, there was a handicap that the investigators, with one or two possible exceptions, had not read the book and were otherwise uncertain as to what they attacked. The department, including the members most sceptical of Keynes's analysis – no one accepted all of it and some very little – unanimously rejected the committee's finding. So, as one of his last official acts before becoming High Commissioner to Germany, did President James Bryant Conant. There was much bad blood.

In ensuing years there was further discussion of the role of Keynes at Harvard and of related issues. But it became increasingly amicable, for the original investigators had been caught up in one of those fascinating and paradoxical developments with which the history of the Keynesian (and doubtless all other) revolutions is replete. Shortly after the committee reached its disturbing conclusion the Eisenhower administration came to power.

Mr Randall became a Presidential assistant and adviser. Mr Weeks became Secretary of Commerce and almost immediately was preoccupied with the firing of the head of the Bureau of Standards over the question of the efficacy of Glauber's salts as a battery additive. Having staked his public reputation against the nation's scientists and engineers on the issue (as the late Bernard De Voto put it) that a battery could be improved by giving it a laxative, Mr Weeks could hardly be expected to keep open another front against the economists. But much worse, both he and Mr Randall were acquiring a heavy contingent liability for the policies of the Eisenhower administration. And these, it soon developed, had almost as strong a Keynesian coloration as the department at Harvard.

President Eisenhower's first Chairman of the Council of Economic Advisers was Arthur F. Burns of Columbia University and the National Bureau of Economic Research. Mr Burns had credentials as a critic of Keynes. In his introduction to the 1946 annual report of the National Bureau, called 'Economic Research and the Keynesian Thinking of Our Times', he had criticised a version of the Keynesian underemployment equilibrium and concluded a little heavily that 'the imposing schemes for governmental action that are being bottomed on Keynes's equilibrium theory must be viewed with scepticism'. Alvin Hansen had replied rather sharply.

But Burns was an able economist. If he regarded Keynes with scepticism, he viewed recessions (including ones for which he might be held responsible) with positive antipathy. In his 1955 Economic Report, he said, 'Budget policies can help promote the objective of maximum production by wisely allocating resources *first between private and public uses*; second, among various governmental programmes.' (Italics added.) Keynes, reading these words carefully, would have strongly applauded. And, indeed, a spokesman for the N.A.M. told the Joint Economic Committee that they pointed 'directly toward the planned and eventually the socialized economy'.

After the departure of Burns, the Eisenhower administration incurred a deficit of no less than $9.4 thousand millions in the national income accounts in the course of overcoming the recession of 1958. This was by far the largest deficit ever incurred by an American government in peacetime; it exceeded the *total* peacetime expenditure by F.D.R. in any year up to 1940. No administration before or since has given the economy such a massive dose of Keynesian medicine. With a Republican administration, guided by men like Mr Randall and Mr Weeks, following such policies, the academic Keynesians were no longer vulnerable. Keynes ceased to be a wholly tactful topic of conversation with such critics.

Presidents Kennedy and Johnson continued what is now commonplace policy. Advised by Walter Heller, a remarkably skilful exponent of Keynes's ideas, they added the new device of the deliberate tax reduction to sustain aggregate demand. And they abandoned, at long last, the doubletalk by which advocates of Keynesian policies combined advocacy of measures to promote full employment and economic growth with promises of a promptly balanced budget. 'We have recognised as self-defeating the effort to balance our budget too quickly in an economy operating well below its potential', President Johnson said in his 1965 report.

Now, as noted, Keynesian policies are the new orthodoxy. Economists are everywhere to be seen enjoying their new and pleasantly uncontroversial role. Like their predecessors who averted their eyes from unemployment, many are now able to ignore – often with some slight note of scholarly righteousness – the new problem, which is an atrocious allocation of resources between private wants and public needs, especially those of our cities. (In a sense, the Keynesian success has brought back an older problem of economics, that of resource allocation, in a new form.)

We have yet to pay proper respect to those who pioneered the Keynesian Revolution. Everyone now takes pride in the resulting performance of the economy. We should take a little pride in the men who brought it about. It is hardly fitting that they should have been celebrated only by the reactionaries. The debt to the courage and intelligence of Alvin Hansen is especially great. Next only to Keynes, his is the credit for saving what even conservatives still call capitalism.

15

Keynes and the finance of the First World War

N. H. DIMSDALE

Finance in the early stages of the war

Although Keynes did not join the Treasury officially until January
1915, he was actively concerned with war finance from the outbreak
of hostilities. His first intervention was rather unorthodox. It arose
from a request from Basil Blackett at the Treasury, dated 1 August
1914, 'to pick your brains for your country's benefit'.[1] The Treasury
needed assistance in resisting the arguments of the joint-stock banks
for the immediate prohibition of gold exports. The banks were also
causing difficulties through their substantial demands for gold at
the Bank of England, in anticipation of a run by their depositors.

On Blackett's suggestion Keynes drafted a memorandum against
the suspension of gold payments.[2] He showed that the difficulties
of the money market at the outbreak of the war arose from the
inability of foreigners to meet obligations in London because of
the interruption of the normal channels for remitting payments. The
solvency of the acceptance houses was threatened by the massive
default of their foreign customers. There was, however, no danger
of an external drain of gold from London and, therefore, no case for
suspending payments. As for the bankers' fears of a run by their
depositors, the internal demand for gold could be reduced by
enabling the Bank of England to increase its note issue, through suspending the Bank Charter Act. The demands of the depositors could
be met in notes, making hoarding of gold by the banks unnecessary.

These arguments convinced Lloyd George, the Chancellor of the
Exchequer, of the undesirability of forbidding gold exports. At a
time when France, Russia and Germany suspended payments,
Britain alone of the belligerents remained on gold. But the need for
internal currency was met by Currency Notes issued by the Treasury
rather than the Bank of England.

Keynes then turned his attention to the plight of the money
market, recognising from the outset that normal working would not

be resumed until the credit of the acceptance houses had been fully restored. A temporary respite had been given by a one-month moratorium on bills of exchange. Keynes's proposal[3] was intended to guarantee the solvency of the acceptance houses and to ensure their ability to take on new business. He considered that the best way of achieving this would be the formation of a syndicate of acceptance houses. New business accepted by it would bear a government guarantee of contingent liability for a high proportion of the total value of new acceptances. While the authorities did not adopt these proposals, measures introduced on 12 August afforded the banks and discount houses generous facilities for discounting pre-moratorium bills at the Bank of England, but did less for the acceptance houses. Their solvency was not ensured until further assistance was given by the Bank of England on 5 September. Only then was the money market restored to working order.[4,5]

Back in Cambridge, he described the financial crisis of 1914 in detail in two articles for the *Economic Journal*.[6] He was critical of the behaviour of the joint-stock banks, particularly over the hoarding of gold, and claimed that: 'The banks held on to what gold they had, and took from the Bank of England in the first three days of the crisis many millions more. Our system was endangered, not by the public running on the banks, but by the banks running on the Bank of England.' He charged the banks with deliberately withholding gold coins from their depositors, who despite all, showed no signs of panic. His criticism may have been too severe in view of the extensive freezing of the banks' liquid assets. There was some moderation of the harshness of his judgement in his second article.

He was also critical of the handling of the issue of the First War Loan in December 1914 and set out his own ideas on government borrowing in a note to Sir John Bradbury, Joint Permanent Secretary to the Treasury.[7] He suggested that loans should cater for the needs of the different sections of the market, which he identified as the banks, the ordinary investor and the small investor. The banks would be attracted by Exchequer bonds of five to ten years to maturity. The needs of the ordinary investor would be met by long-dated securities with a generous yield and protection against early conversion, since 'redeemability, both early and optional, is giving the investor, as distinguished from the patriotic citizen too little'. The appeal to the small investor, who would not think of subscribing to loans, should be made through £5 and £10 bonds available through the Post Office.

Keynes appears to have been seeking official employment for some months. In January 1915 he was appointed as assistant to Sir George Paish, special adviser to the Chancellor of the Exchequer. His experience at the India Office and on the Royal Commission on

Indian Currency and Finance proved to be of great value. He was already well known and trusted by Sir Robert Chalmers, Joint Permanent Secretary with Bradbury, and Basil Blackett, with both of whom he had worked closely on the Commission.[8]

Arrived in the Treasury, Keynes became concerned that low interest rates would discourage foreigners from holding balances in London and so have adverse effects on the gold position. His remedy, suggested in March, was the issue of Treasury bills to compete with trade bills and other measures to reduce bankers' balances at the Bank of England.[9] However, by May the growth of borrowing by Treasury bills was causing concern. His main objection to heavy reliance upon Treasury bills was that they were taken up by the banks and not the public. Borrowing from the banks expanded the volume of deposits held by the public: 'From the individual point of view this money is *unspent*: it is lying idle waiting to be spent or to be invested. In these circumstances it is not safe to rely on these funds finding no outlet.'[10] What was needed was a second War Loan designed to secure the public's money. The terms of the issue should be generous, 'since investors who do not usually go into the gilt-edged market have got to be attracted'.[11]

Keynes's monetary theory at this time was broadly Marshallian. He had acknowledged his debt to Marshall and to the Cambridge oral tradition generally in a review of Fisher's *The Purchasing Power of Money*. In this, after references to Marshall's evidence before the Gold and Silver Commission and the Indian Currency Committee, he wrote: 'It is hardly an exaggeration to say that monetary theory, in its most accurate form, has become in England a matter of oral tradition. These preliminary remarks are necessary to explain that it is from the standpoint of this oral tradition, rather than from any printed book, that an English economist must approach Professor Fisher's very important contribution to the subject.'[12] Whereas Marshall had mainly analysed problems arising from long-run trends in the price level, Keynes concentrated on the short period.[13,14] He was particularly interested in short-run variations in the demand for money and their implications for monetary policy and debt management. He made extensive use of the traditional Quantity Theory, although he made qualifications to allow for the effects of hoarding. An increase in the money supply was not necessarily a matter for concern, as he pointed out when criticising the undue importance attached to the note issue by the Bank of France. 'In so far as the notes are hoarded, they do no harm at all, in whatever quantities, and constitute in effect a *loan to the State without interest*. When these notes are ready to emerge from their hoards, then it ought to be possible to reabsorb them by floating a public loan.'[15]

Internal Finance

By August 1915 Keynes and his colleagues in No. 1 Division at the Treasury were becoming concerned about reconciling the demand of the army for recruits with commitments to subsidise the Allies. Kitchener was pressing for an army of seventy divisions. But an army of this size, Keynes thought, could not be supported unless other expenditure was reduced. He set out the position in a memorandum for McKenna, the Chancellor of the Exchequer.[16] It measured in terms of manpower the amount of the aggregate contribution of the United Kingdom to the war in men, ships, subsidies and munitions, and argued that the labour force of the United Kingdom was so fully engaged in useful activities that any considerable further diversion of it to military uses must be *alternative* and not *additional* to the other means by which the United Kingdom was assisting the Allied cause. Thus increased recruitment must, he emphasised, be at the expense of subsidies to the allies, which had a cost in terms of manpower. According to Keynes's calculations, if France were subsidising Britain to the extent that Britain was subsidising France, Britain would be relieved of claims on resources equivalent to nearly 500,000 men. The use of manpower as a measure of resources is interesting in view of the extensive application of manpower budgeting during the Second World War. Keynes argued that it was erroneous to distinguish between those in essential and less essential types of employment and to assume that the latter could be spared for military duties. Labour would continue to be drawn into the less necessary occupations and away from essential employment as long as the power of the public to consume was not reduced by taxation. He therefore pressed for substantial increases in taxation if the targets for recruitment and subsidies were to be achieved.

Keynes's paper did not lead to any change in the target for army recruitment, and he returned to the growing pressures on resources in a memorandum on the financial prospects, written in September 1915.[17] He distinguished between finance provided by 'real resources' and 'inflationist borrowing'. 'Real resources' included 'that part of their current income which individuals and corporations in the United Kingdom do not spend but hand over to the Treasury in taxes and loans', capital goods consumed, or sold abroad, and borrowing from abroad. Expenditure in excess of real resources would be financed by 'inflationism' which amounted to increasing the money supply.

The prospective budget deficit for the financial years 1915–16 was £700 million, allowing for receipts from current taxation and long-term borrowing to date. Real resources might produce an additional £620 million, assuming £450 million from additional loans and taxation, £90 million from the sale of gold and securities and £80 million from foreign loans; £500 million would be a more realistic figure, leaving between £80 million and £200 million to be found through 'inflationism'. In estimating the proceeds from loans and taxation no mention was made of the price level. But it seems reasonable to suppose that the yield from taxes and loans was calculated assuming that the price level would be constant with the effects of 'inflationism' being considered separately. This is an important assumption, since, as Keynes was to emphasise in *How to Pay for the War* (1940), the yield from taxes and voluntary savings can always be increased, if money incomes rise sufficiently through inflation.

Keynes discussed in more detail the extent to which the authorities should use inflationist methods of finance in a separate paper on 'The Meaning of Inflation'.[18] By 'inflation' he meant increasing the money supply rather than raising the price level. In so far as the increase in the money supply was accompanied by a desire of the public to hold an increased proportion of their resources in the form of notes or bank deposits, there would be no effect on their expenditure. The uncertainty engendered by war conditions might well induce people to hold more money than usual. If the government expanded the money supply beyond this, the public might be induced to increase their money balances temporarily. But issue of a loan should not be long delayed, otherwise there would be a danger of the public using their enlarged money balances to bid away resources from the war effort. If employed with care a measure of 'inflationism' could be a useful financial device. Much depended upon whether the additional balances came into the hands of those who would spend them or those who would use them to subscribe to a loan. In Britain the additional money would go mainly to the working class who would spend it. The main effect of the increased expenditure would be a rise in imports and a worsening of the trade balance. The scope for inflationist methods was therefore limited by the need to maintain gold payments and to finance the allies. By contrast, in a comparatively self-sufficient economy, such as Germany, inflationary finance could be used deliberately to raise prices relative to wages and so benefit the social classes who would subscribe to public loans.

In his *War Memoirs* Lloyd George bitterly attacked Keynes's memoranda on financial prospects for being excessively alarmist.[19] However, it would appear that Keynes's call for a substantial increase in taxation was justified by the state of the economy in the second half of 1915. In the early stages war resources were provided by increased output, reduced investment and lower exports, but there was no decline in consumption.[20] During 1915 national product ceased to rise and the balance of payments began causing concern. Additional resources for the war could be made available, if consumption were reduced. Increased taxation and inflation were alternative ways of achieving this, and Keynes had good reasons for preferring the former.

Keynes's memorandum on financial prospects had some practical results in the increased taxation introduced in McKenna's budget of September 1915. But the increases could hardly be regarded as an adequate contribution to the finance of the war, although there was some reduction of consumption in 1916.[20] Keynes calculated the effect of levying taxes to reduce the consumption of wage earners in Britain to the same level as in Germany. He estimated that this could produce £400–500 million of additional revenue in 1915. In a talk given at the Admiralty in March 1916 he noted that 'these resources cannot be seriously increased except by severe taxing of the working classes. If they consumed *pari passu* with Germany we could save £400 million and just do it.'[21]

Treasury opinion was, however, less optimistic about the possibilities of taxation. Although the proposed increase in revenue for 1916–17 was only about £100 million, Keynes commented: 'The Treasury hold that any increased taxation beyond this extreme limit would defeat its own object by destroying the sources of revenue and loans through over-taxation.'[22] This meant that there would be heavy dependence on borrowing. Treasury experience indicated that the best way of raising the money was issuing big loans interspaced with short-term borrowing. Keynes seems to have favoured greater emphasis on taxation. But the management of internal finance was not his concern, his main responsibilities by this time being Allied finance and the sterling–dollar exchange.

When he discussed the finance of the First World War fifteen years later in *A Treatise on Money* (1930) he distinguished between the two approaches which arise in his wartime memoranda.[23] The government may increase taxation so that the burden falls heavily on the working class and reduces their level of consumption – the possibility which he discussed in his first talk at the Admiralty. But he regarded this as raising insuperable political problems. The alternative approach depended upon letting prices rise relative to wages. The exceptional profits of entrepreneurs could then be tapped by high rates of taxation on profits and sales of government bonds. Entrepreneurs would be acting as tax gatherers for the authorities through a policy of deliberate profit inflation. He concluded that 'to allow prices to rise by permitting a profit inflation is, in time of war, both inevitable and wise' and noted that this was the policy evolved by the Treasury by trial and error during the war. When he wrote *How to Pay for the War* in 1940 Keynes argued that voluntary savings can be relied upon to finance war expenditure, so long as the government is willing to tolerate the subsequent inflation. But he emphasised the disadvantages of relying on voluntary saving compared with his own proposals for deferred pay: 'It (voluntary saving) is a method of compulsorily converting the appropriate part of the earnings of the worker which he does not save voluntarily into the voluntary savings (and taxation) of the entrepreneur. "We shall depend on the voluntary system" is another way of saying "We shall depend on inflation to the extent which is necessary".'[24] After examining the tight wage–price spiral observed during the First World War, he commented: 'But what a ridiculous system with wages and prices chasing one another upwards in this manner! No one benefited except the profiteer.'

The main argument against inflationary finance in *How to Pay for the War* was social. The distribution of income and wealth would shift in favour of entrepreneurs at the expense of workers and rentiers. His principal objection to inflation while at the Treasury in the First World War was that it might force Britain to suspend payments. His attitude is hardly surprising in view of his responsibilities for external finance.

Keynes continually pointed out the consequences of full employment for the war economy. When advising late in 1915 on the shortage of freight which was impeding the movement of war supplies, he noted that the major bottleneck was the shortage of labour at the ports. This reflected the excessive demand for labour throughout the economy. 'But we ought to realise quite clearly that we have now reached the point where any new project must necessarily be *alternative* and not additional to what we are already doing in other directions. To carry overseas each new division of an expeditionary force is *alternative* to carrying food, munitions or other necessary commodities to the Allies or to ourselves. We have to decide not merely that one more division would be useful, but that it would be so useful that it is worthwhile to incur a deficiency in one of these other directions.'[25]

The full commitment of manpower resources provided a strong economic argument against conscription, which Keynes advanced in the press under the pseudonym of 'Politicus'. He wanted to claim personal exemption from military service on grounds of conscientious objection, even though his work in the Treasury protected him from conscription. He was active in supporting the claims for exemption of those of his friends who were also conscientious objectors.

Finance of the Allies

As soon as he entered the Treasury Keynes began dealing with the problems of lending to the Allies. One of his early assignments was to accompany Lloyd George, E. S. Montagu, Financial Secretary of the Treasury, and Lord Cunliffe, the Governor of the Bank of England, to the joint financial conference of the Allies at Paris in February 1915. The division of the burden of Allied finance was discussed, and it was agreed that France and Britain would contribute equally to the assistance of Russia. Keynes suggested that Russian gold be deposited at the Bank of England, earmarked for the Russian account. By this device the gold could still appear as part of the Russian reserves, while being available to the Bank of England, if needed for the support of the pound. He also sought to make assistance to Russia conditional upon release of some of the Russian wheat crop. Both these proposals were accepted, and a proposal for a joint loan bearing the guarantees of all three Allies was resisted. Keynes argued that a joint guarantee might cast doubt upon British issues and would weaken the authorities' ability to regulate the access of the Allies to our capital market. It would also imply British acceptance of responsibility for servicing part of the national debt of France and Russia without securing any worthwhile advantage in return.[26] In these, as in subsequent negotiations with the Allies, Keynes showed skill and determination in protecting Britain's financial interests.

In May 1915 Keynes went with McKenna, the new Chancellor of the Exchequer, to Nice to confer with the Italians over Allied financial arrangements. He underwent an operation for acute appendicitis in June, but by August he was sufficiently recovered to attend another Allied conference at Boulogne. The main topic for discussion at this meeting was the issue of a joint Allied loan in America. Keynes urged most strongly that some of the gold reserves of France and Russia be released for use as collateral for the loan.[27] This was agreed, as was also that the proceeds of the loan be divided according to the amount of gold contributed by each Ally.

The Russians demanded additional credits in return for remitting gold to support the Allied loan. There was some misunderstanding here, since Russian purchases in America were already straining Britain's ability to pay and this was the main reason for the urgency of the loan. Britain was unable to increase credits for Russia, particularly since the French had withdrawn from their undertaking given at the Paris conference to share equally in the finance of Russia. Excessive Russian orders also threatened to disrupt the production of munitions and to lead to wasteful competition for resources among the Allies. Keynes did much of the necessary negotiating with the Russian government. The outcome was an agreement providing for the shipment of Russian gold and establishing a procedure which required Treasury approval for Russian expenditure financed through British credits. The agreement enabled a comprehensive system of control to be introduced gradually with an increasing proportion of Russian orders being placed through British government departments.

Keynes negotiated a similar arrangement for the control of Italian expenditure financed by British credits in November and December 1915. Heavy buying of wool, jute and wheat by the Italian government, well in excess of current requirements, had necessitated the introduction of some form of financial control. Treasury supervision of Italian expenditure was, however, less stringent than for the Russians.

The high level of expenditure by the Allies created acute problems for the Treasury particularly in 1916. Shortage of freight provided some relief, causing actual outlay to fall short of planned expenditure. These attempts by the Treasury to enforce some economies on the Russians led, however, to an allegation by Lloyd George, then Minister for Munitions, that the Russians were being deprived of necessary war material. Lloyd George, who meanwhile had become Prime Minister, did not forget the incident. He intervened to deny Keynes the award of the C.B. early in 1917, but Keynes received the honour four months later.

Keynes described his work as paymaster to the Allies in a talk given at the Admiralty in March 1916: 'We bribe whole populations. It is our money which keeps the allies sweet. It is my business to deal with our financial relations to the allies day by day, and help to steer the line between too much and too little. I venture to say that not half of what we give had the smallest direct military significance. The rest is a *douceur*. Food for Italy. Pigs for Paris.'[28]

When he came to write 'Notes on Exchange Control' at the beginning of the Second World War he recalled: 'It is far more trouble than it is worth to be too logical about controls. (I remember how the day after I had established the principle that Russian credits should be for munitions only, M. Routkowsky came round for my initials to a Bond Street bill for a Grand Duchess's underclothing; and there was the case of the beeswax for the little Fathers.)'[29]

The sterling–dollar exchange

The disruption of the exchanges at the beginning of the war caused a temporary weakness of the dollar because of the inability of Americans to make payments in London. The strength of the pound did not last for long but declined as recruitment drew labour away from export industries and war expenditure swelled the demand for imports. The trade balance deteriorated, the adverse balance rising from £170 million in 1914 to £368 million in 1915, while the deficit with the United States grew from £74 million to £181 million in the same period.[30]

Initially war purchases in America were financed by sales of sterling in New York, but this led to strain, particularly over the finance of Russian expenditure. There was a break in the exchange in August 1915. The situation was restored by raising a joint Anglo-French loan, mobilising U.S. securities owned by British citizens and the sale of gold. The proceeds from these sources were paid into the Treasury account in New York. From the account payments were made for purchases of supplies, assistance to the Allies, and buying sterling to support the exchange.[31] Early in 1916 the Treasury, acting through Messrs J. P. Morgan, pegged sterling at $4.76. The pegged sterling–dollar exchange became the pivot of the Allied financial system. It stabilised the exchanges of the Allies in New York and in all neutral countries.[32] The support of the exchange was to be one of Keynes's major responsibilities. It was appropriate that much of the task should fall upon him in view of his spirited defence of maintaining payments in the initial crisis.

In October 1915 Keynes wrote a memorandum on the prospects for the trade balance. He warned that: 'It would be foolish to assert that we have any reasonable prospect of getting through the six months April–October 1916 without a catastrophe.'[33] This gloomy prediction led to the suggestion that Britain might suspend payments. But Keynes was swift to the defence of the gold standard, opposing both complete suspension and restrictions on the export of gold. He emphasised the advantages of attracting foreign balances and the damaging effects of suspension on the international banking business of the City. An additional reason for maintaining payments was that only through the pegged rate could Britain finance the overseas expenditure of the Allies. This was a direct consequence of their leaving the gold standard. He concluded that: 'A limitation on the export of gold may in fact be forced upon this country. We may not be able to help it. But there is little to be said for courting it or adopting it before the last possible moment.'[34]

Exchange difficulties were postponed for several months in the first half of 1916 because of underspending by both government departments and the Allies. Expenditure was delayed by shortage of freight and lengthening lags of deliveries behind orders. As Keynes noted in March 1916: 'Last October we took the spending departments at their word, and we took the allies at their word. If they had spent all they threatened, we should have been ruined', and predicted: 'We may be able to stand the racket 9 (months). We cannot stand it for 18.'[35] From May the exchange situation deteriorated, necessitating large sales of U. S. securities and gold. Writing in October, Keynes underlined Britain's growing financial dependence on the United States: 'Of the £5 million which the Treasury have to find daily for the prosecution of the war, about £2 million has to be found in North America.'[36]

There was no prospect of this dependence being reduced. On the contrary it would increase as Britain exhausted her stocks of gold and marketable securities and needed to issue more loans on the American market. A detailed report he prepared for McKenna showed that during the five months May–September 1916 Treasury expenditure in America was at the rate of $207 million per month, two-fifths being financed by loan and the remainder by sales of gold and securities. During the six months from October 1916 to March 1917 expenditure was conservatively estimated at $250 million per month of which five-sixths would have to be financed by loan. The borrowing of $80 million per month was causing strain; there would be great difficulty in raising it to $200 million. Even if the Americans were willing to lend, there would be a danger of British overdraft requirements exceeding the capacity of the New York market. It was a matter of whether funds could be raised in America fast enough to keep up with expenditure. A rise in the rate of interest would not assist the borrowing since it might raise doubts about Britain's creditworthiness.

An exchange crisis occurred in November 1916 when the Federal Reserve Board advised American banks to restrict their lending to foreign governments. During the three weeks ending on 16 December, an average of $107 million was paid out of the Treasury account in support of the exchange against a weekly allotment of $12 million. As Keynes remarked in a talk given at the Admiralty early in 1917: 'Another ten days of this and we should have been finished.'[37] The Treasury were determined to hold the rate until the reserves were exhausted. Fortunately the drain dried up suddenly and the pegged rate was held. Underspending by departments again helped the Treasury to spread the meagre reserves available after the crisis. These were, however, barely sufficient to finance purchases in America for more than a month.

The question of suspension of payments was revived and Keynes repeated his defence of maintaining the peg. But on this occasion he explored how exchange control might operate. The exchange authority would have far-reaching powers, since it would examine requests for foreign exchange not only from within Britain but from the Allies and all parts of the Empire except Canada. It would be a powerful body for achieving economies and reinforcing Treasury control. Suspension might be more effective than Treasury arguments in persuading departments to reduce expenditure. 'In short the abandonment of the gold standard might effect some economies by striking terror into the hearts of the spending departments through the tremendous consternation which it would produce in the Press and the City, a terror which cannot be produced by quieter methods.' But there would be great drawbacks: 'An official control of exchange can be introduced at Petrograd and even at Berlin without serious consequences, but for this country to follow suit is to evacuate a position of unique advantage.' Our credit would be seriously damaged and the enemy would be given encouragement. ' "If England has gone off the gold standard, she can't last six months", is what everybody would say, *whether it is true or not.*'[38]

In February 1917 Keynes was promoted to be head of the newly formed 'A' Division, which was responsible for external finance. He reported directly to Sir Robert Chalmers, Joint Permanent Secretary, and to Bonar Law, who had replaced McKenna as Chancellor of the Exchequer in Lloyd George's War Cabinet. The staff of 'A' Division included men of great ability, such as Dudley Ward and Oswald Falk, who relieved Keynes of much of the detailed work he had done previously.

Although the entry of the United States into the war in April greatly relieved the situation, the difficulties of managing the exchange were by no means over. Keynes sought assurance that expenditure by Britain in America on behalf of the Allies would be a first charge on credits granted by the U.S. Treasury. This seemed to be agreed, but misunderstandings soon arose. Congress intended that American advances should be used only for the direct purchase of American goods, which would preclude the use of American funds to support the sterling–dollar exchange. The movement of a large quantity of wheat in June caused a crisis in the exchange as it coincided with the withdrawal of funds from London by American banks subscribing to the Liberty Loan. Requests for American assistance proved fruitless as the Secretary of the U.S. Treasury, W. G. McAdoo, held that he was not empowered to provide funds for the support of sterling. He complained that America was being asked to bear the entire burden of financing the war, and insisted that there could be no assurance of continuing American aid unless an inter-Allied council was set up for assessing needs and allocating credits.

Keynes drafted a reply for Bonar Law seeking to clear up the misunderstandings which had arisen. Britain accepted that the U.S. Treasury had given no undertaking to repay our overdraft at Morgan's from the proceeds of the Liberty Loan, and that an inter-Allied council should be set up to allot American aid. However, the American impression that they were bearing the full burden of financing the war was incorrect. Since the entry of the United States into the war, Britain had given twice as much assistance to the Allies as the United States. Whereas American credits could be used only for purchases within the United States, Britain financed Allied expenditure throughout the world. We were now at the end of our resources and could not continue giving aid as in the past.

'In short our resources available for payment in America are exhausted. Unless the United States Government can meet in full our expenses in America, including exchange, the whole financial fabric of the alliance will collapse. This conclusion will be a matter not of months but of days.'[39]

The question of support for the exchange remained unsettled. In the absence of American assistance, the Treasury could not maintain the pegged rate. Keynes recommended that Sir Hardman Lever, the Treasury's representative in Washington, be instructed to support the exchange so long as there were dollars in the Treasury account, but not to draw on the remaining gold reserves in Washington. When the supply of dollars was exhausted, he should request American help, so throwing the onus for the breakdown of the exchange on to the U.S. Treasury.[40] This policy was communicated to the Americans at the end of July in the course of a long memorandum drafted by Keynes and amended by Bonar Law. It ended with an urgent request for funds to support the exchange. It had the desired effect in that the U.S. Treasury now understood the British position. They sought to provide the dollars which were needed, despite the concern of Congress about unrestricted use of American funds.

In September, Keynes visited the United States with Lord Reading to discuss outstanding financial issues. The initial impression which he made on the Americans was not entirely favourable. Blackett reported confidentially that 'he made a terrible reputation for his rudeness out here', a view which was modified on closer acquaintance.

On his return, Keynes represented the Treasury 'in a newly established monkey house, the Inter-Allied Council for War Purchases and Finance', set up at American insistence. He pursued the matter of dollar reimbursement of British expenditure on behalf of the Allies and sought some relaxation of the ruling that American funds could be used only for direct purchase from the United States. He proposed that the Allies be permitted to pay in dollars for wheat supplied from British Empire sources provided that Britain undertook to spend the dollars in America. This proposal proved unacceptable to the Americans but a compromise allowing for some measure of reimbursement was agreed upon. Keynes was also concerned about the American policy of preferring to lend to Britain, leaving us to re-lend to the Allies. In this way Britain became a conduit for American funds, enabling the United States to receive British financial obligations of high quality, while Britain accumulated claims of doubtful value against the Allies.[41] As his own contribution to reimbursement from France, he suggested that the National Gallery be given a grant to enable it to bid for pictures at the sale at Degas' studio in Paris in March 1918, which he attended with the Director of the National Gallery.

Post-war arrangements: reparations, war debts and the exchange rate

In January 1916 Keynes was asked by the Board of Trade to write a joint memorandum with Sir William Ashley on the effect of an indemnity. Their paper began by examining the payment of the French indemnity after the Franco-Prussian war.[42] Although the greater part of the indemnity of £212 million was paid in the form of bills, the transfer of resources had been brought about by French sales of foreign securities. This occurred as French investors financed their subscriptions to two issues of government stock by disposing of foreign securities. The receipt of the indemnity was beneficial to Germany but its use for debt repayment had aggravated speculation prior to the crisis of 1873.

The memorandum went on to distinguish between the payment of an indemnity through the transfer of securities and capital goods and the payment of an annual sum over an extended period. The annual tribute would be paid in the form of a surplus of exports over imports without specifying the quantities of commodities to be transferred. No recommendation was made for imposing an indemnity on Germany. It was assumed that Britain would make no claim for reparation and that payments would go only to countries overrun by Germany.

The suggestion of an annual payment over a number of years was seized upon by those who wanted to claim the full cost of the war from Germany, notably the Committee of Indemnity, chaired by W. M. Hughes, the Australian Prime Minister. They did not, however, appreciate the limitation of this method of payment. The annual tribute could not exceed the trade surplus of the indemnity paying country, if the transfer of commodities was to be effected. Lord Cunliffe, formerly Governor of the Bank of England, who advised the Hughes Committee, was prepared to recommend an annual payment of £1,200 million without considering how such a sum could be paid by Germany.[43]

Keynes made a preliminary estimate of Germany's capacity to pay reparations in October 1918.[44] He suggested that £500 million might be obtained from the transfer of moveable property, such as securities and capital goods, and from assets in ceded territory. An annual payment of £25 million, capitalised at 5%, would provide an additional £500 million, making a total of £1,000 million, which would be obtained 'without crushing Germany'.

The problem was examined in greater detail in the Treasury indemnity memorandum, which was largely the work of 'A' Division.[45] The cost of the war to the Allies, including war pensions, was estimated to be £25,000 million, which was far in excess of Germany's ability to pay reparations. There could, therefore, be no question of recovering from Germany the full cost of the war.

The maximum value of transferable property, including gold, foreign securities, ships, railways rolling stock and raw materials and of assets in ceded territory was put at £1,370 million. In addition, there could be an annual payment spread over a number of years. But this method would be alternative to extracting the maximum amount of transferable property. Germany could not achieve a substantial trade surplus unless the Allies were prepared to moderate their claims for capital goods and raw materials. 'If Germany is to be "milked" she must not first of all be ruined.' The alternative policy of assisting a recovery of German exports would enable £1,900 million to be paid over thirty years. In any event the grand total of reparations could not exceed £3,000 million and £2,000 million would be a more realistic estimate.

There would be a considerable disadvantage to Britain in a policy of promoting German exports, which would increase competition for British industry in world markets. Since Britain could expect to receive only a small share of reparations, the bulk of the payments going to the Allies, she would not receive adequate compensation for the increased competition. The report concluded that transfer of moveable property would be a better way of exacting reparations than maximising the tribute payable over a long period. It is not clear how much of the memorandum was written by Keynes himself.

But his authorship of much of it can be inferred from the fact that the section analysing Germany's capacity to pay reappeared in chapter 5 of *The Economic Consequences of the Peace*.[46]

While working on the indemnity memorandum Keynes prepared a scheme for the cancellation of war debts.[47] He suggested that at the opening of the Peace Conference Britain should propose to the United States the complete cancellation of inter-Allied war debt. Britain would also offer to forgo her share of reparations, which should be put at the disposal of the Conference for the assistance of the newly created states. Although we were on paper a net creditor, having lent £1,450 million to the Allies and borrowed £800 million from the United States, we would gain from cancellation. We should be giving up paper claims against the Allies, while being relieved of real debts to America. The proposal would impose some sacrifice on the United States which had loaned £1,670 million. This was mainly in the form of sound financial claims, because of American policy of lending to countries whose credit was relatively good, such as Britain and France. But America had emerged from the war richer and could better afford to make the sacrifice than Britain and the Allies.

When the proposal was considered at the Peace Conference in March 1919, Keynes emphasised the connection between the settlement of reparations and inter-Allied war debt. The demand for large indemnities against Germany was closely related to the heavy indebtedness of countries such as France and Italy. He argued that: 'A settlement of inter-ally indebtedness is, therefore, an indispensable preliminary to the peoples of the allied countries facing, with other than a maddened and exasperated heart the inevitable truth about the prospects of an indemnity from the enemy.'[48]

However, the Americans were not prepared to accept an outright cancellation of war debts. Within two weeks Keynes proposed a scheme for the issue of reparation bonds, guaranteed by both the enemy states and Allied governments.[49] The bonds would be issued by the enemy states with a present value of £1,500 million and yielding 4%. Allied governments would receive bonds worth £1,000 million as payment of the first instalment of reparations. They could be used to settle war debts, to provide collateral for international loans, or to finance much needed imports from Britain and the United States. But the scheme foundered when the Americans refused to guarantee interest on foreign debt and showed unwillingness to give further assistance to France and Italy. Both of Keynes's proposals proved unacceptable, but a minor concession was gained in the American agreement to remit interest on war debts for a period of three years. War debts and reparations were left to encumber post-war finance, confirming Keynes's view that 'the existence of the great war debts is a menace to financial stability everywhere'.

Early in 1919 Keynes suggested that the peg be discontinued and sterling be allowed to float.[50] He argued that some depreciation of the pound would be desirable when Britain was seeking to repay debts expressed in terms of sterling. Exports would be stimulated and imports retarded, while the burden of debt repayment would be reduced. 'If sterling is 10% depreciated, a given volume of exports goes 10% further than it would do otherwise in paying off this debt.' Recognising that depreciation must not be so great as to undermine confidence, he suggested that a duty of 10% be imposed on gold exports to limit the extent to which the currency could depreciate. Importers of gold would receive rebate certificates, conferring exemption from the duty, which could be sold to gold exporters. Gold up to the amount imported might be available to exporters at less than the official export price, if competition for the rebate certificates were not strong enough to maintain the 10% margin. A free market in gold would be re-established with the probable addition of a parallel market in rebate certificates. When, however, the exchange was freed in March 1919 gold exports were prohibited without the refinements of Keynes's proposal, and other measures were taken to restore the London gold market.[51]

Conclusion

By the end of the war in 1918 Keynes, still only thirty-six, had made a considerable reputation for himself in the Treasury. Under Chalmers and Bradbury he was responsible for much of the external finance of the war, including financial relations with America, and he worked directly with successive Chancellors of the Exchequer in this area. As he and his Division had done most of the initial work on reparations and Allied war debts it was natural that he should become the Treasury representative at the Peace Conference. His subsequent disillusion with the negotiations and resignation from the Civil Service are the subject of another chapter. His experience at Versailles was, however, to prove invaluable. It meant that as commentator and outside critic of official policies he had an unrivalled knowledge of the financial problems which were to hinder post-war reconstruction.

Keynes was highly perceptive in the analysis of situations, but he remained fairly conventional in the instruments of policy which he advocated. He urged the use of the interest rate to attract foreign balances to London and to encourage public subscriptions to War Loans. He did not favour the imposition of controls either on foreign exchange or in the domestic economy. He sought solutions in a market situation by influencing the market. A typical example of this was his advocacy of official intervention in the wheat market, not to effect bulk purchases, but to influence market sentiment.

His defence of the sterling–dollar peg did not arise from mere reverence for the gold standard. He believed that Britain could only finance her imports and fulfil commitments to the Allies with a fixed exchange rate. He had not changed his view in 1939 when he wrote of exchange management in the First World War: 'To have abandoned the peg would have destroyed our credit and brought chaos to business; and would have done no real good.'[52]

He applied Marshallian economics to the problems of the war economy, only extending the theory when a problem required it, as in his discussion of manpower and fiscal policy. In his numerous memoranda he appears as a practical and resourceful civil servant, ready with an ingenious proposal to solve almost any financial problem.[53]

NOTES

This chapter is based on *Collected Writings of John Maynard Keynes*, Vol. XVI, *Activities 1914–1919, The Treasury and Versailles*, edited by Elizabeth Johnson (London: Macmillan, 1971) and on the Keynes papers in the Marshall Library, Cambridge.

1. *Collected Writings*, Vol. XVI, p. 3.
2. *Ibid.*, pp. 7–15.
3. *Ibid.*, pp. 16–19.
4. E. V. Morgan, *Studies in British Financial Policy 1914–1925* (London: Macmillan, 1952), ch. I.
5. W. A. Brown Jr, *The International Gold Standard Reinterpreted 1914–1934* (New York: National Bureau of Economic Research, 1940), Vol. I, ch. I and II.
6. J. M. Keynes, 'War and the Financial System', *Economic Journal* (September 1914), and 'The Prospects of Money, November 1914', *Economic Journal* (December 1914).
7. *Collected Writings*, Vol. XVI, pp. 40–2.
8. *Collected Writings*, Vol. XV, *Activities and associated Writings: India and Cambridge, 1906–14*.
9. *Collected Writings*, Vol. XVI, p. 95.
10. *Ibid.*, p. 100.
11. *Ibid.*, p. 107.
12. J. M. Keynes, 'Review of I. Fisher, *The Purchasing Power of Money*', *Economic Journal* (September 1911).
13. A. Marshall, *Official Papers* (London: Macmillan, 1926).

14. E. Eshag, *From Marshall to Keynes: An Essay on the Monetary Theory of the Cambridge School* (Oxford: Basil Blackwell, 1963).
15. *Collected Writings*, Vol. XVI, p. 49.
16. *Ibid.*, p. 110.
17. *Ibid.*, p. 117
18. *Ibid.*, p. 125
19. D. Lloyd George *War Memoirs* (London: Ivor Nicholson and Watson, 1933), pp. 681–6.
20. Some figures may be helpful here.

Gross domestic product 1914–16 (1938 market prices; £ million)

	Consumers' expenditure	Government current expenditure	Gross investment (including stockbuilding)	Exports less imports	Gross domestic product
1914	3,560	530	354	182	4,626
1915	3,637	1,590	−118	−18	5,091
1916	3,335	1,810	−220	159	5,084

C. S. Feinstein, *National Income, Expenditure and Output of the United Kingdom 1855–1965* (Cambridge: Cambridge University Press, 1972), Appendix Table 5.
21. *Collected Writings*, Vol. XVI, pp. 184–8.
22. *Ibid.*, p. 167.
23. J. M. Keynes, *A Treatise on Money* (London: Macmillan, 1930), Vol. II, pp. 173–4.
24. J. M. Keynes, *How to Pay for the War* (London: Macmillan, 1940), p. 69.
25. *Collected Writings*, Vol. XVI, pp. 154–5.
26. *Ibid.*, pp. 67–74.
27. *Ibid.*, p. 189.
28. *Ibid.*, p. 187.
29. *Ibid.*, p. 213.
30. Morgan, *British Financial Policy*, Table 45.
31. *Ibid.*, pp. 344–59.
32. Brown, *International Gold Standard*, ch. III.
   M. Friedman and A. J. Schwartz, *A Monetary History of the United States 1867–1960* (Princeton: Princeton University Press, 1963), pp. 199–200.
   D. E. Moggridge, *British Monetary Policy 1924–1931* (Cambridge: Cambridge University Press, 1972), pp. 16–17.
33. *Collected Writings*, Vol. XVI, p. 140.
34. *Ibid.*, p. 149.
35. *Ibid.*, p. 185–6.
36. *Ibid.*, p. 197.
37. *Ibid.*, p. 210.
38. *Ibid.*, p. 221.
39. *Ibid.*, p. 250.

40. *Ibid.*, pp. 253–4.
41. *Ibid.*, pp. 274–85.
    Brown, *International Gold Standard*, p. 74.
42. *Collected Writings*, Vol. XVI, pp. 313–34.
43. R. F. Harrod, *The Life of John Maynard Keynes* (London: Macmillan, 1951), p. 230.
44. *Collected Writings*, Vol. XVI, pp. 338–43.
45. *Ibid.*, pp. 344–83.
46. J. M. Keynes, *The Economic Consequences of the Peace* (London: Macmillan, 1919), pp. 106–31.
47. *Collected Writings*, Vol. XVI, pp. 418–19.
48. *Ibid.*, p. 422.
49. *Ibid.*, pp. 429–31.
50. Keynes Papers T/7.
    Moggridge, *British Monetary Policy*, pp. 19–23.
51. Morgan, *British Financial Policy*, pp. 197–8.
52. *Collected Writings*, Vol. XVI, p. 211.
53. The author is grateful to D. E. Moggridge and E. A. G. Robinson for helpful comments on an earlier draft.

16

J. M. Keynes at the Paris Peace Conference

HOWARD ELCOCK

J. M. Keynes attended the Paris Peace Conference of 1919 as the chief representative of the British Treasury at the age of thirty-six. From the beginning he was uneasy about the atmosphere of the Conference, and he became increasingly disillusioned about the motives of its chief participants as it dragged on. Later, he was to write a polemical account of the Conference as bitter as it was brilliant, and above all he believed that Paris in 1919 was cursed with a miasma of deceit and hypocrisy which rendered vain all attempts to prepare a good or even a decent peace treaty.

> The word was issued to the witches of all Paris:
> > 'Fair is foul and foul is fair,
> > Hover through the fog and filthy air.'
> The subtlest sophisters and most hypocritical draftsmen were set to work, and produced many ingenious exercises which might have deceived for more than an hour a cleverer man than the President.[1]

Much later, Keynes recalled that in January 1919 'the feverish, persistent and boring gossip of that hellish place had already developed in full measure the peculiar flavour of smallness, cynicism, self-importance and bored excitement that it was never to lose'.[2] Keynes also examined the principal statesmen at Paris in brilliant, if unfair, portraits,[3] and summed up their relationship thus: 'The President, the Tiger and the Welsh witch were shut up in a room together for six months and the Treaty was what came out.'[4] He believed that the evils and follies of the Treaty were the result of the weaknesses in the characters of each of the 'Big Four' compounded with the nature of their relationship and the atmosphere in which they worked. In any consideration of the life of John Maynard Keynes, the part he played in an event which made so deep and lasting an impression on him deserves attention.

Keynes's interest in the peace which would follow the First World War was, of course, primarily a specialist one. He was concerned that after the war the economy of Europe should be able quickly to return to stability and thus the peoples of Europe be able to recover their former prosperity. He was concerned with the dynamic aspect of the economic settlement, that it should speedily allow trade and manufacture to revive and employment to grow; that this should happen was in the hands of the politicians who made the peace, especially in the size of the indemnity they demanded from Germany and the way in which it was extracted. In January 1916 he circulated a memorandum which he had prepared jointly with Sir W. Ashley in which they pointed out that the indemnity extracted by Germany from France after the Franco-Prussian War had damaged not only the loser but also the victor, since the payments had distorted Germany's balance of payments and her financial markets by producing an excess of paper money and securities not backed by real assets, which had led to inflation and a growth of unsound investment schemes whose collapse had brought about a financial crisis in Germany in 1873. Furthermore, if Germany were now to be asked to make good the damage wrought by her troops in France and Belgium, the effect would be to increase employment and prosperity in Germany herself, since large-scale employment and demand would be created; thus Germany might increase her prosperity more rapidly than the Allies. Clearly the question of how to extract an indemnity and reparations payments or work was an extremely complicated one if the victor powers were not themselves to suffer damage.[5]

As the war drew to a close, however, it increasingly became apparent that such a view was unlikely to be easily acceptable to many members of the government. British politicians were particularly anxious to secure vengeance and payment from Germany, and this was a principal theme in the General Election campaign in December 1918.[6] At this time Keynes prepared memoranda on the subjects of reparations and inter-Allied war debts. In the first,[7] he assessed the significance of the restrictions on Allied claims against Germany arising from President Wilson's speeches and from the Armistice terms,[8] and concluded that a claim for war costs was definitely excluded. In any case, Germany's capacity to pay would be limited, because of her exhaustion at the end of the war, the territorial losses she would suffer under the terms of the Peace Treaty, and the difficulty of extracting large sums without damaging the economies of the Allied powers. He assessed Germany's capacity to pay under four heads: immediately transferable wealth, raw materials, the probable value of property in ceded territory, and a series of annual payments, and concluded that whilst it might be possible to extract £3,000 million, it would probably not be prudent to extract more than £2,000 million. He pointed out that the more that was taken from Germany immediately in the form of

gold, raw materials and capital goods such as ships, railway loco-
motives and rolling stock, and industrial plant, the less could be
extracted from her in the future: 'If Germany is to be "milked" she
must not first of all be ruined',[9] and he also showed a rare appreciation of the human problems involved in the extraction of reparations:

It is ... generally supposed that if the whole of a man's surplus production
is taken from him, his efficiency and his industry are diminished. The
entrepreneur and the inventor will not contrive, the trader and shopkeeper
will not save, the labourer will not sweat and hasten, if the fruits of
their industry are set aside, not for the benefit of their children, their
old age, their pride, or their status, but for the enjoyment of a foreign
conqueror.[10]

Finally he warned again of the difficulty of transferring money
payments without damaging the victor powers: if Germany was to
make a trade surplus to pay reparations, she must be able to compete effectively in other countries, which would damage their
industries and reduce the employment available to their workers.
Thus moderation in the Allied claim for reparations would be both
prudent and humane.

Keynes's concern for post-war economic stability and development was also a dominant motive for his memorandum of November
1918 urging the cancellation of inter-Allied war debts.[11] He urged
that Britain should forgo her share of the indemnity in order that
it might be used to benefit the new states or for other purposes. He
pointed out that reparations claims were to some extent paper debts
in view of Germany's limited capacity to pay, whereas Allied debts
to America would have to be paid in real money; altruism on the
British part might encourage American generosity. This proposal
was dismissed at this time by Bonar Law as 'too altruistic at all
events till we see more clearly than at present what total sum it
would be possible for Germany to pay',[12] but would be revived later.

The extent of the claim for reparations became a cause of great
controversy within the British government. Keynes had urged
moderation on behalf of the Treasury and was supported by the
Board of Trade, but the War Cabinet had also established a committee under the chairmanship of William Hughes, the Australian
Prime Minister, to consider the reparations question, and in December 1918 this Committee presented a report to the Cabinet which
recommended that Germany should pay the Allies' entire war costs,
a sum of £24,000 million: Keynes had thought it prudent to extract
only £2,000 million. Keynes's biographer commented that the
Hughes report was 'written in total ignorance of the most elemen-

tary points'[13] especially on the question of the transfer of payments from Germany to the Allies:

In this utter nescience Hughes may not have been different from many other politicians of the time, who conceived of the indemnity simply in terms of writing a cheque for that amount and levying it upon citizens. The transfer problem was not envisaged. Keynes told them about it, but they turned a deaf ear.[14]

Unlike Keynes, Hughes, supported by Lord Cunliffe, the Governor of the Bank of England, was not prepared to recognise the danger to the Allied trade balances and to their prospects of prosperity and full employment inherent in a large claim; all that mattered was extracting as much money as possible from the defeated enemy. The Cabinet refused to resolve the dilemma posed by the differences between Keynes's views and those of the Hughes Committee, with the result that it divided the British delegation at Paris throughout the Conference.

When Keynes arrived in Paris in January 1919, there were more immediate problems awaiting solutions. Under the terms of the Armistice the Allies were maintaining their naval blockade of Germany, but had undertaken to supply food as necessary to the enemy.[15] The difficulty was how Germany was to pay for it. The Americans were not merely anxious but eager to feed Germany since they had a surplus of pig products which they wished to dispose of in this way: 'When Mr Hoover sleeps at night visions of pigs float across his bedclothes and he frankly admits that at all hazards the nightmare must be dissipated.'[16] The Americans wished to be paid for their surplus foods, but the French wished to block the use of Germany's liquid assets for such purposes in order that they might be available for reparations payments. In reply to President Wilson's plea in the Council of Ten that the Germans should be fed, the French Finance Minister, M. Klotz, said that he

... would appeal to President Wilson to consider also the question of justice. He was quite willing to admit that German foreign securities should be earmarked for this purpose. But they were creating a new German debt. There were other German debts which were just as honourable and noble. Therefore, he would ask, as a matter of justice, why Germany should pay for food in preference to paying off debts incurred for the restoration and for the reparation of damage committed elsewhere.[17]

Despite temporary agreement the French continued to obstruct the use of German foreign reserves to pay for food, partly because of what they saw as German deceit in delaying the surrender of their mercantile marine as required under the terms of the Armistice.

Keynes represented the Treasury at a number of meetings with German representatives at Trèves and Spa, at which methods of paying for food supplies were discussed, and at which it became evident that the only practicable and acceptable method of payment was to allow Germany to use part of her liquid assets for this purpose; the only other method the Germans suggested was a loan from the Allies, which Keynes and the other Allied representatives turned down as politically impossible.[18] During these meetings Keynes built up a friendly relationship with Dr Carl Melchior, one of the German delegates, which was later to assume some importance: at the meeting at Spa in February at which deadlock seemed inevitable on the issue of the surrender of the German merchant fleet, Keynes met Melchior informally, but to no effect. The Allied representatives decided that a dramatic rupture with the Germans was the only way to bring the food crisis to the attention of the 'Great Ones' in Paris and abruptly left Spa in the early hours of the morning of 5 March.[19]

The breakdown of negotiations had the desired effect. Keynes and his colleagues gained the attention of the principal statesmen at Paris, and Keynes himself pressed Lloyd George to overcome French opposition to the use of the gold in the Reichsbank to pay for food supplies: 'Everything turned on the gold ... I had got this clearly and definitely into the Prime Minister's head.'[20] What is not recorded either in Keynes's writings or in his published papers is that Lloyd George, Clemenceau and Colonel House had a preliminary discussion of the subject on 7 March, a day before the famous meeting of the Council of Ten at which Klotz was humiliated. (See below.) Indeed, the only record of this meeting of 7 March is to be found in Lloyd George's personal papers.[21] The question of German food supplies was one of the most hotly debated issues between Lloyd George and Clemenceau at this meeting, the former speaking of 'the deplorable condition of the German population and the danger of spreading Bolshevism unless Germany was fed', the latter dismissing German tales of suffering and of the increasing danger to the Government posed by the *Spartakusbund* as German propaganda designed to get food and a lenient peace.[22] No agreement was possible, and the following day the French renewed their opposition to the use of the German gold to pay for food in the Council of Ten, in a discussion arising out of the breakdown of the negotiations at Spa. The British representatives emphasised the danger of Bolshevism in Germany; the French wanted the gold for reparations and thought that the Germans should be compelled to work for their food; Clemenceau said that 'this was not an unreasonable request and it would be found to be in agreement with the teachings of Christianity'.[23] Lloyd George spoke of the reports he was receiving from the commander of the British army of occupation in Germany of the evident starvation of the people and the distress it was causing to his men. The French refused to yield. M. Klotz felt that to make the gold available to pay for food would destroy the incentive for the Germans to work and would 'use up all the funds which might eventually become available for the payment of reparations. This was what he objected to.'[24] At this point Lloyd George exploded with wrath; according to Keynes he had been 'working himself up, shaking himself and frowning as he does on these occasions'.[25] First he spoke of the honour of the Allies; then he turned on Klotz: in reply to Klotz's remarks he

... appealed to M. Clemenceau to intervene in the matter ... He would not have raised the matter, but for the fact that during the past few months in spite of the decision reached by the Supreme War Council in January last, obstacles had continually been put in the way, with the result that nothing had been done. He appealed to M. Clemenceau to put a stop to these obstructive tactics, otherwise M. Klotz would rank with Lenin and Trotsky among those who had spread Bolshevism in Europe.[26]

Keynes's memory of this speech and the impression it made on those present is worth quoting: of Klotz Keynes wrote: 'Lloyd George had always hated and despised him, and now saw that he could kill him. Women and children were starving, he cried, and here was M. Klotz prating and prating of his "Goold". He leant forward and with a gesture of his hands he indicated to everyone the image of a hideous Jew clutching a money-bag.'[27] When he concluded by coupling Klotz's name with the leaders of the Bolshevik Revolution in Russia, 'All round the room you could see each one grinning and whispering to his neighbour "Klotzky"'.[28] Clemenceau attempted to recover lost ground; France had been ravaged and ruined and 'she merely possessed a few pieces of gold, a few securities, which it was now proposed to take away in order to pay those who would supply food to Germany; and that food would certainly not come from France'.[29] Indeed not: the gold would be used to assuage Mr Hoover's nightmare about the American pig surplus. (See p. 165.) However, all he won was a provision that the Germans must agree to surrender their merchant ships before they were told that they could use their gold resources as collateral for the purchase of food supplies.[30] Once more the Allied representatives were despatched, this time to Brussels, to meet the Germans

The British delegation was led by the First Sea Lord, Admiral Wemyss, who was anxious lest the French block the agreement by a rigid insistence that the Germans must declare their intention immediately to surrender their merchant ships before they were given any word of the food agreement, a demand which the Germans, distrustful of Allied intentions, would almost certainly refuse to meet. Wemyss authorised Keynes to drop a hint privately to Melchior about the food agreement in order to ensure that there was no difficulty over the ships. As a result, the Conference proceeded without a hitch and the victualling of Germany began.[31] Keynes's friendship with Melchior had paid a dividend and meant that the demands of honour and humanity prevailed over French obstruction and obstinacy.

Keynes had played a major part in securing agreement to reasonable terms for the feeding of Germany; at the same time a far more major and serious crisis was brewing within the Peace Conference itself, namely, disagreement over the amount of reparations it was proper and possible to claim in the Peace Treaty. American and French positions were, of course, poles apart; the French wanted to claim the full cost of the war, which the Americans said was forbidden under the terms of the Armistice. Unfortunately, Keynes was not appointed to the Commission on Reparations established by the Peace Conference in Germany: the British representatives were Hughes and Cunliffe, who had prepared the report for the War Cabinet which recommended an enormous demand (see pp. 164–5) together with Lord Sumner, a Lord of Appeal who was to give legal advice, but was a third supporter of a severe demand. These British representatives supported the French to the exasperation of the Americans; on 25 February Keynes told Philip Kerr, one of Lloyd George's private secretaries and a confidant, that the chief representative of the American Treasury, Norman Davis, had expressed strong views as to the uselessness of the Reparations Commission, arising largely from the presence on it of Cunliffe and Sumner, whom he dubbed 'the Heavenly Twins': Davis had said, 'If we can wind down the Heavenly Twins by agreeing any fool report for the Three and then get rid of them by winding up the Commission we can get around with some human beings and start quite afresh.'[32] In February the Americans threatened to forgo any claim to reparations themselves, which would mean that no American help would be available to the Europeans to enforce the Reparations Chapter,[33] but in March the deadlock was still complete; Colonel House told his diary on 3 March that 'all our Commissioners, experts and economists tell of the same impasse and come almost hourly for consultations'.[34] American irritation at the apparently unlimited obstinacy of the Europeans in insisting on a large claim was to have its effect in other fields.

Keynes could play little part in these discussions; as British representative on the Supreme Economic Council he was concerned more with immediate economic problems such as feeding the Germans and restoring trade relations than with the drafting of the Treaty; he could only make his views known unofficially on occasions such as Foreign Office tea parties at the Hotel Majestic (the headquarters of the British delegation in Paris), and when he was consulted by Lloyd George.[35] The statesman faced the problems of inflamed parliamentary and public opinions, coupled with the extreme views of Hughes, Sumner and Cunliffe.[36] Nonetheless some members of the British government became anxious at the lack of progress, and in early March Keynes circulated a paper suggesting that the only way of escape was to leave the figures to be extracted undetermined in the Treaty. The amount should instead be determined by an inter-Allied expert Commission and should be related to the amount Germany could pay in thirty years, the period during which the generation of Germans that had been responsible for starting and prosecuting the war would be alive to suffer the consequences.[37] This was to be the solution ultimately adopted, though before this General Smuts and Lord Sumner persuaded first Lloyd George and then Wilson that it would be proper to include in the reparations demand pensions for the dependants of those killed in the war and for those disabled, and the separation allowances paid to the families of servicemen on active service during the war.[38] There was also an unseemly squabble between the British and the French over how to divide up the spoils.[39] At this stage, however, Britain and France seemed to be allied in favour of an extreme demand, against American pleas for moderation.

It was at this stage in the proceedings that Keynes revived his proposals that the inter-Allied war debts should be cancelled.[40] Since the Americans were the principal, indeed almost the sole, creditors they would be the chief losers and an exceptionally cooperative and generous spirit would be required of them, and for this the time was scarcely propitious. Nonetheless, Keynes argued that it was right to suggest it now, as it would remove an important European motive for insisting on making heavy reparation claims:

The question of inter-Allied indebtedness is closely bound up with the intense popular feeling amongst the European Allies on the question of indemnities – a feeling which is based not on any reasonable calculation of what Germany can, in fact, pay, but on a well-founded appreciation of the intolerable financial situation in which these countries will find themselves *unless* she pays.[41]

This was indeed an important problem for the Allies, especially for the French,[42] but Keynes's main concern was once more that Europe's economies should be able to return to stability and prosperity after the war; he feared that the payment of war debts would give rise not only to economic difficulties but also to political crises, both within European countries, where repudiation of these debts would 'soon become an important political issue'[43] and between debtor and creditor nations: 'A debtor nation does not love its creditor, and it is futile to expect feelings of goodwill from France, Italy and Russia towards this country, or towards America, if their future development is stifled for many years to come by the annual tribute which they must pay us.'[44] The scheme had much to commend it, but it was flatly rejected by the American delegation in Paris owing to fears that it would be impossible to secure the approval of Congress, and also to some extent as a result of American irritation at the British attitude on reparations. Keynes was forced to think again.

The problem now was to find a reparations proposal which all parties could accept. On 28 March Klotz proposed that the fixing of the Allies' total demands should be deferred to a later date, a proposal which Lloyd George enthusiastically accepted, saying that Keynes had already suggested this to him.[45] In particular, it would be a means of avoiding trouble in parliament, which was bound to follow the announcement of a moderate claim. When it came to details, however, a gap opened between the British and the French. The British wished to limit the demand to the amount the proposed Reparations Commission found that Germany could pay over a period of thirty years, while the French wanted to add up all that Germany owed, divide it into thirty instalments, and then, if Germany could not pay them, extend the period until all was paid.[46] The French position was vividly put by Klotz to the Council of Four: 'I recognise that it is highly desirable that Germany should be able to get herself out of debt in thirty years, but if this is impossible, we should not be the victims',[47] while Lloyd George and the Americans wished the Commission to consider Germany's capacity to pay within thirty years. The French were obstinate, with the result that President Wilson sent his famous telegram to Admiral Benson ordering the *George Washington* back to Brest so that he could walk out of the Conference.[48] In the end, the French reluctantly gave way, but Lloyd George was attacked in the House of Commons for being too lenient with the Germans, an attack to which he replied with a brilliant speech in his own defence. He also faced opposition from within his own delegation, notably from Hughes, who threatened to refuse to sign the Reparations Chapter of the Treaty. Lloyd George retorted bitterly: 'I quite understand

Plate 9   The philosopher G. E. Moore in 1899, aged 26.

Plate 10   Lytton Strachey and Duncan Grant at Charleston, 1922.

your attitude. It is a very well-known one. It is generally called "Heads I win, tails you lose".[49] However, Lloyd George's view prevailed and the scheme was substantially the one which Keynes had originally proposed.

If the amount Germany owed in reparations were to be left undetermined for a time, however, she would not be able to give any guarantee on the basis of which she could obtain credit to resume industrial investment and production. In any case, Europe was still in a desperate economic plight with starvation and unemployment rampant in many of its countries. One-third of the children of Vienna had to stay indoors because they were naked[50] while in Germany the only way people could keep warm in the evenings was to go to public places of entertainment – the middle classes to the opera or the theatre, the working class to political meetings, including those of the Spartacists, to which admission was free.[51] The trade and industry of Europe must be restarted as soon as possible, and having seen his proposals for inter-Allied debt cancellation rejected by the Americans, Keynes prepared a scheme for providing credit to restart industry; in a letter to his mother on 17 April he described it as 'a grand scheme for the rehabilitation of Europe'.[52] This proposal, which the Chancellor of the Exchequer, Austen Chamberlain, sent to Lloyd George with his approval on 17 April, was that the governments of the Central European powers should issue bonds, the largest proportion to be German bonds to the value of £1,000 million. The security backing those bonds was to be reparations and they should be guaranteed by the Allied and Associated Powers in agreed proportions, Britain, the United States and France each guaranteeing 20% of the bond issue.[53] In a covering letter to the statesmen at Paris drafted by Keynes, Lloyd George declared that 'the economic mechanism of Europe is jammed' and this would be a way to free it, coupled with an early lifting of the blockade of Germany and other measures.[54] On 23 April, Lloyd George sent the proposal to Wilson, urging that the assistance of governments was needed to revive Europe: 'The more prostrate a country is and the nearer to Bolshevism the more presumably it requires assistance. But the less likely is private enterprise to do it.'[55] Keynes's plan provided a fair and reasonable way for the victor powers to re-establish European credit.

Initial reactions by the American experts in Paris were apparently favourable, but when they asked the United States Treasury for authority to accept it, they met with strong opposition. Keynes informed his Treasury superiors early in May that the American Treasury have cabled many thousands of words of criticism and horror, and have formally interdicted Mr Davis and Mr Lamont from discussing any such question with us even in private conversation. Amongst the objections Mr Leffingwell has discovered that the scheme would require an alteration of the Constitution of the United States.[56]

On 3 May Wilson wrote to Lloyd George informing him that he must reject Keynes's proposal, partly because Congress would not approve the necessary legislation, but partly because of his impatience with European attitudes on the reparations issue; it was grossly improper for the European Allies to insist on taking away all Germany's working capital and then to ask the Americans to provide Germany with new capital.[57] The obstinacy of Hughes, Cunliffe and Sumner earlier in the Conference had so alienated the Americans that they would not now cooperate in assisting Europe to her feet.

Keynes was immensely dismayed by Wilson's reaction to his scheme, which, he told Philip Kerr, 'indicates a spirit far too harsh for the human situation facing us', and his embitterment can be seen in a letter to a friend in which he described the American reaction: 'They had a chance of taking a large, or at least humane view of the world, but unhesitatingly refused it'; he described Wilson himself as 'the greatest fraud on earth'.[58] In these letters we see the beginning of the bitter spirit of reproach which characterised Keynes's portrait of President Wilson in *The Economic Consequences of the Peace*. He continued unofficial conversations with the American experts in Paris, but to little effect, finding further evidence of American irritation at the Allied attitude to reparations: he commented of the American officials that

in fighting week after week preposterous demands on the part of ourselves and the French they have got into a habit of arguing and working in the interest of the enemy which is not likely to disappear in the future. So far as finance goes it is no exaggeration to say that the sympathies of the Americans are far more with the enemy than with any of us.[59]

In view of this, the Americans were not likely to prove cooperative on the Commission to be set up to assess reparations, or to assist in the rehabilitation of European credit.

At the same time as Keynes's scheme was being rejected, the Treaty as a whole became available for the first time. Like many others Keynes was appalled by the cumulative effect of its provisions, a feeling expressed by other members of the British delegation during May.[60] Harold Nicolson and Keynes both blamed Cunliffe and Sumner – 'the Twins' – for many of the Treaty's defects, and Keynes made up his mind to resign from the Treasury in protest.

He wrote to Austen Chamberlain on 26 May tendering his resignation but offering to stay on for another two or three weeks if it was decided 'to discuss the Treaty with the Germans with a view to making substantial changes'.[61] Lloyd George, moved by the protests of the German delegates at Versailles and others, made up his mind to demand concessions for them from his colleagues, obtained the support of the Imperial War Cabinet, and on 2 June told the other members of the Council of Four that unless the Treaty was modified Britain would not take part in a renewal of hostilities, or of the blockade of Germany, for which the Royal Navy was essential.[62] Keynes believed, however, that it was all too late; he wrote to his mother on 3 June that

The P.M., poor man, would like now at the eleventh hour to alter the damned Treaty, for which no-one has a word of defence, but it's too late in my belief and for all his wrigglings Fate must now march on to its conclusion,[63]

and on 5 June he wrote to Lloyd George telling him that he was 'slipping away from this scene of nightmare'.[64] Disillusion had turned to despair, and Keynes retired to Cambridge to prepare his attacks on the Treaty and its makers. The only subject upon which he was prepared to lecture at Cambridge in the following academic session was economic aspects of the Treaty,[65] and within three years he had published his criticisms of the Treaty and his proposals for its alteration[66] which were influential in turning people's minds, especially in Britain and America, against the Versailles Settlement.

The time has now come to attempt to sum up John Maynard Keynes's role at Paris. In 1919 he was thirty-six years old and still a comparatively junior member of the Treasury. He could not, therefore, expect to play a major role in the deliberations of the Conference and was mainly confined to specialist areas of its work, such as German trade and supplies on the Supreme Economic Council. Nonetheless, his briefings provided Lloyd George with the policies he adopted and pursued on the feeding of Germany and on reparations, and in both cases his proposals were substantially adopted. His plan for the rehabilitation of European credit was accepted by Lloyd George and Austen Chamberlain and was admired by some Americans, although collectively they turned it down; he thus achieved more than most men of his age at Paris in 1919. He was adept at briefing his superiors; as Dudley Ward recalled for Sir Roy Harrod, Keynes and Lloyd George were 'two master minds' who could cooperate 'to achieve what at first seemed quite impossible'.[87] His attitude to Lloyd George was ambivalent; he admired the Prime

Minister's fluency and ability in arguing a case, as when he over-
threw the French in the argument over the feeding of Germany on
8 March, but he disliked Lloyd George's fickleness and his predilection for informality and secrecy.[68] It was significant that he re-
frained from publishing his portrait of Lloyd George as 'the Welsh
Witch' with his portraits of Clemenceau and Wilson, in *The Economic Consequences of the Peace*, and indeed did not publish it until
1933. He admired Lloyd George's ability, but blamed him at the
end for the Treaty's defects: 'The Prime Minister is leading us all
into a morass of destruction,' he wrote to Austen Chamberlain at
the end of May: 'How can you expect me to assist at this tragic
farce any longer, seeking to lay the foundation, as a Frenchman put
it, "d'une guerre juste et durable".' His ideas and sentiments had
been heeded, but had not prevailed: he could not reasonably have
expected that they should, but that did not reduce his bitterness or
his sense of betrayal by his colleagues and his superiors. One cannot
read any of Keynes's writings on the Conference and its members
without a realisation of the depth of the emotions engendered in
Keynes by his experiences in Paris in the first six months of 1919.

NOTES

1. *The Economic Consequences of the Peace* (London, 1919), p. 47.
2. 'Dr Melchior: A Defeated Enemy' in *Two Memoirs* (London, 1949),
   pp. 12–13. The Memoir was probably read in 1931 or 1932.
3. For a discussion of these portraits see Howard Elcock, *Portrait of a
   Decision, The Council of Four and the Treaty of Versailles* (London,
   1972), pp. 1–3 and 305–22.
4. *Essays in Biography* (London, 1933), p. 34.
5. *Collected Writings of John Maynard Keynes*, Vol. XVI, *Activities
   1914–1919* (London, 1971), pp. 313–34.
6. See Elcock, *op. cit.*, p. 6.
7. *Collected Writings*, Vol. XVI, pp. 344–83.
8. See Elcock, *op. cit.*, for details of the Armistice terms and Wilson's
   attitude to them.
9. *Collected Writings*, Vol. XVI, p. 375.
10. *Ibid.*, pp. 376–7.
11. *Ibid.*, pp. 418–19.
12. *Ibid.*, p. 419.
13. R. F. Harrod, *The Life of John Maynard Keynes* (London, 1951),
    p. 230.
14. *Ibid.*, p. 231.
15. Elcock, *op. cit.*, p. 37.
16. Keynes to Sir John Bradley (Joint Permanent Secretary to the
    Treasury), 14 January 1919, *Collected Writings*, Vol. XVI, p. 394.

17. *Foreign Relations of the United States: The Paris Peace Conference, 1919* (Washington D.C., U.S. Department of State, 1943–7), Vol. IV, pp. 288–9.
18. *Collected Writings*, Vol. XVI, pp. 394–404; 'Dr Melchior', pp. 22–52.
19. 'Dr Melchior', pp. 48–52.
20. *Ibid.*, p. 55.
21. Lloyd George Papers: Beaverbrook Library F 147 1. See Elcock, *op. cit.*, pp. 142–6.
22. Elcock, *op. cit.*, p. 145.
23. *Paris Peace Conference*, Vol. IV, p. 283.
24. *Ibid.*, p. 290.
25. 'Dr Melchior', p. 56.
26. *Paris Peace Conference*, Vol. IV, p. 290.
27. 'Dr Melchior', p. 61.
28. *Ibid.*, p. 62.
29. *Paris Peace Conference*, Vol. IV, p. 290.
30. *Ibid.*, pp. 292–3.
31. 'Dr Melchior', pp. 63–7.
32. Quoted in Harrod, *op. cit.*, p. 236.
33. For a detailed account of the negotiations on reparations at this time, see Elcock, *op. cit.*, pp. 123–30.
34. Quoted in *ibid.*, p. 127.
35. Harrod, *op. cit.*, pp. 237–8.
36. See Elcock, *op. cit.*, p. 161.
37. Elcock, *op. cit.*, p. 128.
38. Harrod, *op. cit.*, pp. 255–65; Elcock, *op. cit.*, p. 173.
39. Elcock, *op. cit.*, pp. 160–2.
40. *Collected Writings*, Vol. XVI, pp. 420–8.
41. *Collected Writings*, Vol. XVI, p. 421.
42. Elcock, *op. cit.*, p. 129.
43. *Collected Writings*, Vol. XVI, p. 423.
44. *Ibid.*
45. Elcock, *op. cit.*, p. 172.
46. *Ibid.*, pp. 203–8.
47. Quoted in *ibid.*, p. 203.
48. *Ibid.*, pp. 204–5.
49. Lloyd George Papers: Beaverbrook Library F/28/3/27.
50. *Collected Writings*, Vol. XVI, p. 463.
51. Elcock, *op. cit.*, pp. 141–2.
52. Quoted in Harrod, *op. cit.*, p. 246.
53. *Collected Writings*, Vol. XVI, pp. 429–30.
54. Lloyd George Papers: Beaverbrook Library F/7/2/27; *Collected Writings*, Vol. XVI, pp. 431–6.
55. Lloyd George Papers: Beaverbrook Library F/7/3/34, Document 1.
56. *Collected Writings*, Vol. XVI, p. 438.
57. Lloyd George Papers: Beaverbrook Library F/7/2/34, Document 2. See Elcock, *op. cit.*, pp. 208–10.
58. Quoted in Harrod, *op. cit.*, p. 250.
59. *Collected Writings*, Vol. XVI, p. 453.

60. See Elcock, *op. cit.*, p. 25f. for a fuller discussion of reactions to the draft Treaty.
61. Quoted in Harrod, *op. cit.*, p. 25.
62. See Elcock, *op. cit.*, pp. 270–5 for details of Lloyd George's initiative.
63. Quoted in Harrod, *op. cit.*, p. 252.
64. *Ibid.*, p. 253.
65. Harrod, *op. cit.*, p. 286.
66. *The Economic Consequences of the Peace* appeared in 1919, and *A Revision of the Treaty* was published by Macmillan in 1922.
67. Harrod, *op. cit.*, p. 240.
68. See 'Mr Lloyd George' in Keynes's *Essays in Biography* (London, 1933), pp. 32–9; and 'Dr Melchior', p. 11.

17

Economic policy in the Second World War*

D. E. MOGGRIDGE

As in the First World War, the period of the second great war of this century saw Keynes deeply involved in the formulation of economic policy, at first as a semi-outsider, later as an official and rather irregular insider.

During the Second World War, Keynes's role differed considerably from that of his earlier wartime experience. In 1939 Keynes was by far the most distinguished economist of his generation, both within 'the profession' and amongst the larger public. (The latter fact is attested to by his mother's scrapbook collection for the period, which, despite the limitations imposed by his semi-official position for much of the time, was as large as that for the 1930s.) This public stature, plus the connections forged over previous years, gave Keynes much greater access to and opportunities to influence official and unofficial opinion.[1] On the other hand, during the Second World War, Keynes held no formal position in the official hierarchy beyond his membership of the Chancellor of the Exchequer's Consultative Council.[2] He was, in fact, cheaper than the American 'dollar a year man', for he received nothing for his services beyond his expenses for official missions abroad.

These changes from the 1914–18 arrangements meant that Keynes's forms of involvement during the 1939–45 war differed considerably from those of the earlier period: 'he was just "Keynes", free to shoot at anybody – and anybody, regardless of rank, was free to go to him with his troubles'.[3] Being 'just "Keynes"' had its advantages, of course, for it meant that he could, and did, take his troubles where they mattered. Thus, a matter might come to his attention from members of the Treasury, from friends and colleagues (both economist and non-economist) in other departments, from

* I should like to thank Austin Robinson and Susan Howson for useful comments on an earlier draft of this essay. In addition to the evidence presented here in the notes, more material on Keynes's Second World War activities will appear in Vol. xxii and xxiii of *Collected Writings of John Maynard Keynes*.

friends outside Whitehall, or from his own voracious (but often selective) reading of official papers from all sources. The result might be a volley of minutes (often supported by forthcoming or recently published articles in the *Economic Journal* or the press) directed at several in-trays, a word with a friend in high places that would lead to further enquiries from a higher level, or a personal letter. Thus, for example, Keynes's concern with developments in Anglo-Greek financial arrangements received a hearing through Brendan Bracken who took it up with Churchill; his concern with the growth of Indian sterling balances, and India Office unwillingness to consider the problem seriously, led to a conversation with Churchill in an informal setting and requests for full Cabinet discussion; and his unhappiness with the Beveridge coal rationing scheme (stimulated in part by Professor Lionel Robbins of the Cabinet Office) led to discussions with Oliver Lyttleton, the Minister of Production. Similarly, his connections with the National Institute of Economic and Social Research and his editorship of the *Economic Journal* brought the Madge social surveys to the attention of officials concerned with budgetary policy well before publication.[4] As a 'demi-semi-official'[5] Keynes was free to square other departments or politicians on emerging policies at a much earlier stage than normally – a practice followed, for example, with Lord Beaverbrook over the approach to the 1945 American loan negotiations.[6] As 'Keynes' he found himself regularly consulted by and consulting the American Ambassador Mr Winant and his adviser E. F. Penrose,[7] visiting American officials such as Harry Hopkins and Oscar Cox, journalists such as Walter Lippmann (many of whose letters on American conditions and opinion went via Keynes to senior officials and ministers), and foreign officials and ambassadors such as Mr Maisky. As 'Keynes' he could, and did, consult the General Council of the T.U.C. and leaders of opinion. The upshot was that, even more than in the 1930s, Keynes was very much a 'political' economist, whose influence, although it never matched the brilliance of his pen,[8] played a role unique in the annals of modern British economic policy.[9]

Keynes's views on the economic problems of the war and his influence on their solution are the subject of this essay. If only because the range of subjects that interested him in the six years of war and the eight months of peace following the war and preceding his death in April 1946 was vast, I must be selective.[10] All I can hope to do in this context is, by example, to give some of the flavour of the principles and practice of the wartime Keynes at work. To do this, I shall examine Keynes's activities in four areas: internal war finance, post-war internal economic policy, external war finance and post-war external economic policy. For these were his major concerns, despite his frequent forays elsewhere, and they provide us with a good indication both of his views and of his methods of getting them adopted.

I

Wartime financial policy is concerned with a rather limited range of general principles. Any policy proposal must satisfy, in various ways, four criteria: it must intensify the war effort of the nation by mobilising domestic resources for war and maintaining that mobilisation; it must increase the resources available by drawing, as far as possible, on unused resources at home and resources from abroad; it must make the burdens resulting from these transfers of resources from their normal uses as tolerable as possible; and it must minimise the complications of the war that spill over into the post-war world. All these criteria involve both action and persuasion, for what is possible within given limits, and even the limits themselves, depend on what is tolerable – on what public opinion in both its inner and outer forms believes just.[11] From the outset, Keynes involved himself in the problems of war finance on two fronts – maximising the possible under existing constraints and easing the constraints themselves.

Internal wartime finance

Keynes's contributions to discussions of the problems of wartime finance began well before the outbreak of the war in 1939. For more than two years previously, in the Committee on Economic Information of the Economic Advisory Council, in memoranda to ministers and officials, and in articles, broadcasts and letters to the press, he had discussed the economics of preparing for war – the economics, in Britain of the 1930s, of the movement towards full employment.[12] However, the outbreak of the war, which Keynes does not seem to have expected as late as 25 August 1939,[13] brought a rapid response, at first in a letter to *The Times* on loan policy,[14] and subsequently in the ideas of *How to Pay for the War* (1940). As the story of the evolution of these ideas and their tactics of presentation provide a classic example of Keynes the political economist at work, it is worth tracing the evolution and presentation in more detail.

Keynes first broached the ideas of *How to Pay for the War* in a talk on 20 October 1939, to the Marshall Society, the Cambridge undergraduate economics society, entitled 'War Potential and War Finance'. Four days later, he sent copies of his proposals, now entitled 'The Limitation of Purchasing Power: High Prices, Taxation and Compulsory Savings', to the editor of *The Times* (with whom he wished to place it as a single article), Sir John Simon (the Chancellor of the Exchequer), Mr Attlee, Sir Josiah Stamp, R. H. Brand and H. D. Henderson. On 27 October, he spoke to a dinner of officials, ministers and M.P.s, later circulating copies of the draft proposals to those interested. As a result of the ensuing discussions and comments, he modified his proposals, dropping, for example, the suggestion of guaranteeing the real value of compulsory savings because it might deflect subsequent discussion from his substantive proposals, before they appeared in *The Times* on 14 and 15 November 1939 under the title 'Paying for the War'. Between the appearance of the articles and the publication of his pamphlet *How to Pay for the War* at the end of February 1940, Keynes entered into extensive discussions with his supporters and his critics to make his scheme more generally acceptable. In particular, he directly (and indirectly through Professor Laski, G. D. H. Cole and Kingsley Martin) attempted to alter the scheme to make it acceptable to both Labour and trade union leaders, who had been unenthusiastic about the details of his original proposals, while convincing them of the soundness of his underlying principles.[15] Thus, for example, on 24 January he spent the morning with members of the Labour front bench, before going on in the afternoon to a committee of the General Council of the T.U.C. In the weeks that followed, he spoke to members of the House of Commons, the Fabian Society and the National Trade Union Club, and continued his discussions with fellow economists of all persuasions, City representatives and friends. As a result of this process of discussion, he introduced several modifications into his original scheme for deferred pay – family allowances, stabilisation of the prices of most basic articles of consumption and a post-war capital levy to repay the compulsory savings.

After publication, which coincided with a debate in the House of Lords that Keynes had arranged through Lord Balfour of Burleigh, and a broadcast on 11 March, Keynes continued to press for the adoption of his policy both privately and publicly. However, early May brought a change in tactics, as he told Clement Davies, a sympathetic M.P., on 3 May:

There is not the slightest hope of getting any useful attention at this stage. Things have clearly got to stew for a bit yet. ... I feel one must wait until the progress of events is making some new action obviously necessary.

At the present stage I believe there is a good deal to be said for concentrating on the inadequacy of the spending programme rather than the inadequacy of the fiscal programme. If we can get what is wanted in the former respect, the inadequacy of the latter will soon be shown up.

Keynes proceeded to do just that.

The German campaign in the West and the fall of France provided the necessary stimulus, bringing with them a sharp rise in expenditure. They also brought about the political crisis, the fall of Neville Chamberlain and the Cabinet changes which took Keynes into the Treasury as a member of the new Chancellor Sir Kingsley Wood's Consultative Council and unofficial adviser. Once within the Whitehall machine, with the new ministers and climate prepared by his previous persuasion and the turn of events, Keynes was extremely successful in gaining official acceptance of his principles and methods of analysis, if not his exact proposals. The 1941 budget, which dominated subsequent wartime financial policy, was Keynesian in inspiration and presentation.

So much for the background, which shows Keynes the 'political' economist at his prime. What of the principles involved? Throughout the discussions after the outbreak of the war, Keynes's main concern was with the best method of transferring resources from peacetime to wartime uses, especially from consumption.[16] Before the outbreak of war, this had not been a problem, as the authorities had been able to draw on previously unused resources to meet both the needs of rearmament and the multiplier repercussions of the increased government expenditure. In those circumstances, Keynes's main concern had been on ensuring that the financial market implications of the expansion of demand and its financing did not upset the long-term policy of cheaper money which he believed necessary for the economy.[17] War, however, made the problem of transferring resources acute, for not only would the war effort require any remaining increases in output but it would also require real resources that would normally be devoted to other uses, particularly consumption. From Keynes's point of view, the authorities could gain command of the additional resources from consumption in four ways:[18]

(1) Individuals could voluntarily reduce their consumption expenditure and directly or indirectly make their savings available to the authorities by taking up loans or idle balances.

(2) Inflationary official policies could bid resources away from those who might use them and place them in the hands of those who would pass them on to the authorities either through profits taxation or through voluntary savings.

(3) A policy of comprehensive rationing could reduce consumption by fiat.

(4) Increased taxation could reduce the resources available to the public for consumption and transfer them to the authorities.

Given the sums involved and the consequent need for a sharp rise in the average (and marginal) propensity to save, especially among groups that had not previously saved much, Keynes believed that voluntary savings would not provide the resources required for the successful prosecution of the war without inflation. However, although inflation might prove effective up to a point in reducing consumption, after this point further price rises would lead, with a lag, to offsetting wage claims. Given the likely lags, prosecution of the war through this means of finance would necessitate substantial and *continuous* price rises.[19] As for rationing *by itself* as a means of restricting consumption, Keynes believed that it would prove much too restrictive of personal choice and therefore give rise to dissatisfaction, that it would prove socially divisive as those with higher incomes could get round any less than comprehensive scheme, and that the complexities of a comprehensive scheme (in the days before the idea of points rationing had become common)[20] would prove too great an administrative burden at a time when the object of any measure was to release the maximum volume of resources for wartime purposes.

Thus by elimination Keynes found fiscal measures at the centre of his wartime financial vision. Through taxation, the authorities would take command over current resources from present income earners for wartime purposes. A portion of such command over resources, credit to the taxpayer as post-war deferred pay, would be released to expand consumption in the first post-war slump. The deferred pay scheme and the release of credits financed by a capital levy after the war would ensure a more equitable distribution of wealth after the war than would the voluntary savings or inflationary methods of war finance.

At the same time, a scheme of subsidies on the basic articles of consumption, largely subject to rationing, would stabilise the basic demands on family budgets, and, along with family allowances, provide for an element of social justice during the war. This set of arrangements, with the assistance of rationing, of inessential consumption and voluntary savings, would provide the resources from personal consumption to wage total war successfully, while physical and financial controls would restrict unnecessary wartime investment.

Keynes's proposals lay at the heart of the policy eventually adopted by the authorities, as did his macroeconomic method of analysing the extent of the problem and the impact of particular measures. After the 1941 budget, the first British budget cast in an explicit macroeconomic rather than a Treasury accounting sense, Keynes spent the rest of the war attempting to improve on the details of his fiscal vision, not always with success,[21] until the prospects of peace turned him towards proposals designed to ease the eventual transition.[22] It is significant that on the day of his death he was engaged in writing a memorandum on budgetary policy designed to continue the transition to normal conditions rather than engaged on some of his other activities, for the Keynesian approach to public finance represents perhaps his most enduring contribution to the conduct of public affairs.

One of the implications of the fiscal and strict exchange control policies adopted by the authorities after 1939 was that the rate of interest was not expected to play either of its 1914–18 roles of transferring real resources to the authorities from residents and foreigners holding short-time sterling balances. Keynes's views on the rate of interest in the 1930s, in both his more formal academic writings and his policy advice and public persuasion, which encouraged a policy of long-term interest rates and attacked the rise in rates that official passivity and post-1932 funding had engendered, proved remarkably influential in creating a climate of opinions which made war and cheap money seem compatible to the authorities even before he entered the Treasury.[23] However, Keynes's arrival in the Treasury, after market expectations of continuing cheap money had been disturbed by the brief doubling of bank rate at the outbreak of war and the relative failure of the first large war loan, toughened the Treasury's nerves as regards cheap money and encouraged it to groom the market for better terms from a Treasury point of view with each successive issue, thus keeping up the demand for debt and encouraging expectations of lower long-term interest rates after the war. In addition, Keynes's understanding of the determinants of the structure of interest rates[24] encouraged the Treasury to tailor its available issues to market preferences to ensure the structure of rates consistent with the Treasury's longer-term policy goals. This concern was to carry itself over into Keynes's proposals for post-war monetary policy, as was his view of the role of financial controls.[25]

External wartime finance

Soon after the outbreak of war, Keynes also became involved in discussions of external financial policy, sending the Treasury a memorandum on exchange control policy, the Ministry of Economic Warfare a memorandum on financial aspects of the blockade against Germany, and drafting a memorandum intended for President Roosevelt, which never found use owing to the pressure of events, on America's financial role in the war.[26] After the publication of *How to Pay for the War*, Keynes returned to this area, arguing that a more effective exchange control policy was necessary to conserve Britain's overseas assets for the prosecution of the war. Thus even before he entered the Treasury, Keynes had developed a set of principles which he proceeded to apply as cases arose. The principles and their application often bore the stamp of bitter experience, for in many of his memoranda and minutes on external financial matters 'last time' often came in as a justification for avoiding or undertaking certain courses of action.[27] Briefly summarised, the principles were:

(1) Through an effective exchange control, Britain should husband her exchange reserves and other external assets for use in obtaining wartime resources. Careful overseas purchasing policy would further assist this policy's effects.

(2) The adverse post-war consequences of any wartime sale of foreign assets under (1) should be minimised.

(3) Britain should try to obtain access to the maximum volume of foreign resources from sterling area countries and elsewhere, again taking care to minimise the post-war consequences and consequent liabilities.

(4) In her economic warfare against the enemy, Britain should encourage financial as against physical measures. In particular, as it was unlikely she could prevent the enemy using its foreign assets, she should through pre-emptive buying, price policies, and other controls attempt to ensure that the enemy authorities were 'tempted' to waste their resources on inessential or very expensive products. At the same time, through similar policies, Britain should minimise the financial gains possible from enemy exports.

Keynes's policy as regards 'temptation' of the enemy was rejected at the outbreak of war.[28] All of the other principles found ready adoption. Within the limits of the space available in this essay, only a few examples are necessary.

By the time Keynes entered the Treasury, to some extent as a result of his agitation (through memoranda and speeches on his part, as well as his encouraging sympathetic M.P.s to ask questions in the House), most of the gaps in Britain's foreign exchange controls had disappeared. Those which had not were the subject of one of Keynes's first memoranda on entering the Treasury. Subsequent discussion at the Exchange Control Conference, set up to consider the memorandum and take action to it and similar questions as they arose later, closed many of the remaining gaps. In addition, the fall of France and the hope (which Keynes had shared from the outbreak of war) that the United States would come to Britain's aid in solving the external financial problem had led to the abandonment of the principle that Britain's external assets would have to last a three-year war, if only because Britain's survival was at stake.

Thus Keynes's first eighteen months at the Treasury, despite the passage of the Lend–Lease Act in March 1941, were more often concerned with finding foreign assets to keep the British war effort afloat than in conserving them.[29] A counterpart to this process was the attempt to minimise the post-war consequences of any use of current assets to finance the war effort. Even before he had entered the Treasury, Keynes had attempted to convince Samuel Courtauld to use the assets of Courtauld's American subsidiary, American Viscose Corporation, as security for a dollar bond issue, the proceeds of which would accrue to the Treasury. Such an issue would provide the British authorities with dollars while leaving Courtaulds in control of the firm and make attempts to force a sale unattractive.[30] Despite his failure to get a positive response from Courtaulds on this occasion, Keynes continued to press the alternative of borrowing against existing assets, in particular direct investments, as against outright sale, both before and after Mr Morgenthau's announcement of his intention to insist on the sale of such assets prior to the receipt of Lend–Lease aid. Keynes's emphasis on this alternative, which maximised the value of such assets, given the importance of trade connections, patents and other intra-firm links, was not entirely successful, as the 'show sale' of American Viscose at a knockdown price indicates.[31] However, the repeated suggestion of this alternative created a climate of opinion in London that made it possible to float the idea in informal discussions with American officials in London early in 1941. These discussions, along with later discussions in Washington, some of which involved Keynes during his visit in the summer of 1941, resulted in two large pledges of British assets as security for American loans, thus raising over $425 million for Britain at a crucial stage of the war.[32] Similarly, Keynes's repeated emphasis on the undesirability of Britain's being stripped of all her foreign assets and thus being open to American pressure as to the shape of her overseas commitments helped, along with the views of other Treasury advisers and officials, to prevent the sale of many sterling-denominated overseas assets to the United States in the dark days of the autumn of 1940, when Britain was perpetually 'scraping the bottom of the box' while carrying on the war alone.

This continual concern with the post-war consequences of wartime acts and agreements permeated Keynes's advice in other areas. It saw him successfully urge the refusal to grant a large dollar loan to Newfoundland; attempt to guide the negotiations with France and other European allies (who had come through the war with substantially larger gold and foreign exchange reserves in relation to their liabilities) so that the post-occupation payments agreements minimised the volume of credit granted by Britain and maximised the gold payments she received; it saw him negotiate a transition through Stage II Lend–Lease (the period after the defeat of Germany but prior to the defeat of Japan) which would allow Britain to use her available foreign resources to maximise her export potential while using American aid to meet other needs; and temper Britain's post-war commitments to her prospective post-war position.

Almost inevitably, the concern with Britain's post-war position involved Keynes in discussions of the problems of Britain's growing sterling indebtedness to various parts of the world. From the beginning of his period of wartime Treasury service he had been concerned with the problem, but at first it took the form of worrying about accumulations of sterling by 'allies' such as Greece and China, who demanded assistance in forms that would leave them with large post-war sterling assets.[33] Keynes opposed such arrangements, unless the sums involved were in purely 'psychological' rather than usable sterling, However, the initial lack of concern with wartime sterling area balances was not peculiar to Keynes, for even as late as January 1942 some senior Treasury officials were still worried about the possibility that India might end the war with insufficient sterling balances for normal trade, despite already substantial Indian reparation of the sterling securities.[34]

It appears from the papers that Keynes's concern with the potential problems of post-war sterling area balances nevertheless antedated that of his Treasury colleagues. For prior to the comment cited above, Keynes was writing to R. F. Kahn, then Economic Adviser to the Minister of State in the Middle East, about the growing problem of Egyptian sterling balances which he suggested had not received adequate attention in either the Treasury or the Bank of England.[35] From January 1942, moreover, Keynes's concern with the problem of sterling area balances showed itself in a long series of proposals to reduce the rate of growth of such balances or so to immobilise them that they would not threaten Britain's post-war external position. These proposals covered all sterling area countries in various ways,[36] but their major concern was the position in the two largest areas of difficulty, India and the Middle East.

As regards India, an early Keynes-inspired Treasury attempt to raise the problem with the India Office and obtain a revision of Britain's financial arrangements for the Indian Army or other measures failed. Keynes then attempted to raise the issue above the interdepartmental level. He mentioned the matter to Mr Churchill, probably at a meeting of the Other Club on 16 July 1942, with the result that the Prime Minister asked the Chancellor for the facts and put the matter on the agenda of the War Cabinet. The subsequent Cabinet discussions lasted much of the summer, but given India Office (and Indian) reactions to Treasury proposals, the Cabinet (and the Treasury) agreed to drop the matter for the time being, despite an Indian offer of some minimal assistance. In the end, Keynes's advocacy of this course of action within the Treasury, in the hope of a more comprehensive settlement later, probably cost Britain £100 million in additional post-war debt.[37]

For the rest of the war, the Treasury, largely at Keynes's and Lord Catto's instigation, attempted to get agreement on other means of immobilising the balances through various devices. However, nothing came of the various proposals, beyond a general agreement in some sections of the Treasury[38] that the Indian, Middle Eastern and other sterling balances would be funded, written off or released in various proportions. The only major bite into the balances came through gold (and silver) sales at premium prices on bazaar markets designed to attract idle balances previously hoarded in commodities, thus reducing inflationary pressures while financing local currency expenditures by the British (and Americans) at little cost to the British gold and foreign exchange reserves. Although the proposals for gold sales did not come from Keynes directly,[39] when Britain's reserves could stand the strain, particularly while the Lend–Lease authorities were worried about the growth of Britain's reserves while considering their materials allocations, he repeatedly pushed for an experiment. The result was one of the most successful experiments in war finance, which for the expenditure of £55 million from the reserves directly reduced sterling balances by £99 million and probably indirectly reduced them further, as the sales increased economic stability in the areas concerned by reducing inflation and restoring confidence in the local currency (thus increasing currency hoarding and allowing the authorities to obtain increased resources in a non-inflationary manner through credit expansion). Thus, although Keynes's efforts to deal with sterling on a large scale during the war came to nought, his concern for the post-war consequences of wartime policy did have some important effects.

II

However, Keynes's concern with the post-war world did not cease with a consideration of the possible post-war consequences of policies related to the maximisation of the war effort. Even in *How to Pay for the War* Keynes went well beyond what was necessary for the purposes of wartime financial policy. Keynes also took the opportunities his position in the Treasury gave him to ensure that the shaping of the post-war world would see positive steps to avoid a disastrous repetition of the economic events of the inter-war years. From 'Proposals to Counter the German "New Order"' in the autumn of 1940 to his efforts at Savannah in 1946, Keynes was continuously and heavily involved in preparations for an improved post-war world.

Internal post-war financial policy

Keynes's influence on the development of post-war internal economic policy in Britain emerged most clearly in three directions: the methods of analysis used in assessing the impact of various post-war policies, the 1944 White Paper on Employment Policy, and the 1945 National Debt Enquiry.

After he had successfully introduced the apparatus into budget discussions in 1940/41, Keynes's macroeconomic approach to many economic problems came to be used in other areas of policy formation. Initially, the users tended to work from the supply side only, but under the pressure of Keynes's increasing optimism as to the level of demand during the transition they turned to consider both sides of the relationship.[40] Such estimates of post-war incomes and activity came to be used extensively in enquiries such as the Treasury's and Economic Section's evaluation of the Beveridge proposals prior to their publication, for they provided the authorities with a crude view as to what the nation could 'afford' in the post-war world, given other claims upon resources. One result of the Beveridge discussions was a series of representations to Beveridge by Keynes, Professor Robbins and the Government Actuary, which led to a marked trimming of the original Beveridge proposals in the drafting stage.

However, the most frequent use of Keynesian types of analysis came in discussions of post-war employment policy. From *How to Pay for the War* onwards, Keynes was convinced of the need to avoid repetition of Britain's inter-war experience. The permanent Treasury officials, however, perhaps partly because of inter-war experience and partly as a result of the absence of Sir Frederick Phillips, the most 'Keynesian' of the senior officials, in America for most of the time after 1940, were generally pessimistic as to post-war prospects.[41] One senior official even went to the length of asking J. E. Meade of the Economic Section in 1941 about the Section's attitude towards a policy of post-war deflation.

In these circumstances, it is, perhaps, surprising that Keynes did not push on his own for a more active approach to the problems of post-war employment. However, given his other extremely time-consuming preoccupations, Keynes apparently believed such an effort was unnecessary. This belief seems to have rested on four premises: a successful post-war employment policy, unlike, say, social security policy, required little in the way of concrete planning and even less in terms of actual legislation; such a policy would depend heavily on Britain's post-war external position; the necessary ingredients for such a policy were under consideration in various reconstruction committees, even if these were not specifically directed to the employment problem; and unemployment would not be the problem facing the authorities for several years after the war.[42]

As a result of Keynes's relatively minor involvement, the early Treasury documents for the Committee on Post-war Internal Economic Problems were the work of H. D. Henderson, one of the Treasury's leading pessimists as to the possibility of providing any solution to the problem of employment in the post-war world.[43] It was the Economic Section, in particular James Meade, which provided the impetus from 1941 onwards. Granted Keynes used his considerable influence to ease the passage of certain proposals, in particular Meade's counter-cyclical variations in social insurance contributions, which he pushed to inclusion in the Beveridge report, the 1944 White Paper on Employment Policy and the 1944 White Paper on Social Insurance. However, within the Treasury, he appears to have felt that he need do no more than prevent major Treasury blunders as officials drafted meliorative replies, one of which Keynes characterised as 'not much more than Neville Chamberlain disguised in a little modern fancy dress',[44] to successive activist Economic Section papers for official committees, while preventing the Economic Section documents themselves from becoming too academic.[45] When, however, the Steering Committee on Post-war Employment reported early in 1944, Keynes welcomed the document, despite its Treasury sections with their 'air of having been written some years before the rest of the report', as representing 'a revolution in official opinion'. Proclaiming that 'theoretical economic analysis has now reached a point where it is fit to be applied', he foresaw 'a new era of "Joy through Statistics"' as the policy came into operation.[46]

Nevertheless, even after this welcome, Keynes's drafting contributions to the White Paper which followed were minimal, largely one suspects because of his contemporaneous involvement in an extensive official and ministerial debate on post-war economic policy and his illness during March and April 1944, the period of most extensive drafting. However, two comments to outsiders towards the end of the war seem to indicate the point his own thinking had reached:[47]

189

No harm in aiming at 3 per cent unemployment, but I shall be surprised if we succeed [owing to the openness of British economy].

It may turn out, I suppose, that vested interests and personal selfishness may stand in the way [of a successful full employment policy]. But the main task is producing first the intellectual conviction and then intellectually to devise the means. Insufficiency of cleverness, not of goodness, is the main trouble.

Interestingly enough, Keynes's most substantial contribution to the working out of the post-war employment policy came in the area of monetary policy. For when, in response to a request from Mr Attlee for an investigation of a post-war capital levy, the Treasury agreed to a National Debt Enquiry Committee with wide-ranging terms of reference, Keynes became a member.[48] As with the Macmillan Committee fifteen years before, Keynes dominated much of the proceedings, giving evidence on monetary and debt managment policy for three meetings before submitting his own proposals. These proposals were incorporated by Sir Richard Hopkins into the Committee's first report, which went to the Chancellor in May 1945.[49] In fact, Keynes's recommendation of a post-war cheap money policy incorporated in the report can be regarded as the basis of Dr Dalton's post-1945 experiments, even if one wonders whether Keynes would have approved of the tactics.[50]

External post-war policy

Keynes's contributions to official discussions of post-war external economic policy centred around the creation of the Bretton Woods Institutions (the International Monetary Fund and the World Bank), a scheme for the international regulation of primary product prices, Britain's post-war commercial policy, and Allied reparations policy.[51] As the first three subjects have received extensive discussion elsewhere, detailed discussion seems unnecessary here (beyond a brief look at the principles involved).[52] However, Keynes's involvement in discussions on the last subject are much less well known, despite its links with his 1914–19 and inter-war concerns, and is thus worth a more extended discussion.

Between the beginning of the war and his entry into the Treasury, Keynes did not give much thought to the shape of the post-war international economy. However, at the end of 1940 a request from Mr Eden for a statement in reply to Germany's plans for a New Order in Europe, eventually used in a speech at the end of May 1941, led Keynes to give the issues more thought. The resulting 'Proposals to Counter the German "New Order"' provide a good indication of the shape of the specific plans followed.[58] The proposals set out the following principles:

(1) Friendly collaboration with the United States was essential in the creation of a better post-war world, as she was the only country likely to have the means to make many plans come to fruition and as her size and wealth would make any solution that lacked American support almost unworkable.

For Keynes this principle carried with it two corollaries:

(a) It was an advantage for Britain to initiate ambitious schemes for many facets of the post-war world, for such schemes would stimulate the Americans to develop counter-proposals for international collaboration and, over time, to commit themselves to such principles. If this commitment did not come and the Americans rejected a course of international collaboration, they would feel obliged to support alternative British proposals for a less internationalist solution.

(b) In most cases, even after putting forward a set of proposals, British negotiators would have considerable room for manoeuvre in subsequent discussions, if only because one of the primary goals of the negotiators was American collaboration.

(2) Any post-war international currency arrangements would depart markedly from the *laissez-faire* practices of the period 1920–33.

(3) Within a framework that maximised national autonomy, measures and institutions to prevent wild fluctuations in employment, prices and markets would be necessary.

(4) Post-war institutional arrangements for currency and demand management would be compatible with extensive international trade and equal access for all to the markets of the world.

(5) There would be organised relief and reconstruction aid for post-war Europe.

This framework of ideas served Keynes well in all the subsequent discussions of post-war international economic arrangements. In the eighteen months after their original drafting, Britain produced plans for post-war currency arrangements, commodity policy and international trade. Behind the first two plans was the pen of Keynes, while the third was the work of James Meade. In all three cases, Keynes took an active part in the departmental and inter-departmental discussions, which, along with preliminary consultations, preceded their presentation to the Americans in the course of 1942 and 1943, arguing powerfully for a multilateral, internationalist, solution to the problems involved rather than the Imperial, bilateral arrangements favoured by others. Throughout these discussions, however, Keynes remained sceptical of merely doctrinaire principles, wherever they emerged, getting himself into considerable hot water with the Americans and some of his colleagues in other departments as a result.[54] Throughout the discussions, Keynes also made it clear that the extent of his concessions to *laissez-faire* principles depended almost entirely on the arrangements made to solve Britain's problems during the transition from war to peace, for, without an adequate solution to these, Britain would be unable, after the losses of the war, to accept the risks of an international economy organised on liberal lines.

However, getting the British plans to the Americans represented only the first stage in the process of shaping the post-war world. There followed lengthy international negotiations, on these and on the American proposals on investment and reconstruction, with frequent delays to allow ministers to give their blessings to the progress so far. On the British side, these periods between bouts of negotiation normally required Keynes and others who supported his type of post-war arrangements to reargue the case for liberal multilateral international settlements in place of the bilateral, sterling area-based arrangements for trade, currency and commodities favoured by some Treasury officials, several ministers and the Bank of England. The further the negotiations got, the more gruelling these intervening periods became, as those who opposed the evolving consensus realised they had fewer remaining opportunities to prevent its realisation. Thus between December 1943 and May 1944 Keynes was continuously involved in discussions on the International Monetary Fund. At one stage, he conveyed the situation to a colleague who was ill as follows:[55]

It is absolutely impossible to keep you up to date with the comings and goings here. It has been a complete bedlam, which only Hoppy's [Sir Richard Hopkins] calm hand keeps in any sort of order. Ministers are in perpetual session, driving one another crazy with their mutual ravings, the Beaver [Lord Beaverbrook] being mainly responsible, his approach and mentality being nothing short of criminal.... Ministers have now left Currency for Commercial Policy, and, as you may suppose, confusion is still worse compounded.

The next year saw another session involving commercial policy, the International Monetary Fund, and the terms of the British approach to the Americans for transitional assistance, while the last three months of 1945 saw another period of dispute as the terms of the loan negotiations and the commercial policy settlement became clearer.

Again, Keynes's personal letter to a colleague best sets the stage:[56]

The ignorance was all-embracing. So far as the public was concerned, no-one had been at any pains to explain, far less demand, what had been done. And as for the insiders, so dense a fog screen had been created that such as the Chancellor and the Governor of the Bank had only the dimmest idea of what we had given away and what we had not. . . .

However, the ignorance was not the real trouble – I suppose that is normal among the great, and inevitable and indeed quite proper among the public. Both political parties were split on issues which had nothing to do with the technical details; and both sets of party leaders decided that a complete abdication of leadership would be the happiest way out. A section of the Socialists thought they detected too definite a smell of *laissez-faire*, at any rate of anti-planning . . . At any rate, it was easy to argue that, as extreme versions of foreign trade planning through barter agreements were ruled out, our policy was no better than a specious revival of nineteenth century liberalism.

A section of the Conservatives, led by Max [Beaverbrook] and supported by others too near to Winston [Churchill], were convinced, with some reason, that the proposed Commercial Policy ruled out Preference as a serious, substantial policy for the future; and that this, taken in conjunction with the opening of the Sterling Area, doomed the idea of an Empire economic bloc. It annoyed them, of course, to have me pointing out that the Empire in question would not include Canada (or possibly South Africa) and would have to be built on the British loyalty and goodwill of India, Palestine, Egypt and Eire.

By Keynes's death in April 1946, agreement on the American loan, the International Monetary Fund and a draft outline on commercial policy had been reached. However, the attitudes that underlay the disputes of the previous years undoubtedly survived him, complicating the settlement of such issues as the post-war sterling balances.

Keynes's involvement in the issues surrounding the post-war treatment of Germany and her Allies had begun with his 'Proposals to Counter the German "New Order"'. There, in the first draft, he suggested Allied post-war policy should be to rebuild the German economy so it could play its usual role in the economic life of central Europe. If the Allies did not do so, he argued, the only alternative dominant power in the area was the Soviet Union. In these circumstances, he advocated no punitive post-war economic settlement, a policy which had obvious implications for reparations policy.[57]

However, it was another year before reparations issues began seriously to occupy him. At first, Keynes's efforts were directed towards persuading ministers and officials to agree to provide the officials involved in this area of post-war planning with a series of general principles through their answers to a series of questions, which carried the following general rider: 'The chief thing that matters is that Ministers should not suppose that the chief thing that matters is to avoid the mistakes made last time.'[58] This attempt to stimulate discussion fell rather flat, and as far as one can gather, beyond some informal official discussions nothing happened until the end of August 1942, when Dr Dalton circulated a memorandum on the subject to his colleagues. This memorandum, after some discussion, led to the setting up of an Interdepartmental Committee on Reparations and Economic Security (the Malkin Committee). Keynes and Edward Playfair were the Treasury representatives on the Committee during its thirty-eight meetings between November 1942 and August 1943.[59]

In the course of the Committee's discussions Keynes clearly set out the principles. which he thought should govern future policy, successfully convincing his colleagues in the process. His approach to the problem made a threefold distinction between restitution, occupation and relief costs, and reparations. He saw the end of the war would bring a return of looted property, where identifiable, and a clearing up of all pre-war and wartime financial relationships and commitments through what was effectively an act of bankruptcy on the part of the enemy. During the period of occupation that would follow, the first charge on Germany would be local occupation and relief and reconstruction expenses. During this period, which he assumed would be relatively short, the Allies, if they did not reduce Germany's standard of living below a stipulated level or impair, disproportionately to their value, Germany's productive capacity, could receive deliveries of stipulated goods and services in kind up to a predetermined maximum amount. Of course, the occupation, relief and rehabilitation expenses might make such deliveries completely impossible within the limitations proposed. After the occupation, the Germans, who would be unable to have their own armed forces under the peace treaty and would therefore avoid the burden of defence expenditure, should contribute through an export levy to the defence and peacekeeping costs of the world as undertaken by the great powers or an international agency.[60] This framework served the Committee well in its discussions and underlay its report of 31 August 1943.[61] Keynes used the report as the basis for a long talk to American officials concerned with post-war problems, during his 1943 visit to America, despite the Cabinet's objections to his doing so.[62]

Although the Malkin Report might have served as the basis for British reparations policy, it did not do so. In fact, although officials continued to discuss alternative approaches to the problem during the next year, especially through the Economic and Industrial Planning Staff, Ministers did not settle on, or even extensively discuss, the issues involved. However, Keynes maintained an interest in the issues, often intervening in an informal way on particular aspects of the work of Treasury officials involved in the continuing discussions, particularly those concerning the dismemberment of Germany. It was with this background that he became involved in the course of the Stage II negotiations with the American Treasury's plan for the de-industrialisation of Germany, the Morgenthau plan. His initial reactions appear best in his own words.[63]

Both Morgenthau and Harry White were considerably more interested in their plan for de-industrialising Germany than in anything else. . . . I took the line that all plans relating to Germany which I had seen so far struck me as equally bad, and the only matter I was concerned with was that it should not be the British Treasury who had to pay reparations to support Germany. I gathered that the plan is not quite as crude as it appeared in the reports from Quebec. All the same, it seems pretty mad, and I asked White how the inhabitants of the Ruhr were to be kept from starvation: he said that there would have to be bread lines but on a very low level of subsistence. When I asked if the British, as being responsible for that area would also be responsible for the bread, he said that the U.S. Treasury would, if necessary, pay for the bread, provided always it was on a low level of subsistence. So whilst the hills are being turned into a sheep run, the valleys will be filled for some years to come with a closely packed bread line on a very low level of subsistence at American expense. How I am to keep a straight face when it comes to the roundtable talk I cannot imagine.

Morgenthau eventually passed Keynes a copy of his plan. There is no record of Keynes's having discussed it with him, but Keynes's comments to the Chancellor suggest that the de-industrialisation proposals still struck him as unacceptable, as did the proposals concerning education, even though some details struck him as quite sensible.[64] However, the plan, plus previous ministerial acts and a discussion with President Roosevelt on the subject of the post-war treatment of Germany later in his visit, seem to have made him more pessimistic, for soon after his return to London he wrote:[65]

What frightens me most in the whole problem is that these issues are extremely likely to be settled by those (as I know by first hand conversations) who have not given continuous or concentrated thought to it. . . .
. . . For, in fact, there is *no* good solution. *All* the solutions which are being talked about are not only bad, but very bad.
No doubt we shall refrain from making the *same mistakes* as last time. But that is not much comfort.

Despite his pessimism, Keynes maintained his involvement in discussions of the problems, attempting throughout to clarify the issues, to keep Germany intact, and to ask for more precise thought on the financial implications of the various proposals being canvassed. As a result, he became involved in drafting the instructions for the British delegation to the Moscow conference that would implement the Yalta decisions by ministers on reparations – decisions which, as usual, took little account of official planning.

The results of Yalta, Potsdam and the early stages of the military occupation of Germany left him very disheartened. Therefore, when Professor Calvin Hoover wrote to him in November 1945, asking him to speak out against existing policy, as reparations deliveries were inconsistent with the Allies' guarantee of a minimum standard of life for the Germans, Keynes replied:[66]

At an earlier stage I was considerably concerned in discussions on this matter. But eventually I got to feel so hopeless about any sensible or even possible result, that I disengaged myself from so distasteful a subject. Our original ideas on this matter a year or more ago were in my opinion not too bad. But, for reasons which are only too obvious, they have fallen by the way . . . and only a change in policy can prevent great misfortunes.

All the same, I am afraid that this expression of opinion must remain private and personal to yourself. I can only regain complete freedom of public expression by ceasing to be officially connected with other matters. Perhaps that day may not be far off, but, at the moment, I have to behave like, at any rate, a demi-semi-official. This time I have not too bad a conscience about that, because, as I have mentioned, I am not, as I was last time, personally mixed up in responsibility for the subject. And also, because I believe that this time, both here in the U.S.A. and also in England, the majority share my views; whereas, last time, I was a voice crying in the wilderness and had, therefore, to cry loudly.

Certainly, by that time Keynes was hoping to disengage himself gradually from his wartime level of Treasury activity. He never succeeded in doing so. Just over four months later he was dead.

NOTES

1. Keynes's views on the formation of public opinion do not seem to have changed greatly after he set them out in *A Revision of the Treaty*. See *Collected Writings of John Maynard Keynes* (London, 1971), Vol. II, ch. 1. On Keynes's view of public opinion, see also D. E. Moggridge, 'Keynes: The Economist', in Moggridge (ed.), *Keynes: Aspects of the Man and his Work* (London, 1974).
2. The other members of Sir Kingsley Wood's Council were S. R. Beale, C. F. Campbell, H. D. Henderson, G. Riddle, Sir Walter Citrine, Sir Bertram Hornsby and Lord Riversdale.
3. P. D. Proctor, 'At the Treasury, 1940–1946', in *John Maynard Keynes 1883–1946* (Cambridge, 1949), p. 27.
4. One official summarised Keynes's working habits and their irregularity in a letter to a colleague at the time of the setting up of the Arts Council as follows: 'Keynes pushes the Minister: the Minister pushes

Wood, and Wood is, therefore, constrained to write this letter to you. In short, both Keynes and the Minister ask why . . .' Wood to Barlow, 14 February 1945.
5. Keynes to C. B. Hoover, 6 December 1945.
6. Although he deals with Keynes's discussions with Beaverbrook over the International Monetary Fund in March 1944, even going so far as to quote from one part of one letter, A. J. P. Taylor does not deal with the Keynes–Beaverbrook discussions of April 1945 when Beaverbrook agreed with the Keynes approach to the forthcoming loan negotiations with the Americans. But, of course, that would have spoiled the run of his story. See A. J. P. Taylor, *Beaverbrook* (London, 1972), p. 556; Beaverbrook to Keynes, 18 and 20 April 1945; Keynes to Beaverbrook, 27 April 1945; Keynes to Brand, 3 May 1945.
7. Keynes had known Penrose fifteen years earlier as an undergraduate.
8. R. S. Sayers, *Financial Policy 1939–1945* (London, 1956), p. xiii.
9. In passing, it is worth noting that Keynes, on occasion, was over-devious and over-irregular in his attempts to make his influence felt, most particularly in his attempts to sabotage the Board of Trade–State Department negotiations for an extension of the 1938 Anglo-American Trade Agreement. In this instance, some of his behaviour, plus that of the relevant Board of Trade official, verged on the childish, while some of his comments on the possible post-war British trade policy, although logically founded and well-meant, certainly increased Britain's difficulties in subsequent negotiations. Full details will be available in *Collected Writings*, Vols. XXII and XXIII.
10. In addition to the more well-known matters of war finance and post-war planning referred to in the literature, Keynes's interests and influence extend to such matters as the post-war rebuilding of London, colonial development policy, the preservation of art treasures in Italy, war aims, the future of the Export Credit Guarantee Department, the post-war cotton trade and post-war trends in labour management relations.
11. For a fuller discussion of these issues, see Sayers, *Financial Policy*, ch. 1.
12. See, for example, 'Borrowing for Defence: Is it Inflation?' *The Times*, 11 March 1937; Sayers, *Financial Policy*, pp. 153–5; PRO Cab58/30, Committee on Economic Information, 26th and 27th Reports, 16 December 1938 and 20 July 1939; PRO T177/47, Keynes to the Chancellor, 28 May 1939; 'Crisis Finance', *The Times*, 17 and 18 April 1939; 'Will Rearmament Cure Unemployment', *The Listener*, 1 June 1939; 'Borrowing by the State', *The Times*, 25 and 26 July 1939; letters to *The Times*, 24 April 1937, 28 April 1939, 4 May 1939.
13. Letter to R. F. Kahn, 25 August 1939.
14. 29 September 1939.
15. Labour's lack of enthusiasm is clear from the newspaper clippings of the period, as well as from reports that reached Keynes from his contacts within the party. Further details will be available in *Collected Writings*, Vols. XXII and XXIII.
16. Keynes also allowed for decreases in investment and sales of overseas

assets or increases in overseas liabilities. To give some indication of what happened, a comparison of 1938 and the peak war effort year of 1944 is instructive. Taking the national accounts for the two years (plus the intervening years for stockbuilding) the figures look as follows: increased output (largely achieved by 1940/41) £1,320 million, decreased consumers' expenditure £530 million, decreased investment £140 million, deterioration on current account £140 million. Figures, at constant 1938 prices, from C. H. Feinstein, *National Income, Expenditure and Output of the United Kingdom 1855–1965* (Cambridge 1972), Appendix Table 5.

17. On this matter see D. E. Moggridge and S. K. Howson, 'Keynes on Monetary Policy, 1910–45', *Oxford Economic Papers* (July 1974).

18. Additional resources would come to the authorities from decreased investment and a deterioration in the current account as a result of controls.

19. See *Collected Writings*, Vol. IX, pp. 413–25. Keynes believed that the workers would accept a fall of up to 10% in their standard of living before pressing for higher money wages. After that point, wages would follow prices, with a lag largely determined by the institutional conditions surrounding wage bargaining. In the First World War, the lag had been about six months to a year, but in the conditions of 1939–40, with the trade unions more index conscious, the lag would be shorter and, hence, the price rises necessary for a given transfer of resources larger than had been the case during 1914–18.

20. See W. B. Reddaway, 'Rationing', in D. N. Chester (ed.), *Lessons of the British War Economy* (Cambridge, 1951), pp. 183–4.

21. Keynes's 1942 proposals for a social policy budget, which included flat-rate taxes on employees in service and non-essential occupations, sharp increases in taxes on luxuries, encouragements to the employment of married women and family allowances for the lower paid, drew what is perhaps the classic retort from the Inland Revenue. 'the purpose of the income tax is not the redistribution of income'. (Sayers, *Financial Policy*, pp. 97–8.) Nevertheless, many of the proposals found their place in the statute book.

22. *Ibid.*, ch. IV.

23. *Ibid.*, ch. V, pp. ii–iii; Moggridge and Howson, 'Keynes on Monetary Policy'.

24. Even as late as 1939, despite the work of Keynes and others in the field, 'the Treasury had no coherent theory of any relation between short and long rates' (Sayers, *Financial Policy*, pp. 156–7).

25. *Ibid.*, pp. 181–2; 'New Issues Control', 29 January 1945.

26. These memoranda and the discussions associated with them all predate the preparation of the final version of 'Paying for the War', thus giving another indication of Keynes's range of interests and energy, although at the time he was far from fit physically.

27. This dependence on 'last time' comes out heavily in Keynes's initial memorandum on exchange control, the historical portions of which appear in *Collected Writings*, Vol. XVI, pp. 210–14. It also appears in the discussions of the blockade against Germany, Greek finance,

American finance, and ultimately, of course, reparations. On the reparations issue, see pp. 193–6.
28. W. N. Medlicott, *The Economic Blockade*, Vol. 1 (London, 1952), p. 39.
29. Thus Keynes's 1941 mission to the United States was primarily concerned with an attempt to get the Americans to take over many of Britain's outstanding pre-Lend–Lease commitments. Though apparently successful at the time, Keynes's efforts, then as so often later, particularly in Stage II, came to less than expected when the Americans turned to executing the understanding, and the 'old commitments' returned time and time again as British claims for compensation in Anglo-American negotiations, finally appearing as the various 'half-dead cats' in the Stage II and Lend–Lease settlements.
30. Keynes to Courtauld, 29 April and 1 May 1940; Courtauld to Keynes, 30 April 1940.
31. For the rest of the story see Sayers, *Financial Policy*, pp. 387–9; D. C. Coleman, *Courtaulds: An Economic and Social History, Vol.* II, *Rayon* (Oxford, 1969), ch. xv.
32. Sayers, *Financial Policy*, pp. 392–6.
33. In both cases the demand was for some sterling backing for internal expenditure rather than the purchase of overseas supplies.
34. Sayers, *Financial Policy*, p. 258.
35. Keynes to Kahn, 31 October and 2 December 1941.
36. For more details see D. E. Moggridge, 'From War to Peace – The Sterling Balances', *The Banker*, August 1972.
37. Sayers, *Financial Policy*, p. 261n.
38. This lack of general agreement within the Treasury on sterling balances policy played an important part in the Treasury's post-war behaviour after Keynes, the strongest proponent of the policy embodied in the 1945 American Loan Agreement passed from the scene.
39. R. A. Harri, Chief Economic Adviser, G.H.Q. Middle East, originated the proposals which R. F. Kahn passed on to Keynes in London.
40. In *How to Pay for the War*, Keynes appears to have believed that a slump would follow soon after the end of the war. Hence his suggestion for the repayment of deferred pay in such circumstances and the emphasis he gave it, on F. A. Hayek's suggestion, in the pamphlet. By 1943, he had come to expect that high levels of demand would be the norm for ten to fifteen years after the war. ('The Long Term Problem of Full Employment', 25 May 1943.) By that stage, he was coming to regard unemployment as high as 800,000 as a very pessimistic assumption for post-war forecasts of national income. When his colleagues, estimating from the supply side tended to assume unemployment as high as 1,200,000 to 1,500,00 in their forecasts, Keynes was moved to protest strongly that demand conditions would probably make such a forecast nonsensical. See PRO Premier 4/16/13, Estimate of the National Income, 25 June 1943.
41. Sir Alan Barlow, for example, thought that 'the pre-war optimum of 10%' would prove to be the minimum post-war unemployment figure.

Sir Hubert Henderson was equally pessimistic, as was Sir Richard Hopkins.
42. Keynes to Meade, 11 January 1943.
43. Henderson's papers from this period on the subject, reprinted in *The Inter-war Years and Other Essays* (Oxford, 1955), provide a very accurate picture of his views as to the post-war prospects.
44. Keynes to Eady, 30 June 1943.
45. Keynes to Robbins, 29 March 1943; Keynes to Meade, 27 May 1943.
46. 'Post-war Employment', 14 February 1944.
47. Keynes to Beveridge, 16 December 1944; Keynes to T. S. Eliot, 5 April 1945.
48. The other members of the Committee were Professor Lionel Robbins, James Meade, Sir Wilfred Eady, Sir Herbert Brittain, Sir Cornelius Gregg, Sir Richard Hopkins, Paul Chambers, Sir Edward Bridges (Chairman).
49. For the Committee's deliberations and Keynes's part see Moggridge and Howson, 'Keynes on Monetary Policy'.
50. In his evidence and memorandum to the Committee, Keynes emphasised the importance of flexibility in policy and of maintaining market uncertainty. Dalton appears to have done neither.
51. Keynes's wartime interests in the first, second and fourth topics were carryovers from his earlier work. Even the third had concerned him during the 1930s, particularly in connection with the work of the Economic Advisory Council. In fact, the links were so close in the case of primary products that he wrote the first draft of his post-war scheme with a copy of his 1938 article 'The Policy of Government Storage of Foodstuffs and Raw Materials' (*Economic Journal*, September 1938) in front of him.
52. See, in particular, R. F. Harrod, *The Life of John Maynard Keynes* (London, 1951), chs. XIII and XIV; R. N. Gardner, *Sterling–Dollar Diplomacy*, revised edn (New York, 1969); E. F. Penrose, *Economic Planning for the Peace* (Princeton, 1953); J. K. Horsefield, *The International Monetary Fund 1945–1965*, Vol. 1 (Washington, 1969), Part I.
53. The first draft is dated 25 November 1940.
54. See, for example, Gardner, *Sterling–Dollar Diplomacy*, pp. 41–2; D. Acheson, *Present at the Creation* (London, 1970), pp. 29–30.
55. Keynes to Waley, 17 February 1944.
56. Keynes to Halifax (then British Ambassador to the United States), 1 January 1946.
57. 25 November 1940.
58. Keynes to Wilson, 20 October 1941.
59. The other economists on the Committee were Professor Robbins and James Meade.
60. 'Germany's Contribution to the Cost of Keeping the Peace of the World', 21 December 1942; 'Reparation and Restitution', 1 and 31 March 1943.
61. The report is available on PRO FO371/35305.
62. Mr Richard Law (the leader of the delegation) asked London for permission for Keynes to give the talk on 16 September 1943. The

request was rejected at a meeting of Ministers on 29 September, partly owing to Keynes's previous views on the matter and partly owing to the report's assumption that Germany would not be dismembered after the war. However, Mr Law took silence to mean consent and Keynes spoke on 28 September.

63. Keynes to the Chancellor, 4 October 1944.
64. Keynes to the Chancellor, 6 October 1944. In the light of these letters it seems difficult to understand Harry White's comment that Keynes supported the plan (J. M. Blum, *From the Morgenthau Diaries,* Vol. III, *Years of War* (Boston, 1967), p. 343).
65. Keynes to Passant, 30 December 1944.
66. Keynes to Hoover, 6 December 1945.

18

Bretton Woods

RICHARD N. GARDNER

'History', it has been said, 'is lived forward but is written in retrospect. We know the end before the beginning and we can never
wholly recapture what it was to know the beginning only.' It is
difficult to reconstruct the intellectual, political, and economic setting
of the Bretton Woods Conference a quarter of a century later. But
it is useful to try. The effort may help explain the international
financial system we have inherited from the past – and it may even
tell us something about the steps we can take to improve that system
today. According to the old cliché, those who ignore history are
condemned to repeat it. I doubt that this is any less true in the field
of international monetary policy than in other areas.

Perhaps the first important thing to note at the outset is that the
Bretton Woods Conference and the crucial negotiations that preceded it were very much an Anglo-American affair, with Canada
playing a useful mediating role. For historical reasons that were
unique, these three countries had an unusually large influence in
the negotiations. Germany, Italy, and Japan, countries that today
hold a large measure of economic power, were then enemy countries
and thus not represented at Bretton Woods. France was still under
German occupation; its government-in-exile played only a marginal
role. The less developed countries played nothing like the part they
play today in international economic conferences. The Soviet Union
came only at the last minute and sat on the sidelines.

The United States, of course, was the dominant element. For
better or worse only the U.S. had the resources to make these institutions work. Moreover – and people often forget this in recalling
the Bretton Woods Conference – the war was still on. The Normandy
landings took place only a month before the conference opened.
The Allies had not yet broken out of the Normandy beachhead;
nobody knew when the war would end or how it would be won.
There was almost complete dependence on the U.S. militarily,
politically, and economically. No wonder, then that the U.S. role at
Bretton Woods was decisive. It is unlikely that there will ever be

Plate 11 Lydia and Maynard Keynes in 1929. Cézanne's 'L'oncle Dominique' can be seen in the background

Plate 12   Front cover by David Low of a pamphlet published in 1934 by the *New Statesman* and reprinted here by permission. The annotations are by Maynard Keynes and show his excruciating handwriting. Stalin says: 'I suppose they're all talking about something to do with Russia – as usual.' G. B. Shaw says: 'I marry Lopokova! Certainly not.' H. G. Wells says: 'It seems to me that it's what any man of sense would do.' Keynes says: 'My dear Sirs, as a matter of fact I happen to know it's too late.'

another world conference in which American power is so preponderant.

Since the U.S. role was so decisive at Bretton Woods, it is worth examining in some detail the political and economic factors that influenced the American delegation. The U.S. negotiators operated with certain basic preconceptions. One was that the mistakes made after the First World War must be avoided. To begin with, this meant that planning for the post-war period should begin early – indeed, it began as early as 1941 and 1942. Secondly, the U.S. should join a system of world organisations and play a leading part in building a new world order. Unfortunately, thinking about the kind of world in which international organisations would operate tended to be somewhat naïve. Cordell Hull, for example, could say at the time of Bretton Woods that once a United Nations was created, 'there will no longer be need for spheres of influence, for alliances, for balance of power, or any other of the special arrangements through which, in the unhappy past, natives strove to safeguard their security or to promote their interests'.* Harry White described as follows the assumptions under which he laboured in wartime Washington:

It was expected that the early post-war world would witness a degree of unity and good-will in international political relationships among the victorious allies never before reached in peace time. It was expected that the world would move rapidly . . . toward 'One World' . . . No influential persons, as far as I can remember, expressed the expectation or the fear that international relations would worsen during these years.

The widely shared assumption, in other words, was that there would be a new political deal – 'one world' – with power somehow exorcised from the system. There was no anticipation of the Cold War. Nobody foresaw the need for huge U.S. overseas expenditures for military defence and foreign aid; no one foresaw the magnitude of Britain's overseas spending. The working-papers for the Anglo-American financial negotiations in the autumn of 1945 estimated British government overseas expenditures after the transitional period at $250 million. (British overseas government expenditures were seven times that by the early 1960s.) The political assumptions behind Bretton Woods were thus very far from the post-war realities.

A related element in U.S. thinking was the preoccupation with economics – with the economic basis of a durable peace. Here again the post-war planners drew lessons from the inter-war history. Profoundly influenced by the writings of Keynes and others, they believed the Versailles settlement had collapsed because of its

*References for this quotation and the others that follow may be found in my *Sterling-Dollar Diplomacy* (2nd edition, 1969).

inadequate foundation. They were determined not to make that mistake again. This time there would be an adequate economic underpinning for the post-war arrangements.

The emphasis on economics was welcome up to a point; but it tended to be overdone. Leo Pasvolsky, for example, stated that unwillingness to abandon policies of economic warfare would constitute 'the *greatest* danger that will confront us after the war' (emphasis added). Arthur Krock, summarising the mood in Washington at the time, said 'economic freedom for all is the basic American foreign policy for the prevention of war'. The old cliché, 'if goods can't cross borders, soldiers will', seemed to underline much of the thinking of the State Department under Cordell Hull. The Secretary of State actually believed that the fundamental causes of the world wars lay in economic discrimination and trade warfare. Some of his aides went so far as to propose a trade agreement with Nazi Germany in 1939 as a means of avoiding the Second World War!

Another element in American thinking was the very great emphasis on the concept of multilateralism or non-discrimination in trade and payments. The U.S. was preoccupied with the imperial preference system. (The U.S. in those days was on the anti-imperialist crusade. It is ironic to note that twenty-five years later the U.S. is the country most on the receiving end of this charge.) Economic spheres of influence were regarded as a threat to peace, and particularly to the American concept of 'one world'. The Ottawa Agreements were also considered very harmful to American trade interests.

There was also a strong American desire to get rid of exchange controls and quotas. Here the U.S. commitment was not to free trade as such, but rather to preserve a role for the price mechanism. Thus, tariffs were permissible, but not direct controls. The concept was practical as well as ideological. The U.S. wanted an environment in which American trade could expand – in which the comparative advantages of the U.S. in key sectors could make its impact, free from unreasonable burdens and restrictions.

Still another element – one that looks particularly curious in retrospect – was the strong feeling of many of the New Dealers against bankers. Henry Morgenthau proudly declared at Bretton Woods that the Fund and Bank would 'drive the usurious money lenders from the temple of international finance'. (It would be interesting to know what Morgenthau thought in the very final months of his life when the 'usurious money lenders' led by the Federal Reserve Bank of New York mobilised several billion dollars in forty-eight hours to rescue sterling.) The close collaboration between central bankers and governments that has characterised the post-war period was neither foreseen nor even encouraged by the wartime planners. Indeed, on U.S. initiative, the Bretton Woods Conference adopted a resolution asking the Bank for International Settlements to go out of existence.

A particularly important feature of the American setting that needs to be noted was the rivalry between the Treasury and the State Department. Treasury had the upper hand because Morgenthau was a close friend of President Roosevelt. This helps explain why primacy was given to the financial side of post-war planning. (Had Hull been Roosevelt's Dutchess County neighbour instead of Morgenthau, we might have ended up with an I.T.O. and not an I.M.F.!) Another result of the division between State and Treasury was that problems of trade and finance were dealt with in virtually watertight compartments. These divisions were carried over into our international economic organisations, with results that still afflict us. It is anomalous that if a country is in balance of payments difficulty and resorts to trade restrictions – quotas or import surcharges – its problems are discussed in G.A.T.T., while if it comes for financial aid or employs exchange controls, its problems are discussed in the I.M.F. There is no adequate coordination or integration of policy between these two institutions. This is traceable right back to the divisions within the U.S. executive branch during the Second World War.

So far I have concentrated on the executive branch. What about Congress and the public at large? We tend now to forget the lingering isolationist tradition that was still very strong at the time of Bretton Woods. It was a tremendous undertaking to bring the U.S. into the I.M.F. and Bank. Up to that time the U.S. had not joined any universal world organisation. There was real doubt that the American Congress would approve membership in international financial organisations, or even in the United Nations itself.

There was also a strong *laissez-faire* tradition, which complicated the task of bringing the U.S. into the Fund and Bank. It is extraordinary to reread some of the things that were said at the time about the White plan and the Keynes plan in the press and in the U.S. financial community. The Guaranty Trust Company, for example, could say that both the Keynes and White plans were 'dangerous' because they would 'enable nations to buy merchandise without being able to pay for it' and would 'substitute fallible human judgment and discretion for the impersonal action of the markets in regulating balances of international payments and foreign exchange rates'. The American Bankers Association declared that 'a system of quotas or shares in a pool which gives debtor countries the impression that they have a right to credits up to some amount is unsound in principle, and raises hopes that cannot be realized.' The *New York Times* thought neither plan was necessary because 'the gold standard was, without any international agreements, the most satisfactory international standard that has ever been devised'.

There was, finally, the pervasive feeling that the U.S. was the world's perennial surplus country and had to protect itself against too liberal access to international credits. Senator Taft rose on the floor of the Senate to complain that the U.S. was 'putting ... all the valuable money in the Fund' and that U.S. participation would mean 'pouring money down a rat hole'. The U.S. negotiators did not hold these extreme views, but they had to take account of them. Moreover, even they may have been victims of an 'arrogance of power' when it came to economics; they hardly imagined that the U.S. might some day need international assistance in dealing with its own payments problems.

Let us look now at the other side of the Atlantic – at the political and economic setting in Britain. Several factors were working on behalf of cooperation with the U.S. in a post-war financial arrangement. The most obvious was the complete British dependence on the U.S. This was not a negotiation between equals or between two fully independent countries. The U.S. was giving $30 billion of Lend–Lease aid to Britain; there was no equivalent British leverage on the U.S. In the last analysis the British had to accept what the Americans wanted. But there were also reasons based on Britain's own perceived self-interest for working with the U.S. for the kind of economic system envisaged at Bretton Woods. British opinion was strongly committed to the concept of world organisation in the economic as well as in the political field. The liberal economic tradition still had a good deal of vitality. Academics in government like James Meade and Lionel Robbins, civil servants like Richard Hopkins, ministers like Richard Law, were committed to liberal economic principles. Keynes, as Sir Roy Harrod has brought out so brilliantly in his biography, was doubtful at first, but came around to a liberal approach on the assurance of a generous liquidity package and an American commitment to help in British reconstruction.

Yet throughout the negotiations there were three important British reservations. The first was a concern – one might almost say a fixation – with full employment. The trauma of the 1930s had a profound effect on British thinking: freedom to maintain full employment at home had to be safeguarded in any post-war financial plan. No one today would quarrel with that as an objective, but rereading British comments of a generation ago one is struck by the extent to which this one theme was exalted over all others. Herbert Morrison could say, for example, that 'one of the biggest contributions' Britain could make to world trade after the war would be to 'have a *shortage* of labour' (emphasis added). The British government could argue in international meetings that full employment was 'the main condition for the maintenance of satis-factory levels of living'. Very little, if anything, was said about employment being *productive* as well as *full* – and even less was said about how the necessary productivity could be achieved. Keynes sometimes talked as if exchange rate changes by themselves could provide a satisfactory method of adjustment. He told the House of Lords that under the Bretton Woods agreement the external value of sterling could be altered 'to conform to whatever *de facto* internal value results from domestic policies which them-selves shall be immune from criticism'. Not only during the wartime period but for years thereafter, the focus of political discussion in Britain was on the responsibilities which the U.S. would have to undertake to restore equilibrium to Britain's balance of payments. It would have been better for all concerned if equal efforts had been given to educating the British people on British responsibilities for restoring equilibrium. (The failure to do this has proved costly. Keynes would have thought it incredible if someone had told him the hard facts of the 1960s – that the United Kingdom would run huge balance of payments deficits when the U.S. was also running huge balance of payments deficits. The British leaders simply assumed that if the U.S. ran deficits, Britain would run surpluses, and the adjustment problem would be solved.)

A second British reservation concerned Commonwealth trade and financial arrangements. Lord Beaverbrook wrote me a rather angry letter after the first edition of *Sterling–Dollar Diplomacy*, saying: 'You may have the idea that my opposition ... was contentious or obscurantist. It was, as I see it, the attitude of one who sought to reconcile his belief in the Empire with his hope that a strong Empire was the best ally the United States could have. Was I wrong?' Well, of course, he was. Empire was not a viable economic or political concept for Britain after the Second World War. It took a long time for some members of the British public and political leadership to recognise that fact. Keynes scathingly denounced such members of the House of Commons as wanting to 'build up a separate economic bloc which excludes Canada and consists of countries to which we already owe more than we can pay, on the basis of their agreeing to lend us money they have not got and buy only from us and one another goods we are unable to supply'. Yet despite Keynes's eloquence, there remained a lingering commitment to the sterling area and preference. Part of the explanation was the failure to recognise the full and terrible weight of the war on Britain, to realise that the post-war situation would be radically different and that Britain could no longer run a reserve currency. Perhaps there was also the feeling that the sterling balances and the preferences would be useful things to have because they might guarantee Britain assured exports in the post-war period. On the part of some there was also the desire to maintain Commonwealth economic and financial ties as a means of maintaining Commonwealth political relationships.

Perhaps most important of all there was in Britain no less than in the U.S. an 'arrogance of economic power'. Neither country, when it came down to it, wanted to surrender its reserve currency status and throw itself unreservedly into an international financial arrangement. If that statement was not true for Keynes himself, it certainly applied to the people in the Bank of England and others in London with whom Keynes had to deal and whose acquiescence was required for a Bretton Woods settlement.

In hindsight, we may say that the reluctance of the United Kingdom to surrender or share its reserve currency role has been one of the major causes of its post-war difficulties. During the war-time negotiations U.S. officials suggested the possibility of a multi-lateral effort to scale down and fund the sterling balances (the funding was to be through the I.M.F.). Admittedly, the suggestion was hardly more than a hint, but history might have been very different – and very much better for both sides – if the hint had been picked up. Of course, a scaling down and funding of the balances would have been politically possible only if the U.S. had been willing to offer a big chunk of direct aid to holders of the balances like India, Pakistan, and Egypt. It is possible that the American negotiators were not prepared to face up to the full implications of a genuine solution to the sterling problem.

Let us now try to draw these threads together. How, in summary, did the intellectual, economic and political forces on both sides of the Atlantic affect the final outcome at Bretton Woods? In what major respects does the Bretton Woods compromise need revision today? In answering these questions I would focus on four main points:

First, the emphasis on universal organisation on both sides of the Atlantic led to the neglect of regional arrangements, a neglect that had to be corrected later, beginning with the Marshall Plan. We are still struggling with the question of how regional arrangements can be accommodated to the universal design.

Second, there was an underestimate on both sides of the magnitude of the liquidity problem. Neither side foresaw that inflation would double the price of commodities over the pre-war level and that the stock of gold would be inadequate to finance world trade and payments. Nobody foresaw the extent to which new gold production would be discouraged by the concurrence of inflation with a fixed gold price. The liquidity problem was not understood in the same way that we understand it today.

The lack of foresight was particularly striking, of course, on the American side. The U.S. negotiators were worried about Congress; they could not take for granted that even the modest White plan would be accepted. They fought the overdraft concept of the Clearing Union, pressed for a depository scheme in which drawing rights were strictly related to contributions, insisted on conditional rather than unconditional liquidity and smaller quotas for countries like France than those countries wanted. All of these policies worked against U.S. interests and had to be reversed by American negotiators two decades later.

If the U.S. had accepted the Keynes plan in its original form and had undertaken post-war aid to Europe through the Clearing Union rather than through Marshall Aid, the U.S. would have accumulated over $30 billion of overdraft facilities which would have financed nearly all of the U.S. deficits in the 1950s and the 1960s. Admittedly, too much should not be made of that point. The Keynes plan would not have been the right device for post-war reconstruction. Still, it would have served the long-term U.S. interest to have negotiated on the basis of the Keynes plan, adapting it as necessary to remove its inflationary bias and its other defects. Fortunately, this failure has been remedied a quarter of a century later by the activation of the facility for Special Drawing Rights in the I.M.F. At long last we have achieved what Keynes wanted – a quantum of international reserves automatically available to all countries that can be increased in accordance with the needs of world trade. However, we still have to solve the problem of assuring the orderly coexistence of different reserve assets – gold, dollars, sterling, and S.D.R.S.

Third, the interaction of American and British forces left us with no adequate solution to the adjustment problem. In a way this is curious, because the first drafts of the White and Keynes plans did deal boldly with this issue. In their original form, the American and British currency plans faced the adjustment issue squarely – they provided for far-reaching international control over the economic policies of deficit and surplus countries. Under the first (unpublished) draft of the White plan, members were obliged 'not to adopt any monetary or banking measure without the consent of a majority of members' votes of the Fund'. The published version omitted this far-reaching (and politically unrealistic) provision, but authorised the Fund to make recommendations for changes in the economic policy of countries going too far toward deficit or surplus. Moreover, recommendations could be reinforced by sanctions – the denial of the use of Fund resources beyond a certain point for a deficit country, the rationing of the 'scarce currency' in the case of a country in surplus. Under the Keynes plan, the Clearing Union could *require* a deficit country that drew more than one-half of its overdraft facilities to deposit collateral, depreciate its currency, control outward capital movements, or surrender liquid reserves in reduction of its debit balance. It could recommend to that country internal economic measures needed to restore equilibrium. It could *require* a surplus country whose credit balance exceeded half its quota to carry out such measures as the stimulation of domestic demand, the appreciation of its currency, the reduction of import barriers, and the making of international development loans.

With the notable exception of the 'scarce currency' clause, most of these references to international supervision of the economic policies of deficit and surplus countries were eliminated during negotiation of the Fund articles. In part this was owing to differences between the U.S. and Britain on the relative emphasis to be accorded to deficit and surplus country responsibilities; it was also because of the fact that explicit qualifications of economic sovereignty would alienate congressional and parliamentary opinion. Thus the Bretton Woods compromise left a good deal of ambiguity about the responsibilities for adjustment of surplus and deficit countries. It ruled out adjustment through freely fluctuating exchange rates or by controls on payments for current transactions – since exchange stability and multilateral trade were two primary Bretton Woods objectives. But it said very little about how adjustment *was* to be achieved. The architects at Bretton Woods apparently hoped that, with the aid of Fund resources, deficit and surplus countries could be relied on to restore a balance within a relatively short time by reasonable domestic policies and by occasional changes in exchange rates to correct a 'fundamental disequilibrium'. Unfortunately, however, this system just has not worked out.

The inadequacies of the Bretton Woods adjustment mechanism were camouflaged in the early post-war years when the U.S. was in surplus and the rest of the world was in deficit. Nobody paid much attention to the problem of how the Fund would 'police' surplus and deficit nations to assure their good behaviour. In effect, the U.S. 'policed' itself – adopting liberal aid and trade policies appropriate to a surplus nation because it quickly recognised that if it failed to do so the rest of the world would go broke. This was not a question of American altruism, but rather of enlightened self-interest. The U.S. was the economic giant among nations; there was no one with whom to share responsibility; it alone had the power to save the wartime multilateral dream and assure the survival of freedom in the West. The political costs of failure were unacceptable to it and, consequently, it was willing to pay the price in the Marshall Plan, other measures of post-war aid, and unrequited tariff cuts. Nobody had to invoke the principal Fund sanction envisaged for 'policing' the creditor – the 'scarce currency' clause considered so important by Keynes. It was unavailable, in any case, since the Fund was inactive during the period of U.S. reconstruction aid and dollars in the Fund were not technically 'scarce'. But for the reasons mentioned above it was not needed.

When 'dollar shortage' gave way to 'dollar glut' and a U.S.-centred system was replaced by a more balanced distribution of economic power, the shortcomings in the Bretton Woods design became apparent. The countries of continental Europe did not 'police' themselves in the direction of creditor-country responsibility following the earlier American model. It was not that they were more 'wicked' than the U.S.; but because none of them was big enough to be decisive, they did not assume the same responsibility the U.S. had done for 'saving the system'. The French used growing gold reserves to support an independent economic and political role, with little heed to cooperation through the Fund. (France un-willingly had to disgorge half of its $6 billion gold stock after the May 1968 disorders, but student rioters such as Cohn-Bendit can hardly be considered part of the permanent adjustment mechanism!) The Germans were equally reluctant to accept the Fund's concept of creditor-country responsibility.

As they face the 1970s, therefore, the U.S., Britain, Canada and other countries are still struggling with the difficult adjustment issue they confronted at Bretton Woods a quarter of a century ago. The United States is seeking to improve its payments position by a total of about $10 billion a year. Which are the countries prepared to see their payments positions reduced by this amount (or even by this amount minus allocations of S.D.R.S)? And, quite apart from the specific American payments problem, just what methods of adjust-ment are countries agreed to use? Are they to place primary reliance on trade and capital controls, on fluctuating exchange rates, or on the harmonisation of domestic and foreign economic policies? Until greater progress is made in resolving these questions, we are likely to stumble from crisis to crisis.

One way to improve the international adjustment process would be to give international agencies the kind of influence over the economic policies of deficit and surplus countries that was envisaged in the original U.S. and British currency plans. For example, there could be more regular and systematic consultation among senior government officials so that international adjustment is given greater weight in national policy-making. More progress could also be made in the adjustment of national policies on military spending, foreign aid and private capital flows to help reduce imbalances of payments.

In the years immediately ahead, however, it is unlikely that the adjustment problem will be fully resolved by measures of this kind. Economic sovereignty dies hard. Deficit and surplus countries are reluctant to sacrifice domestic economic objectives for the purpose of external balance; even when prepared to do so they do not always have the policy instruments available to get sufficiently quick results. And there are limits to their willingness to adjust foreign spending in the interest of payments balance.

For these reasons, it is encouraging that the international community is taking a new look at the possibilities of easing the adjustment problem through greater flexibility in exchange rates. The present adjustable peg system of the I.M.F. permits changes to take place, but only after the political leaders of a country find them necessary to cure a 'fundamental disequilibrium'. For reasons of prestige or domestic politics, national leaders are frequently reluctant to devalue or revalue a currency; as in the case of the pound sterling and the mark, they tend to postpone changes too long and to make them only after a currency crisis has developed.

Like many others, I believe the best way to provide for greater flexibility in exchange rates is through the 'crawling peg', under which a currency could move up or down one or two percentage points a year through a series of tiny changes every week or so. The changes would take place in response to a formula designed to move the rate in the direction necessary to restore balance, thus taking the responsibility off the shoulders of the political leaders. In addition, we should permit exchange rates to fluctuate within a 'wider band' (such as the $2\frac{1}{4}\%$ on either side of parity agreed to at the end of 1971).

Although some have argued that greater exchange flexibility will unsettle the confidence of international traders and investors, a modest combination of crawling peg and wider band should commend itself to the financial community as a desirable substitute for the present arrangement. After all, a substantial risk of a very small rate change may be preferable to the small (but far from negligible) possibility of a very substantial rate change that exists at present, particularly if the new system makes exchange and trade restrictions less likely and eases the adjustment problem of a troubled world economy.

My fourth and final observation has to do with our international arrangements for monetary decision-making. It was envisaged at Bretton Woods by both the U.S. and Britain as well as everybody else that the International Monetary Fund would be the central place for taking decisions on the liquidity and adjustment problems. It has not worked out that way, for several reasons. One, I believe, was the decision, taken at the Savannah Conference two years after Bretton Woods at the insistence of Fred Vinson, the U.S. secretary of the Treasury, to have full-time executive directors. As a result of this decision, we have a rather inadequate system for managing our international monetary affairs. There are the annual meetings of the Fund in which the responsible decision-makers get together for a week, and they pass a lot of resolutions; but with more than one hundred countries represented, the amount of real business that can be done is limited. And these meetings are only once a year. The rest of the time you have the executive directors permanently resident in Washington and, meaning no disrespect to them, they are not the people with responsibility for making the real decisions in capitals. This has left a serious gap.

In recent years we have developed a parallel structure for decision-making on liquidity and adjustment problems outside the Fund – the Group of Ten, the Basle Club, and the O.E.C.D. This has meant a diffusion of responsibility among a number of forums for monetary policy-making. Moreover, these new forums are all 'rich men's clubs', with the less developed countries excluded from decision-making on very important matters. They resent this – and with some justice. Countries like India and Brazil have an important stake in how these questions are resolved – on how much liquidity is created, on how adjustment is to take place. The way these matters are resolved affects the amount of foreign aid the less developed countries get and the extent to which they will have a chance to sell their exports in the markets of the developed world.

One way to correct this situation would be to create a Group of Twenty-One consisting of the countries with nationals on the executive board of the Fund, plus Switzerland. They could meet at the ministerial level every three months, alternately at the headquarters of the Fund and at the Fund office in Paris or at other places. This consultative Group of Twenty-One operating at the ministerial level would provide the element we now lack – a mechanism for the continuous high-level discussion of international financial problems with the participation of key countries from the Third World.

Ansel Luxford, the chief Treasury lawyer in the American delegation at Bretton Woods, sent me a letter some years ago containing a good deal of wisdom. It may be appropriate to quote part of it today:

> To me, then as now, the major significance of Bretton Woods was the death blow it represented in victory over the economic isolationism of the prewar period and the serious threat that with military victory this country would again revert to economic nationalism. Thus, the question of how effective the Bank and Fund may have been in the light of postwar events (many of them not foreseeable except by hindsight) is not nearly so important as having established the principle of u.s. cooperation in the solution of the international economic problems of the future.
>
> Let me admit that Bretton Woods' sails had to be trimmed to the point where public and Congressional acceptance might be possible – but only then after a life and death fight. Let me admit that the package was wrapped in the glittering generalities of a hard political fight designed to get public acceptance and force Congressional approval. My answer is that both courses in my opinion were essential to establishing the major principle and are entirely in harmony with what we all know to be the realities of mobilizing political action in this country.
>
> Having established the principle and having obtained public acceptance thereof, the ground was paved for the British Loan, Marshall Aid etc. To my way of thinking, the basic differences between the British and u.s. approaches were not matters of economic theory or even disagreements over the major economic factors involved. The real question was how to equate economic principle with the realities of both British and u.s. political life (to say nothing of the other interested countries).

I believe this historical judgement will be convincing to anyone who understands the conditions in which the Bretton Woods negotiations took place. We can criticise the negotiators for excessive preoccupation with economics, but surely we are fortunate that they used the occasion of the Second World War to create the economic institutions that made our extraordinary post-war recovery possible. Had there been no Bretton Woods Conference during the Second World War, it might not have been possible to negotiate a Fund or Bank at all; the solidarity and idealism of the war would have been dissipated. We can criticise the post-war planners, too, for unrealistic universalist dreams. But surely we are fortunate that they established universal institutions linking the developed countries of the West to the developing countries and potentially to the countries of Eastern Europe.

'There is', Keynes warned at Savannah, 'scarcely any enduringly successful experience of an international body which has fulfilled the hopes of its progenitors. Either an institution has become diverted to the instrument of a limited group, or it has been a puppet of sawdust through which the breath of life does not blow.' One cannot escape the conclusion that Keynes, perfectionist though he was, would have been the first to acknowledge the service to the general interest and the continuing vitality of the institutions in whose conception he played such a decisive part.

PART THREE

19

The international negotiator

F. G. LEE

Letter from F. G. Lee, member of the United Kingdom Treasury Delegation to the Stage II negotiations on Lend–Lease in Washington, D.C., to F. E. Harmer, Temporary Assistant Secretary at H.M. Treasury, London, December 1944.

My dear Freddie,

> 'This is the way the world ends
> This is the way the world ends
> Not with a bang, but a whimper . . .'

Now that the campaign is officially over, the general staff has gone away, and only the second line troops are left to deal with tedious mopping up operations, it may be of interest if I send you some brief personal impressions of the struggle. I am not, of course, going to attempt in any way to write a history of the negotiations – that would take more time and historical perspective than I possess. So you must be content with a hastily dictated and incoherent letter. (Of course, in so far as it is incoherent it is in a style appropriate to much of the negotiations. You will remember someone's comment on Carlyle's *French Revolution* – that most of the events described in it appeared to be taking place at night amid dense smoke and complete confusion. Perhaps you ought to advise Hawtrey[1] to reread his Carlyle before he comes to deal with this particular segment of financial history.)

The main difficulty in writing you this letter is to know where to begin. I think, however, that I can best give you an idea of the atmosphere if I say that for most of the time there were no negotiations in the ordinary sense of the word at all. That is to say, we scarcely ever had, or ever approached, a proper discussion with the American team on the questions at issue. The setting in which the meetings of the so-called Main Committee took place was such as to preclude anything in the nature of a discussion. There was never any agenda: the two groups sat round the wall in Mr Morgenthau's[2] room and made speeches at each other: once the question before the meeting became at all complicated, it was obvious that it had passed beyond Mr Morgenthau's comprehension and it was impossible in such a setting to try to make him understand what it was all about. It is true that with some difficulty Mr Morgenthau was persuaded to agree to joint sub-committee meetings under Harry White's[3] chairmanship. But although Harry White proved an admirable chairman, the meetings were nearly always much too large, there was great difficulty in getting any agreement beforehand on the agenda, while the Americans found great difficulty in keeping a team in the field for as much as ten minutes at a stretch. People were always being called away to the telephone, to see the Secretary, to see a man about a dog, and so on. Consequently proceedings were always being held up while Mr Currie[4] or Mr Acheson[5] was found and persuaded to come back to the meeting.

The great misfortune was, in my view, the failure to establish at the beginning of the negotiations a small high-powered combined committee at the 'official' level to act as a clearing house for the negotiations generally, to deal with points of principle, and to act as a channel through which really important issues could have been submitted to the 'ministerial' committee presided over by Mr Morgenthau. Admittedly, on our side this would have meant some overlap, since presumably Keynes would have figured on both the 'official' and 'ministerial' committees, but I do not think that this would have mattered: and if there could have been a body consisting of, say, Keynes, Sinclair[6] and Brand[7] on our side and Acheson, Harry White and Currie on the American side, I believe that much more rapid and more satisfactory progress would have been made. As it was, for a very large part of the time we were completely in the dark about what the Americans were doing. It usually transpired that they were having prolonged, exhausting and difficult meetings among themselves about points in regard to which, if only they had consulted us informally beforehand, we could probably have saved them a great deal of needless anxiety and trouble. As it was, they usually emerged from these meetings breathless, but proudly bringing out as a trophy a document drawn up by one of their lawyers – which we at once rejected as either irrelevant or unacceptable, or both. They then had to begin all over again.

The trouble largely arose, of course, from Mr Morgenthau's determination to remain in personal control of the negotiations. In the event, I think that the fact that he did so and that we were at great pains always to regard him as the leader on the American side, redounded to our advantage in the negotiations and will continue to help us in the future. But, as I have said, it meant that devolution to an effective combined body at the official level proved impossible. The chances of getting such a body established were in any event weakened by what one may call the Cherwell[8] delusions on our side. As you probably know, Cherwell persisted in believing that if only Mr Morgenthau and he could be left in a room together for about five minutes, untrammelled by officials and 'legalistic' documents, he (Lord Cherwell) would emerge with a definite promise of $5-6 billions and no questions asked. I cannot tell you what an immense relief it was to all of us here when the Cabinet decided to send Maynard out: until he came we were little better than disorganised rabble. The news of his coming made all the difference to our spirits:

'Et l'espoir, malgré moi, s'est glissé dans mon coeur.'

Even given the initial failure to establish an effective combined committee at the official level, a great deal of the confusion could have been avoided had the Americans had a really effective Secretary for their group. But Frank Coe[9] must, I think, be written off as a failure. He is never exactly a ball of fire – Maynard at one time said that the trouble with Coe was that he was bone lazy and in addition his glands were wrong. Certainly he is the only Secretary I know who has fallen fast asleep at a meeting of which he was supposed to be taking the minutes and had to be woken up by the Chairman. The main trouble was that he himself was very elusive and, when finally tracked down, had very little real knowledge of what was going on or was likely to happen on the American side. It was here that we missed Denby[10] so badly – in fact the absence of Denby throughout the negotiations was our greatest handicap. I feel that if Denby had been there, we could have ascertained from him informally what were the snags immediately ahead and could have suggested ways and means of by-passing them. As it was, the only *effective* off-the-record contacts we had with the American side was when Maynard used to get hold of Harry White informally. Otherwise there was no one at what I may call the second-eleven level who was sufficiently in the know to be able to tell us what was going on behind the scenes. I ought perhaps to make it clear that in saying this I am not in any way criticising the way in which the actual discussions of the programmes themselves were conducted. I was not present at any of these, but my impression is that (apart from the difficulties with the Navy Department) the discussion of the military programme was admirably conducted, while Griffin,[11] Appel[12] and others did their best to expedite discussions of the non-munition programmes and in general were cooperative and reasonable in their attitude.

Who then were the heroes of the negotiation – accepting the thesis that it was an episode which had its heroes. On our side, one name stands quite alone. Maynard's performance was truly wonderful. I think that occasionally he over-played his hand and occasionally wore himself out in struggling for points which were not worth winning. But in general he was an inspiration to us all: it is no exaggeration to say that we felt like Lucifer's followers in Milton 'Rejoicing in their matchless chief'. His industry was prodigious, his resilience and continuous optimism constant wonder to those of us more inclined to pessimism, while I doubt whether he has ever written or spoken with more lucidity and charm. And, of course, the impression which he makes on the Americans gives us an enormous initial advantage in any negotiation in which he participates. Take Harry White, for instance – that difficult nature unfolds like a flower when Maynard is there, and he is quite different to deal with when under the spell than he is in our normal day-to-day relations with him. I think that everyone on the United Kingdom side would agree that we could not have hoped to have got anywhere near the results which have actually been achieved had it not been for Maynard's genius and inspired leadership.

There are three other people on the U.K. side whom I should like to mention briefly. The first is Charles Hambro.[13] He was given the rather tiresome job of being Chairman of the Non-munitions Committee. This involved protracted discussions with the U.S. Foreign Economic Administration, often on boring points of detail and wording. Charles devoted himself to this work with great industry and constant good temper. His was, I think, a very notable contribution. Secondly, I think that Helmore[14] did an extremely good job for the Board of Trade. He did so by assiduously attending every meeting he could. He kept the export question where it ought to have been – right in the middle of the picture. He got on excellently with Maynard and worked most harmoniously with us in the Treasury Delegation – always being ready to help us out in odd jobs if we were pressed for staff or time. I cannot believe that any other possible representative of the Board of Trade could have achieved for himself the position that Helmore did. Lastly, I should like to say what an excellent job, in my view, was done by Stevens[15] and the Secretarial Staff under him. For the most part they simply had humdrum work to do, but they were always cheerful and ready to rally if we wanted some extra copying done late at night or some long telegram despatched on a Sunday. Keynes paid a tribute to them at one of the official steering committees, but I hope very much that it will be possible for the Treasury to give them a separate pat on the back for what they did.

On the American side I think that Morgenthau is definitely

entitled to a place. It is quite true that for a large part of the time he had very little idea of what was going on. But his discussions with the Chancellor and subsequently with Keynes had left him with clear conviction that the United Kingdom must be helped to make the first steps towards economic recovery, and he cast himself for the role of the U.K. champion. And although he was on occasions both tiresome and timorous, I think that he sincerely stuck to the role in the face of opposition from other quarters in the U.S. administration. He had one great triumph – when after terrific efforts he brought the Navy Department into line and made them discuss details of our naval requirements with the Admiralty Delegation. This great effort plus the excitement of the election and the 6th War Bond Drive left him exhausted, and in the last battle (about the date from which export freedom should begin) he was worsted by Crowley.[16] But the willingness to help us is, I think, now definitely there. Here again, of course, we owe a very great deal to the charm of Maynard and the memories of Bretton Woods.

A second figure who stood on the American side was Harry White. I have already referred to his unwonted geniality. But apart from this he was most impressive on the occasions when he acted as Chairman of the Combined Sub-Committee. Admittedly he did not succeed in making the meetings very coherent, but he showed great ability in getting to the heart of the issues and in something of the action to be taken on them.

Dean Acheson played a comparatively minor role, although he saved the situation on one most tiresome question – that of the so-called 'Reciprocal Aid' clauses in the military agreements. In this case he presided over a meeting with the War Department and insisted upon their accepting as satisfactory the assurances which were given on behalf of Australia, New Zealand and India, instead of their sticking grimly to clauses which we had constantly declared to be unacceptable. The primary trouble with Acheson has been, of course, that he has been greatly overworked and that his subordinates are pretty poor. . . .

Lastly I would add, but with a good many reservations, Oscar Cox.[17] He did not play any very prominent part in the earlier negotiations since he was preoccupied with preparations of the President's Lend–Lease Report. In the later stages of the negotiations his political judgement was, I think, very definitely at fault, and it was he who was primarily responsible for urging Crowley to come out in opposition against the proposal to give us export freedom as from 1 January 1945. In short, I think that Oscar has again shown that he is willing to subordinate any question of principle to political expediency . . .

Finally, what can one say about the outcome of the negotiations? For my part, while life in Washington naturally makes one more and more a believer in what Sir Thomas Browne would call the mutability of any human arrangements, I think that the negotiation was an unqualified success. Certainly if one contrasts what we achieved at the end of November with what some of us hoped to achieve at the end of August, I think that we can be well satisfied. In particular, I think that we achieved success in four definite directions:

(a) The fact that the military programmes were accepted to the extent that they have been was a significant success, despite our failure to get protocol status...

(b) I think that at the U.S. Treasury there is now a pretty clear recognition that the U.S. dollar balance is serious and that we have got to be helped, if possible, to safeguard it...

(c) On the question of export freedom, which was, to my mind, very largely the crux of the negotiations, we have achieved a settlement which is at least a long way better than anything that appeared likely to emerge from the abortive negotiations of the spring and early summer...

(d) Lastly I think that in what I may call the intermediate ranks of the U.S. Foreign Economic Administration there has been something like a rally to our side and a recognition that we have had less than a fair deal over Lend–Lease during recent months...

As I said at the beginning, I am afraid that this is a very incoherent letter which I have had to dictate in the intervals of rather urgent work. But you may find it of some interest as a humdrum supplement to the brilliant, racy accounts of the negotiations which you will, no doubt, get from Maynard.

Yours ever,
Frank

NOTES

1. R. G. Hawtrey, Director of Financial Enquiries, H.M. Treasury.
2. H. Morgenthau, Secretary of the U.S. Treasury.
3. H. D. White, Assistant to the Secretary of the U.S. Treasury.
4. L. Currie, Deputy Administrator, U.S. Foreign Economic Administration; Administrative Assistant to the President.
5. Dean Acheson, U.S. Assistant Secretary of State.
6. Sir Robert Sinclair, Chief Executive, Ministry of Production.
7. R. H. Brand, H.M. Treasury's Representative in Washington.
8. Lord Cherwell, Paymaster General.
9. F. Coe, Assistant Administrator, U.S. Foreign Economic Administration.

10. C. Denby, Head, General Areas Branch, U.S. Foreign Economic Administration.
11. Mr Griffin, Member, U.S. Foreign Economic Administration.
12. G. Appel, Member, U.S. Foreign Economic Administration.
13. Sir Charles Hambro, Head, British Raw Materials Mission, Washington.
14. J. C. Helmore, Under Secretary, Board of Trade.
15. R. B. Stevens, Secretary, British Civil Secretariat, Washington.
16. L. T. Crowley, Administrator, U.S. Foreign Economic Administration.
17. O. Cox, General Counsel, U.S. Foreign Economic Administration.

20

Keynes in the City

NICHOLAS DAVENPORT

One of the oldest investment institutions in the City of London is the National Mutual Life Assurance Society. It was an amalgamation of two 'mutual' societies – the National dating back to 1830 and the Mutual to 1834. Each was founded to carry out 'the principles of mutual life assurance'. The beginnings were small, the growth of the joint Society was slow, the investment policies were conservative. Prudence was the key-note. Nothing sensational ever happened – apart from the installation of the telephone in the Society's office in May 1896 – until the greatest economist of our age, Maynard Keynes, was elected to the board of directors in 1919 and to the chair in 1921. Thereafter the Society emerged from local obscurity into national prominence. The new chairman's annual speeches to the policy-holders became headline news in the press. This went on for seventeen years – until his resignation in October 1938.

The man responsible for Keynes's election to the National Mutual Board in 1919 was Geoffrey Marks, one of the country's outstanding actuaries. He had been Chief Officer of the Mutual Society since 1893 and his word was law. Fortunately he was an intellectual with forward ideas and a great admirer of Keynes, having been greatly impressed by the essays on monetary reform. He had secured the election to the board in 1918 of Keynes's close friend and collaborator, Oswald Toynbee Falk. Head of a stockbroking firm, Buckmaster and Moore, Falk was a man of intellectual distinction and had been a member of the Society's actuarial staff before the First World War. He had served with Keynes at the Treasury during the war and at the subsequent Versailles conference. To complete his intellectual team Geoffrey Marks in 1921 managed to get another Cambridge economist elected to the board – Walter Layton, who was then Editor of *The Economist*.

One can imagine the fierce financial arguments which flew across the board-room table, for the first time in the history of this conventional mutual life office, when two or more economists of the advanced Keynesian school of thought were gathered together.

Fortunately I was able later on to witness it myself because in 1932 I was elected to the board to replace my friend Sidney Russell Cooke – a pupil and friend of Keynes – who had died suddenly in 1930. Geoffrey Marks had sent for me and said: 'I want some one on this blasted board who can answer Keynes back.' That, of course, was an impossibility. Maynard could always get the better of any financial argument. Besides I was a student of Keynesian economics and was at that time writing the finance column of the *New Statesman and Nation* under Keynes's supervision.

In the Society's official history it is drily recorded: 'At the beginning of 1919 the Society entered upon a period of the greatest importance in its history . . . Keynes's association with the Society has given distinction to the National Mutual and it is he who is largely responsible for the development of the financial policy which has resulted in the Society's present high standard among British life offices.'

What the authors meant to say was that Keynes had revolutionised their ideas of investment. It had hitherto been actuarial practice in the life offices to distribute their assets between money at call, government bonds, loans and mortgages, debentures and reversions in more or less fixed proportions. Ordinary shares with fluctuating dividends were not considered respectable. Board rooms were scared of economic cycles and oblivious of equity growth. When Geoffrey Marks was explaining this conventional practice to Keynes on their first interview Maynard listened with amazement. 'Incredible!' he said. 'I would have thought that the right investment policy for the National Mutual would be to hold one security only and change it every week at the board meeting.'

This would not have been considered such a speculative orgy by the 'go-go' managers today, for at the end of the quinquennium in 1919 the invested funds of the National Mutual were only a little over £3 million. I hasten to add that the conventional prudence of its board had enabled the Society to write off out of the actuarial profits of this quinquennium its entire war losses and still declare a good bonus on the with-profit policies. These war losses were stated to be 'Depreciation of investments 1914–18 £203,000, claims under policies due to war casualties £99,100, increase in income tax £75,700.' The financial scale of horror in those days was clearly manageable for actuaries.

At his first quinquennial meeting as Chairman of the Board in 1924 Keynes told the policy holders: 'Life assurance societies must stand or fall mainly with the success or failure of their investment policy . . . While actuarial practice is much the same in all well-conducted Societies today investment provides more pitfalls and

225

also more opportunities than it formerly did . . . The board of the National Mutual believes that the gradual building up of a sound investment policy is the most vital part of their duties.' This indicated that Keynes had made the National Mutual board adopt what is known as 'an active investment policy'.

Most life office directors had been content hitherto to sleep on their investments, leaving their management to their professional hidebound actuaries. A breath of fresh air now swept through the National Mutual office. Keynes at that time was extremely busy on his own account, speculating in forward exchange and commodities – more often than not in partnership with Falk – but this, of course, was not what he expected the National Mutual to do. An 'active investment policy' for a life office meant primarily active dealings in the money and government bond markets. And Keynes added a second dimension – active 'switching' in the equity share markets.

In the money and bond markets Keynes was able to apply his professional knowledge as an economist and monetary expert. The National Mutual would place its money on 'the street' on a day-to-day basis when some crisis had driven money rates sharply upward. Then it would move into the government bond market when it foresaw money rates turning downwards. Finally, it would gather in its capital profits when it considered that the gilt-edged market had reached its peak. That was the theory of the exercise but, of course, it was not always easy to carry it out in practice.

Exploitation of the money cycle in the 1920s and 1930s – covering boom and slump – certainly required expertise. Keynes could foresee the course of monetary events long before the Governor of the Bank, Montagu Norman, had put the controls into operation. Not only that – he could influence the course of events by his annual speeches at the National Mutual. In 1934, for example, in his speech to the policyholders he had elaborated on the crying economic need for cheaper money and the national press next day headlined his cogent arguments. The gilt-edged market immediately soared upwards. Such was his great influence in the City.

An active investment policy in equities in this period was a much more difficult affair. The Western economies were being caught up in the American boom and were heading for the crash which fell upon Wall Street in the autumn of 1929.

It is generally believed that Keynes was responsible for inducing the life offices to invest in equity shares for the first time. This is not strictly true, for the National Mutual had acquired a large block of Prudential Assurance ordinary shares long before he joined the board. But it is certainly correct to say that it was Keynes who demonstrated to the life offices that investment in industrial and commercial ordinary shares as well as in insurance and investment trust equities was a desirable investment policy for the growth of a life fund and that the trade cycle could be exploited for the timing of their entries into or their exits from equity shares. I am not suggesting that Keynes persuaded life offices to trade in equity shares, as some managers do today, but it was something to persuade the actuaries of the life offices to keep equities in their portfolios as a fixed and permanent proportion of their assets and to contemplate 'switching' not only when management problems arose but when economic trends pointed to a 'bear' market.

In his speech at the annual general meeting of the National Mutual in January 1929 Keynes was able to declare record profits and bonuses. In the first decade over which he had presided at the board he was able to announce that the average annual bonus earned was in excess of 95 shillings – the highest so far ever achieved in any life office. The surplus carried forward was equal to 20.7% of the liabilities.

Came the Great Depression and much trouble followed for those who had plunged heavily into equity investment. The National Mutual had invested in dollar equities as well as British – at one time the division was 50/50 – and there was much disputing on the board about the virtues of equity investments. Falk was the great advocate of dollar equity growth. Unfortunately he had induced Keynes to join in the launching on the market, and to act as Chairman, of the Independent Investment Trust in 1924. The propectus appealed for institutional money in a somewhat arrogant manner, saying, in effect, that the directors would not bother to estimate their future profits because they understood the money system and would be able to exploit the movements in the rate of interest. In six years the Independent Investment Trust had virtually lost its entire capital – around £1 million – because it had invested heavily in the preferred stocks of American investment trusts and utilities. Keynes and Falk were obliged by their institutional shareholders to hand over the management of the Company to a city merchant bank, Helbert Wagg. There was a flaming quarrel between Keynes and Falk – not the 'some disagreement' which Harrod records (p. 302) in his life of Keynes – and my personal knowledge is that Keynes and Falk never again worked closely together in investment affairs except on the board of the National Mutual.

And we went on having our board-room rows. Intellectuals on City boards of directors always generate rows and it was a delight to watch Maynard handling and sometimes provoking them. Maynard despised conventional bankers. In his articles in the *Nation* and later in the *New Statesman and Nation* he never lost an opportunity to pour scorn on orthodox finance and ridicule the bankers. This came to the boil, first, during the 1925 return to gold, when he called Winston Churchill, then Chancellor of the Exchequer, and the Governor of the Bank, Montagu Norman, 'feather-brained' in his pamphlet 'The Economic Consequences of Mr Churchill', secondly, during the 1931 sterling crisis when he inveighed against the bankers' deflationism expressed in the May report. Unfortunately we had a banker on our board – Francis Curzon, the brother of the great Marquess Curzon. He was deputy Chairman of the Westminster Bank. On one occasion when there was an awkward dispute over investment policy Keynes turned on him and said: 'Really, Curzon, you have all the pomposity of your brother and not a scrap of his intelligence.'

The 1930s were very difficult times for the security markets. After the first crash of September 1929 there was a sizeable recovery in Wall Street in 1930. It was the long subsequent fall to the end of 1932, bringing most investment trusts and holding companies down to around 10% of their 1929 peaks, which brought disaster to the investment world. The portfolio of the National Mutual Life, being better balanced and more widely distributed, escaped the tragedy of the Independent Investment Trust, but it had to postpone the valuation of 1929/30. However, the depreciation it suffered on its portfolio was completely recovered by the end of 1934 – and a handsome surplus added. It is typical of the man that Keynes always insisted on having the truth revealed about its portfolio – by taking current market values – in defiance of the actuarial custom of the life offices which was to show their portfolios at cost.

My recollection of the later thirties is that Maynard was getting tired of having to carry disputatious board-room colleagues with him in an active investment policy. You cannot as a rule be successful in the management of an investment portfolio if you have to work through a committee. You have to trust your own judgement and be quick to reverse your position if it is necessary. Maynard proved that he could be successful when acting alone. His own portfolio was worth £506,450 by the beginning of 1937. But I came across a minute of his in the books of the National Mutual which expressed his doubts about collective management. It was dated 12 October 1937, and it ran as follows: 'Investment results largely depend on how one behaves near the top and near the bottom. We have failed to be successful near the top. But that is no reason why we should be equally unsuccessful in the slump.' And we were not.

I think Maynard in the end began to get disillusioned with an 'active investment policy' and more inclined to accept the policy of the more cautious actuaries, namely, that for a long-term investment institution, like a life office, it was wise to concentrate on long-term equity holdings, choosing only those of the best managed companies. The Wall Street crash made everyone less inclined to play the market game and it brought the following caution in Keynes's classic *General Theory*: 'Speculators may do no harm as bubbles on a steady stream of enterprise, but the position is serious when enterprise becomes the bubble on a whirlpool of speculation. When the capital development of a country becomes a by-product of the activities of a Casino the job is likely to be ill-done.'

In his last speech as Chairman of the National Mutual Life in May 1938, he spoke as usual to a wider audience and protested against the deflationary techniques of the Bank of England which had just issued a wad of long-dated debt, instead of Treasury bills, thus causing a slump in the gilt-edged market. He requested the Bank of England 'to add to our knowledge of the actual facts and figures which alone can make the working of the economic system intelligible. A great deal is at stake. We have to show that a free system can be made to work.' He expressed confidence that the Great Depression would soon be over but it was clear that his patience with argumentative investment committees was getting exhausted. He resigned from the board of the National Mutual in October 1938 when the assets of the Society had reached £7½ million. They are now over £90 million.

Curiously enough he went on as Chairman of the Provincial Insurance Company, which he had joined in 1923, for the rest of his life because he found the Scott family atmosphere more agreeable. I think he always despised the City and its stiff-necked Establishment. Although he was elected to the Court of the Bank of England in 1941 – his old enemy was later prostrate at his feet after he had exhausted himself over Bretton Woods and in securing the American and Canadian loans – it cannot be said that he was ever a popular figure in the City. He would have felt very ashamed in Bloomsbury if he had been.

21

Keynes and economic history

CHARLES WILSON

In the Cambridge of the early twentieth century history was much in the air. In King's College it was the air that Keynes breathed as an undergraduate. Two of King's history dons came, like Keynes, from dissenting stock: John Clapham and W. F. Reddaway. Reddaway, like Keynes, was Cambridge born. As time went on, there was Lowes Dickinson, Charles Webster and Frank Adcock.

Closer still, on the same staircase indeed, was Charles Ryle Fay who was later to be Reader in Economic History in the Faculty of Economics. Fay – eccentric, wayward, crusty but somehow lovable – was a close friend of Keynes in those days. Later they grew apart. The reason was not far to seek. Fay was a committed historian. His God was Adam Smith. His published lectures are still fascinating reading if you like exceptions to the rules of economic conduct, historical peculiarities, colourful anecdote. This, for Fay, was the stuff of history. Keynes, a social scientist, saw things very differently, searching always in history for foreshadowings of the present, mirrors of current problems. 'Keynes', Fay once exploded to me, 'didn't believe in *history*. He only wanted to use bits of it for his own purposes.'

I suspect that in his heart of hearts, John Clapham sympathised with Fay. True, it was the great economist Alfred Marshall who had put Clapham on to the paths of economic history, but Clapham was taught by Archdeacon Cunningham, Dean of Trinity and father of Cambridge economic history, as well as by Marshall the economist. Clapham's history reflected the second more than the first. His attitude, too, was sceptical towards theory (though he was a good theorist). He once confessed he never read Keynes's *General Theory* because conversation with Keynes convinced him he would not understand it.

This may seem an odd introduction to a note on Keynes the historian. Yet, *pace* Clapham and Fay, Keynes wrote two pieces which demonstrated his deep interest in history, economic history especially. They are the 'historical' chapters in the *Treatise on*

Money (1930) and in *The General Theory* (1936). Both have stimulated long controversy. Both have been influential and (I believe) beneficial to the study of economic history.

In the *Treatise*, after some characteristically brilliantly epigrammatic flourishes on prices, profits and enterprise, he breaks off for an historical digression – equally characteristic in its imaginative sweep and refreshingly old-fashioned in its audacious rejection of narrow specialisation.

> It would be a fascinating task to re-write economic history in the light of these ideas ... to conjecture whether the civilizations of Sumeria and Egypt drew their stimulus from the gold of Arabia and the copper of Africa which, being monetary metals, left a trail of profit behind them in the course of their distribution through the lands between the Mediterranean and the Persian Gulf ... in what degree the greatness of Athens depended on the silver mines of Laurium ... how far the dispersal by Alexander of the bank reserves of Persia . . . was responsible for the outburst of economic progress in the Mediterranean basin of which Carthage attempted and Rome ultimately succeeded to reap the fruits; whether it was coincidence that the decline and fall of Rome was contemporaneous with the most prolonged and drastic deflation yet recorded; if the long stagnation of the Middle Ages may not have been more surely and inevitably caused by Europe's meagre supply of the monetary metals than by monastic or Gothic frenzy; and how much the glorious Revolution owed to Mr Phipps.

(Mr Phipps was a bold adventurer who fished up a record haul of £$\frac{1}{4}$ million in bullion from a wrecked galleon off Hispaniola in 1688. Did this provoke the Stock Exchange boom recorded by the historian of the Joint Stock Companies, W. R. Scott?)

Then followed a rather more serious examination of a case study in the evolution of capitalism. The source was the work of the American economic historian, Earl J. Hamilton, whose industrious researches into the mining and export of Central American silver to Spain and the ensuing price revolution of the sixteenth century had fascinated Keynes. The suggestion was that down to the 1580s, the influx of treasure had created a great profit inflation in Spain, only to be followed by ineluctable decline as wages caught up with and overtook prices, turning profits into losses. Elaborating the tenuous theoretical basis of Hamilton, Keynes enlarged spaciously upon the original. And unquestionably, as another American historian wrote later, Keynes's 'great authority' undoubtedly brought great support and prestige to Hamilton's thesis.

Time and research have dimmed the light which Keynes's gloss on Hamilton seemed at one time to cast on the mysteries underlying the causes of the sixteenth-century price revolution. The American critic already quoted, Professor J. U. Nef, in a paper delivered to the Anglo-American Historians' Conference in 1936, and reprinted many times since, challenged the accuracy of Keynes's figures and the plausibility of his theories. Why, if we are properly advised to seek for the origins of modern capitalism in a widening gap between low labour costs and rising prices which create high profit margins, did *France* not enjoy such an early capitalist boom? For was not the gap there also large? Yet France remained, capitalistically speaking, backward. Steadily, Nef and others eroded the Hamilton–Keynes 'thesis'.

Few historians today would feel able to accept the Keynes thesis without drastic modification. Yet here, as in other instances, Keynes did something important for the study of history. He asked the right questions; he saw the problem in a wide context; he provoked good and fruitful controversy; his was not the whole truth by a long chalk, but he was the means by which a greater degree of truth was to be achieved. In passing, it is worth noticing that the footnotes acknowledge his debt to Clapham – not that Clapham shared his views but he provided Keynes with historical material, such as evidence of wage levels in sixteenth-century England. Did Keynes also borrow from Clapham ideas of the *stimulus* which discoveries of gold and silver may give to enterprise? There is a remarkable paragraph in Clapham's *Economic Development of France and Germany* published just before the *Treatise*, in which he deals in his usual masterly fashion with this problem (pp. 381–2). The two minds thought remarkably alike on this occasion. But who was the originator? It is impossible to know. Both in their different ways were realists: perhaps that is why their ideas sometimes coincided.

Keynes's second excursion into history was even more striking. At the end of *The General Theory* he prints some 'Notes on Mercantilism'. He had been reading the great 2-volume work on *Mercantilism* (1935) by the distinguished Swedish historian (and strictly classical) economist, Eli Heckscher. This had just appeared in English translation as Keynes was writing *The General Theory*, and it provoked him into some reflections on the balance of trade, bullion, saving and investment in their historical aspect. There emerged a sharp attack on the orthodox economists who (he believed) had 'been guilty of presumptuous error in treating as a puerile obsession what for centuries has been a prime object of statecraft'. Then followed a characteristically elegant model by way of justification. The only practical inducement to investment in the past was a low rate of interest. That in turn depended on a plentiful supply of precious metals and this in turn on a favourable balance of payments. The favourable balances could only be achieved by

Plate 13   Maynard Keynes in 1930.

Plate 14   George Bernard Shaw and Maynard Keynes on the steps of the Fitzwilliam Museum, Cambridge, in 1936 after the opening of two new galleries (*Cambridge Evening News*).

either diminishing imports or boosting exports, and for the latter full, or at least fuller, employment was needed. Thus the mercantilists nobbled the rate of investment, economic growth and higher employment at one go. Were they not far, far better men than had been supposed? Were they not 'realists' who had grasped the fundamentals of the economic predicament of their age – that 'throughout human history there has been a chronic tendency for the propensity to save to be stronger than the inducement to invest'?

Once again, Keynes had asked some pertinent questions. Once again he had placed an old problem on a new and larger setting. Once again he had brushed the dust off an historical monument and thrown new light on its real significance. And, of course, once again, and quite inevitably, he had touched off a lively controversy. In his 'Notes' he had paid scrupulously courteous deference to Heckscher's historical eminence, the quality of his work and in particular the grand scope of the two volumes on *Mercantilism*, only observing lightly and in passing that it was hardly likely that the author, a member of the classical school, would find himself in full agreement with his (Keynes's) conclusions on the subject.

This was to prove a masterpiece of understatement. Keynes's polite references, far from softening the asperity of Heckscher's reaction to the Keynesian heresy, did the reverse. After rumbling critically over the 'Notes' in reviews for some years, Heckscher's final Olympian thunder rolled out in full majesty in the shape of a completely new Appendix to a revised English edition of *Mercantilism* published in 1955. All the orthodox objections were brought into play. He probed, skilfully and up to a point successfully, Keynes's weaknesses – especially the tenuous relationship at certain points between Keynes's theoretical assumptions about governments, entrepreneurs and their policies, objectives and motives in the historic past and the actualities of history. Inevitably some of his shots landed on target; but in one general sense, Keynes's 'rehabilitation' of mercantilism remained substantially intact. However partial or unsuccessful might be their ideas in detail, were 40,000 English politicians, merchants, pamphleteers and publicists all wholly and hopelessly wrong in their belief in the efficiency of some measure of *dirigisme*, and that deriving from balance of payments considerations? To this, the orthodox school had no reply which was likely to convince any but the committed classical theorist.

I had myself in 1949 put forward a note on *Treasure and Trade Balances: the Mercantilist Problem*. Starting with quotations from Keynes's 'Notes' to *The General Theory* I had attempted to refine and extend the Keynesian thesis, broadening its basis and trying to relate it more closely and empirically to historical evidence. But, like Keynes himself, I too – and equally inadvertently – provoked a sharp and aggrieved rejoinder from Heckscher. Unlike Keynes I did not suffer the all-out blockbuster with which Heckscher concluded his Appendix on *The General Theory*. For not content to stop at history, Heckscher here advanced on to a general anti-Keynes offensive along the whole economic front. As an economist, it appeared, Keynes scarcely deserved to be considered in the long term. His whole work 'was dominated by the problems of employment and unemployment'. His thinking was relevant essentially, and perhaps only, to an age of massive fixed capital investment and was itself merely a product of depression between the two world wars. These added up to 'a phenomenon with which Keynes seems almost to be obsessed' – employment. 'Seldom has a work with pretensions to universal applicability been based to such an extent on a single, narrow point of view.' *The General Theory*, Heckscher concluded (Vol. II, pp. 357–8), was not general at all: it was highly and narrowly particular.

So much, it would seem, for economists who leave their straight-and-narrow and get mixed up with history.

With another historical excursion of a rather different kind – the two essays on Malthus – I shall not concern myself at length, for Keynes as a biographer is dealt with elsewhere in this book by David Garnett. I will only say of them that though Keynes uses Malthus and his theories (as he often uses historical phenomena and ideas) for his own purposes, the essays are alive with historical sensibility. They were originally read as a paper to a luncheon gathering in King's on the centenary of Malthus's death. Malthus was not a King's man: he was a Jesus man and a product of the ancient Yorkshire connection of that College. (The name was a contraction of the North Country name 'Malthouse' and not, as is often thought, some strange if unspecific continental surname.) Jesus were accordingly invited to send a representative for the Malthusian occasion. He was Sir Arthur Quiller-Couch – 'Q' – novelist, critic, Professor of English Literature and a Fellow of Malthus's old College. The luncheon and paper together ensured that it was late afternoon before the guests dispersed. As they did, Q met Scholfield, University Librarian and Fellow of King's. The following dialogue ensued:

Scholfield: Surely it's too late to go back to dinner at Jesus, Q? Why don't you stay on and have dinner with me here?

Q: Thank you kindly, Scholfield, but no. You must remember Malthus was a Jesus man and we have our own little Feast of the Contraception. I must get back to it!

Views on Keynes as historian will continue to differ. There is something, certainly, in Fay's *dictum*. Keynes *did* use history for his own purposes. It *was* often a kind of tactical support weapon, brought up to give weight to the generalities of logic and analysis. At other times it was an intellectual toy, a plaything of the mind. The mathematical side of his mind enjoyed playing with historical evidence just to see what could be done with it. In the chapter of the *Treatise on Money* quoted above, he digresses on the matter of Francis Drake's privateering booty brought back in *The Golden Hind* for the Queen. This he describes as the 'fountain and origin of British foreign investment'. £42,000 invested in 1580 (Keynes calculated) would have accumulated by 1930 to approximately the aggregate of British foreign investment at the time he was writing – £4,200,000,000, or one hundred thousand times the original investment. At moments like these the historian can hardly help feeling the gap growing between his conceptual world and that of Keynes the mathematical economist.

Yet there is a real sense in which Keynes did economic history a great service. Just because he was a mathematician, a theorist, an applied economist, a bibliophile, an artist, a polymath – everything, in fact, except a professional historian – he could look at history from the wings, knowing enough not to be irrelevant, yet not knowing so much by rote that he was overwhelmed either by antiquarian facts or by an undue sense of professional responsibility. As an economist and statistician he knew which questions needed asking – better, perhaps, than many economic historians. He read with great diligence and perception the kinds of economic history that seemed to him to say something important – or perhaps *almost* to say it. And he completed its articulation with that mixture of elegance and masterly persuasion which, if it did not always convince, never failed to stamp itself on the mind. His propositions were often unacceptable but his methods made historians ask themselves new questions – about the origins of capitalism, the role of money and government, the significance of balance of trade theories, the functions of precious metals, the operations of prices etc., etc. He stimulated and provoked by breaking down the old images and clearing away the debris of ancient received doctrine – doctrine which historians often found themselves enunciating without knowing they were doing so. But he was also the historical *amateur* in the best and original meaning of the word. Perhaps he did *use* history, but he did so not only because it served his purpose but because he valued the added dimension it afforded to the imagination. In many ways, he contributed to the art and science of economic history, revivifying and strengthening it with the powerful resources of his mind, imagination and style.

22

Keynes as a philosopher

R. B. BRAITHWAITE

Keynes wrote one philosophical book, *A Treatise on Probability* (1921 and Vol. VIII of the *Collected Writings*); and qualified his view of probability in a book review of 1931 (included in *Collected Writings*, Vol. X). These exhaust his published writings which were deliberately philosophical; they form the subject of the first part of this essay, which draws heavily on what I wrote as an 'editorial foreword' to *Collected Writings*, Vol. VIII. The second part of the essay comments on the puzzling account which Keynes gave of the development of his own moral philosophy in the memoir 'My Early Beliefs', posthumously published in 1949 (included in *Collected Writings*, Vol. X).

I

The story of the writing of the *Treatise on Probability* has been fully told in R. F. Harrod's biography of Keynes. Keynes started work on Probability in 1906 when he was in the India Office, and devoted most of his intellectual energy to it for the next five years until the book was nearly completed. After 1911 Keynes undertook commitments which delayed his completing the book; and although much of the *Treatise on Probability* had been set up in type by August 1914, it was not published until August 1921 after Keynes had spent most of 1920 on his final revision.

The *Treatise* was enthusiastically received by philosophers in the empiricist tradition, then reviving in the English-speaking countries. Keynes's name was already known to them by the acknowledgement for the use of some of his ideas made in the preface to Bertrand Russell's *The Problems of Philosophy* (1912) in the Home University Library series, a little book which became, as it were, the manual of the empiricist and realist revival. The welcome given to Keynes's book was largely due to the fact that his doctrine of probability filled an obvious gap in the empiricist theory of knowledge. Empiricists had divided knowledge into that which is 'intuitive' and that which is 'derivative' (to use Russell's terms), and had regarded the latter as being based upon the former by virtue of there being a logical relationship between them. Keynes extended the notion of logical relation to include probability relations, which enabled a similar account to be given of how intuitive knowledge could form the basis for rational belief which fell short of knowledge.

Keynes's thesis is that a probability statement expresses a logical relationship (i.e. the holding of a logical relation) between a proposition p and a proposition h (h is usually a conjunction of propositions). A man who knows h and perceives the logical relationship between p and h is justified in believing p with a degree of belief which corresponds to that of the logical relationship. If this logical relationship is that of p being a logical consequence of h, he is justified in being certain of the truth of p; if the logical relationship is that of the falsity of p being a logical consequence of h, he is justified in being certain of the falsity of p; if neither of these is the case, he is justified in having a degree of partial belief in p intermediate between certain belief and certain disbelief.

The originality of Keynes's approach lay in his insistence that probability, in its fundamental sense, is a logical relation holding between propositions which is similar to, although weaker than, that of logical consequence. The way in which the creators of the mathematical theory of probability (Bernoulli, Bayes, Laplace etc.) used the concept suggests that, like Keynes, they thought of it as concerned with justified degree of belief; but (except for an article by Dorothy Wrinch and Harold Jeffreys in 1919, which Keynes had not seen) the *Treatise* contains the first publication of the view that a partial belief is to be justified by knowledge of a logical probability relationship, and that these logical relationships form the subject matter of probability theory.

If Keynes's theory is regarded as a clarification of the concepts used by the classical mathematicians of probability, the only serious rival in 1921 to Keynes's 'logical' interpretation was the 'frequency' interpretation popular among statisticians. According to this the probability (for example) of a new-born child being a boy is concerned with the proportion among births of those which are births of boys. A theory of this sort had been expounded informally in John Venn's *Logic of Chance* (1866), but by 1921 the problem of how to formulate a mathematically satisfactory frequency theory was only beginning to be tackled. Keynes's criticism of the frequency theory is not directed at its mathematics, but is a cogent refutation of the claim that a frequency theory (of any sort) could provide a logic of partial belief. However, Keynes did not convert many statisticians to his own view; and with hindsight one can say that this was largely because he overstated his case. Both Keynes and his frequentist opponents believed that there is one unique concept of probability, the same in every context in which it occurs. Keynes took every probability to be a logical relation between two propositions so that whether or not the relation held was always a logical and never an empirical question. The frequentists took every probability to be a proportion (or in the more sophisticated forms, to be a number determined by proportions). Except in special cases these proportions are empirically given, and it is an empirical fact that a probability has the value which it has. If the frequentists cannot explain the probabilities which justify partial belief, Keynes cannot explain the probabilities (chances) which appear to be empirical facts. He makes a valiant attempt to derive a notion of chance which is to be 'objective' from a probability concerned with a degree of rational belief. But, apart from other difficulties, his account presupposes determinism. It is possible to argue that the 54% probability of a birth being the birth of a boy measures the degree of our ignorance as to whether the pre-natal causes determine that the child should be a boy or that it should be a girl. But this cannot be argued in the case of the 50% probability that a radium atom will disintegrate within 1,622 years (which physicists express by saying that 1,622 years is the 'half-life' of a radium atom), for it may well be that there is no cause for the atom to disintegrate at any one moment rather than at another. Keynes wrote before irreducibly statistical laws had come to be generally accepted in physics. Their advent makes it almost impossible to maintain that the proposition about the half-life of a radium atom is not an empirical proposition.

So most recent writers on probability who have followed Keynes and Jeffreys in holding something like a logical interpretation for probability in the context of partial belief have parted from them in holding a frequency interpretation of some sort for contexts in which probabilities are used inside the empirical propositions of a natural or social science. Probability in the logical interpretation has been called 'degree of confirmation' or 'credibility' or 'acceptability'; in the latter interpretation it has been called 'long-run frequency' or 'statistical probability' or 'chance'. Sometimes both interpretations are involved in the same sentence: to say that it is highly probable that a particular radium atom will not disintegrate within a year is to say that the statistical hypothesis that there is a high chance of the radium atom not disintegrating within a year is a hypothesis which is confirmed to a high degree on the present evidence.

But though students of probability who are sympathetic to

Keynes's approach have mostly felt compelled to separate off a distinct field, that of chance, to which Keynes's interpretation does not apply, conversely many of the statisticians for whom chance is the primary interest have been unable to avoid using something very much like Keynes's interpretation when they are attacking the problem of how to select the best statistical hypothesis to account for observed statistical data. Those who are now called 'Bayesians' would compare statistical hypotheses by comparing their Keynesian probabilities, given the data. Indeed almost any plausible principle for preferring one statistical hypothesis to another is equivalent to a Bayesian procedure with suitable prior probabilities ascribed to the hypotheses. For example, if these are taken to be equal, we have R. A. Fisher's 'Maximum Likelihood' principle.

Thus the logical interpretation of probability, developed fifty years ago by Keynes, Wrinch, Jeffreys (W. E. Johnson, who influenced Keynes, should also be mentioned) flourishes today when the term is used in the context of reasonable partial belief. However most of those today who would accept this sort of interpretation would not develop it in Keynes's way. Keynes takes the logical probability relationship between two propositions as fundamental to his explanation of rational partial belief, and he maintains that in suitable cases this relationship can be perceived, directly recognised, intuited. When he wrote his book most logicians would have been willing to use these verbs to describe one way of knowing that one proposition was a logical consequence of another; and Keynes thought that he was merely pointing to a wider class of logical relationships which could also be perceived. But most present-day logicians would be chary of using such verbs as 'perceive' to describe knowledge of logical-consequence relationships: many would instead describe such knowledge in terms of the structure and use of language systems. They would be even more chary of claiming to perceive probability relationships.

Consequently many of those today who think about the logic of partial belief would not start with a probability relationship and take a degree of belief as being justified by knowledge that a probability relation holds, but would start with the degree of belief and consider what conditions this must satisfy in order to be regarded as one which a rational man would have under given circumstances. To start this way requires a notion of degrees of belief which is independent of rationality, and this was provided by F. P. Ramsey in a paper of 1926 written deliberately as a constructive criticism of Keynes's view. Ramsey proposed to measure the degree of belief in a proposition p which a particular man has at a particular time by the rate at which he would be prepared to bet upon p being true, which is to say that a belief is of degree q (with $0 \leqslant q \leqslant 1$) if the man is prepared to pay a proportion q of one unit of value (but no more) for the right to receive one unit of value if p is true but nothing if p is false. Degrees of belief measured in this way will be called (following Rudolf Carnap) 'betting quotients'. A betting quotient measures a man's actual partial belief at a particular time and in no way depends upon whether or not the man has a good reason for holding a partial belief of that degree. To confine the partial belief to being one which is rational is effected by imposing restrictions upon the betting quotients.

To treat the logic of partial belief as the theory of the rationality of betting quotients may seem a far cry from Keynes's logical interpretation of probability. But there is no doubt that Keynes's main motive in writing the *Treatise* was to explain how a degree of belief could be rational, and thus not merely a matter of the believer's psychological make-up but one which all rational men under similar circumstances would share. Keynes's logical probability relations were introduced solely as a means to that end; and in a paragraph in which he speaks of probability as being 'relative in a sense to the principles of *human* reason' he throws over entirely his doctrine of specific objective probability-relations. The only publication of Keynes after 1921 which had a bearing upon his theory of probability was his comment on Ramsey's 1926 paper when it was posthumously published in *The Foundations of Mathematics and other logical essays* (1931). In a review of this book Keynes, in response to Ramsey's criticism, was prepared 'as against the view which I had put forward' to agree with Ramsey that 'probability is concerned not with objective relations between propositions but (in some sense) with degrees of belief'. So Keynes might not be unsympathetic to the 'restricted betting-quotient' approach.

However, restrictions on betting quotients do not seem able to provide the justification for inductive inference which Keynes hoped to achieve. Keynes was one of the first to realise clearly that any justification for assigning a positive probability to an empirical hypothesis on the basis of the knowledge of some (but not all) instances of it must presuppose that a probability was assigned to the hypothesis prior to any knowledge of instances of it. He proposed a 'principle of limited independent variety' to provide these prior probabilities, and many philosophers since 1921 have suggested variations and improvements on it. But even if we are not making the inference to a general hypothesis but only to a new instance of the hypothesis, a belief (full or partial) in some proposition about the universe appears to be essential in order to yield prior probabilities which would justify inductive inference.

Ramsey, following C. S. Peirce, believed that induction needed no justification of this sort; but he failed to convert Keynes. Keynes would go along with Ramsey in thinking (to quote from the review again) that 'the basis of our degrees of belief [which correspond to the prior probabilities] is part of our human outfit, perhaps given us merely by natural selection'. But he would wish to say more than this. 'It is not getting to the bottom of the principle of induction merely to say that it is a useful mental habit.' The debate on the status of inductive reasoning, opened by Hume and given a new turn in Keynes's *Treatise*, continues.

II

G. E. Moore's *Principia Ethica* (1903) appeared at the end of Keynes's first undergraduate year at Cambridge, and was received as the new gospel by him and his circle of friends. One cause of Keynes's taking to the study of probability was the large part this played in Moore's theory of right conduct, and part of one chapter of *A Treatise on Probability* (1921) is devoted to working out Moore's theory in more detail. Keynes, in his lifetime, published nothing specifically about his own moral philosophy; and in a short obituary note, published in *Mind* in 1946, I said without qualification that his ethic was essentially that of *Principia Ethica*, and called him a most 'humane Utilitarian'.

It was therefore with great surprise that I read Keynes's memoir 'My Early Beliefs' when it was posthumously published in 1949. This memoir had been read to a small group of intimate friends in 1938 following on a memoir by David Garnett describing D. H. Lawrence's rejection of Garnett's friends as 'black beetles'. Since Keynes's memoir describes his meeting with Lawrence in 1914 or 1915, and comments on Lawrence's reaction, it has become a key document in the socio-literary controversy about Lawrence's relations with 'Bloomsbury'. This is not my concern; but in the memoir, how relevant to Lawrence's 1915 reactions is questionable, Keynes describes and makes some criticisms of the 'new heaven' which (so he says) he and his friends in 1903 found in the teaching of *Principia Ethica*. This, he alleges, had little to do with actions and consequences, and nothing to do with 'morals'. Keynes concludes by depicting the circle of friends as graceful 'water-spiders' and admitting that 'there may have been just a grain of truth' when Lawrence said that 'we were done for'.

Keynes's memoir raises several puzzles, which do not entirely vanish if one takes Keynes to be pulling the legs of his 1938 hearers (as Quentin Bell, one of these, has suggested). For why then should

Keynes so explicitly have requested that it should be posthumously published? Some of my puzzlement vanished, however, when I worked out to my own satisfaction what might have been Keynes's reasons for saying some of the things in the memoir which seemed particularly perverse.

Why did Keynes select as he did from the contents of *Principia Ethica*? There are three strands of thought in this book. The first is Moore's argument for holding that the notion of intrinsic goodness – goodness for its own sake – is an unanalysable concept and that the word 'good', used in this sense, is indefinable. This thesis in the logic of ethics has been of great interest to academic philosophers; but it was not one to excite the young Keynes. What excited him was what he calls the 'religion', contained in the last chapter – the list of things good in themselves, good for their own sakes. Moore's ethical pluralism is the second strand of his thought. Instead of the one thing – pleasure – which the Utilitarians had allowed to be good in itself, Moore postulated a plurality of such things, of which 'by far the most valuable' are states of mind involving either 'the pleasures of human intercourse' or 'the enjoyment of beautiful objects'. This thesis pointed to 'the life of passionate contemplation and communion' as the 'Ideal' for Keynes and his friends. Moore's third strand of thought, expounded in the penultimate chapter 'Ethics in relation to conduct', argued for the classical Utilitarian doctrine that the rightness of an action derives from the character of its consequences – in Moore's language, an action is 'good as a means'. It is because this doctrine (which I shall, for convenience, call 'consequentialism') is common to Moore and the Utilitarians that the ethics of *Principia Ethica* has been called 'Ideal Utilitarianism' as contrasted with the 'Hedonistic Utilitarianism' of Bentham, the Mills and Sidgwick.

Of this 'consequentialist' chapter of Moore's book Keynes says that 'we took not the slightest notice. We accepted Moore's religion, so to speak, and discarded his morals.' After Keynes's memoir was published two of the Cambridge circle have given evidence about the impact of *Principia Ethica*. Clive Bell agrees with Keynes, but Leonard Woolf flatly contradicts him. And contemporary letters of Lytton Strachey, the nearest to Keynes in the group, extolled the chapter on ethics in relation to conduct equally with that on the Ideal. 'The last two chapters – glory alleluiah!' Strachey wrote to Woolf.

Whether or not Keynes was right as to the extent to which his friends shared his attitude, why did he himself take 'not the slightest notice' of the consequentialist chapter, qualified later in the memoir to 'did not pay attention to this aspect of the book or bother much about it'? My explanation is that the consequentialist teaching in *Principia Ethica* was no exhilarating novelty, since it was part of the classical Utilitarianism which Keynes had absorbed throughout his childhood. Moore's influence made him spew out the hedonism, but left the consequentialism intact. We all know people brought up as Christians who, when they lose their faith, declare that they have rejected the whole of Christianity when in fact they have discarded Christian beliefs while retaining Christian principles of conduct. My thesis is that similarly Keynes's rejection of 'Benthamism' (the word 'Utilitarianism' does not occur in the memoir) did not in fact carry over to the consequentialist part of the classical doctrine.

This explanation accounts for Keynes's inconsistencies in talking about consequences in the memoir. He says that 'we' had 'not begun to play the game of consequences', but gives problems about the relative values of consequences (their actual value or their probable value?) as examples of what was discussed. And my explanation fits the fact that Leonard Woolf, who had a Jewish family background, reacted quite differently to *Principia Ethica*.

There may have been another personal factor in Keynes's attitude to classical Utilitarianism. In one place Sidgwick is named along with the Benthamite calculus and the general rules of correct behaviour in order to specify the discarded part of Moore's teaching. Henry Sidgwick had been a frequent and revered visitor to the Keynes household during Maynard's childhood, and Maynard had played golf with the great man in 1900 shortly before his death. Moore has said that he found Sidgwick's personality unattractive; and I suspect that so did Keynes. At any rate Keynes's comments (in letters to his friends) after reading the biography of Sidgwick published in 1906 have been regarded as an early specimen of the debunking of an eminent Victorian.

My explanation, perhaps, does not account for the violence of Keynes's invective against the 'Benthamite tradition' – 'the worm which has been gnawing at the insides of modern civilisation and is responsible for its present moral decay'. Here, in line with Quentin Bell, I suspect that Keynes said this, and connected Benthamism to Marxism a few sentences later, chiefly *pour épater les jeunes*. However Keynes does offer as a reason that the Benthamite calculus was 'based on an over-valuation of the economic criterion' – not, be it noted, because the Benthamite calculus considered consequences of actions, but because it only considered consequences of one sort. Keynes's rejection of this over-valuation is the core of his optimistic sermon 'Economic possibilities for our grandchildren' published in 1930 in the depth of the slump. However it did not stop him from entitling two of his political works the *economic* consequences of the peace (1919) and of Mr Churchill (1925) respectively, since in each case the economic consequences would be counter productive of the ultimate ends he valued.

What I am maintaining is that, whatever Keynes implies to the contrary in his memoir, he always kept to that part of the 'morals' of *Principia Ethica* which requires that actions should be judged by their consequences. Indeed when Keynes asserts proudly that he and his friends were 'in the strict sense of the term, immoralists', this strict sense must be taken as being specified by the preceding declarations – that 'we entirely repudiated a personal liability on us to obey general rules' and that 'we claimed the right to judge every individual case on its merits'. The latter is no more than the claim to liberty of conscience; the former is no more than the negative part of consequentialism – that there are no general rules which ought always to be obeyed. Anyone who thinks that every general rule will have exceptions, and that in any particular case he will have to decide whether it is an exception or not, will be a Keynesian immoralist – a strange term to apply to an especially conscientious man.

It is true that some consequentialist moral philosophers, including Moore, have allowed a derivative authority to some moral rules; and Keynes, *qua* 'immoralist', would not agree to this. However he did not refuse any function to 'the laws and rules of an ordered society': in an obituary notice of 1937, he praised W. H. Macaulay for knowing 'by instinct exactly the right position that rules should occupy in a moral society'.

On my reading (or, if you like, de-rhetoricising) of 'My Early Beliefs', Keynes was brought up in, and never departed from, a consequentialist moral philosophy; he learned from Moore the 'religion' of 'passionate contemplation and communion', but later realised that there were more and richer ways in which states of mind could be valuable than those mentioned in *Principia Ethica* (where the list was not intended by Moore to be exhaustive). The genuine volte-face reported in the memoir is the abandonment of the belief that 'human nature is reasonable'. It was Keynes's psychological beliefs that changed in the course of time, not his fundamental ethical ones. Keynes says that the 'pseudo-rational view of human nature' which he and his circle held at the beginning of the century 'led to a thinness, a superficiality, not only of judgment, but also of feeling'. If it was of this superficiality that Keynes was thinking when he saw himself and his Cambridge friends as 'water-spiders, gracefully skimming . . . the surface of the stream without any contact at all with the eddies and currents underneath', the comparison makes good sense.

23

Maynard Keynes as a teacher

A. F. W. PLUMPTRE

Travelling from Toronto, together with a Canadian friend, we reached Cambridge on Thursday, 2 October 1928. In my first letter home I wrote:

Our train arrived at 4 p.m. and I went straight to King's. That evening we went to see Dr Clapham. He was most genial and welcoming. He gave me about the best news I've ever had! I am under the joint supervision of a well-known economist by the name of Shove and *the* biggest man in English economics – J. M. Keynes.

Two days later I wrote:

I did my first work and handed the results to Shove today ... Yesterday I saw Keynes, my other supervisor. I shall be seeing him three times every fortnight: every second Saturday for reading essays and also at the weekly meetings of the 'Economic Club' on Monday nights. He is a very interesting person, with most amazing rooms – white and orange ceilings, extraordinary drapings, modernistic sort of frescoes, semi-futuristic pictures and so forth. I hope to study them at greater length in the future!

Over the next two years, what with supervisions, club meetings and occasional luncheons, I found myself increasingly at home in these rooms. But, as for the frescoes, whether you loved them or not, they were not to be overlooked. Professor Pigou referred to them as 'somewhat austere and melancholy figures, representing the Tripos Examinations'.[1] Roy Harrod who had arrived for his first supervision some six years earlier, observed that the rooms 'were elegantly furnished, and one long wall had been adorned, shortly after the war, with frescoes of nude figures, flowers and fruit by Duncan Grant and Vanessa Bell'.[2]

Climbing to the top of the staircase from Webb's Court one entered a long and rather narrow room, with a high ceiling and a large window at each end. To the right was a table with a number of chairs that were drawn into service for club meetings. To the left, between the window and the fireplace, was Keynes's special winged chair where he always sat, somewhat slouched, with his long legs

247

out in front of the fire and his eyes twinkling from between bushy eyebrows and a bushy moustache. A small footstool for books and papers always stood beside him. So he has been immortalised in one of David Low's more famous cartoons. Other chairs and small sofas made up an informal circle. In those days Keynes almost always wore a dark blue double-breasted suit which gave him an urban air and differentiated him from the rest of us, undergraduates and dons alike, who normally wore grey flannel 'bags' with jackets or blazers. I was puzzled that he should also wear brown shoes because, at least in Toronto, with a blue suit only black shoes were acceptable; I set it down as one more interesting idiosyncracy.

In my letter home on 24 October I wrote:

The only mark I have received so far was on an essay I did for Keynes on 'Capitalism'. He gave me 'B plus', but remarked he wasn't satisfied with any of our papers because we did not say 'what one feels one means' by the word 'capitalism'; he then spent an hour explaining to the four of us what he felt he meant. Keynes is far beyond my hopes and expectations – cleverer, wittier, and more genial. I believe that there are only eight in Cambridge whom he supervises. He takes us in two groups of four.

This particular supervision, I was to learn, was typical of those with Keynes in two important respects: the topic for discussion was one of public policy, and he himself did almost all the talking.

The essays which we wrote each fortnight, and pushed under his door on Friday evenings so that he could read them before we met him late the next afternoon, were all on topics of current economic and political interest. In most cases, we discovered, he himself was preparing to publish his views on them. Harrod records that in 1922 'the essays were on such topics as rent and quasi-rent and covered the ground of Marshall's *Principles*'.[2] Not so six years later. The subjects to which I find references in my weekly letters home include:

- How and in what ways can Trade Unions raise wages? (November 1928)
- The desirability of control of foreign investment (February 1929).
- Free Trade v. protection (February 1929). 'Contrary to the usual ideas free trade breaks down in theory, but protection when you try to apply it. . . . However I wouldn't say as much outside this room!'
- The Treasury doctrine that a government (unlike a private firm) 'cannot materially or permanently reduce unemployment' by borrowing and spending. (April 1929, when Keynes was actively supporting Lloyd George and the Liberal Party in their advocacy of public works.)

Early in 1929 also there was an essay on 'Analyse theoretically the distinction between the budgetary problem and the transfer problem in German reparation payments. What are the chief economic factors which determine Germany's capacity to pay? If you wanted to get as near that capacity as possible, how would you amend the Dawes Plan (of 1924)?' Faced with this problem for our fortnightly essay, none of us achieved any great measures of success.

He greeted our entry with the remark: 'You are all as incompetent as a bunch of Frenchmen! The English and Germans attending the present [Young Plan] Conference of experts on reparations know what it's all about; the Americans don't know but are capable of understanding when it is explained to them; but the French are incapable of understanding it!'

The reference to reparations recalls an episode, or pair of episodes, which could scarcely have occurred had our supervisor been anyone else. Early in November 1929, I wrote:

Our group of four is to be movie-toned (talking-moving-pictured) with Mr Keynes in a film on the sights and sounds of Cambridge, this particular sight-and-sound being *the* Mr Keynes giving private supervision. We shall be picture-recorded in Keynes's private room with the Great Man in his own chair and ourselves lounging on the sofas discussing some weighty subject.

That effort ended in failure; such was the state of the American art of the 'talkies' in those days that the light proved insufficient (the English November sun failed to provide adequate interior illumination) and the noise of the camera drowned the discussion. Accordingly, there was a repeat performance four months later. In order to ensure adequate lighting the scene was laid in the Fellows' Garden of the College. So we found ourselves discussing German reparations against an idyllic vernal background; Lydia joined us and stood watching it all, amused and motionless, in a short black dress and red Russian boots. My letter of 9 March 1930, recorded:

The photographer was a typical uneducated American – very pleased with himself and his machine. Some of his remarks to Keynes which I jotted down were: 'When I lower my hand, you give the answer, Professor, cold and sweet.' Again, to a subordinate daring to make a suggestion: 'Say, the Professor and I are running this show.' Keynes was rather bored, I think, and said to one of the men: 'Don't let them put "Professor" on the screen. I don't want the indignity without the emoluments' – a typical Keynes remark.*

* Roy Harrod, *op. cit.*, p. 438, says that the first record of this riposte that he had discovered (about the indignity and emoluments of a Professor) occurred in 1931. I suspect that the episode which I described in 1930 was in fact the original; it had every appearance of spontaneity.

The following month I wrote home: 'On Tuesday evening I proposed a motion in the Union: "Resolved that Films should be Seen and not Heard"; there was a very meagre audience.'

There was, as I remarked above, a second respect in which my first supervision with Keynes was typical: he spent virtually all of the available hour explaining to us his own interpretation of the topic. In this regard I could, perhaps, repeat what I wrote retrospectively in 1947:[3]

There was a great difference between Keynes's supervision of undergraduates in economics while I was in King's and other supervision which was given at the same time, and there is something to be learned from the contrast. Mr Gerald Shove was bearing the brunt of it. He is, in many ways, the best teacher I ever had; he always took pains to discuss our written work in detail and to make us talk about it. He would choose subjects that were not too far beyond us; often they would involve examination of some limited but important points in the theory of value. He talked easily and, almost more important, he was easy to talk to. Not so Keynes! His overwhelming brilliance made interruption undesirable and argument almost out of the question. It was amazingly exciting and inspiring but it was not – and was not intended to be – enough. In fact, after many months, it became almost too much. Pearls make pleasant fodder, but in large quantities they are indigestible.

Looking back, I do not think that his undergraduates need have felt badly about being rather overawed by him. The editor of the *New Statesman and Nation*, in an obituary article (27 April 1946, p. 295) said: 'A mutual friend once remarked that in conversation when Keynes was present there was never any point in saying anything because he always thought of a better remark than yours before you had time to think of it. His wit was shattering and his capacity for rudeness [which he never vented on undergraduates] was unequalled. But he was completely disinterested, bore no malice however fierce the controversy, and was so charming that even those wounded could not bear a grudge.'

Early in 1930 when my two years at King's were drawing to a close, I began to take some supervision from Professor Pigou. He was just recovering from a long illness and I was the first undergraduate to have such an opportunity for some years. My letters home show that supervision with him was a relaxed affair, accompanied by tea and toast, and that he had a strong inclination to talk about cricket in Kent (my father's County as well as his own), and mountain-climbing (to which he was vastly addicted), and about almost anything other than economics; indeed he claimed to be unable to think except with pencil in hand. And so I wrote:

Professor Pigou has an entirely false reputation for being unapproachable. He is really easier to get on with than Keynes, the latter being almost too brilliant besides giving rather an impression of greatness. The Professor is the most pleasant of people, full of good humour and friendliness. He is, of course, an outstanding man; but he has none of the assertive confidence of Keynes. It is usually 'Well, I think so and so to be the case, but of course I'm probably wrong.'

In addition to the fortnightly supervisions with Keynes, there were the weekly meetings of his Political Economy Club. May I again quote from my earlier paper:[4]

While Keynes was, in Cambridge, primarily a Kingsman, he came to know all the abler economic undergraduates and graduate students, regardless of their Colleges. This he did, during the 1920s and 1930s, through his 'Political Economy Club'. It met every Monday evening. Besides the undergraduate and graduate members several dons would usually attend: Dennis Robertson, Richard Kahn, Piero Sraffa, Austin Robinson, and others less regularly. Before settling down to business each undergraduate member of the club had to draw a number out of a bowl; then a member of the club would read a paper; then other members would stand up in front of the fireplace and comment on the paper in the order of the numbers they had drawn; then some of the dons would make some remarks; and finally Keynes would sum it all up, stressing the essentials, taking sides in any dispute, introducing new points of view, pursuing some arguments to their logical conclusions and others to their ultimate absurdities, laughing at lapses and mocking at muddles, with epigrams and paradoxes tumbling over each other. Nothing annoyed him more than a muddle; nothing pleased him more than a paradox. It was all very intoxicating for us undergraduates; and also terrifying. It was an ordeal to read a paper in that gathering; it was, at least for some of us, an even worse ordeal to sit through an abstruse paper, in which the author was extending his own intellectual powers to the utmost, knowing that, as one's number was up, one would have to stand in front of the fireplace and make some intelligent and intelligible comment.

Both Austin Robinson and Roy Harrod have provided their own accounts of the meetings of the Political Economy Club and I am glad to find that they closely resemble the one given above. Austin describes participation in the Club as 'fascinating and alarming' and adds: 'Through his Club Keynes knew intimately all the best of each generation of Cambridge economists, and exercised a more personal influence on them than anyone else.' Roy says: 'Keynes, without preparation and out of his own stock, seemed to know so very much more [than the rest of us], whatever the subject might be.'[5]

During my two years I read two papers to the Political Economy Club. The second, which proposed some extensions of the theory of international trade, ran into heavy 'flak', some of it from some of the dons. I was vastly relieved when Keynes began his concluding remarks with the words, 'Well, I am a Plumptre man'; Richard

Kahn, with whom I walked, talked and played tennis a great deal in those days, also gave me moral and intellectual support. Of the earlier paper, on international implications of overhead costs, which I read a few weeks after my arrival in Cambridge, I wrote home as follows:

Last night I read my paper to Keynes's Club. The Club was depleted because 5 November seems a proper day for celebrations on the basis of fireworks and firewater. However, six of the best members turned up, together with Keynes and (Dennis) Robertson.... The discussion lasted for 2¼ hours; the small congenial group made it very pleasant. Keynes was in very good form, amusing and witty.

Of Keynes's lectures I can say little. Time had been when he carried a full load. Harrod writes that 'In the Lent and Summer Terms of 1909 Keynes lectured on Money, Credit and Prices three times a week. He at once made a great impression.'[6] That year he also had twenty-four private pupils.[7] However, during my two years as an undergraduate, he lectured for one term only. For lecture notes he used galley-proofs of theoretical sections of the *Treatise on Money* on which he had been labouring for some five years. A number of dons and research students attended these lectures, but I doubt that many undergraduates were able to get a great deal out of them.

Keynes, in those days, spent weekdays (Tuesdays to Fridays) attending to his affairs and developing his political and financial interests in London; the weekends (Saturdays to Mondays), at least in term-time, he spent in Cambridge. From time to time he had little luncheon parties in his room. Delicacies were carried up from King's kitchens, on the opposite side of Webb's Court, and consumed under the envious eyes of the Tripos frescoes. These were always gay occasions. I find the following account in a letter dated 4 May 1930, just before my undergraduate days came to an end:

Lunch with Keynes, where Kahn and Morris (newly elected Fellows) and Wilkinson (4th-year undergraduate) were the other guests, was very pleasant. The main subject of conversation was quite large, viz. eternity: what it was and why people wanted it. Keynes explained that he had been trying to tell his wife 'who knew little of these matters' what the beliefs of Christianity were, and that he couldn't do it 'without seeming too burlesque'.

In any pedantic sense Keynes was not my best teacher, but in terms of impact and influence he was incomparable. As an economist, his dominant concern, as he explained in his introduction to the Cambridge Economic Handbooks, was not with a body of doctrine to be imbibed and duly regurgitated by students, but rather with methods of thought which would reduce to rationality and manageability whatever might be the pressing economic issues of the day. When he discussed these issues, whether in supervisions or in his Club or elsewhere, he was developing and refining his own thoughts. He was, moreover, happy to involve in his thought-development process, not a group of students to be indoctrinated, but rather a group of junior members of his own much beloved College and University who might in some measure make a contribution. Happily, no little of his method of thought rubbed off on a number of us. And for this favoured few it was indeed a mind-expanding experience!

NOTES

1. A. C. Pigou, 'John Maynard Keynes, 1883–1946', *Cambridge Review*, 18 May 1946.
2. R. F. Harrod, *The Life of John Maynard Keynes* (London, 1951), p. 323.
3. A. F. W. Plumptre, 'Keynes in Cambridge', *Canadian Journal of Economics and Political Science* (1947), pp. 367–8.
4. *Ibid.*, pp. 370–1.
5. Harrod, *The Life of John Maynard Keynes*, pp. 151–2.
6. *Ibid.*, p. 145.
7. *Ibid.*, p. 149.

24

Maynard Keynes as a biographer

DAVID GARNETT

Plutarch enjoyed comparing the subjects of his *Lives*: Romulus and Theseus, Hannibal and Scipio Africanus are examples. But as he despised the arts as occupations which should be reserved for slaves he would only have been interested in a comparison of those life-long friends, Maynard Keynes, Lytton Strachey and Virginia Woolf, in respect of their political activities. It is, however, as writers and biographers that it is interesting to compare them, for in that most difficult branch of literature they each excelled. I do not wish to place these friends in order of precedence, even if it were possible, but rather to suggest their similarities and their differences in order to appreciate better the quality which gives each a charac-teristic flavour. They were all three writers, but while Lytton and Virginia were professional writers and nothing else, Maynard was endowed with such a variety of talents that he certainly would not have described himself as 'Author' on his passport; Lytton probably did and my guess is that Virginia would have done so if she had filled up the form herself. Leonard may have put 'Married woman'.

Yet Maynard was much the most prolific writer of the three as the Royal Economic Society has somewhat ruthlessly set out to prove. The contents of the majority of the twenty-six volumes which will gather dust in the libraries of the world, are either ephemeral journalism or pamphleteering, or specialist scientific writing, if poli-tical economy ranks as a science.

In character the friends could scarcely have been more different. Lytton was an introvert who occupied himself with continual self-analysis, looking backwards with amused doubtings, subtle devalua-tions, and positively enjoying brooding on the record of his own absurdities. Virginia also, in spite of her vanity, was able to relish the humour of her own social *gaffes* and enjoyed describing herself in ridiculous situations. Maynard, an extrovert, and with far less vanity, did not. He preferred his triumphs to his failures. He was by nature intensely *loyal*, with a life-long love for the friends of his youth and a tendency also to be loyal to established institutions which he was never eager to jettison. Lytton was by contrast a revolutionary, whose motto was that of the whiting in *Alice,*

What matters it how far we go? The further off from England the nearer is to France.

In 1918 Lytton struck a new note, reviving biography as an art, for it had sunk into an exercise in piety, laborious for the author and tedious for the reader. Lytton changed the perspective in which the Victorians were viewed. Whether Dr Arnold had short or long legs can now only be discovered by the exhumation of his skeleton, but after the publication of *Eminent Victorians* his ghost could no longer use them to bestride the educational world. The Victorians shrank in stature when Lytton wrote of them, but in becoming smaller they became alive, able to excite our sympathy and our pity. We realised that the waxworks in Madame Tussaud's had once been real and extraordinarily interesting people. Lytton's method in achieving this transformation was not simply to survey his speci-mens through the wrong end of his opera glasses, but to pick out salient trifles: the dirt in the ears of Italian Cardinals or (as has been proved correct in the case of Gordon) brandies and sodas early in the day. Incidentally it is amusing to note that what was so deeply resented in the case of Gordon was, twenty years later, generally admired in Winston Churchill, though he dispensed with the soda.

Yet, partly because of his assumed detachment, partly because of his wit, the reader often feels that Lytton's judgements are 'slanted' like the B.B.C. foreign services in wartime. Too much emphasis in one place while another aspect has been skated over or ignored, shows that Lytton was very much a propagandist. It is a great loss to literature that he never carried out his original intention of writing parallel lives of those Eminent Victorians whom he whole-heartedly admired. Darwin, Faraday, Lister might have been his choice. Such lives, had they been written, would have been strictly comparable with Maynard's biographies of the founders of Political Economy in Cambridge, Malthus, Jevons, Marshall and Edgeworth, men whose contributions to knowledge he explained and whose characters he admired. Contrariwise Maynard should have written a life of Marx and an assessment of *Das Kapital.*

Virginia Woolf's best biographical work is to be found in her essays and short assessments of writers, most of which were pub-lished in periodicals. This was Maynard's opinion; for when I was about to write an article on Virginia's achievements as a writer soon after her death, Maynard urged me to read these biographical essays and to note how brilliantly she could suit her style to her

subject and what a 'professional' writer she was. In her longest
biography – that of Roger Fry – much was omitted out of consideration for the feelings of Roger's sisters – and also of her own sister.
But in her short essays she sparkles, often identifying herself with
her subject by a sympathy, a love of life, by her humour and her
understanding, so that the reader puts down her sketch with the
sensation of having had a breathless interview. Only later he
sometimes wonders if he has been imposed on. Was Virginia playing
a game of make-believe, dressing herself up – as Jack Mytton who
went duck-shooting by moonlight in the snow wearing only his
nightshirt, or as Laetitia Pilkington the dwarf who amused Swift as
a little girl and remained always a lady in the difficult circumstances of being a 'call girl' for the Great Duke of Marlborough and
his staff? Occasionally I think I detect Virginia's love of the farcical
in one of Maynard's sketches. Take Henry Higgs:

> ... extremely deaf and unable to hear the comments of others present, in
> which indeed he seemed to take no interest, his argument would continue
> as an entirely solo performance, frequently on some other item of the
> agenda than that under discussion; the only Chairman, in my experience,
> who was able to make him desist being Edwin Cannan, who used to take
> him almost by the throat, shouting down his ear that we were not discussing
> that matter and putting his hand over his mouth until he gave up. On
> other occasions when he had more curiosity as to what was going on, he
> would push towards whoever was speaking his highly unreliable electrical
> machine which would proceed to deliver a thunder-and-lightning storm
> above which nothing could be heard.

I have been told that Lytton persuaded Maynard to keep the
sentence in which he wrote that President Wilson's hands were
lacking in sensitiveness and finesse which he had intended to omit.
Incidentally that sentence tells us at least as much about Maynard
as it does about the President. It reinforces what I shall say later.
I think a comparison between Lytton's description of Gladstone
and Maynard's of Lloyd George, written two or three years later,
shows Lytton's influence. Each of them was writing about the complex character of a Prime Minister, but Maynard was drawing from
life. Lytton wrote:

In the physical world there are no chimeras. But man is more various
than nature; was Mr Gladstone, perhaps, a chimera of the spirit? Did his
very essence lie in the confusion of incompatibles? His very essence? It
eludes the hand that seems to grasp it. One is baffled as his political
opponents were baffled fifty years ago. The soft serpent coils harden into
quick strength that has vanished leaving only emptiness and perplexity
behind. Speech was the fibre of his being and when he spoke the ambiguity
of ambiguity was revealed. ... But here also was a contradiction. In spite

of the involutions of his intellect and the contortions of his spirit it is impossible not to perceive a strain of *naïveté* in Mr Gladstone. . . . His very egoism was simple-minded: through all the labyrinth of his passions there ran a single thread. But the centre of the labyrinth? Ah, the thread might lead there through those wandering mazes at last. Only with the last corner turned, the last step taken, the explorer might find that he was looking down into the gulf of a crater. The flame shot out on every side scorching and brilliant, but in the midst there was a darkness.

And here is Maynard on Lloyd George:

How can I convey to the reader who does not know him any just impression of this extraordinary figure of our time? This syren, this goat-footed bard, half-human visitor to our age from the hag-ridden magic and enchanted woods of Celtic antiquity? One catches in his company that flavour of final purposelessness, inner irresponsibility, existence outside and away from our Saxon good and evil, mixed with cunning, remorselessness, love of power, that lend fascination, enthralment and terror to the fair-seeming magicians of North European folklore. . . . Lloyd George is rooted in nothing, he is void and without content; he lives and feeds on his immediate surroundings; he is an instrument and a player at the same time which plays on the company and is played on by them too; he is a prism, as I have heard him described, which collects light and distorts it and is most brilliant if the light comes from many quarters at once; a vampire and a medium in one.

I do not think Maynard would have written that passage *in quite that way* if he had not read *Eminent Victorians*. But how much better it is! How much better written for one thing. There is no hand seeming to grasp an elusive essence – a messy image. And it does convey something genuine and felt whereas all Lytton tells us is that Gladstone was contradictory and incomprehensible. Nevertheless I believe that Lytton's influence on Maynard was a wholly good one. It tempted him to be more indiscreet than he was by nature: to have the courage to print what he would have said in conversation. In Maynard's best writing there is an element inevitably absent from Lytton at his best: a *visual* quality. Maynard had the enormous advantage of writing of what he had seen with his own eyes, and those beautiful deep blue eyes noticed every detail. All through the *Essays in Biography* there are passages in which his eyes have been caught by what is significant and which tell everything in a dozen words. 'Charlie Chaplin with the forehead of Shakespeare' is the best description of Einstein.

Again the portrait of Clemenceau in *The Council of Four* could only have been drawn by someone who had studied him from life and had eyes for every significant detail. It is not only that Maynard had the enormous advantage of having met and talked with most of the men he was writing about, but that he had a much more acute visual sense. He cared more for pictures than Lytton and learned more from Duncan Grant and Vanessa Bell than Lytton ever learned from Carrington. Maynard's Clemenceau has the solidity of a portrait by Ingres. There he sits on his brocaded chair, his hands gloved, in his thick black square-tailed coat of good broadcloth, tired and patient, listening to the Anglo-Saxon humbug and Maynard has eyes that see that: 'His boots were of thick black leather, very good, but of a country style, and sometimes fastened in front, curiously by a buckle instead of laces.' And as another example of his keeping down to earth, how significant is this sentence in his delightful and loving account of Mary Paley Marshall:

> Every morning till close on her ninetieth year, when, to her extreme dissatisfaction, her doctor prohibited her (partly at her friends instigation, but more on account of the dangers of the Cambridge traffic even to the most able-bodied than to any failure of her physical powers) she bicycled the considerable distance from Madingley Road to the Library ... wearing as she always did the sandals which were a legacy of her pre-Raphaelite period sixty years before.

Like Lytton, Maynard was often most profound when he was wittiest. For example he visited General Haking of the Armistice Commission, who had installed himself, his wife and two marriageable daughters in what had been Lüdendorff's villa until the collapse of Germany amid a semicircle of pine trees. In this Wagnerian setting General Haking's A.D.C. and his fellow-subalterns had imported a pack of hounds. *The Times* arrived regularly on the breakfast table. But for Maynard the ghost of Lüdendorff haunted the spot: he imagined him unbuckling his bright breast-plate – a figure in opera - and calling to the soughing pines. And he adds: 'Miss Bates had vanquished Brünnhilde and Mr Weston's foot was firmly planted on the neck of Wotan.'

That joke is sheer genius. It symbolises and sums up the unbridgeable gulf between England and Germany which makes it next to impossible for the countries to understand each other. On the basis of that joke a composer and librettist might compose a very amusing light opera.

Later on in 'Dr Melchior' Maynard returns to the same theme when he describes a Conference presided over by Admiral Sir Rosslyn Wemyss who, goggling at Maynard with the look of a seasick porpoise, astonished the Germans by '. . . total abandonment of the faintest attempt to keep up appearances of knowing what this Conference was about, coupled with his supreme self-possession and unassailable, as it were, social superiority, like a humorous and good-natured duchess presiding over the financial business of a local charity – which somehow made *them*, so serious and pompous, seem to be a little absurd.'

'Dr Melchior: A Defeated Enemy' is the finest of Maynard's writings: It combines deep personal feeling, a passion for humanity and justice, the unravelling of all the tangled threads in the negotiations, wit and an almost uncanny observation of tiny but very significant detail. It is so real and so profoundly moving that I would compare it not to any other piece of historical writing that I know, but to a chapter from some great work of the imagination – by Tolstoy perhaps. It is a work of art.

Perhaps it is the best of Maynard's writings because it was composed to be read to the small group of old friends to whom he could reveal everything in his nature.

Maynard himself would not have been happy if I did not mention his mastery of historical detail and the carefulness of his research in such matters as the explanation of character by the influence of heredity and environment which he employed to put each of his subjects into his social and intellectual frame. In such work he was meticulous. In conclusion I would say that his greatness as a writer is not only because of his intellectual eminence and versatility; it is also moral.

He realised in time what was being done in the Peace Treaty. It outraged his sense of honour, his sense of humanity and his sense of what was possible. He resigned and wrote *The Economic Consequences of the Peace*. By doing so he became a moral force.

His resignation was due not only to his intelligence and his clear-sightedness but also to the ethos of the Cambridge in which he grew up, and to the influence of the friends whom he loved, whose judgements he respected and whose basic unworldliness he shared. It is because he did not betray his own and their values that he was able to go on and have a continually increasing influence.

25

The concept of the Arts Council

MARY GLASGOW

In May 1940, Maynard Keynes wrote to the Council for the Encouragement of Music and the Arts. He appealed on behalf of the actor-manager, Donald Wolfit, whose company had recently presented a series of plays at the Arts Theatre, Cambridge, and who now sought advice about a provincial tour and a possible Shakespeare season in London. It was a gallant proposal, with air-raids and invasion looming and most London theatres already closed.

Wolfit had not heard of C.E.M.A., then barely five months old, but Keynes had. The correspondence he started quickly developed into an attack, in which he accused the Council, first politely, then not so politely, of wasting its resources and of spending money on drama tours financed by itself instead of offering guarantees against loss to existing managements:

> It is easy to fritter money in that manner... The considerations on the other side [i.e. the guarantee system] are, first of all, that it is likely to be a good deal more economical and that the liability of the Council would be limited, whereas under its own management it is unlimited; and also that no one can run a provincial tour successfully without a high degree of discretion and freedom, when once he has started, from management by a London committee.

The Council demurred. It had not envisaged making grants of any kind to 'commercial' companies, nor had it intended to support ventures based on London. Keynes pressed hard. He was not mollified when he heard, two months later, that C.E.M.A. had agreed to finance tours by the Old Vic and Sadler's Wells, led by Tyrone Guthrie. Finally, he proposed that Wolfit be given a guarantee of which he himself would promise a quarter. He wrote to the secretary:

> My suggestion is that your Committee should guarantee Mr Wolfit an amount equal to the deficiency of his average weekly share of receipts below £170, subject to a maximum of £400 altogether... I should be prepared myself to find a quarter of the guarantee... This means that the

Plate 15   Cartoon by David Low (by arrangement with the Trustees and the London *Evening Standard*), 1938.

Plate 16　Maynard Keynes in the library of his London house in Gordon Square in 1940 (*Radio Times Hulton Picture Library*).

sum to be found by your Committee would be £300, or 5 per cent of the sum guaranteed to the Vic–Wells companies. Could not Mr Guthrie be persuaded to release 5 per cent of his guarantee, either by making some slight economy, or by basing his estimates on the assumption that it is just conceivable that someone may attend one or other of his performances? I think he would be a legitimate subject for general execration if he won't!

Keynes won. His offer was accepted and the guarantee was given.

I have described this first confrontation of Keynes and C.E.M.A. at length because it illustrates so many facets of his method of working. It was typical of him to take up an individual case when it came his way and to act vigorously, even capriciously, in its support. It was typical of him to be tenacious – he himself called it 'obstinate' – and to pursue his end until he achieved it. The elaborate satire is typical, and so is the detailed spelling-out of terms – he was often accused of making complications over subsidies just for the fun of it. Typical again is the personal generosity which brought about the solution of that particular argument; and perhaps most typical of all the insistence that artists must be allowed freedom in their own sphere. When, in 1945, the time came for C.E.M.A. to be superseded by the Arts Council of Great Britain, Keynes delivered a broadcast to herald the establishment of the permanent, chartered body for which he had striven, and in the course of it he said: 'The work of the artist in all its aspects is, of its nature, individual and free, undisciplined, unregimented, uncontrolled. The artist walks where the breath of the spirit blows him. He cannot be told his direction; he does not know it himself.' I cannot help wondering whether the purpose of Keynes's approach in 1940 did not, in fact, go further than the immediate issue. There is no evidence to suggest that it did; yet he must have seen the possibilities implied by the tentative C.E.M.A. experiment in subsidising the arts. Did he want it to be known that he was interested?

C.E.M.A. came into existence at the end of December 1939, to administer a sum of £25,000 provided by the Pilgrim Trust. It had an office and a secretary lent by the Board of Education, and it announced that its money would be spent on 'encouraging' with financial help musicians, actors and artists whose livelihood was endangered by the war. At the same time, it would provide the solace of 'music and the arts' for people throughout the country who were scattered and cut off from their normal life during the first winter black-out. The initiative came from the President of the Board of Education, Lord De La Warr; but the driving force behind C.E.M.A., once launched, was the secretary of the Pilgrim Trust, Dr Thomas Jones. T.J. saw in the new body an extension of the social service which had sent music and drama organisers and travelling art exhibitions to relieve the drabness of unemployment in mining areas during the thirties. Of the two purposes proclaimed, helping artists and serving audiences, there is no doubt that the second was uppermost in his mind.*

There was a built-in conflict between the claims of art and those of social service, and in the lifetime of C.E.M.A. it was never fully resolved. With Keynes's coming, the emphasis shifted, as we shall see. At the beginning, under T.J., much of the help provided was for amateur activities. The programme was, understandably, an emergency one and there was no long-term plan in view. A leader in *The Times* of 15 July 1940 attacked C.E.M.A. for spending too much time on amateur activities, to the detriment of the professional symphony orchestras and of opera and ballet at Sadler's Wells. Keynes was not alone in wanting a change of emphasis.

When Keynes wrote his initial letter, he told a friend that if he wanted something he believed in going to the bottom, to the secretary of an organisation, not its chairman. The bottom, in this case, was myself, a junior civil servant seconded to the job. The letter came, and I was duly flattered. I summoned up my courage and asked if I might go and see him.

I went, one summer evening in 1940, to 46 Gordon Square. Keynes lay on a sofa, propped up by white pillows against a background of heavy red velvet curtains. (His doctors insisted that he spend as much time as possible lying down.) He began at once asking awkward questions with alarming courtesy. He wanted to know why the council was spending so much money on amateur effort. Why was it missing this obvious opportunity to support artistic ventures of standing? Could it not see how many important things were waiting to be done? It was standards that mattered, and the preservation of serious professional enterprise, not obscure concerts in village halls. He was never one to mince words and, hearing him for the first time, I found him formidable. I noticed a trick he had, when he wanted to stress a point, of curling the little finger of one hand over the fourth, and that was somehow formidable too. I tried to keep my head, because I was sure he was only partly right and in any case my allegiance was to T.J. I came away battered but exhilarated.

Eighteen months later, in 1942, having seen their experiment well rooted with an annual grant-in-aid from the Exchequer, the Pilgrim Trustees withdrew their patronage. The President of the Board of Education, then Mr R. A. Butler, invited Keynes to be Chairman

* The Chairman of C.E.M.A. was Lord Macmillan of the Pilgrim Trust, and Thomas Jones was the Vice-Chairman.

of C.E.M.A. In official circles it was said that his acceptance was unlikely, that he was not only excessively busy but also far from well. Roy Harrod, in his admirable biography, records that he hesitated. But he did accept, and personally I believe that he had hoped the offer would be made.

There can hardly have been two men more dissimilar in background or outlook than Keynes and T.J., but one thing they shared – a delight in 'action', and with it a horror of bureaucracy. Early on, T.J. spurned an offer of money from a well-endowed public source because it was made conditional upon the appointment of various committees, according to whose reports eventual plans would be drawn up. Keynes too once received a suggestion that aid for the arts should be given on the basis of recommendations made after a detailed national survey: he welcomed the offer of research, in this case sponsored by a private benefactor, and said he looked forward to seeing the results in six months' time. When, after a year, evidence came of a proliferation of working parties, no member of which had yet put pen to paper, he broke off relations. His letters to the C.E.M.A. staff are punctuated by rude remarks about 'red tape': 'Yes, I suppose we ought to have a firm of solicitors. . . If other people insist on going into all this nonsense, I suppose we have to also.' More constructively: 'We have been wonderfully free from cut-and-dried organisation so far, and I hope we shall stick to it.' He describes the coming Arts Council as 'independent in organisation, free from red tape'; and once, in an interview, he told the press: 'The arts owe no vow of obedience.'

The pattern of activity at C.E.M.A. did not immediately change with Keynes's coming. There was no abatement of the emergency work with which it had all started. Factory concerts, performances in small halls and touring exhibitions of paintings continued and multiplied, and there was by 1942 a team of regional officers responsible for their organisation. Keynes was appreciative, but this was not where his sympathies lay. He caused some resentment when he suggested hiving off the 'educational' activities into a separate department; it was a reasonable idea, but he did not pursue it at the time. What he did, as his consistent policy, was to guide the Council towards giving more attention to the arts as such. The old conflict between art and social service went on, but now the bias was reversed; just as, at the beginning, T.J. had been criticised for favouring amateur effort, so now Keynes was attacked for spending too much of the Council's resources on established professional bodies, and on London. Later, he summed up his intentions diplomatically: 'We . . . are greatly concerned to decentralise and disperse the dramatic and musical and artistic life of the country, to build up provincial centres and to promote corporate life in these matters in every town and county . . . But it is also our business to make London a great artistic metropolis, a place to visit and to wonder at.'

It would be difficult, as well as boring, to attempt to list the vast number of different projects which came before the Council for consideration. I shall choose just a few, those which figure most prominently in the Chairman's correspondence. Some of them clearly reflect his personal interests, not to say prejudices. Keynes had a strong predilection in favour of the ballet; it could hardly have been otherwise for the husband of Lydia Lopokova and the founder of the Camargo Society. But there were people who felt that it was going too far to insist, as he did, on bringing the Ballets Jooss back from South America in the middle of the war – especially when the results, in terms of the success of the company's perform-ances, were not outstanding. Kurt Jooss's satire of the 1920s, *The Green Table*, did not greatly appeal to British audiences of the 1940s; yet Keynes was impatient of criticism and persisted in championing Jooss's work.

There was a moment of excitement in 1944 when it seemed that the Russian Ballet might be persuaded to come to London. Keynes was at Bretton Woods, and he responded at once to the hopeful cable he received by talking to the Russian delegates on the Inter-national Monetary Commission and laying detailed plans with them for the visit. He longed to be able to offer the Covent Garden Opera House for the performance, although the building was only just then being restored after serving as a dance hall during the war. The plan fell through for political reasons. Keynes directed his energies to negotiating the transfer of the Sadler's Wells Ballet to Covent Garden, an end which was achieved in time for the re-opening, but which badly strained relations with the Vic–Wells Governors in the process.

In spite of his special interest in the ballet, it is the theatre which occupies most space in the letters which Keynes wrote to me as secretary of C.E.M.A. He rarely mentions an individual painter or work of art; never, I think, any musical work or even any particular ballet; but detailed attention is given to plays and players. Keynes liked to have a say in what the companies associated with us chose to perform, and I have the impression that play-going was at that time his chief pleasure. Surely it came from his involvement with the Cambridge Arts Theatre. It was an informed, precise pleasure. I remember a moment when Turgenev's *A Month in the Country* was presented at the St James's Theatre in London: Keynes settled into his seat on the first night with a blissful sigh, saying:

'Ah, this is the loveliest play in all the world!' One of the nicest things about working for him was witnessing the enjoyment he got from the arts. The words 'enjoyment' and 'fun' appear again and again in his letters. In the 1945 broadcast he said: 'We do not think of the Arts Council as a schoolmaster. Your enjoyment is our first aim.'

A major preoccupation of his was finding buildings to house the arts, and here his concern for the provinces was genuine and urgent. Really he knew very little of Britain outside Cambridge and London, but he had friends in all manner of unlikely places who wrote to put forward their ideas, and he was eager to follow any clue, from a report of a derelict warehouse which might be turned into a theatre to an appeal to save some building of historic beauty. Most of the proposals came to nothing; it was not the easiest period for planning, in terms of real estate. Sometimes the initial cost was too great, sometimes the buildings were too small to be run economically – one such was the lovely little eighteenth-century theatre at Richmond, in Yorkshire; but suggestions came in thick and fast, from Plymouth, Swindon and Bridgwater, Lewes, Luton and Wigan, about which Keynes wrote: 'It would be great fun to start a new theatre up there.'

A plan which did come to fruition was the restoration of the Theatre Royal, Bristol. It was the oldest building in England with a continuous record of dramatic performances, but in 1942 it was damaged in an air raid and there was a danger it might have to be sold and pulled down. In a minimum of time, less than a year, C.E.M.A. took a lease of the theatre and launched it again as a going concern.

The choice of plays at Bristol, during the three years of C.E.M.A. management, was designed to give straightforward entertainment, and this was in keeping with Keynes's policy of giving the public pleasure rather than instruction. He openly combated the school of drama enthusiasts who seemed to believe that only plays which lost money were worthy of official support; the box office, he would say, was not an entirely despicable measure of value. When he was planning the new Covent Garden, in 1944, he wrote: 'Personally, I should like to add to the programme . . . a three months' season every year of Gilbert and Sullivan.'

I have spoken of the reluctance shown by the pre-Keynes Council to have dealings with the commercial theatre. It was understandable that T.J. and his colleagues should have felt safer working with educational trusts like the Old Vic than with managements belonging to the entertainment industry. Wolfit had invaded the 'educational' field in 1940, turning his company into a non-profit-sharing one for the occasion; in 1942, one of the giants of the West End, H. M. Tennent, prepared to follow suit. Hugh Beaumont, the Managing Director, set up a special company called 'Tennent Plays' to function alongside the parent body, and was given a guarantee against loss by C.E.M.A. for a London season. He agreed to pay his actors a fixed salary, regardless of takings, and to plough back any profits into a fund for future work. The success of the scheme depended upon the productions being exempt from Entertainments Tax, which was levied at that time, and to achieve this end it was necessary to satisfy the Board of Customs and Excise that their object was 'partly educational', as the relevant Act of Parliament put it. Tennent Plays got their exemption, and the season started. ·

The first play was a production by John Gielgud of *Macbeth*, which had been touring under the parent company and so needed no extra capital outlay. It was followed by other classics, including a lavish production of Congreve's *Love for Love*. Performances began in the early evening, so that Londoners could go to the theatre straight from work and be home before the onset of air raids at night. If things had gone wrong, the management would have lost much more than the £5,000 guaranteed by C.E.M.A. In the event, the season turned out to be exactly what the public wanted. Tennent Plays made money and the guarantee was not called.

Unfortunately, Hugh Beaumont's success resulted in trouble for C.E.M.A. and a good deal of hostility towards its Chairman. Other managements decided to do what Tennent's had done and set up their own non-profit-sharing subsidiaries. They, too, prospered, and in turn provoked recriminations. There were critical articles in the press, and disputes within the C.E.M.A. camp. The commercial theatre was accused of feathering its nest at the taxpayer's expense.

Oddly, criticism of Keynes in this matter of support for commercial enterprise took the form of calling him an amateur, one who did not understand the theatre and allowed himself to be taken in by the unscrupulous. There were, of course, people who took advantage of the situation; abuses did develop, and had to be sorted out; but the accusation of amateurism seemed hard to Keynes. There is a querulous note in some of his letters. 'What, if anything, am I to reply to this letter?' he asks, after an attack by one critic. 'Why he is so angry, I am not perfectly clear.' And 'Why does this fearful emotional tension get set up, when all people are trying to do is to give some harmless and moderately experienced advice?'

Meanwhile, it remained true that not a penny of C.E.M.A. money was spent on the Tennent Plays season or on any of the subsequent non-profit-sharing ventures. The managements took risks, C.E.M.A. sponsored them, and the system of guarantee against loss came into its own. Keynes once said that if a subsidising body were 100% successful it would end up by spending nothing at all, except on administration. It would choose so well and back such uniformly certain winners that all its loans would be repaid in full and none of its guarantees ever called . . .

He had his own, stern view of how public money should be spent, and on this subject there was a continuing battle between him and John Christie of Glyndebourne. Christie pleaded hard for a C.E.M.A. subsidy when the Glyndebourne Opera reopened after the war, and his resentment when it was refused was great and lasting. Keynes, supported by Steuart Wilson, who was at that time Music Director of C.E.M.A., considered that Glyndebourne, however glorious, was a rich man's pleasure, with no claim upon the taxpayer, and he maintained his stand.

It is a little disconcerting to find how often the progress of C.E.M.A. was marred by disputes. Sometimes they were simple squabbles about who should get what; sometimes they started with attacks from outside by people who thought they were better qualified than the Council to distribute public funds; quite often they raged (it is not too strong a word) among the C.E.M.A. directors and members of Council, most of whom held determined views in their own fields and were eager to defend them. There were professional battles, like the one concerning the commercial theatre, when Lewis Casson, as drama director, fought hard to prevent the powerful West End managements from gaining what seemed to him an unfair advantage over their less wealthy competitors. There were territorial struggles over the claims of different parts of the country and particularly of Scotland, where Osborne Mavor (the playwright, James Bridie), as Chairman of the Scottish Committee, showed a cantankerous behaviour curiously at odds with his benign and generous nature.

Probably it was inevitable. So many emotions were involved, so many hopes at stake and so many vested interests on the defensive. But there was, in addition, the personality of the Chairman. Supremely intelligent himself, he was impatient of anything less than clear thinking and well-defined aims. He knew what he wanted, and why, and he liked to have his own way. He could be very rude on occasion, and he did antagonise a number of people. Faced with an issue on which he felt deeply – and there were many such – he never hesitated to declare war.

It must also be said that he had strong likes and dislikes, both among individuals and among institutions. Just as his own favourites were apt to get special treatment, so he was, in the nature of things, suspicious of some of the activities he inherited from the original

C.E.M.A. One was the system of touring exhibitions called 'Art for the People', run by the British Institute of Adult Education. He thought the Institute had been pampered by T.J. (as indeed it may have been) and he questioned its methods in what must have seemed a vexing, even insulting way. And he never really came to terms with the Old Vic. There is evidence in his letters of persisting antagonism: 'It seems to me that the Sadler's Wells and Old Vic people are difficult, reluctant and aloof. What about dropping them?' If this comment had ever got beyond the stage of speculation, it would have seemed like treachery to a number of people.

A particular source of irritation was the Scottish Committee, with its insistent demand for a 'Goschen Formula' share of funds. Keynes did his best to be conciliatory: 'So long as they do not require the Chairman to wear a kilt at one meeting out of ten, it is, I think, all a matter of words'; but: 'I always find the question of Scotland . . . too tiresome to concentrate on easily', and: 'I would rather hand them over their share of the money, leaving them to stew in their own feeble juice, than agree to a separatist precedent which would allow them to get the best of both worlds.' The Scots were often difficult, but such an outburst as that was unjust.

The name C.E.M.A. itself annoyed Keynes. He inserted a final allusion to it when he announced the setting up of the Arts Council: 'I hope you will not try to turn our initials into a false, invented word. We have selected initials which we hope are unpronounceable.'

Much of all this sparring was light-hearted, at least on Keynes's side. But in 1944, half-way through his Chairmanship, it began to worry him. He wrote to his friend Samuel Courtauld to complain that 'As things are at the moment, there is nothing I should better like than to escape.' The effort of running C.E.M.A. at the height of its growing pains seemed to be becoming too much for him, and this was hardly surprising considering the claims of his work at the Treasury. 'I do not see how anyone can fulfil the proper functions of Chairman unless he gives something like a quarter of his time to it, rather than, as I do, about a twentieth.' However, the mood of depression did not last. 'Things' improved and, if the quarrels which weighed on him did not disappear, at least they fell into place behind the satisfaction of what was being achieved.

Gradually, C.E.M.A. evolved towards the Arts Council. Keynes and his colleagues began to work for the future, and the future of the arts was closely bound up with his personal philosophy. He really believed that the creative artist was more important than the economist or the politician, and he said so in so many words: 'The day is not far off when the Economic Problem will take the back seat where it belongs, and the arena of the heart and head will be occupied, or reoccupied, by our real problems – the problems of life and of human relations, of creation and behaviour and religion.' Meanwhile, he worked closely with the Treasury advisers on the wording of the new Charter and was himself responsible for the final draft.

The climax of his work for the future came with the opening of the Royal Opera House, Covent Garden. It was a kind of symbol of what he stood for, and an earnest of what he hoped would be realised. He himself was Chairman of the Covent Garden Trustees and he fostered every aspect of the preparations, from the negotiation of a special Treasury grant to the redecoration of the auditorium. The Opera House was opened on 20 February 1946. Lord and Lady Keynes were in their box, the Royal Family in theirs; and the ballet chosen for the first production was *The Sleeping Beauty*, in which Lydia Lopokova had danced the title part, years before. The evening was a national triumph. It was also the last public occasion on which Keynes appeared in this country.

Whatever he may have felt to the contrary, Keynes did give a remarkable amount of time to C.E.M.A. There were frequent meetings at Gordon Square, when the directors of music, art and drama were invited to dine and discuss their plans round the table in the basement dining-room. Lady Keynes would preside – I remember her especially on winter nights, swathed in woollens and wearing high, fleece-lined boots – and she usually gave us carrots to eat, because she said they would help us to see in the black-out. The artistic directors changed over the years, but the personalities which figured most were Reginald Jacques, for music, and Steuart Wilson who succeeded him; Ivor Brown and then Lewis Casson for drama; Philip James for art. All of these were powerful men of vision and expertise. Ivor Brown I remember particularly for the part he played in shaping early policy and helping forward the transition from the pre-Keynes period. Lewis Casson was argumentative and acted as a valuable catalyst. Steuart Wilson brought a kind of soaring imagination which Keynes appreciated because it so often defied the rules, just as he valued Philip James's grasp of affairs. Conversation ranged over all the arts, and over the individuals connected with them. Practical matters were to the fore, and the talks were as firmly based as they were stimulating. We would go back to our desks next day with our instructions clear, ready to perform marvels.

Then there were his letters. When Keynes was in London he wrote to me nearly every day, not only to approve minutes and agenda, which he did with drastic thoroughness, and to dictate procedure, about which he was always precise, but also to go into the minutiae of administration. Because he was obliged to spend time lying down and needed to be spared the weariness of personal interviews, he wrote instead, and the result is an archive of recorded material which might not have been available otherwise. Many of the letters have seven or eight different headings, setting out the matters he wished to discuss, from 'Wigmore Hall' to 'Finance officer' and from 'Factory concerts' to 'Our future home'. I have a feeling he enjoyed the details as much as the grand planning; I am sure this was true of the later years, when he became less worried by the quarrels I have described and began to see his policies taking shape. It may even have been that this side of his life helped to balance the other, and that the government's financial delegate found a certain refreshment in ordering the affairs of the London theatre and the national symphony orchestras from his desk in Whitehall, from his cabin in mid-Atlantic or his hotel room in Washington, New York or Ottawa. Certainly the letters continued to come in regularly during the American journeys. He asked that all minutes of meetings be sent to him without delay, wherever he was, and instructed me to write him full reports of everything that happened. These he dissected at once and returned them with comments of devastating frankness.

The letters are an immensely readable mixture of enthusiasm and hard-headedness. Many of them are far longer than they need have been and are written with a savouring of language which makes them much more than formal documents. They are full of quirks and prejudices, and a kind of Edwardian puckishness. About a disputed tour by Wolfit's company, he counsels letting the manager have his way: 'He will always be a lone Wolfit.' About the first, rather amorphous plan for an Edinburgh Festival, presented by Rudolf Bing: 'I fear that I may find myself being rude to Rudi.' About Glyndebourne: 'John Christie is holding out to me a very amiable, leafy and well-grown olive branch. I am proposing to accept it.' About a threatened resignation by a Council member: 'The worst of people who are always saying that they are considering resignation is that they never do resign. If he does resign, we, I think, would feel resigned.' Some references are to projects since forgotten: 'By all means let us become little elephants in Apsley House'; and 'Children's Theatre: I look forward to the idea of Mr Gwatkin and Mr Christie going out to sea together in a sieve! I am sure the children will enjoy the sight.'

I cannot help noticing, as I reread the thick files, how expansive and long my own letters to him were. They became more so as my confidence increased and my awe of him subsided. He did not seem to mind; but his answers could be pungent. One, written from Washington in October 1943, which begins: 'I particularly congratulate you on the account of the relation of the Council to the associated theatre companies', continues in another context: 'I was . . . deeply shocked by what you were proposing . . . You must forgive me if I characterise it as being (a) untruthful in fact, (b) dangerously hampering in practice, and (c) seriously and deliberately misleading in the present case!' He softened these strictures by adding the exclamation mark, in ink.

He hated anything that smacked of muddle – his favourite term of abuse: 'Any half and half, unclear, anomalous arrangements . . . will only lead to trouble.' That is what he constantly tried to teach us. In November 1945, he wrote from America, after receiving the minutes of a Council meeting held in his absence:

I was considerably shocked by the lightheartedly enthusiastic way in which the Council gave the Executive Committee authority without, so far as I can see, any of the necessary information before them . . . For heaven's sake, keep this at bay until I return . . . There is rather too much of an air of 'warm endorsement' and half-baked ideas in these minutes to leave me quite happy!

Again there is an inked-in exclamation mark.

It is pleasant to read, in yet another letter from across the Atlantic – almost the last, in the spring of 1946 – that he was proud of our achievement: 'The air-mail edition of *The Times* reaches me, so I am fairly up-to-date about the two repertory seasons. It all seems very glorious, far in advance of anything that is happening in New York, and for that result London certainly has to thank C.E.M.A. for having been an indispensable contributory factor.'

Keynes took office as Chairman of C.E.M.A. on 1 April 1942. He died on Easter Sunday 1946. In the course of those four years he fashioned the Arts Council-to-be and laid the foundations of permanent State patronage of the arts in Great Britain. He did not found C.E.M.A. and he did not live to see the Arts Council incorporated under Charter; but it was he who turned the one into the other.

26

The Cambridge Arts Theatre

NORMAN HIGGINS

In 1934, as First Bursar of King's College, Mr Maynard Keynes completed arrangements for rebuilding the College hostel fronting Peas Hill and St Edward's Passage. These plans left an irregular plot of land belonging to the College totally enclosed by existing buildings except for a single storey access to another lodging house at 7 Peas Hill. At this time Cambridge was a theatreless town; the New Theatre had become Cambridge's tenth cinema, while the Festival Theatre had run out of sponsors wealthy enough to finance its operation. Keynes seized the opportunity to provide a centrally-sited theatre on this irregular plot by negotiating a 99-year building lease from his College, together with possession of three lodging houses in St Edward's Passage. The planning of the hostel had been entrusted to George Kennedy & Nightingale, architects with offices in the Chenil Galleries, Chelsea, and the main building contract to the local firm of Rattee & Kett, and Keynes employed both for the theatre project.

A year earlier, with financial aid from friends, I had founded the Cosmopolitan Cinema in Market Passage – the first provincial specialist cinema giving public performances of films in foreign dialogue: the Academy Cinema in London was the only other cinema with this policy. After an uncertain start the project began to flourish. In May 1934 Mr and Mrs Keynes told me of their plans for the proposed theatre; they thought suitable stage productions could be obtained for about twenty-six weeks in each year with the remainder devoted to film programmes. Keynes then surprised me with a proposal that I should close the Cinema, move its equipment to the new theatre, and accept the post of General Manager there on a salary and profit-sharing basis. He discounted my lack of knowledge of the professional theatre, commenting 'we shall learn by experience unencumbered by notions which may prove inappropriate to the present venture'.

This proposal was accepted by the Cinema board, and I began my new duties at the end of the 1935 academic year: but two members of the Cinema board then repudiated the agreement and decided to continue to operate the Cinema, a decision which in 1947, when stage productions monopolised the Arts Theatre stage, proved a blessing in disguise when the theatre management obtained a long lease of the premises, where its film activities have since been concentrated.

The first planning conference took place during the summer at the Keynes's country retreat at Tilton, Sussex, when Kennedy produced his outline drawings and a rough estimate of cost – £18,000; appropriate clauses were drafted for a Memorandum and Articles of an operating company, and in December The Arts Theatre of Cambridge Limited was registered as a private company with a share capital of £15,000 divided into 7,500 £1 ordinary shares and 7,500 6% redeemable preference shares. The first Directors were Keynes, Miss J. M. Harvey (Secretary of the Camargo Society and Secretary of the London Film Society) and G. H. W. Rylands (a Fellow of King's College, and principal pillar of The Marlowe Dramatic Society and the Amateur Dramatic Club), with myself as Secretary. Keynes took up all the ordinary shares, and 100 preference shares were allotted to Miss Harvey and 100 to Rylands to cover Director's qualification. Thereafter a letter outlining the project was circulated under confidential cover to a carefully selected list of Cambridge residents, with an invitation to apply for preference shares: but the response was meagre, only 2,100 shares being applied for despite Keynes's assurance that he would provide additional finance to build and equip the theatre.

Influenced by experience of backstage conditions during the latter part of his wife's career as a ballerina, Keynes imposed firm conditions at the outset of planning, specifying *inter alia* that backstage comfort should match that provided for patrons. It was all too clear that the irregular site would present daunting problems: suffice it to say that Kennedy brilliantly surmounted them. Plans were extended from time to time including the provision of a Restaurant* on the first floor of the St Edward's Passage houses, and the installation of up-to-the-minute projection and sound reproducing equipment. The final cost proved to be just over twice the original estimate, and the nominal capital of the Company was increased by the creation of a further 2,500 £1 ordinary shares, taken up by Keynes, giving a subscribed capital of £12,300: cash to meet the balance was provided as required by Keynes as an interest-free loan.

From the start of the project throughout the remainder of his

* Keynes argued that a civilised theatre-goer must be able to dine within the building.

life, Keynes, despite his many other commitments and the stress of his voluntary Treasury work during the war years, always found time to discuss details of management, and his interest in every aspect was insatiable – the make-up of audiences (scanning a capacity audience he remarked 'strange, I don't recognise half a dozen faces'), their drinking habits (coffee and squash for ballet, and gin and tonic for a farce), and in the Restaurant the proportion of wine drinkers and what they drank. From the outset he tried to encourage undergraduates to drink wine rather than spirits by charging the usual prices for the latter, but adding a modest 50% (instead of the customary 100% to 150%) to the cost price of wine. His encouragement was all embracing and his dedication quickly persuaded colleagues and staff that they were partners in an important public enterprise. A long queue would entice him into the box office where his belief that the task was perfectly simple proved mistaken, and his efforts to help something of an embarrassment.

After a lively discussion the building was christened The Arts Theatre: apt in contemporary times, the title was assumed by the Cambridge public to indicate 'a highbrow temple not for the likes of us', and it took some years for a catholic programme policy to dispel this erroneous impression.

Following the apparently inevitable delays in completion, the Theatre opened in February 1936 with a Gala performance by the Vic–Wells Ballet, followed the next evening by a Gala film programme. With the clarity which distinguished his writings Keynes explained his purpose

The object of the Arts Theatre of Cambridge is the entertainment of the University and Town. Its name describes, and the form of a Pentagon given to its auditorium by the architect symbolises, its purpose of providing a home in Cambridge for the five arts of drama, opera, ballet, music and cinema.

No permanent company will be maintained, but the Theatre and its organisation will provide opportunities for at least four classes of production

  (i) In the first place, the Theatre will be available for dramatic and musical enterprises staged and produced in Cambridge.
  (ii) From time to time the management of the Theatre will itself take the responsibility of producing plays.
  (iii) It is hoped that plays from the West End with their London casts will be available from time to time, either immediately before, or immediately after, their appearance in London.
  (iv) It is hoped that some of the leading repertory companies of the country and international touring companies will come to Cambridge to give some of the more successful items in their repertoire.
On the Cinema side the films given will be of the character already associ-

ated with the name of our General Manager, Mr Norman Higgins: that is to say, European productions of conspicuous merit will take a more prominent part in the programme than is usual in other picture houses.

On Sunday evenings some concerts and lectures will be arranged each term.

At the conclusion of the Gala ballet performance, attended by the numerous members of his family and relations, Keynes insisted that Kennedy and I should accompany him on to the stage, and in a speech beginning 'My Lord Lieutenant, Mr Mayor, Mr Vice-Chancellor, Mr Chairman of the County Council, Venerable Heads of Colleges, Learned Professors, My Lords, Ladies and Gentlemen' he thanked us in turn in the most generous terms for our pre-opening work. This speech also demonstrated the perfect acoustic qualities of the auditorium for the spoken word, to which such as Ruth Draper, John Gielgud, Peggy Ashcroft and Sybil Thorndike have paid tribute. Mr and Mrs Keynes later that evening acted as host and hostess at a delightful supper party in the Restaurant which concluded with a speech of thanks from Provost Sheppard praising their public-spirited enterprise.

Public response during the early years was spasmodic: annual visits by the Vic–Wells Ballet, the Sadler's Wells Opera, a few West End productions of the Marlowe Society and the Footlights attracted capacity audiences, but other stage productions averaged only 25% of financial capacity: film programmes fared a little better although it appeared to take half the week before the public realised the switch from stage to screen.

A serious illness in 1937 prompted Keynes to anticipate his long-term plans for the eventual ownership of the undertaking: from Ruthin Castle where he had been taken for treatment he unfolded his plans in letters to the Mayor and the Vice-Chancellor, to which he received encouraging replies. A Trust Deed was then prepared and approved at the most unconventional board meeting I have experienced, which took place in a lovely Welsh valley with Keynes, his wife, Rylands and myself seated on travelling rugs spread on the grass.

Keynes's plan was to make a gift of his ordinary shares to Trustees representing the University and Town, supplemented by a covenant to purchase for the Trustees the 5,000 unallotted preference shares. As part of the financial tidying-up a £12,000 mortgage was obtained from Barclays Bank utilised to repay the balance of his interest-free loan to Keynes. This mortgage was paid off in full within a few years. For some years after the founding of the Trust the existing holders of preference shares remained members of the company, but these were eventually redeemed (at a premium of 3s.

a share, dividends having been paid from allotment to redemption) and reallotted to the Trustees, who thus became the sole owners of the undertaking.

In his letters to the Mayor and the Vice-Chancellor the donor explained that he regarded his gift 'as in some sense a memorial to my parents who have served the University and the Town for upwards of half a century'. Keynes and Rylands were appointed Trustees representing the theatre management, and, subject to their consent to serve, the Mayor and Deputy Mayor, the Professors of English Literature and Music and the Provost of King's College were appointed *ex officio* Trustees, with myself as Secretary. It is of interest to record that during the intervening years no one qualified by virtue of his office to serve as an *ex officio* Trustee has refused to do so.

During the drafting of the Trust Deed the closest liaison was maintained with Customs and Excise and Inland Revenue to ensure that the undertaking qualified as a properly constituted charitable trust with a partly educational basis. On its execution it became possible to make application for exemption from the payment of entertainment duty on admissions to partly educational programmes, and this brought increasing improvement to the Trust finances, enabling the arrangement of many programmes which otherwise would have proved too expensive.

Shortly after Keynes returned to Cambridge he approved my suggestion concerning future approved productions by amateur societies, who hitherto had rented the Theatre. Experience had shown that too much time was being expended on fund-raising to the detriment of rehearsal, while exemption from entertainment duty could be applied for only if the Trust itself was financially responsible. From that time it became standard practice for the Trust to assume direct financial responsibility for approved amateur productions subject to the acceptance of an overall budget: any loss was borne by Trust funds, but in the event of a profit the Trust made a donation of half the surplus of income over expenditure to the society concerned. This new procedure was unanimously welcomed by University and Town societies, and has been mainly responsible for ensuring a regular continuity of productions which have been a stabilising factor in the always changing national theatrical scene.

The outbreak of war brought appreciable changes: many Army and R.A.F. stations within a few miles of Cambridge were built or extended, while several government departments were evacuated from London to temporary offices within the borough boundary, incidentally bringing an influx of sophisticated theatre-goers. Allied to the curtailment of most peacetime leisure activities the theatre became increasingly popular, and when the blitz began, involving the closure of most of the West End theatres, we were able to pick and choose star-studded productions instead of having to go in search of them. With several other cinemas functioning in Cambridge, the Arts Theatre ceased to show films and became exclusively concerned with stage productions. But in the choice of programmes quality remained the decisive factor.

Throughout the war years Cambridge enjoyed theatrical fare never before possible in the provinces. It is impossible in the space available to attempt to mention the galaxy of stars who appeared in plays, opera, ballet and Sunday evening programmes organised for H.M.'s Forces during that period: it will perhaps suffice to say that Laurence Olivier was the one notable exception. During the worst of the blitz many Londoners came to Cambridge whenever possible for a quiet, if short, weekend: amongst them were Peggy Ashcroft, Natasha Litvin and Angus Morrison, and at pre-lunch gatherings over a glass of sherry at Merton Hall discussions led to the launching of the Apollo Society. Rylands, Provost Sheppard and I joined the above trio as founder directors, and the first Apollo Recital of Poetry and Music was given in the Arts Theatre on a Sunday evening, following an introductory speech by the Poet Laureate, who then joined Keynes in his private box. Another Cambridge start of a movement now nationally famous.

Keynes was a firm believer in building future audiences by arousing the interest of schoolchildren in music and drama: from the opening of the Theatre special matinées of suitable plays, ballets and programmes of music were arranged for school parties as guests of the management, while parties of senior pupils were accommodated as guests at public performances of suitable plays whenever advance booking indicated that seats could be made available. From the founding of the Trust these activities increased in line with the improvement in Trust finances. It became the custom for me to go to London on Fridays when Keynes was coming from the Treasury to Cambridge for the weekend: I left Wardour Street or Shaftesbury Avenue in good time to arrive at Liverpool Street station early enough to claim a place in the front row of the scrum which assembled opposite where the restaurant car of the Fenman would stop: when the train arrived the usual concerted scramble ensued but I always managed to secure a gangway seat and place my overcoat and bag on the adjacent seat. When those 'beaten to it' had dispersed along the corridor Keynes would quietly approach with his heavy bag of Treasury papers. Discussion of theatre matters would proceed while tea was served and eaten, when Keynes would reach for his bag and become immersed in its contents. It was on one of these occasions that I asked him to give me a guideline for expenditure for schools events: his response was as clear as it was generous – 'spend in each financial year up to half the surplus of income over expenditure revealed in the previous year's accounts' – a decision which resulted in upwards of £10,000 being spent under this head, as well as providing me with a most rewarding task.

Up to the beginning of the war catering charges had been maintained at the lowest level commensurate with the catering account breaking even: the Company therefore had no profit standard to set against the wartime introduction of Excess Profits Tax, resulting in payments to the Exchequer for this tax of some £14,000.

The Footlights activities were in abeyance during the war years, but the Marlowe Society continued to mount Lent Term productions of high quality due to the devoted efforts of Rylands and Donald Beves, while drama companies were liberally interspersed with visits of ballet and opera companies. Throughout these years a series of Sunday recitals was arranged annually with artists of the calibre of Solomon, Moiseiwitsch, Myra Hess, Segovia, Cortot, Benjamin Britten, Peter Pears, Gerald Moore, Joan Cross, Elisabeth Schwarzkopf and Elisabeth Schumann, while from ten to twelve symphony concerts were mounted annually by the B.B.C. Symphony, B.B.C. Concert, London Philharmonic, Hallé and the Royal Philharmonic Orchestras, of which twenty-five were broadcast.

During his absence in America on Treasury business Keynes maintained a close watch on artistic projects both as Chairman of the Cambridge Trust and as Chairman of C.E.M.A. (later the Arts Council), and later he set up the Covent Garden Opera House Trust. A typical example of his perseverance resulted in the return to this country of the Ballets Jooss Company who had been stranded in America for over two years: the Company reassembled in Cambridge where the Trust provided storage accommodation for scenery and costumes and repair facilities. At Keynes's request I set up a non-profit-distributing company of which I acted as unpaid Managing Director, and for some years negotiated London and provincial tours for them. The Trust also joined with the Arts Council in providing funds for the reorganisation of Intimate Opera, whose affairs were also conducted from Cambridge on a voluntary basis for some three years.

Some disappointments were suffered: Associated British Cinemas eventually refused Keynes's offer to take over the lease of the New Theatre (then closed) which would have provided a much larger stage and seating capacity for ballet, opera, pantomime and other large-scale productions, while the purchase of the theatres in Bedford and Luton was brought to an abrupt halt by Keynes's untimely death.

In the space available only a bare, factual account of the Arts Theatre has been possible, and fails to convey the abiding memories of a courageous man who dismissed difficulties with a witty phrase and a friendly gleam. His hospitality, which mixed colleagues, visiting artists and undergraduate guests at hilarious supper parties, added a sparkle to Cambridge life: he insisted that my wife and I should take any brief holidays possible at Tilton whether or not he and his wife were there, and I remember the considerable trouble he took to alter his weekend plans so that he and his wife could come to Cambridge to dine in our flat with Kennedy, Rylands, my wife and me to celebrate the tenth anniversary of the opening of the Theatre.

The loss of a beloved Chairman was a shattering blow at a time when expansion schemes were in active preparation, but which had to be abandoned in the absence of his financial backing, and it became essential to concentrate all our energies in ensuring the continuance of the purpose which led to his munificent gift to Cambridge. He blazed a trail increasingly copied by local authorities in many parts of the United Kingdom, and it is a lasting tribute to his initial planning that forty years later the Trust continues to implement the policy he laid down.

27

The picture collector

RICHARD SHONE with DUNCAN GRANT

'Fine Cézanne £900 cheap and fine Seurat £350 will you buy or advise Vanessa to buy they go tomorrow Duncan.' So runs a characteristic telegram from Duncan Grant to Maynard Keynes. There were to be many more such communications over the years until Keynes's death. Here is a postcard which goes even further, from Duncan Grant in Paris (9 May 1920): 'We have bought you a picture by Thiesson* for 1,200 francs. We like it very much but it is not exactly what most people would say to be exciting. But then it is very cheap. Nessa says she will buy it if you don't want it. We have seen two very fine Segonzacs – 1 landscape and 1 still-life. What about them?'

When he died, Keynes left a large and valuable collection of mainly modern French and English pictures with fine examples of work by Ingres, Degas, Seurat, Cézanne, Picasso, Matisse, Derain and Braque. Among the English artists there were of course numerous pictures by Grant and Vanessa Bell as well as a wide range of other work by Sickert, Dobson, Roberts, Spencer Gore and Ivon Hitchens. Keynes loved his pictures, was reluctant to lend them to exhibitions and often repeated what a joy it was to return home after a visit abroad and see the familiar works – the Sickert 'Bar-Parlour' above the piano in Gordon Square, the Cézanne in his bedroom at Tilton. They were an essential and invigorating part of his life, a visible representation to him of an ingredient in the civilisation to which his gifts were dedicated.

The collecting 'lust' ran in his family, and indeed still does. Before he turned his attention to pictures, Maynard had already begun to buy books. His Cambridge contemporaries would not have been surprised to hear in later years of his valuable book collection, but they would almost certainly have been curious to learn that Picasso and Braque, Sickert and Hitchens were hung on his walls. As an undergraduate he showed no interest in painting in a university not especially noted for any such enthusiasm. Among his

* Gaston Thiesson, a French painter (1882–1920).

friends were mathematicians, historians and classical scholars. Of course one admired Greek sculpture and architecture, one paid lip-service to Italian and Dutch pictures and usually one stopped there.

As the 'dumped grass-orphan of an Anglo-Indian Major', to use his own description, Duncan Grant lived with his Strachey cousins in London and was on particularly close terms with Lytton and James. After leaving St Paul's when he was seventeen, he attended the Westminster School of Art. In Lytton's world he was uneducated, but with his natural intelligence and refreshingly unexpected views he was soon accepted as a regular and welcome guest in Cambridge. It was at about this time (*c.* 1905), before he left to study in Paris, that he met through Lytton many of those friends who were later to constitute Old Bloomsbury – Leonard Woolf, Clive Bell, Norton, Sydney-Turner, E. M. Forster and Desmond MacCarthy. And of course he met Maynard who became an intimate friend on his return from Paris.

One of the fascinating features of Duncan Grant's friendship with this generation of Cambridge men was his introduction into the cult of the secret society, the Apostles. Maynard and Lytton's life revolved for some time around the fortunes of the Apostles and thus it was only natural that Duncan, being close to Lytton, should have been initiated into the intrigues and dramas that swirled about each fresh election. His knowledge of Apostolic affairs shocked some of its old members. In London, talk was free – how could it be otherwise with Roger Fry or Virginia Woolf in the company – and the Society was openly discussed if a little uneasily by such as Maynard who all his life retained a kind of adolescent loyalty to the Society, its cult of secrecy still vividly impressive.

It is against such a background that we must see the friendship of Keynes and Duncan Grant. For the former, here was a different point of view in that it was completely unacademic, free from the somewhat narrow and stultifying vision of life that tended to irritate him in some of his university friends. On his part, Duncan Grant developed a highly personal taste in literature, picked his way through the maze of intellectual opportunities that Keynes and his friends offered him, absorbing much that he heard and taking nothing on trust – to the point of asking his mother for *Principia Ethica* for his birthday. Though not at all given to philosophical and abstract argument, his presence was found uninhibiting during the high-powered dialectical discussions which invariably occurred in London and Cambridge. Something of the atmosphere of those years is to be found in his early portraits of Lytton and James Strachey, and in the 1908 painting of Maynard at King's College.

Until Keynes's marriage to Lydia Lopokova in 1925, Duncan and Vanessa Bell were his closest friends in London, his chief confidants and the 'keepers of his conscience'. Maynard shared rooms with Duncan in Fitzroy Square and later in Brunswick Square, and in 1910 they travelled together to Greece and Constantinople, and in the following year went to Tunis and Sicily. During the war, Maynard was a regular guest at Charleston, a farmhouse in Sussex where Vanessa Bell with her children and Duncan and David Garnett went to live. He would come with bundles of papers from the Treasury, a fund of amusing stories about the famous and not so famous, sympathy and encouragement and the luxury perhaps of a bottle of whisky or port; for physical exercise he would strenuously indulge in his passion for weeding. In 1920, he, Duncan and Vanessa spent several weeks in Rome on a gigantic spending spree and went for some days to the Berensons' villa 'I Tatti', where at a party Maynard was mistaken for 'Il Pittore Grant' and shown the pictures, and Duncan 'l'Economisto Keynes' and asked about the European financial situation.

It was during these immediate post-war years that many of the best pictures came into Maynard's collection on the advice of Duncan and Vanessa. His early purchases were fairly conventional – a John drawing, for example, from the Chenil Galleries in 1908 and a small 'Mother and Child' by Eric Gill for £25 also from the Chenil. (Maynard's brother Geoffrey had given Gill one of his earliest commissions.) With the advent of the two Post-Impressionist Exhibitions, Maynard modestly branched out into modern French art with a water-colour by André Lhote, 'La Seine'. Among the English pictures at the Second Exhibition, he lent Frederick Etchells's 'The Dead Mole'. Etchells came to a summer camp at Everleigh, Surrey, organised by Maynard in 1912, and they saw a good deal of each other at this time. But the turning point in his career as a collector came in 1918 when there was a sale of the contents of Degas' studio. Not only was this sale important for Maynard, but through him several fine pictures entered the National Gallery. It is worth recounting the circumstances of the sale in some detail.

On one of his infrequent holidays in London from wartime agricultural work in Sussex, Duncan Grant picked up a catalogue in Roger Fry's studio of the forthcoming sale of Degas' collection at the Gallerie Georges Petit in Paris. He was greatly excited by some of the illustrations and at a dinner on the same evening, he tackled Maynard. Might he persuade the Treasury to draft money into the National Gallery to buy some of the paintings? Maynard liked the idea. A few days later he went through the catalogue with

Duncan and Vanessa at Charleston and became most enthusiastic, especially over the Cézannes. On 21 March, Duncan was gloomily working on the farm when he was handed a telegram from Maynard: 'Money secured for pictures.' Two days later Maynard wrote to Vanessa that he was leaving for Paris, for it so happened that the sale coincided with a financial conference which Maynard was to attend.

My picture coup was a whirlwind affair – carried through in a day and a half before anyone had time to reflect what they were doing. I have secured 550,000 francs to play with; Holmes* is travelling out with us and I hope we shall be able to attend the sale together. The prime object is to buy Ingres; his portrait of himself being first choice; after that the Perroneau. I think Holmes also has his eye on a Greco but admits there would be another chance for this. I am fairly sure I can persuade him to go for the Delacroix 'Schwiter'; I shall try very hard on the journey out to persuade him to buy a Cézanne as a personal reward to me for having got him the money, but I think his present intention is not to buy a Cézanne; I have not yet discussed the question of Corot with him.

Duncan and Vanessa's original intention was to get Roger Fry to see Sir Charles Holmes and advise him over the purchases. But Fry was down at Poole throwing pots for the Omega Workshops, so their hopes were placed – a little uneasily – on Maynard's powers of persuasion. The sale took place on 26 and 27 March with Paris under fire at the time from 'Big Bertha', the Germans having broken through the Allied lines. Consequently, bidding was timid and slow until excitement mounted when the National Gallery secured Delacroix's 'Baron Schwiter' against keen competition from the Louvre. Maynard bought for himself an Ingres drawing 'Femme Nue' for 1,900 francs, a small painting of a horse 'Cheval au Pâturage' by Delacroix, a study by Delacroix for the Palais Bourbon decorations and a still-life 'Pommes' by Cézanne for 9,000 francs.

On 28 March, Duncan, Vanessa, Clive Bell and David Garnett were finishing dinner at Charleston, when a tired and hungry Maynard arrived. Vanessa takes up the story in a letter to Roger Fry:

Maynard came back suddenly and unexpectedly late at night having been dropped at the bottom of the lane by Austen Chamberlain in a Government motor and said he had left a Cézanne by the roadside! Duncan rushed off to get it and you can imagine how exciting it all was. . . . Holmes's purchases are idiotic considering his chances. He wouldn't hear of Cézanne and in the end didn't spend all the money, but came back with £5,000 unspent and no El Greco which he might easily have had. He did

* Sir Charles Holmes (1868–1936), Director of the National Gallery, 1916–28.

get the Delacroix 'Baron de Norvins' – [Vanessa has here confused the 'Baron de Schwiter' with another purchase, Ingres' 'M. de Norvine'] – 'Angelica and Roger' by Ingres and I think some drawings, a Corot landscape, Manet's 'Lady with a Cat', a Gauguin still-life. I can't remember the rest. Maynard got for himself the Cézanne 'Apples', a wonderful Ingres drawing, a small picture by Delacroix and a drawing by Delacroix which he's given to Duncan. The Cézanne is really amazing and it's most exciting to have in the house.

A Cézanne in a private collection in England was rare indeed; there was none in a public collection and Maynard's small study of seven apples soon became an object of pilgrimage by the younger painters like Mark Gertler. Other pictures bought by the National Gallery – news of whose purchases was kept secret until after the war – included two other Ingres paintings, another Delacroix, Manet's 'L'Exécution de Maximilien' and a painting each by Forain, Rousseau and Ricard and drawings by David, Ingres and Delacroix.

This was the real beginning of Maynard's collection and pictures were swiftly added over the next few years. Those bought at the 'Vente Degas' were the unexpected benefits of shrewd wartime speculation. The later ones belonged to the period of growing personal wealth. To have Maynard and his money there on the spot, to be able to persuade him to buy, was a splendid compensation for relative poverty. But of course Maynard fully appreciated the situation and was only too willing to concede. His love and respect for Vanessa and Duncan as creative artists, amounting it seems to a kind of humility, was all-embracing. A similar feeling, though inevitably on a different scale and with a different focus, ran through his relationship with Lydia Lopokova, especially in the years before their marriage. Maynard had, perhaps, little innate feeling and understanding of painting, but his discrimination and knowledge grew over the years and was aided by Lydia's more quickly responsive feelings and definite if somewhat idiosyncratic views. But with this growing knowledge, a characteristic quality of Maynard's came into play: he attempted to speak and pronounce upon painting on occasion with an authority that was ill-founded. His roving mind and quick imagination could not be stopped and it led him to make comments that might be pretentious and even absurd. Naturally this irritated those of his friends who thought they knew what they were talking about.

Acting on the telegram quoted at the beginning, Maynard bought one of his best and most impressive pictures. Duncan Grant had seen a Seurat study for the 'Promenade à la Grande Jatte' hanging outside the Chelsea Book Club in the King's Road. It was being

sold by a German refugee at the remarkably reasonable price of
£350. Keynes not only liked the painting but found such a bargain
irresistible. Sometime later Maynard heard from the dealer P. M.
Turner that 'La Grande Jatte' itself was for sale in Paris. Duncan,
Maynard and Turner went over to see it in a private house with the
plan that Maynard and Turner should buy it together at the
relatively cheap price that was asked. In spite of all Duncan's
exhortations, he could not persuade them to buy the picture and it
soon found its way to America.

In the same month as the Seurat study joined his collection,
Maynard bought a Matisse, 'Déshabillé'. Under Oliver Brown, the
Leicester Galleries were rapidly established as a centre for shows
of advanced English and French painting. Their first post-war
exhibition of a French painter was given over to Matisse. It was an
unexpected success and Matisse, who was in London at the time,
was amazed to find English people buying his work. 'The Matisses
are lovely', wrote Vanessa Bell to Roger Fry (30 November 1919),
'but for the most part rather slight sketches. We have induced
Maynard to buy one of the best, a small seated figure with bare
arms, very sober in colour, for 175 gns. All are sold. He's evidently a
great success nowadays.' Fry's advocacy of Matisse was of course
greatly responsible for this volte-face.

In the following year, a Derain still-life and a Friesz landscape
were added to the collection. His friends were not forgotten –
Duncan's 'Paper Flowers' was bought from his first one-man show
(1920) and Vanessa's 'Gulf of St Tropez', also came from her first
show in 1922. A few months later, at Vanessa's command, Maynard
bought the best of his several Sickerts, 'The Bar Parlour', from the
annual London Group show. The sale of this important work was
particularly heartening to Sickert. He had only recently returned,
grief-stricken and incognito from Dieppe after the death there of
his second wife, Christine. He was very short of money, hampered
by colds and undernourishment, living first of all in the 'Bachelor
Hotel', Aldersgate – the bar of which inspired this painting – and
later in a comfortless bedsitting-room next to his studio in Fitzroy
Street. But he soon began to go out again, wrote a favourable review
of Vanessa's pictures and was made welcome in Bloomsbury, especially at Gordon Square when Lydia and Maynard gave a party. He
later painted a charming profile of Lydia.* In 1934, again Maynard

* For a description of Sickert at such a party by Virginia Woolf, see
Leonard Woolf, 'Downhill All the Way' (1967), pp. 115–17. The portrait
of Lydia Lopokova (c. 1923) has inscribed on the back by Sickert: 'To
J.M.K. from a hereditary mathematician' – the painter referring to one of
his forebears.

came to the rescue and contributed £25 to a fund set up by Sir Alec Martin, Sylvia Gosse and others to help Sickert out of serious financial difficulties. Among other Sickert paintings and drawings, Maynard owned the 1900 'Théâtre de Montmartre' painted when Sickert ran a school in Paris. It was bought from the Goupil Gallery in 1924.

Towards the end of the First World War, Maynard had commissioned Duncan and Vanessa to decorate his rooms at 46 Gordon Square. An amusing feature was two large cupboards with panels depicting English, French, Italian and Turkish life – from the plump Florentine housewife to the fried eggs and fat brown teapot of an English breakfast. More sober treatment was accorded to Maynard's next commission – decorations for his rooms in King's. Duncan had previously painted one of the walls, but had despairingly given up on a large composition in the manner of his 'Lemon Gatherers' now in the Tate Gallery. This time, he and Vanessa undertook eight life-size panels, four each, of male and female figures representing the various triposes: draped females and undraped males whose arts and sciences are somewhat obscure. They were completed at Charleston and installed in 1922, when the whole room was painted in an appropriate colour scheme and Vanessa worked appliqué curtains for the windows.

In the 1920s and right up to his death, Maynard was involved in one way or another – though usually financially – in many organisations concerning painting and the ballet. His involvement was never dilatory or self-seeking; his well-known capacity for hard work, his attention to detail and overall vision were together concentrated on whatever project was at hand. One of his most cherished was the London Artists Association. In Maynard's own words it

came into being towards the end of the year 1925, as the result of a meeting with a group of artists, who had found themselves without an efficient organisation for dealing with their work and had consequently sold almost incredibly few pictures during the previous year or two.... The result of our conversation was to make us feel that a small organisation formed on co-operative principles might, even if it had no great financial backing, at least do something to reduce the anxieties of promising painters and perhaps help to get a better market in the long run for their works. The idea was that an organisation could be formed which, acting as agent to a group of artists, would allow them to work in greater freedom from continually pressing financial considerations by providing them with a small guaranteed income and taking upon itself the entire management of the business side of their affairs.

The Association held regular group and one-man shows; it also sent exhibitions to the provinces and made sure its artists were well represented abroad in shows of English painting. It was through the Association that Keynes commissioned the portrait of himself and Lydia by William Roberts in 1935, reproduced as the frontispiece to this book. Maynard was generous to Roberts, buying several more paintings and drawings, finding him patrons and giving him continued financial support after the liquidation of the group. By that time such painters as Pasmore, Coldstream, Rogers, Medley and du Plessis had become members of the Association.

There were occasional disagreements – about financial arrangements, about new members ('I got a dreadful dressing down from Roger [Fry] (and gather you've had one too) for letting Paul Nash into the Association', wrote Maynard to Vanessa, 10 February 1927), about the underpaid and overworked secretaries, the overexposure of some artists' work and certain sales going on behind the Association's back. But generally everything worked smoothly, the artists were paid and the organisation received much complimentary publicity. One of its features was its persuading sympathetic writers to contribute catalogue forewords, such as Raymond Mortimer, Edmund Blunden, David Garnett, Cunninghame-Graham and Virginia Woolf. The guarantors gave whole-heartedly to the enterprise, particularly Samuel Courtauld and Maynard.

From the Association's exhibitions, Maynard added many works to his collection, particularly by the younger painters like Pitchforth and Raymond Coxon. And as a buyer for the Contemporary Arts Society, the Association kept him sensitively aware of when such a sale would particularly help a painter's circumstances – as with Ivon Hitchens who sold two pictures to Maynard, one of which went to the Tate Gallery through the C.A.S. Hitchens had been bombed out of his London home and was living in considerable discomfort in a caravan near Petworth, Sussex.

In 1937, Maynard commissioned from Derain designs for the sets and costumes of the ballet *Harlequin in the Street*, and for Moliere's *Le Misanthrope* staged at the Cambridge Arts Theatre. The Derain drawings are amongst the Keynes papers at King's College. And a small but incalculably valuable project deserves a brief mention: Duncan Grant hit on the happy idea of starting a picture library at King's whereby undergraduates could borrow lithographs and drawings for a small sum each term. Always enthusiastic to enhance the life of his College, Maynard readily agreed and for the first year Duncan was chiefly responsible for buying works. The scheme still flourishes.

In his later years, Maynard became more and more a bibliophile, once remarking to Duncan Grant that he was concentrating on books and was not going to buy pictures any more. Fortunately this was a short-lived resolution and some splendid French paintings were added to the collection. Notable among them was Cézanne's 'Sous-Bois' of about 1880 which the dealer Vollard had bought from the painter. It had then come to Wildenstein's who sold it to Maynard in 1937 along with two small paintings by Delacroix. The three together cost £4,500. A few weeks later, Maynard – who regularly studied sales catalogues in bed after breakfast – bought at Christie's two Braques, a nude and a landscape and two Picassos, both still-lifes. A picture added by Lydia to the collection (now apparently lost) was a drawing of herself from the Diaghilev days by Picasso (see Plate 5a). Another picture by Braque had been bought some years earlier by Duncan and Vanessa from a book shop in Berlin.

During the years of the Second World War Maynard Keynes purchased relatively little, but his collection was constantly borrowed from by exhibition organisers, especially for shows put on by the Council for the Encouragement of Music and the Arts which later became the Arts Council of Great Britain. Realising how important it was for people to see pictures at this time of hardship and austerity, he was well prepared to lend his paintings, and did so freely.

Though containing important pictures, Maynard Keynes's collection was not a scholarly one, and nor was it a personal one in the sense that some painters' collections are highly personal. But among modern collections Keynes's certainly had a place of distinction in the combination of good pictures of the French and English schools and the fruits of an encouraging patronage. It evokes the humane and spirited percipience that went into its formation.

The more important paintings in the Keynes collection are:
Georges Braque,'Femme Nue', 1925
Georges Braque, 'Nature Morte', 1911
Paul Cézanne, 'L'Oncle Dominique', 1865–7
Paul Cézanne, 'Pommes', 1873–7
Paul Cézanne, 'Sous-Bois', 1879–82
Paul Cézanne, 'L'Enlèvement', 1867
F. V. E. Delacroix, 'La Fiancée d'Abydos', c. 1843
F. V. E. Delacroix, 'Cheval au Pâturage', c. 1819
F. V. E. Delacroix, 'Le Lion et la Couleuvre', c. 1847
André Derain, 'Nature Morte'
André Derain, 'Dormeuse aux Mains Croisées'
Henri Matisse, 'Déshabillé', c. 1917
Pablo Picasso, 'Nature Morte avec Fruits', 1924

Pablo Picasso, 'Nature Morte', 1923
Auguste Renoir, 'Paysages avec Oliviers, Cagnes', 1912
Georges Seurat, 'Study for "La Grande Jatte"', 1884
Walter Sickert, 'Théâtre de Montmartre', *c.* 1900
Walter Sickert, 'The Bar-parlour', 1922

28

The book collector

A. N. L. MUNBY

If Keynes had lived for another ten years there is little reason to doubt that he would have become one of the great book collectors, not only of his generation (for he was already this) but, as his younger brother Geoffrey became, of the century. He very early crossed the ill-defined no-man's-land which divides the scholar who buys a few fine books from the book collector proper. To the former category he had always belonged: it was indeed natural that one for whom the arts had such an appeal should not be blind to the attractions of fine printing and binding; and he had little sympathy with the school of thought, not entirely unknown in academic circles, which delights in the self-inflicted austerity of the cheap paperback, announcing that the text is all-important and that its exterior trappings are mere vanity.

Even as an Eton schoolboy Keynes was buying Aldines and Elzevirs. As early as March 1903 he made a handsome present to the College Library in the form of a Latin Psalter of 1547 bearing the signature of Nicholas Udall, author of *Roister Doister*, and a flogging headmaster of Eton, dismissed in 1541. At home in Cambridge he inevitably came under the influence of the well-known Cambridge bookseller, Gustave David, for whom he maintained an affectionate regard until the latter's death in 1936, and whom, as Bursar of King's, Keynes was careful to rehouse when the building of the Arts Theatre evicted him from his premises in St Edward's Passage.

As a first-year undergraduate Keynes adopted a short-lived system of marking his rare books in numerical sequence. The figures show him to have been a substantial book-buyer, even at the age of nineteen; and some of these earliest purchases were noteworthy, Adam Smith's copy of Virgil in three volumes folio, for example, accession number 305 of 1902, which David's code-mark suggests cost him half a guinea.

When Keynes was an undergraduate the Baskerville press was a peculiarly Cambridge cult, and nearly all the long row of Baskervilles in his library also bear David's familiar *sigla*. Keynes was a founder-member of the Baskerville Club in October 1903, together with A. T. Bartholomew, Arthur Cole, Stephen Gaselee, Francis Jenkinson, G. I. H. Lloyd, C. D. Robertson and Charles Sayle. The Club published its *No. 1 Handlist* in 1904, an annotated checklist of Baskerville's publications. Keynes's copy, with his *marginalia*, survives today, and shows that, even at this early date, he was at grips with the problems which beset Baskerville's bibliographers. A modern collector cannot forbear a pang of envy when he reads some of the annotations; as when Keynes notes against the great Kehl edition of Voltaire, printed in Baskerville's types, 'I had a copy in poor calf on approval . . . for 42s. ix. '05.' This he seems to have returned, but a great book-collecting *coup* can be related to this year. One of his copies of the first edition of Newton's *Principia* bears his manuscript note, 'Purchased from David about 1905 for 4s., he having bought it in the Faringdon Rd for 4d.' This must represent one of his earliest excursions into the field of the history of thought in which he was later to excel.

This was indeed the great age of book-collecting in Cambridge, when such bookmen as Keynes's brother Geoffrey and E. P. Goldschmidt were laying the foundations of future bibliographical reputation. When the latter went down from Trinity in 1909 he prefaced a privately printed catalogue of seventy-five of his rare books with an acknowledgement to those who, by their interest and advice, had encouraged and helped him in the pursuit of bookhunting, in particular Charles Sayle, J. M. Keynes and Stephen Gaselee. An older man who may have been influential was H. S. Foxwell (1849–1936), Fellow of St John's and a neighbour in Harvey Road, who from 1875 onwards acquired 80,000 volumes in the history of economics, and of whom Keynes was to write an affectionate memoir. Keynes's own earliest exercise in this kind of subject-collecting in depth dates from 1906 when he assembled a long series of works on probability for the writing of his Fellowship dissertation, mainly modern works but also containing some rare first editions of authors such as Charles Babbage, George Boole, Augustus de Morgan and Laplace.

Up to the early 1930s most of Keynes's older books continued to be bought from David; and these comprised good, but not necessarily first, editions of the poets and dramatists, including rather sketchy author-collections of Wordsworth and Coleridge, together with the works of the philosophers and economists. These latter David would keep on one side for him, and already in the late 1920s his series of Hume, Hobbes and Locke were making a respectable showing. But they were casually acquired at this date and not pursued with the avidity that characterised his book-collecting in the last ten years of his life. For it was not until the mid-1930s that the idea was evolved of forming a really comprehensive collection to illustrate the history of thought. The fashion of ideological collecting is a comparatively recent development in England, and though one cannot claim pioneer status for Keynes, he was well in the van. Until the eighties of the last century, English collectors had been mainly preoccupied with manuscripts, *incunabula*, *editiones principes*, and literature of the Elizabethan and Stuart periods. The notorious Libri, historian of mathematics and book-thief, in his two great sales of 1861, was one of the first who set out to draw English collectors' attention to works important to the history of thought. These two sales of books imported from France contained a magnificent series of manuscripts and books by Galileo, Copernicus, Kepler, Cardan etc., many with long notes pointing out their significance, and we must not allow ourselves to be blinded to the originality of Libri's catalogue by his unenviable reputation. As in the case of T. J. Wise in our own day, Libri has fallen under a cloud which has obscured his very real merits. The immediate financial results of these two sales must have been disappointing, but in them Libri gave an impetus to collecting in the scientific fields which was to culminate in the libraries of Young in the sphere of chemistry, of Osler and Cushing in medicine, of Foxwell in economics and of Keynes in philosophy.

Keynes's scheme can be simply formulated: it was to assemble all the early editions (including variant issues of the same edition) of the authors whom he regarded as important in the development of ideas. To the original texts he added all the translations and all contemporary controversial works involving his chosen authors. Author-collecting alone, however, he felt was not enough; the background must be filled in as well. And so the scheme was extended to include numerous minor works which in any way influenced or illustrated his intellectual giants. A small quarto notebook was used to record accessions to the collection; in it were lists of authors' works with bibliographical details, and each item was ticked off as it was acquired. The main group of authors, in the order in which they are entered, is as follows: Locke and Hume, almost complete, including the latter's extremely rare *Abstract of a Treatise of Human Nature*, 1740, and a group of some thirty of his autograph letters, partially unpublished when Keynes bought them, Spinoza, Hobbes, a remarkably fine and almost complete series, Berkeley, Descartes, Leibnitz, Butler, including a large paper presentation copy of *The Analogy of Religion*, Francis Hutcheson, with Gibbon's copy of the *System of Moral Philosophy*, 1755,

Bentham, Rousseau, Bacon, the scientific and philosophical works almost complete, including the very rare *Opera* of 1623, Mandeville, Henry More, Malebranche, Montesquieu, Kepler, Galileo, Bodin, Sir William Petty, Cardan, Sir Thomas More, Richard Hooker, Boyle, Glanville, Oughtred and Bishop Wilkins. Authors unrecorded in the notebook but amply represented in the library include Copernicus, *De Revolutionibus Orbium Coelestium*, 1543, bought for £150 in 1934, Hegel and Kant, two authors little collected in this country, Malthus, Pascal and Adam Smith; and he assembled at the end of his life a group of the important papers of Einstein, Eddington and Rutherford. Of Newton, Keynes had probably the best collection in private hands, owning his copy of Leibnitz's *Charta Volans*, as well as four copies of the various issues of the first edition of the *Principia*, one in contemporary red morocco and one, the so-called second issue, with edges entirely untrimmed. In his last few years Keynes, at his brother's insistence, was fast acquiring the true collector's appreciation of fine condition and he was beginning to accept a poor 'working' copy only as a temporary expedient. He was indeed not at all indifferent to original wrappers, uncut edges, *minutiae* of 'state' and 'issue' and other matters of importance to the bibliophile but so incomprehensible and even exasperating to the uninitiated. In his chosen field of philosophy and economics there were discoveries to be made. From a bibliographical standpoint the path is comparatively uncharted; it was only in recent years, for example, that the experts decided which in fact is the first edition of so important a book as Hobbes's *Leviathan*, while there is still discussion over the significance of the variant title-pages of the first edition of Newton's *Principia*, a discussion to which Keynes himself made a valuable contribution.*

His Newton manuscripts, some 150 in number, would alone confer distinction on a library. These were purchased in July 1936, when Viscount Lymington's Newton Papers were sold at Sotheby's. Keynes attended the sale and bought about forty lots in person and he followed up many of the others purchased by the book trade. Had the sale come a few years later when his collecting had gained the momentum of the war period there is little doubt that his purchases would have been even more extensive. Keynes liked to look in at a sale, though of course he had not the leisure to attend regularly. In fact the only other sale we recall his sitting right through was the celebrated dispersal of Gibbon's Lausanne library at Sotheby's in July 1934. Here his purchases were on a comparatively modest scale. Normally he tried to view the books before the auction and then gave his commissions to Maggs Brothers. He by no

* *Bibliographical Notes and Queries*, Vol. II, no. 6 (July 1936).

means confined himself, however, to the auction rooms for his purchases, but ordered regularly from the catalogues of English, Continental and American booksellers; and it gave him particular pleasure to buy an expensive book, if the price was a fair one, from some relatively humble member of the trade. If the price was, in his view, unreasonably high, but the book a desirable acquisition, he would occasionally write a long letter of mingled homily and economic theory, which from time to time secured some abatement. Despite a sharp eye for cost he enjoyed to a high degree the goodwill of the bookselling fraternity.

As the gaps in the ranks of the post-Renaissance authors were filled Keynes turned his attention to acquiring a few really finely printed *incunabula* and Aldines. Here too the history of thought was the dominant interest – the Sweynheym and Pannartz Augustine's *De Civitate Dei*, the Jenson Diogenes Laertius' *Vitae Philosophorum*, 1475, the Mentelin edition of Bruni's translation of Aristotle's *Ethics*, 1469, and the great five-volume Aldine *editio princeps* of Aristotle, 1495–8, a bargain for £160 in 1934. In the case of the early Greek Aldines Keynes allowed himself to go beyond his self-imposed limits of subject to take in such books as the *editiones principes* of Theocritus, Aristophanes, Thucydides, Herodotus, Demosthenes and Pindar.

By 1939 Keynes found that he could not add books to the history of thought collection fast enough to satisfy his collector's appetite and since the filling of the last few gaps was only a matter of time he sought another outlet for his energies. He turned his attention to English literature of the Elizabethan and Stuart periods. Three causes probably contributed to this choice. He believed firmly in the permanent value of the literature of this period; he thought, moreover, that many books of the Elizabethans were far rarer than was generally supposed and that his was the last generation which would have an opportunity to buy many of them at any price; he also felt that in the 1930s many of them were absurdly cheap. In all respects he was undeniably right.

The varying rarity of different classes of book from generation to generation is a puzzling phenomenon for the bibliographer. But in the case of the Elizabethans the signs are sinister for their survival on the shelves of private collectors. There are indeed very few young collectors of them, and as each older collection comes under the hammer an ever-increasing proportion finds its way into public libraries. The paucity of private collectors, and the partially non-competitive buying by libraries, had brought them to a lower price in the mid-1930s than they had realised for years. They had indeed had a long run; in the late eighteenth century the discriminating group of collectors round William Herbert brought them into popularity, which was to be magnified by the extravagant enthusiasms of Dibdin and his circle in the first three decades of the nineteenth. Huth and Christie-Miller consolidated their position among the gilt-edged securities of the book world. At the dispersal of the last-named library in the 1920s they reached their zenith; yet within a few years books which at the Britwell sales had realised hundreds of pounds were fetching as little as a tenth of those prices. For this the slump was only partially to blame; pure literature had become unfashionable and a less scholarly generation of collectors was pursuing the more meretricious charms of illustrated books and bindings. Keynes was shrewd enough to know that this could only be a temporary phase and he was prepared to back his judgement to the full extent of his resources. Between 1939 and his death he bought avidly any sixteenth- and seventeenth-century English authors who came his way at prices which he considered to be reasonable. The field was a large one and he could afford to be selective; he considered moreover that greater enjoyment was to be had from buying ten books at £10 apiece than one at £100. In the last two years before his death, however, there were signs that this attitude was being modified and he was prepared to fill in substantial gaps in the ranks of his Milton, Ben Jonson and Spenser first editions.

Keynes's lifelong interest in the theatre led him first to the dramatists, and the two long shelves of quarto plays at Tilton bore testimony to the sense of urgency which he brought to their acquisition. He not only bought these at auction, he ransacked the shelves of the half-dozen booksellers who specialise in such books. His Shakespeare quartos were naturally mostly late ones, yet he contrived to find a copy of the 1608 (1619) copy of *Henry V* and the 1634 *Two Noble Kinsmen*. He had good runs of the plays of Massinger, Ford, Beaumont and Fletcher, Shirley, Davenant, Ben Jonson (including a fine copy of *Sejanus*, 1605), Webster, and Heywood. His restoration dramatists were, as might be expected, even better represented, with a fine shelf of Dryden, and most of Congreve, Farquhar, Otway, Shadwell, Vanbrugh, Wycherley and Nathaniel Lee, this last an author whom Keynes considered underrated. Among the poets was an enviable group of books by Spenser: *Colin Clout*, 1595; *The Shepheards Calendar*, 1597; *The Faerie Queene*, 1590–6 and *Complaints*, 1591. The last was the book which, Sir Roy Harrod records, Keynes diverted from the Folger Library by receiving his copy of Maggs's catalogue at Bretton Woods in the Foreign Office bag and not through the post. The prolific George Wither was well represented, and other desirable books included Chapman's Homer's *Iliad* (1610), Carew's *Poems*, 1640, and a copy of that rare and bibliographically distracting book Benlowes's *Theophila*, 1652. Among the Miltons we find *Paradise Lost* (4th title), 1668, *Paradise Regained*, 1671, and *Poems*, 1673; given a few years, *Lycidas* and the *Poems* of 1645 might have been added, perhaps even *Comus*. But death intervened when only the pattern of the early English collection was becoming plain; nevertheless a solid foundation had been built.

The urgency of his wartime collecting and the solace which his books brought him in those dark days are illuminated in several letters to George Rylands. 'I have been comforting my declining days'. he wrote as he set off for America on 3 September 1943, 'by buying lots of quarto plays from Shakespeare to Congreve, and can now boast that I have more than forty. I should consider 100 a fair collection and 200 a good collection.' He succeeded in assembling about 180. On 6 February 1944 he expounded 'a new theory of Shakespeare's sonnets' and went on to complain that 'the booksellers and the book collectors have been going quite mad lately in relative values', citing recent cases in which a first edition of the *Shropshire Lad* had fetched more than *Paradise Lost* and Masefield's *Everlasting Mercy* more than *The Anatomy of Melancholy*. 'The truth is', he added, 'that it is no use for booksellers to take any interest in books which are really rare. The thing to do is to work up interest where there are plenty of copies to be had.' A postscript to a letter of 19 April 1944 provides testimony to the assiduity with which Keynes studied his early plays.

Two other books of a certain interest I have been reading lately. I wonder if you know them. Have you ever read 'The Cruel Brother' (by Sir William Davenant). I think this is really the most cruel and appalling plot that I have ever read. A pretty thrilling play, but ghastly. The other was a play published posthumously by Lucius, Viscount Falkland [*The Mariage Night*, 1664]. You will remember how all his contemporaries thought him the most brilliant and charming of youths, until he committed what was virtually suicide at, was it?, the Battle of Worcester, and Clarendon's famous notice of him. The play is rather odd, but he clearly has not the faintest idea how to write verse, and the amateurishness is beyond all expectation (for he spent most of his life in the country and talking to learned friends), but there are some charming passages.

Keynes corresponded with his fellow-collectors and booksellers on a large scale, and the reader marvels at how time could have been found for those four-page letters about the frontispieces of Hobbes's *De Cive* or the translations, one by Bentham, of Voltaire's *Le Taureau Blanc*. One extract from a considerably longer letter, written on 21 March 1944 to Ernest Maggs, is quoted here, which illustrates Keynes's altruistic readiness to share his specialised knowledge with a bookseller who had served him well. Keynes was writing from his bed after a heart attack.

I should like, if I may, to draw your attention to Lot 31 in Hodgson's sale of March 30th, namely, the first edition of Hume's *Treatise of Human Nature*. This is a book, the occurrence of which I have been closely watching for the past forty years. In my opinion, its rarity is very much greater than is commonly recognised. Indeed, I do not think there is another book of such fundamental importance in the history of thought which is so scarce. I should say that at least 50 copies of the first edition of *The Wealth of Nations* turn up for every copy of the *Treatise of Human Nature*. It is particularly scarce with all three volumes, which this copy has, since the third volume was published separately a year later. To the best of my knowledge, not above four or five copies at the outside of the three volumes together have changed hands in the last forty years. I wonder if you have ever had a copy through your hands. I should doubt it. A little time ago I asked Quaritch if he had ever had a copy, and he told me that he had no record of ever having had one. It is not generally known that the third volume exists in two states, one with 8 lines of Errata, and the other with 12 lines. Since I already have two copies, acquired over this long period, one with the 8 lines and one with the 12 lines, I scarcely feel entitled to bid for this lot, though, if it is in really good condition, I should nevertheless like to have it. As I am still having to keep to my bed, I shall not have a chance of making a visit. As I happen to have made a special study of Hume editions over a very long period of years, you may be glad to have the above expression of opinion. I am sure that it ought to be acquired at any reasonable price.

As a postscript it may be added that Keynes finally owned four copies of Volumes I and II and two copies of Volume III of this very rare book; and that Mr Maggs was outbid at £31 for the copy at Hodgson's sale.

The cataloguer of Keynes's library encountered some agreeable surprises among books which had not been consciously collected but casually acquired: his annotated copy, for example, of Moore's *Principia Ethica*, 1903, the Bible of the Cambridge intellectuals of his day, or his first editions of early works of E. M. Forster, T. S. Eliot and Virginia Woolf. The last named inscribed to him a copy of Hoole's translation of Ariosto, with Jane Austen's signature, which she had bought at Hastings and sent him as a present, and another gift came from Edith Sitwell, a manuscript of her poem 'Lullaby', handsomely bound and offered in grateful exchange for a folio Ben Jonson which Keynes had generously passed to her.

It is a matter for the deepest regret that Keynes did not live to assemble his library within four walls. Spread over his three places of residence it was awaiting the leisure that the end of war might have been expected to bring, to be arranged in the first-floor room at Gordon Square. This room, already of substantial size, had been extended into the next-door house; several fine bookcases had been bought and it would have made a worthy setting for the collection in its entirety, a place to which book collectors would have made a pilgrimage and where they would have been assured a welcome. For though Keynes took no part in the purely social aspects of book collecting he was ever ready to show or even lend his rare books to the serious student.

The responsibility for providing a suitable setting for the collection and for making it available to students in the way Keynes would have wished has now devolved upon his College. Apart from a selection of his working books, left to the Marshall Library, the whole collection was bequeathed to King's, where it has materially raised the status of the College Library, and where the filling of gaps in the donor's favourite author-collections, such as Hobbes, Locke, Berkeley and Bentham, has provided the present writer with an agreeable exercise in bibliophily, of which Keynes, he hopes, would have approved.

Index

Burns, Arthur F., 140
Bussy, Janie, 61
Butler, R. A., 262

Camargo Society, 264
Cambon, J. M., 25
Cambridge, *see* Apostles, Arts
   Theatre, King's College, Political
   Economy Club
Cambridge Economic Handbooks,
   Keynes's introduction to, 252–3
'Can Lloyd George Do It?, 124
capital levy, post-war, to repay com-
   pulsory savings, 180, 182
capitalism, 91, 92, 111–12; saving of,
   attributed to Keynes, 128, 132,
   141
Carrington, Dora, 66, 71
Casson, Lewis, 267, 269
Cézanne, P., 280, 283–4
Chamberlain, Austen, 171, 173, 283
Chappell, William, 43
Charleston, Sussex, 6, 61, 71, 282,
   283, 286
Cherwell, Lord, 219
Christianity, Keynes's remarks on,
   37, 252
Christie, John, 267, 270
Churchill, Winston, 19, 178, 186,
   228, 255
City, Keynes in the, 70, 224–9
Clapham, John, 230, 232; *Economic
   Development of France and Ger-
   many*, 232
Clearing Union, Keynes's plan for,
   209, 210
Clemenceau, G., 166–7, 257–8
Coe, F., 219
*Collected Writings of John Maynard
   Keynes*, 11, 13, 16, 21, 23, 79, 80,
   106, 107, 125, 159, 160, 161, 174,
   175, 177, 196, 197, 198, 237
Colm, Gerhard, 137
Commission on Reparations, 168
Common Market, Britain's decision
   to join, 115
compulsory savings, 148, 179, 180,
   182; post-war capital levy to re-
   pay, 180, 182
Congreve, *Love for Love*, 265
conscientious objection, 16, 66, 68–
   70, 115, 148–9
conscription, 67, 69, 148
Consultative Council of Chancellor

of the Exchequer, Keynes's ap-
   pointment to, 177, 181
Contemporary Arts Society, 287
Cosmopolitan Cinema, Cambridge,
   272
Council for the Encouragement of
   Music and the Arts (C.E.M.A.),
   260–71, 278, 288
Council of Four, The, 257
Council of Ten, 165, 166
Courtauld, Samuel, 185, 268, 287
Covent Garden, Royal Opera House,
   264, 265, 269
Cox, Oscar, 221
Crowe, Sir Eyre, 3–4, 4–5
Crowley, L. T., 221
Cunliffe, Lord, 149, 156, 165, 168–9,
   172
Cunningham, Archdeacon, 230
Currie, Lauchlin, 135, 218
Curzon, Francis, 228

Dalton, Hugh, 190, 194
Darwin, Charles, and *The Origin of
   Species*, 7
David, Gustave, 15, 30, 290–1
Davis, Norman, 168, 172
De La Warr, Lord, 261
deferred pay, 148, 179, 180, 182
deflationism, 228, 229
Degas sale, 155, 282–3
Delacroix, F. V. E., 283–4
demand, aggregate: definition, 109;
   control of, 87–8, 109, 119–20,
   122, 138
Denby, C., 219
Dennison, Henry S., 137
Depression, the Great, 102, 109–12,
   114, 133, 227, 229
Derain, A., 287
Diaghilev, Serge, 5, 6, 7, 49, 51–2,
   70
Douglas, Constanza (mother of Lydia
   Lopokova), 5
Douglas, Major, 235–6
Durnford, Hugh, 45–8 *passim*
Duse, Eleonora, 7

Eccles, Marriner, 135
*Economic Consequences of Mr
   Churchill*, 77, 115, 133, 228
*Economic Consequences of the
   Peace*, 8, 10, 25, 70, 100, 115, 133,
   172–4, 259

Printed in the United States
150515LV00003B/103/A

9 780521 296960